SEVEN S·E·C·R·E·T·S of a HAPPY MARRIAGE

Wisdom from the Annals of
"Can This Marriage Be Saved?"

by Margery D. Rosen
with the Editors of
LADIES' HOME JOURNAL®

WORKMAN PUBLISHING • NEW YORK

Library of Congress Cataloging-in-Publication Data

Seven secrets of a happy marriage : wisdom from the annals of "Can this marriage be saved?" / [compiled] by Margery D. Rosen and the editors of Ladies' home journal.
    p. cm.
  ISBN 0-7611-2685-6 (alk. paper)
    1. Marriage—United States—Case studies. 2. Marital conflict—United States—Case studies. 3. Married people—United States—Psychology—Case studies. I. Rosen, Margery D. II. Ladies' home journal.

HQ536 .S47 2002
306.81'0973—dc21

2002068998

Workman books are available at special discount when purchased in bulk for special sales promotions as well as fund-raising or educational use. Special book editions or excerpts can also be created to specification. For details, contact the Special Sales Director at the address below.

Workman Publishing Company, Inc.
708 Broadway
New York, NY 10003-9555
www.workman.com

First printing: September 2002
Manufactured in the United States

CONTENTS

SECRET #5   217

BE MONEY SMART
*Discovering What Money Can
and Can't Do for Your Marriage*

SECRET #6   267

MAKE LOVE
Keeping the Marriage Hot

SECRET #7   321

TEAM UP
*Balancing Parenthood
with Partnership*

WORKBOOK   373

CHECKLISTS AND STRATEGIES
*A Workbook for
the Two of You*

FOREWORD

———◆———

I t is a great pleasure to write a foreword to this new book celebrating the fiftieth anniversary of the most enduring magazine feature in the world, "Can This Marriage Be Saved?" The column was initiated in January 1953 by my father, Paul Popenoe, in collaboration with writer Dorothy Cameron Disney. For the first twenty-five years the column included an introduction by my father and was based on cases drawn from the files of the American Institute of Family Relations, the counseling group he founded and headed in Los Angeles. Regarded as America's pioneer marriage counselor, my father established his institute in 1930; it was the first in the nation to provide counseling, education, and research specifically designed to help people cultivate happy, lifelong marriages. "Can This Marriage Be Saved?" represents an obviously fruitful and long-lasting partnership between the institute and the *Ladies' Home Journal,* which has served to popularize the field of marriage counseling and provide hope to millions of Americans whose marriages are encountering the inevitable rocky times.

There is no doubt that "Can This Marriage Be Saved?" met its moment in arriving at the predawn of one of the most dramatic eras of family change in history, an era that has certainly not been very favorable for marital unions. To take but one issue, when the column began in the early 1950s, the chance that a wedding would ultimately lead to divorce was less than 20 percent. Now it is around 50 percent! Despite these figures, there is a new feeling of optimism about marriage today, and a growing realization that healthy marriages are of the utmost importance—for individual happiness, for children, and for the general well-being of our society. The fiftieth year of this column provides a golden opportunity to review just what has happened to marriage in recent decades, and more importantly, what is now being done to revitalize the institution.

A look back at the rapidity of marital change over the past fifty years is sobering. Perhaps the biggest transformation has been in the idea that husbands should be breadwinners and wives should be home-makers. Consider this dramatic shift in attitudes: As late as 1970, 80 percent of married women in the United States agreed that "it is much better for everyone involved if the man is the achiever outside the home and the woman takes care of the home and family." By 1991, a mere 27 percent agreed!

Any social transformation this swift and fundamental is bound to cause problems, and that is what happened. A detailed historical analysis of the content of the first twenty-five years of "Can This Marriage Be Saved?" found that the most frequent problem encountered by the fea-tured couples concerned "role responsibilities." Specifically, a large percentage of the marital problems consisted of complaints by wives (who were increasingly engaged in the workforce and in other outside-the-home activities) that their husbands were not sufficiently involved at home. The wives wanted their husbands to participate more in fathering, help out with housework, and be there for them emotionally. In accurate anticipation of what was to come, the featured marriage counselors typically indicated that full-time homemaking was restric-tive for many women, that marriage was a partnership, and that wives should not have to put up with an absent and domineering man. The message now given to men was the same one that had been tradition-ally reserved for women: Put your marriage and family first. In a sense, these messages worked. While role responsibilities still loom large today as marital problems, they are not on the scale they once were. The young people who marry now enter into relationships that are far more egalitarian and less role-differentiated than those of the past.

The most convincing explanations for why the divorce rate has climbed so far and so fast revolve around this fact that the concept of marriage itself has changed. A hundred years ago marriage was organized in terms of family connections, economic dependence and survival, and largely unbreakable religious and legal covenants. Today, marriage is focused far more on the pursuit of intimacy and companionship. Whereas once we looked for a mate who could be a reliable coworker in the struggle through life, today we look for a best friend, a soulmate, who will make us feel emotionally fulfilled. Divorce used to take place only when a spouse became effectively incapacitated in some way; today, divorce takes place when we find ourselves "falling out of love." Certainly, though, people's emotions are not the most stable or reliable aspects of human nature and, as a result, modern marriage has become more fragile.

Despite high divorce rates, we have witnessed a strong sense of optimism about marriage on many fronts. Marriage is more popular than ever among high school seniors; popular books and television have swung in a pro-marriage direction; and there are significant signs of a national "marriage movement" among professionals such as the clergy, educators, and mental health workers. Even the federal government is getting involved, encouraging marriage within the welfare population. The underlying belief of these ventures is that, yes, marriages can and should be saved—at least many more marriages than we once thought.

The central ingredient of healthy marriages today is good communication between the spouses, and the lack of such communication has become the major reason for divorce. As the columns featured in this book make abundantly clear, communication is a realm in which many of us, especially men, still have a lot to learn. The good news is that communication across the sexes, along with its close companion, conflict resolution, are skills that can in part be taught. This is another area in which "Can This Marriage Be Saved?" has been a national pathfinder. Highlighted for decades by the column, the teaching of these skills has become the stock-in-trade of marriage educators and counselors, the centerpiece of high school marriage courses, and the very basis of the growing marriage movement itself.

Can these new skills save modern marriage? Only if, as this book clearly points out, they are accompanied by a heavy component of trust and long-term commitment. Residing more in the heart than in the mind, trust and commitment are not so easy to teach. And therein lie great personal and societal challenges.

The future of marriage is an unknown. Cutting the divorce rate will not be easy. But if we are to have success, surely it will involve the kind of information and perspectives that we have been getting from "Can This Marriage Be Saved?" for the past fifty years. With that kind of longevity, it seems the column is serving a widely felt need, and that much of the public agrees with my father that lasting marriages give us something of incalculable importance by both enhancing our lives and enriching our society.

—David Popenoe, Ph.D., Professor of Sociology and Co-Director of the National Marriage Project at Rutgers University

INTRODUCTION
Love Lessons across the Generations

———◆———

The year is 1953. For the first time in a generation, a Republican, Dwight D. Eisenhower, sits in the Oval Office . . . the first McDonald's franchise opens in Phoenix, Arizona . . . JFK weds Jackie . . . scientists discover the famous double helix structure of DNA . . . Harvard Law School awards its first bachelor of law to a woman . . . Superman flies onto TV screens and *Playboy* magazine onto newsstands. A nation that eagerly awaits Little Desi's birth on *I Love Lucy* is also introduced to a magazine column that, in its own way, quietly breaks new ground.

Well before the emergence of a self-help culture, daytime talk shows, and Prozac, "Can This Marriage Be Saved?" charted the emotional landscape of marriage. Until its debut, few people even considered the possibility that professional counseling—stigmatized by Freudian theories and pathologizing diagnoses—could possibly be useful in clearing the underbrush from snarled relationships. Yet through the decades, this column not only dismantled roadblocks for couples whose cases it reported, it served as a compass for millions of others. We witness good relationships strengthened and bad ones healed. Take a close look and you will see just how accurately the column has reflected social revolution—and evolution.

Back in the "love-honor-and-obey fifties," spouses largely shared the same view of marriage. Most wives stayed home; their husbands were the undisputed breadwinners—and controlling the purse-strings meant wielding most of the decision-making power in the family, too.

As unprecedented numbers of women moved into the workforce, some reaching its highest echelons, men and women struggled to comprehend the social upheavals set in motion by the women's movement. "Can This Marriage Be Saved?" showed us, up close and personal, how couples wrestled with the difficulties inherent in sustaining a marriage. Some were raising a family in which both parents' paychecks were needed to stay afloat financially, and stressed-to-the-limit wives who worked a second shift at home after one at the office realized they couldn't be all things to all people. We witnessed what happens to the marital balance when he loses his job, or when her salary tops his.

In the seventies, traditional wedding ceremonies gave way to barefoot brides on windswept beaches, and the emergence of the sexual revolution proclaimed a different cultural mantra. So-called "open marriage," with its myriad sexual partners, was in; staying in a relationship that needed work was decidedly not. It was considered better to leave behind the midlife crisis, the kids, and the stale marriage and find the *real* you. Divorce statistics reached an all-time high as nuclear families split apart, and stepfamilies born of their loss struggled with divided loyalties, coparenting, and the emotional wounds that accompanied the separations.

Still, through the next two decades, this column continued to deal unflinchingly with issues long in the shadows—alcoholism and physical and sexual abuse—as well as those increasingly in the headlines today—the growing use of psychotropic medications and new forms of counseling, which included brief group and solution-oriented therapy.

A BRAVE NEW WORLD

Today, those barefoot celebrations seem quaintly old-fashioned. In their place have emerged elaborate show-stopping extravaganzas, replete with designer confections, multiple bridesmaids, and tossed bouquets. Call it a mix of passion and pragmatism, monogamy is more attractive than ever and it remains abundantly clear that Americans are still very much in love with the idea (or the ideal) of blissful coupledom.

But this is not your mother's marriage: Only one quarter of Americans live in the traditional families that "Can This Marriage Be Saved?" first described. In keeping with this trend, just half of all children live in two-parent homes. Between 1950 and 1993 the proportion of households headed by married couples fell from 77 percent to 55 percent. Today, nearly half of all marriages still end in divorce.

And those are only the figures for first-time marriages. The death rate for second marriages hovers around 66 percent. More worrisome, perhaps, are the numbers of young people who may be cohabiting but remain disenchanted with marriage in general. These twenty-somethings know little about how a relationship works. Nearly one in ten twenty-five- to thirty-four-year-olds who walked down the aisle are now divorced, a 40 percent increase in the last thirty years of what the media has recently dubbed "starter marriages." Many are children of divorce themselves, who know firsthand about the heartache of a broken marriage but little about how to sustain a happy, emotionally healthy one of their own.

Yet as social scientists began to study marriage, they corroborated what readers of this column already knew. Most marriages end not with a bang but rather with a gradual separation due to "irreconcilable disappointments," says Diane Sollee, M.S.W., co-founder of Smart Marriages, a Washington, D.C.–based clearinghouse for marital studies and information. Worn down by years of resentment and bitterness, criticism and contempt, unaware of the emotional and relationship skills that could help them, many spouses steadily drift apart until they barely recognize the person sitting opposite them at the breakfast table. Scott Stanley, Ph.D., codirector of the University of Denver's Center for Marital and Family Studies, compares marital breakup to a mudslide in California: It looks like it happened all at once but, in fact, years of erosion led to a final crisis.

Similarly, Linda Waite, Ph.D., and Maggie Gallagher, social scientists and authors of the book *The Case for Marriage,* state that marital stress especially hammers wives, who tend to be more affected physically by stress and arguments. Poorly handled conflict negatively affects the heart and the endocrine and immune systems, adds Stanley. Perhaps most disturbing are findings from Judith S. Wallerstein, Ph.D., of the Center for the Family in Transition at Berkeley, and E. Mavis Hetherington, Ph.D., professor emeritus of psychology at the University of Virginia, whose respective books on marriage and children of divorce—though they reach different conclusions—underscore the fact that children in high-conflict relationships are severely affected by the underlying tension and outright hostility they witness at home.

Today, traditional counseling first reported in "Can This Marriage Be Saved?" has broadened to include relationship-enhancement courses, weekend seminars, day- or weeklong marital education programs in churches and on military bases, as well as courses in high schools and on college campuses. Many experts now insist that teaching the skills that "Can This Marriage Be Saved?" has long promoted—either before or after marriage—can help immunize people against serious marital troubles and divorce. Still, only 5 percent of people in the United States ever seek counseling, notes John Gottman, Ph.D., a sociologist at the University of Washington, who has spent the last thirty years studying why some marriages flourish while others flounder. Most wait an average of six years after problems first surface to even call a therapist. "Would you wait six years after a cancer diagnoses to get treatment?" he asks rhetorically.

At the very least, "Can This Marriage Be Saved?" signals that warring spouses are by no means alone. Certainly a large part of the column's appeal lies in the vicarious thrill we get from reading the sometimes Byzantine sagas of other people's intimate lives. Couples argue—some loudly and bitterly, others with icy silences—each locked in a cycle of blame and accusation that make them feel like adversaries in a never-ending war. And we're always a bit curious to find out what's really happening behind someone else's bedroom door. We're compelled to keep on reading to see how the story will unfold—to see how the pieces of a shattered marriage can possibly be made whole again. (Interestingly, Dorothy Cameron Disney, the woman who wrote the first column, was a longtime author of mystery books and had certainly mastered the fine art of suspense.) Yes, every marriage featured in the column is ultimately saved, but we still want to know how, exactly, and at what emotional cost?

BURNING OUT—OR BURNING ON

The good news is that couples that stay married actually disagree the same amount as those who don't. The fact that they fight is not the problem; how they fight is. But that also means that off-kilter marriages can be set right. By learning trust, communication, decision-making, and conflict-resolution skills, you can become smarter about your own relationship. In fact, one reason this column has remained so popular is that millions of readers see themselves and their marriages reflected in its pages. The column's format—first her turn, then his—shows readers, simply and dramatically, that there are often two sides to an issue, two ways of observing a problem, and neither is necessarily wrong.

Each story told here is true. Each husband and wife is interviewed by the *Journal,* and the words you read are the words they used. Readers can't help but get caught up in the drama: "How could he do that to her?" they think as they read the wife's tale. "Oh, now I understand why he did it," after hearing the husband's version. Rarely do readers have an opportunity to feel someone else's anxiety, frustrations, and pain so keenly. And as they discover how the counselors guide each troubled couple toward a peaceful solution, they find clues to resolving their own domestic dilemmas.

But perhaps the most astonishing lesson is that, while the specifics of the story change from month to month, the underlying issues that can shake the foundation of a marriage—be it in 1953 or 2003—remain fundamentally the same. Particularly intriguing are the ways in which these problems repeat, time and again, from one generation to the next. Clinically and empirically, experts now know that couples often subconsciously pass along the experiences, attitudes, and patterns of behavior they witnessed in childhood. The model for our marriage is our parents' marriage. Though it may be a troubled one, it's at least familiar.

So why do some marriages burn out while others burn on? As the field of marital research expands—and with it a plethora of laboratory and clinical studies, marriage mentors, books, videos, and training programs, it's clear that there is no one answer. Sure, it's a lot harder to stay married these days: women have more options; husbands and wives travel for business, making it more difficult to stay close and easier to meet someone else; economic forces threaten to pull the rug out from under a comfortable life; and there is the fact that time has erased the stigma of divorce that kept a generation of unhappy people together. But the phrase "intentional commitment" comes up often—that is, the conscious desire and choice to make a marriage last.

Commitment and acceptance don't get a lot of press and they're not the stuff of sound bites on the network news, but it's clear that marriages are stronger when couples focus on what they like and appreciate about each other, rather than what irks them. Happy couples argue, get depressed, lose jobs, battle over disciplining the kids—but their sense of *we*-ness over *me*-ness allows them to encourage each other during the good times and empathize during the bad. With a vision aimed toward the future, they can express how they feel and what they want without making it seem as if whatever is missing is the other's fault.

Happy couples are also flexible. Unafraid of change, they not only expect it but prepare for it, too. They recognize that the marriage they now have in their twenties will in fact be different from the relationship they will have in their thirties or forties. Not incidentally, their sense of humor softens the rough edges and replenishes what is lost in the tumult of the outside world.

And what about sex? In a society permeated with sexual images, there is more knowledge about sexual needs and desires than ever before. Many women report that their spouses are finally interested in, and more knowledgeable about, giving them pleasure. Sex, after all, represents the physical attraction two people have for each other; it adds a glow to the marriage and trumps many problems—at least in the short run. For every couple, sexual issues ebb and flow while emotional differences remain. Whether it's how often, how well, who initiates or who pulls away, a couple's sex life is almost always affected by what else is going on in the marriage. Partners may feel so tired and stressed by various job and family problems that sex is the furthest thing from their minds. Yet in a good marriage, they still find ways to give—and get—the attention they need.

While too many people worship the "happily ever after," and give short shrift to the "for better or for worse," every couple chronicled here was at least willing to try to make their marriage a priority and make it work. It takes courage to face problems head-on. But what makes working on a marriage much less frightening is the realization that, while you will never have the power to change your mate, you can change yourself. "Can This Marriage Be Saved?" proves that both partners can transform their actions and reactions. They can make their own choices. And that openness and ability to change brings them a giant step closer to where they both want to be.

—Margery D. Rosen

DEEPEN TRUST
Securing the Anchor of a Good Marriage

———◆———

Trust is the cornerstone of a healthy, deeply satisfying marriage. In a trusting relationship, partners are, quite simply, honest with each other. Their words and actions are not shadowed by deceit; they don't sacrifice a partner's needs for their own or pursue their own goals at the expense of a mate's. Most important, they make a total commitment to each other, a commitment that helps each feel emotionally nourished, comforted, and supported. In fact, over the lifetime of a marriage, couples consistently report that trust is the single most important marker of lasting happiness.

Often, couples become stuck on the most obvious violation of trust—infidelity—and that error in itself can cause them to overlook other problems in their marriage. However, as painful as it is, a marital affair, as we shall see later in this chapter, is usually a symptom of other serious problems in a marriage—often unconscious or

1

unacknowledged. The concept of trust, however, actually goes far beyond sexual fidelity into every aspect of a couple's day-to-day life. Partners should feel safe enough to be their authentic selves. This is a priceless gift—one that partners in a solid union should be assured of and never have to ask for. Paradoxically, trust must also be earned.

In a relationship based on trust, husbands and wives make the marriage a priority. Despite the demands and pressures from children, work, community, or other family responsibilities, the relationship comes first. And that means carving out specific times to do things together—to finish a conversation uninterrupted; even to schedule sex. It also means being able to count on your partner to work through problems, in spite of the difficulties or disappointments that are inevitable in every relationship.

Partners should also be empathic. Empathy means being able to put yourself in another's shoes, to see a situation from your mate's point of view. It's not easy to be empathic, but it is essential to sustaining trust. A trusting partner encourages and supports a mate's goals and dreams; she shows genuine happiness for his joys and successes, concern for his sorrows or setbacks. He respects and accepts a spouse's anxiety, anger, or fear and allows her to be who she is—without judgment, condemnation, or disparagement—even if he doesn't agree. The partner who dismisses or ignores a spouse's feelings, needs, or ideas, or who fails to validate her perceptions, is betraying marital trust.

Seemingly unimportant violations of trust can trigger intense uncertainty and ambivalence in marriage as well, a factor many people fail to realize. In a trusting marriage, you can depend on a mate in ways large and small. It's one thing to rage at infidelity's flagrant breach of trust. It is much harder to justify anger or resentment when a partner repeatedly fails to discipline the children responsibly and consistently . . . to make key decisions about family finances . . . to follow through with promises . . . to keep secret a mate's confidences and insecurities. Yet each of these failures is a violation of trust. What's more, when partners breach the privacy inherent in marriage by parading grievances or embarrassing a mate in front of others, they also violate trust.

Seven Secrets of a Happy Marriage reveals how lack of trust can slip at first unnoticed into an already strained relationship. We hear couples complain bitterly, often publicly, about important dates or anniversaries forgotten, about a partner's constant tardinesss for events that are important to a mate, about key messages that are never given. Slowly but steadily, mistrust chips away at the foundation of a marriage. Unwitting couples wonder what went wrong.

The long-term effects of living with someone you cannot trust are devastating to your sense of self. When a partner doubts a mate's integrity, he or she becomes unsure, insecure, anxious, perhaps even fearful for his or her own physical safety. The person feels trapped, guarded, vulnerable, and may act in unkind ways, which only serves to further push a loved one away.

Nevertheless, time and again in *Seven Secrets of a Happy Marriage* we watch as couples, reeling from the pain of betrayal, pick up the pieces of their marriage. Restoring trust takes time. Perhaps because it is the bedrock of a relationship, it is the most difficult piece to repair. Many fear they won't succeed. But as the following stories poignantly reveal, it is through weathering the crises that couples, given time to heal wounds and share intimacies, often build an even stronger foundation for their relationship.

"My Husband Is Having an Affair"

Eileen's husband met the other woman at church. Why do even the nicest men stray?

"Until last week, if you'd told me that my husband—the Cub Scout leader, the perfect Southern gentleman who doesn't have a mean bone in his body, the man who sings in a church choir—was having an affair, I would have laughed in your face," said Eileen, forty-two, her eyes swollen from days of crying. "We've been married for eight years—this is the second marriage for both of us—and in all that time, I swear there's never been one single problem. Marrying Russell was the most wonderful thing that had ever happened to me. "I was raised in a small coal mining town in Virginia. My father was killed in a train accident when I was in the sixth grade and life was a struggle for my mother. We were poor, but we all had enough to manage. My family is extremely loving, warm, and deeply religious.

"I was nearly eight years older than my brother and sister and I took on a lot of the mothering roles. I was always the good girl, really responsible, the kind of kid who wouldn't go out to play on Saturday until the wash was done.

"After high school, I went to the state university, and when I was twenty, I married my high school sweetheart. Eric was the best-looking guy in the class and brilliant. He's a lawyer now. We were married for thirteen years and he was physically and psychologically abusive to me and to our two boys—not every day, but six or seven times a year he would just beat the daylights out of us.

"I filed for divorce three times. Although I knew that staying together for the kids was a bad idea, I couldn't leave. The way I was brought up, when you get married it's till death do you part. I kept thinking I was doing something that made him behave that way.

"Russell and I were good friends for years before we became involved. I knew his first wife had divorced him after seven years and that they had a very amicable split. Anyway, as the years went by, I realized I was deluding myself about my first marriage. The day after I filed for divorce for the last time, I was feeling really down; I needed someone to talk to, so I gave Russell a call and told him everything. He was shocked; he had no idea that things weren't perfect in my marriage.

"We started seeing each other and our relationship grew intense pretty quickly. My kids adored him. After years of being terrified of their father, Russell was a miracle. We had a big wedding—on Valentine's Day, in fact—and it was beautiful.

"By this time, Russell was getting serious about his music. He wanted to be an opera singer, so a few weeks after the wedding we quit our jobs and moved closer to where this teacher whom he studied with lived. We bought a gorgeous three-bedroom house on a corner lot. Within a few weeks we both found jobs—Russell sold insurance during the day and took classes at night; I got a job at the local library.

"Everything was fine, although Russell had some problems at work. He quit his job because he was disgusted with it; then he got another selling job, but that didn't work out either. He kept changing jobs—once or twice more, I can't remember. He told me there was no growth at either place.

"After a while, he also gave up the idea of being a professional singer. Russell is so gifted, but he didn't think we could manage financially. I was actually making a lot more money than Russell, so I kept my job, although I desperately wanted to spend more time with my boys. I also started going to school a few nights a week. It was tough, but I got straight A's.

"Like I said, things were great. You can count on one hand the number of arguments Russell and I have had in the last eight years. You can't even call them arguments; we just have disagreements, usually over stupid things. Maybe I'll be upset that Russell spends so much time with his fishing club or in his workroom downstairs cleaning the rods or whatever.

"Since Russell also sings in the choir on Sunday morning, we can never get away for a weekend, which I would dearly love to do. But he works so hard and he needs to relax. I don't begrudge him that, although I'm pretty exhausted after working and cleaning the house. It would just be nice to go out to dinner or a movie. No, I've never said anything to Russell about helping out. Well, okay, maybe once in a while I'll slip and say something sarcastic like, 'Russell, is there something bothering you?' And he'd say, 'No, nothing's wrong.'

"You have to understand, my husband is the most honest human being you will ever meet. He will not lie. So if he said everything was fine, it never entered my mind to question him.

"But in my heart, I figured it was something I was doing wrong. I started reading all these books and asking myself what I could do to improve. Keep the house cleaner? Cook more?

"Then, just last week, I sifted through the mail, and for some reason I looked at the phone bill. I don't know what possessed me to open that bill, because usually I put it aside and let Russell deal with it. I noticed there were a lot of calls to this one number in the next town. I knew Russell didn't have any customers there. I stared at the bill for a long time and realized that a lot of the calls were made when Russell was out of town on business. Was he really having an affair? I wondered. I went into the house to look at the old phone bills we keep in the back of Russell's drawer. Sure enough, each showed several calls to the same number, going back over a year.

"I had the operator check the number and she gave me the name and address of a woman I recognized as someone in our church. Oh, my God, I thought, it's been in front of me all this time and I couldn't see it.

"I drove to the church because I knew Russell was going to choir practice that evening. I waited in the car in the parking lot until I saw him. I could tell by the look on Russell's face he knew that I knew. I asked him if he was having an affair and he said yes. I said, 'Do you love her?' And he said, 'Yes.' I said, 'Do you want to marry her?' and he said, 'I don't know.'

"I wanted to die. A lot of that night is a blur, but I know that I started taking every pill in the house—of course, all I had was aspirin and a few diet pills.

"What did I do wrong? I know it's hard to understand this, but I love this man so much; I can't let this relationship go. How can I help him?"

RUSSELL'S TURN

"I love my wife and I know I need help," said Russell, forty-one, as he sank wearily into his chair. "How could I mess up my life so badly? How could I cause this woman, whom I love so deeply, so much pain? She deserves someone better than me.

"Eileen is special. Things just seem to come easy for her. She's a terrific mother, terrific at her job. She gets straight A's in her courses—I was always a poor student. And she has a zillion friends. I still have trouble getting close to people.

"I've always been a real loner. I was born in Alabama and when I was eight my family moved to Ohio. My mother was a housewife, very religious, very soft-spoken, and very subservient to my father, who was a truck driver, so he wasn't home much. When he was, Dad ruled the house as if he were king and everyone else was his servant. He drank a lot and ran around with other women, but my mother would never leave him.

"Mother was very strict with my two younger sisters, but anything I did was fine with her. I was the center of her world. She pampered me and watched over me like a hawk.

"I loved the outdoors and spent much of my childhood roaming the woods by myself. Music was my other love. I sang in the choir and was a member of all the student theater productions. My voice teacher in high school tried to convince me to make music my career—he told me I had a great tenor voice and as good a chance as anyone of making it. But I didn't want to work that hard, and I didn't believe I had the ability.

"I married my high school sweetheart and enrolled in the state university, but I flunked out after freshman year. Failure number one.

"Then I was drafted. It was during Vietnam, so I joined the Navy, but my blood pressure went sky-high and I was discharged after thirty days for hypertension. Failure number two. Soon after that, my marriage broke up. Failure number three.

"I didn't know what I was going to do with my life, but since everyone always told me I'd make a great salesman, I figured I'd try it. I found a job selling life insurance; three months later, I almost went broke. Failure number four. I bounced from one selling job to another, but I kept getting fired because I couldn't keep up with my paperwork. I had so many black marks on my record, no one would hire me. I did construction work to make ends meet, but when I was almost thirty, I thought: You enjoy music so much, let's see if you can make a living out of it. I started taking classes at a music school and got a job in the library. That's when I met Eileen.

"After her marriage broke up, we started to see each other and I knew it was the best thing that had ever happened to me. Three months later, I begged her to marry me.

"Everything was going along just fine. Believe me, until this mess, I'd been true-blue to Eileen. And I love her kids as if they were my own. But I was floundering, so I quit school again, found another sales job, and settled for singing in a small opera company and the choir. I thought about how I was turning forty, and I guess all the failures in my life finally just wore me down.

7

"Then one day while I was singing in the choir I noticed this gorgeous woman in the congregation staring at me. I was flattered by her attention, so I went up to her afterward and started a conversation.

"It turned out that we were on the same fund-raising committee at church; no one else signed up, so it was just the two of us. One afternoon we were meeting at her house and before I knew it we were in bed.

"I felt terrible, but, like an addict, I kept going back for more. I started reminding myself of the things that were wrong with my marriage. How Eileen would always nag me to help out around the house. How our sex life was great, but with this woman, well, it was fantastic. I'd see her maybe twice a week at a motel or at her house before her kids got home from school. She was a bookkeeper and she worked only in the morning; her husband was a workaholic, so he was never home.

"I'll tell you this, though. While Valerie was no match for Eileen, I could talk to her in a way I could never talk to my wife. I would tell her about my problems at work and how I always messed up my life. How could I ever tell these things to Eileen? I'm married to Superwoman. Hell, she even makes more money than I do.

"But seeing Eileen try to kill herself . . . I'm so confused. I can't believe I'm saying this, but I'm torn between the two."

"In my experience," said the counselor, "there are usually three reasons for marital infidelity. It can be a symptom of something wrong in the marriage—not just sex. It can be the result of two people growing and changing so much they are no longer in love or compatible. Or, as in this case, it can be the self-indulgent act of one partner who feels he or she is entitled.

"Initially, I was most concerned about Eileen. Although I did not believe she was suicidal, she was devastated by Russell's betrayal. A conservative, religious woman, she considered her marriage vows sacred, and when her world was shattered, so was she.

"Since childhood, Eileen was the good little girl who tried so hard to please that she lost all sense of self-esteem and self-confidence. She became a doormat for her abusive first husband, then for Russell.

"Russell was the selfish, pampered son who grew up in a household built on religious platitudes but lacking in real moral teaching. He never developed a sense of responsibility and he stumbled through life with the attitude that nothing really mattered.

"Even as an adult, Russell found it difficult to connect with people except on a superficial level. Unassertive and not particularly ambitious, he continued to take the easy way out.

For instance, he did the fun part of his job—schmoozing with customers—but he pushed his paperwork aside.

"Russell's lifelong string of failures came to a head as he approached forty, a birthday when many people take stock of their lives. Russell found himself wanting, and it was at this point that he was particularly vulnerable to an extramarital affair. He simply couldn't say no.

"My first goal in counseling was to convince Eileen that she had done nothing to provoke the abuse in her first marriage or the infidelity in her second. The latter had far more to do with problems Russell refused to deal with. However, she certainly didn't have to stand for it anymore.

"One of my first questions to Eileen was, Where's your anger? Despite her husband's infidelity, she was still wondering, How can I help him? Such continuous self-sacrifice was unhealthy. Instead, I told her to tell Russell exactly how she felt and what she expected of him: He was to end his affair immediately. He was to start helping her around the house. He was to stop spending so much time in his workshop or going fishing, and instead take her antique shopping or out to dinner or whatever else she wanted to do.

"This was very difficult for Eileen, not only because she had spent a lifetime caring for others, but also because she truly believed that 'a good wife doesn't ask.' I explained that many people aren't as perceptive

as she is and that Russell especially had to be told something point-blank before it would occur to him to do it.

"Eileen forced herself to think of her own needs more. When a savings bond came due, she used the money to buy herself a new car—a red Firebird. She had always wanted to cut back her working hours; this time Russell was supportive, although it thrust financial responsibility squarely on his shoulders. He rose to the challenge.

"For the first time in his life, Russell started to look at himself candidly. He truly loved Eileen and he realized how special their relationship was and how close he had come to destroying it. I agreed with him that while extramarital sex could be exciting, the thrill was more akin to the 'forbidden fruit' and was not as satisfying in the long run as the deep and lasting love he and Eileen shared. In fact, I told Eileen and Russell that one reason I felt they could repair the damage was that their marriage was built on a firm foundation.

"Russell promised to take some drastic steps of his own. He broke off the affair and started working diligently at his job, doing the paperwork on weekends if necessary. As the orders started coming in and his boss acknowledged his success, his self-confidence rose. He started helping around the house. He stopped comparing himself to his wife and instead started really talking to her—and that communication has bonded them further.

"This couple was in counseling for a year and a half. By the end of our last session, Eileen told me, 'I know Russell truly loves me as much as I love him; I know he grieved with me through this ordeal.' Do the memories still hurt? I asked her. 'Time has made it easier,' she admitted. 'Although I've forgiven him, there will probably always be a lot of pain. But I do trust him. Believe me, I couldn't live with him if I didn't.'"

AFTERMATH OF AN AFFAIR:
When Trust is Shattered

When trust is irrevocably broken, how can you go on? Most couples who seek counseling after an affair do get their marriage back on track. To help reestablish trust that's been broken, keep the following in mind.

1. First, end the affair. Couples can't begin to rebuild unless they are both motivated to save the marriage.

2. Give the wounded person time to feel angry, vengeful, and hurt after he or she discovers the affair. Their belief system and, along with it, their self-confidence, will be shattered. It can take as long as a year or more to process the pain.

3. Seek professional counseling, preferably together, but if a mate resists, it's imperative to go alone. A skilled therapist can guide patients past self-righteous anger and help them take a microscopic look at the underlying problems in the marriage. What's more, counselors—as well as spouses who have been in therapy— report that once one partner makes a significant change, the relationship is bound to change, too.

4. The persons betrayed must let their partners know that they need to hear some recognition of the pain and hurt they have caused. Time and again, this simple acknowledgment was the turning point for marriage recovery, one that allowed the partner to forgive and move on. Too often, one spouse will say: "It didn't mean anything" or "It was just sex." That's not true. Infidelity is a profound betrayal of trust; continuing to deny it only stalls healing.

5. Don't rush into any major decisions. It's difficult, if not impossible, for anyone to think clearly at a time like this.

6. Partners who have been betrayed must remind themselves that an act of infidelity does not mean that they personally have failed. Rather, they have relationship problems that must, and can, be dealt with.

"I Can't Face Another Christmas with This Man"

Alan had a secret bank account for years. How can Jane ever believe what he tells her?

Jane's Turn

"Alan and I have the shell of a marriage; inside, there's nothing," said Jane, forty-two, a slim, dark-haired woman who spoke so fast it was hard to follow her. "I'm sure everyone thinks things have always been just fine. We go out with friends and have a good time; we're always there for our kids and their activities. On the surface, we function like every other couple. 'Function' is a good word because it is more like a business relationship than a marriage—and a lousy one at that.

"Once we get home, there is no communication or love—only bitterness and resentment. Other than talking about practical things—like who will pick up Tommy, who's ten, at basketball practice or take Eric, eight, to his friend's house—we hardly say two words to each other. I even have to push and prod Alan to do that.

"For a long time, we played 'let's pretend,' but in the past few years I don't think either of us had the energy to do even that. I'm furious and think I have every right to be.

"Until very recently, Alan was out of work again. This is the sixth time in twenty years—wouldn't you wonder? In the beginning I didn't think too much about it, to tell you the truth. But then I noticed a pattern. Every two or three years there would be some insurmountable problem at

11

work and Alan, who's an accountant, would leave on his own or be fired. It was always something different. The boss doesn't appreciate him . . . the work isn't challenging enough . . . whatever. Alan is the kind of guy who gets into a job two hundred percent. He's a workaholic—that's one of the problems, which he never seems to realize. He wears his beeper on his belt, and as soon as that thing goes off, he rushes to the phone and then to the office. I can't tell you how many times he's left in the middle of a basketball game or even on a Sunday night. Nobody is that indispensable. "At first, I accepted his explanations. But what was okay when we were in our twenties, with no kids and no mortgage to worry about, is not okay when we're in our forties and I'm trying to figure out how we can stay afloat, never mind send the kids to college.

"I cannot keep supporting us on my teacher's salary. I've already taken on more consulting projects for the superintendent than I can manage. I'm burned out—and sick and tired of it all. I'm tired of explaining to the boys why Daddy and I aren't talking, and I'm tired of stalling collection agencies. Alan's long periods of unemployment have put a terrible emotional and financial strain on our marriage. We were severely in debt, and if I hadn't been working, I don't know what would have happened. It's a miracle we squeaked by.

"You know, I try to talk about this to Alan, but I get this feeling he never really listens. He argues with me, all right, but he doesn't hear what I'm saying. I get so mad that I lose it sometimes. He's a master at nodding at the appropriate times, but I can tell when he's tuning me out. We replay the same old battles over and over again; I can hear the script in my head.

"I feel as shut out as I did as a kid. I've never gotten along particularly well with my parents. Mother especially was critical and judgmental. My dad was more loving, and there were times when I thought that maybe he understood me. But when push came to shove, guess whose side he always took?

"Dad worked for the town government and never made very much money, which meant that Mother had to work six days a week at a dry-cleaning store. She resented it, but I was thrilled—I got to spend a lot of time by myself. I was one of the original latchkey kids, but I loved it. I'd come home from school and watch TV or do my homework and read. When Mother and Dad were around, there was just so much stress that I'd often go into the bathroom, turn the shower on, and sit there reading magazines just to escape from them.

"I didn't feel good about myself until college. That's when I met Alan. We were best friends for two years, and Alan was very funny and charming. But what I liked most about him was that we would have these monumental talks. He was always there to listen, which is a far cry from the way I feel now. We eloped during my senior year—I couldn't handle making wedding plans with my mother.

"After we graduated, I started teaching and Alan worked as an accountant for a small clothing business. I suppose we felt the real financial pressure once we had children. Our sex life was surprisingly good for a while, but now we never make love.

"Who knows, maybe we would have gone on like this for twenty more years, but last week, something happened that propelled me right over the edge. I was clearing out my desk drawer and found an unfamiliar bank statement. Apparently, Alan had opened an account years ago in his name—and he had twelve thousand dollars in it! I felt as betrayed as if he had had an affair. Here I am worrying and struggling, and he has all this money in this bank. I find this unforgivable. What else is he hiding? How much can I trust him?

"I thought about how the holidays are coming up and I can't make it through another charade of another 'merry' Christmas. This is a time of endings and beginnings, and I want this New Year to be a fresh start. This is my last-ditch effort to make this marriage work."

ALAN'S TURN

"I'm not surprised that Jane has neglected to tell you what a witch she can be," said Alan, forty-two, whose quiet voice and demeanor belied the anger in his words. "She can be so hurtful, dripping with sarcasm, accusing me of being a failure when I've been working my tail off. She says I'm never there for her and the kids— well that's a lot of bunk. The jobs I've had were all important, pivotal positions. I have a responsibility to my boss and the people who work under me. She should understand that. Plenty of men work longer hours than I do. I feel she's never there for me.

"Do you know what it's like to live with a person you know, just know, is convinced you're a screw-up? I feel like there's no support for me at all. I've tried for years to talk to Jane if I had a problem at work, just like we used to. I've always valued her advice; she has a better feel for people and how to get along than I do. But whenever I did, Jane would immediately act as if what I was saying would lead to some awful catastrophe. She never heard what I was saying; she was too busy panicking and obsessing. So maybe I built this wall up around myself, to protect myself from her. What else could I do?

"Jane was the first person who made me feel like I had something genuine to offer. I'd been a loner growing up. When I was ten, I had a bad accident playing baseball—I broke my leg in several places. It never healed properly, and I was in pain for years. There were all sorts of complications that I can't even remember and, as a result, my left leg is still shorter than my right by about two inches.

"Anyway, for two years I had to stay at home, mostly in bed, while it healed. I remember kids coming to talk to me at my bedroom window and I'd beg my mother to let me go out, but she always said no. She was afraid I'd hurt myself. Mother always told me how terrific I was, but I knew better; I knew what she was saying wasn't true. I was a total disappointment to my dad. He worked as a truck driver and he was this real macho kind of guy. Although he was rarely home, I know he was embarrassed to have a son who was such a wimp. By the time I did go back to school, I found it hard to make friends.

"When I met Jane, all that changed. I felt like I had a best friend, and it was a terrific friend-ship that grew into much more. It's hard to say when the problems started for us; all I know is that I've been unhappy for a long time. I don't understand why I do some of the things I do either. Take that bank account. I don't know why I kept it from her. I didn't mean to be hurtful. It made me feel good to know that money was there, that I

could amount to something after all. I don't know why I've made so many job changes either; most of the time, I left on my own. See, I throw myself into work, but after a while my interest fizzles. I hit a plateau and then get bored. I think that's the way you grow, but Jane thinks it's irresponsible.

"You know, occasionally, when we're out with people, I catch glimpses of the old Jane, the funny, energetic woman I fell in love with. But once we get home, that woman becomes a shrew. Maybe I work so much because I hate to come home."

THE COUNSELOR'S TURN

"Alan and Jane were engaged in a dance of anger, blame, and abandonment that had gone on for so long it was difficult to break," said the counselor. "In fact, for the first few weeks, I wasn't sure this marriage could be saved. They had lost the friendship that had been the foundation of their marriage and now were so intent on proving their individual points, and placing the blame squarely on each other, that I was little more than a referee in their cold war.

"Finally, I told them: It's time to decide if you want to make this marriage work. If you do, you each have to take responsibility for having created the problems in your relationship and start acting like allies instead of adversaries.

"My first goal was to help them recognize that many of the patterns in their behavior stemmed from experiences they had as children.

"For instance, Jane's childhood world was not a safe and happy place. She grew up with deep-seated feelings of insecurity and a lack of self-confidence, not surprising considering that her overcontrolling mother rarely showed her any affection. Although Jane's father occasionally was nurturing and gave her the feeling that he understood her, she never knew when he would abandon her and rush to take Mom's side. He made it clear that her mother's feelings and needs, not Jane's, were paramount.

"In a similar way, Jane looked to her husband to rescue her in marriage, and when he created problems rather than saving her from them, her resentment grew deep. To protect herself, Jane withdrew. Like the little girl who used to hide in the shower, she pulled back from Alan, and though she honestly felt she was telling him how she felt, she kept most of her real thoughts to herself. Many of these angry feelings triggered her anxieties and chronic worrying as well as her many harsh, sarcastic attacks against Alan. In counseling, Jane said that unless she made her point as strongly as she did, Alan wouldn't hear her. Alan was a master of emotional withdrawal and, when he pulled back, Jane felt he was abandoning her the way her father used to. Jane promised to hold back the angry words if Alan would promise not to shut her out.

"Many of Alan's problems also stemmed from his childhood. His injury was the first blow to his self-confidence. Because he spent so much time alone with a mother so overprotective that she never placed any demands on him or let him try anything for himself, Alan grew up feeling like an outsider—different, and not as good as others. To him, his mother's constant praise was hollow: He hadn't done anything, so how could he deserve praise? As a result, he never felt challenged and never developed the feelings of self-reliance children need to make their own way in the world. His father's obvious disappointment further reinforced the message that even if he tried, he'd probably fail.

"But in the beginning, this couple's strong and solid friendship served them both. The job now is to reach back to that friendship and relearn how to work together as a team.

"Before we could tackle many of the material problems, however, we needed to shore up Jane's and Alan's self-confidence. I saw them both individually for several sessions to do this. I wanted Jane to see how she was using her anxieties in a controlling way. 'There's a lot of strength in you, Jane,' I told her. 'You don't have to worry at the first hint of a problem.' Because Jane would automatically go into panic mode, I told her to try to concentrate on her abilities and remind herself that she always manages to work through her problems. As she became more confident, her anxieties lessened and Alan felt more comfortable being there for her.

"The focus of Alan's individual session was his lack of confidence in relationships at work. While Jane and Alan both used the term 'workaholic' to describe Alan, I believe he was actually overcompensating for his own feelings of inadequacy. He would pour himself into his job, over and above what is called for, as a way of showing 'See, I am good after all. I am needed. I'm a man.' Then, too, when people at work didn't respond to him or weren't as totally accepting of him as his mother had been, it triggered those old childhood hurts of feeling defeated and rejected. I believe Alan's secret bank account was his way of exerting some control over his life.

"Once they were able to recognize these patterns, Jane and Alan felt more accepting and less hostile toward each other. I told them that the only way that they could continue to make progress was to act this way even when I wasn't there to intervene. They agreed to take the time each day to talk about issues that bothered them, and as soon as the discussion began to

disintegrate, one of them had to call time out. At that point, they both wrote down what they were feeling so they could remember it and talk about it with me at their next session.

"While these two had long argued about Alan's job situation, they had never talked about it in a way that allowed them both to express their feelings honestly and figure out what to do. But now that Alan had heard the hurt in Jane's voice instead of the sarcasm, he vowed to put boundaries on his workload. In time, he understood that he didn't need to work all hours of the day and night, that he could delegate many of his responsibilities, freeing himself to spend more time with Jane and the boys. When Jane saw this, she began to like him better and trust him more. Her anxieties about financial problems lessened. 'She still gets the crazies sometimes,' Alan said at one of our last sessions, 'but I don't take it personally anymore.'

"Such fundamental changes in the way we behave take time. After I had seen this couple for a year and a half, they had stopped trying to compete with each other in their who's-right-who's-wrong game and had begun to feel like friends for the first time in years. Says Jane: 'I realize now that though our problems may not go away, our attitude toward solving them can make all the difference.'"

YOU CAN WORK IT OUT:
Strengthening Trust when You're Shaky

Jane and Alan had been trying to one-up each other for so long that they lost sight of the importance of acting like a team—a key principle for any healthy marriage. The following rules (good advice for every couple) helped them refocus their priorities:

1. Remind yourselves that there are no bosses in a marriage.

2. Mutual respect is essential: Respect your partner's way of thinking and getting things done as well as his or her opinions.

3. Keep a tight rein on your tendency to judge and find fault with your partner's thoughts or ideas when they're different from yours. You're not required to think and feel the same, merely to compromise.

4. Avoid making unilateral decisions. Teamwork means consensus, and consensus is based on sharing.

5. Make sure your common goals and objectives are clear. Repeat them often if necessary.

6. Be on the lookout for competition between you. Marital teamwork is not a contest and you aren't adversaries. Neither has the edge or is better than the other.

7. Teamwork means giving mutual support and encouragement. For instance, instead of negating your spouse's ideas, acknowledge the truth or positive aspects of what he or she is saying. Then you can add your own suggestions to the mix.

"I HAD A FLING WITH MY BOSS"

Exhausted by a new baby and Brian's refusal to help, Amy was only too ready to accept sympathy from another man. Can a young marriage survive the emotional fallout of betrayal?

AMY'S TURN

"It was only a kiss, but it stirred so much passion, I felt my whole body melt," said Amy, a slender thirty-three-year-old with tousled blond hair. "Then reality hit: This is not my husband, Brian; this is my boss, Jed, and we are about to commit adultery.

"'I can't do this!' I cried. I backed away and ran down to my own room, bolted the door, and fell on the bed, sick with guilt, as I thought of Brian waiting trustingly at home during my business trip with Jed. How could I be so stupid, risking everything I really cared about?

"It's ironic: When I first met Brian, at twenty-three, I was excited about my new consulting job—and terrified that he couldn't be trusted. 'He's not the type to settle down,' I told my friends, convinced that a man so handsome, and still unmarried at thirty, had to be vain and shallow. Besides, I wore suits to work, while Brian lived in T-shirts and jeans. I didn't realize that he had built up a very successful plumbing business, which allowed him to dress as he liked yet take time off for his passion, which was scuba diving.

"But Brian pursued me, and proved he was a one-woman guy. He was not only gorgeous but loving and tender—and so much fun! We dated for three years, and then got married. We went diving in Hawaii on our honeymoon and spent weekends on a boat with friends. Each year we'd take a big trip to the Caribbean. I never knew life could be so exciting!

"After seven years of marriage, our only conflict was my yearning for a baby. Brian thought parenthood would ruin our perfect life, but I'd always assumed we'd have kids. I grew up with emotionally chilly parents, and they really froze when my brother, Buddy, died of cancer. I was twelve at the time. My dad, a chemist, withdrew into his work, while Mom spent her days volunteering at the local hospital . . . and her evenings in bed with Buddy's doctor, while I baby-sat for my seven-year-old sister. I promised myself that someday I'd have a real family.

"I knew Brian didn't want kids when we got married. I figured that would change, but he remained adamant. Just after our sixth anniversary, our neighbors adopted a darling baby, and I felt so deprived. That night, I gave Brian an ultimatum: 'If you won't let me have a baby, I'll leave and find a man who will.' Brian looked stricken; he knew I was serious. 'Okay,' he conceded at last. 'But you'll have to do all the work.'

"Having no idea what I was bargaining for, I joyously tossed my diaphragm in the trash. Months later, I was pregnant—and elated. Brian was smitten with little Katie,

too. But the reality that followed was awful! I had no family nearby, and Katie had colic. Every night, she'd scream her head off, arching angrily away from my best efforts to soothe her.

"After six weeks of motherhood, I was so tired every part of me ached, but Brian seemed oblivious. When I said to him, 'This is so hard,' he actually said, 'I know, hon, but we made a deal,' and went off to work. I couldn't help comparing Brian to my boss, Jed, who had three kids whom he adored.

"'If I were Brian, I'd insist that you get some sleep,' Jed sympathized over lunch one day. I tried to smile, but to my embarrassment, I started to sob, and the next thing I knew, Jed was holding me. 'Amy!' he said, stroking my hair. 'I know I could make you so happy if you'd let me. . . .'

"I pulled away, shocked. 'I'm happily married,' I said, thinking I should report this man to human resources, but then I softened. That would be crazy, Jed had been my mentor and my boss for ten years, and he'd never made a pass at me before. I could be generous, pretend this hadn't happened. Jed went out of town for the next week. I felt relieved—but strangely disappointed. I kept thinking of his embrace, and felt a little like a teenager with a crush. I planned to tell Brian what had happened, but somehow I never got around to it.

19

"Then Jed called me at home. It was work-related, but hearing his voice was wonderful. That night, I let myself imagine that the man making sweet, powerful love to me was Jed, not Brian.

"In the next few weeks, Jed and I had many business lunches together and a couple of dinners as we showed a new product line to clients. It was all very proper—except in my mind. Then I got a memo: Jed and I were to make a presentation at a convention in Chicago—an overnight trip. I know I should have refused, but with what excuse? Besides, being away from Katie overnight, I rationalized I'd be able to get some sleep. So I left her with the wonderful woman who takes care of her every day—Brian wouldn't spend a night alone with her—and went to Chicago.

"Our presentation was a huge success. At dinner, Jed ordered a bottle of expensive wine. 'To us—a great team,' he said, raising his glass. Our eyes met, and communicated everything. We didn't want dinner, we wanted each other. In the elevator, he kissed me—a long, slow, passionate kiss that set me on fire. But when the door opened on our floor, I felt a sudden chill. This man I can't wait to make love with is not my husband!

"I tore away to my own room, feeling dirty—as if I'd turned into my mother! Back at the office on Monday, Jed was cool, thank

heavens, but I was a mess. Finally, I called Brian on his pager and said, 'Meet me at home.' I had to tell him, even if it meant losing him. When I heard Brian's car pull up, I ran outside. 'I haven't been honest with you,' I blurted out, and told him everything. Brian got blotchy and his eyes filled up. But when I went to him, he pushed me away. That was so painful. Brian insists that our marriage is over, but I've convinced him to come here and see if counseling will help."

BRIAN'S TURN

"I feel like I've been kicked," said Brian, thirty-nine, a ruggedly good-looking man with green eyes. "In the last few days, I've gone through all kinds of emotions. Right now, I'm feeling very sad for our family, especially Katie. I know what it's like to grow up with divorce.

"I can't believe I was so wrong about Amy. And to think I was the one who had to convince her that I was a good guy, not just a beach bum. Everything was great until she started talking babies—the one thing I really didn't want. As the youngest of four, I saw myself as an inconvenience to my parents. My dad had just made a lot of money in real estate when I came along. He'd always wanted to buy a small boat and sail around the world, but my mom kept reminding him, 'What about Brian and school?' There I was, like an anchor around his neck. One year later my father left us, and my mom went into a depression that lasted until she died a few years ago.

"So I was afraid of having kids. Besides, I thought we had enough with our love affair, our great trips, our careers, and our social life. I was stunned when Amy threatened to leave unless I agreed to a baby. I thought, This child isn't even conceived yet, and already it's coming between us. That was heavy stuff.

"The birth itself was a high, and Katie was beautiful. But instead of a cuddly baby who'd sleep in my arms, she was a full-time screamer. Friends would look at us and say, 'Oh, dear.' One day I walked in and saw Amy all red-faced, crying, miserable. The baby wouldn't breast-feed. Poor Amy—I felt protective toward her, and though I feel ashamed and guilty to admit it, I was furious at Katie for destroying our dreams.

"I admit I haven't been a whole lot of help with Katie, but was that an excuse for Amy to have an affair with that oily S.O.B. she works for? How could she? Last week, I was on my way home from work, but I stopped and parked a block away. I thought, I can't go home for the things I used to count on there, like truthfulness and love and understanding. I've never felt so confused or so alone."

THE COUNSELOR'S TURN

"Amy and Brian were suffering," said the counselor. "And so the first order of business was crisis intervention, to help them avoid doing something they would later regret.

"Brian was furious and deeply disillusioned, and I encouraged him to air those feelings. At the same time, I pointed out that Amy had shown a great deal of integrity in coming to him at an early stage. I suggested, too, that Amy might have created this crisis as a way of telling him that she needed more of his closeness and support. This helped to calm Brian, at least enough to listen as Amy— deeply ashamed—told him how much she loved him and wanted their marriage to work.

"Brian remained wary, but Amy was patient; she even offered to quit the company if it would reassure Brian. To begin rebuilding damaged trust, I gave Amy a task: to call Jed and explain that she was totally committed to her husband and needed to set up strict new boundaries. She would have no more meals with Jed, no late evenings, and no out-of-town activities together—even if it cost her her job. To Brian, she promised to report all of her conversations with Jed for a month—longer if he wanted. This way, there would be no more secrets.

"When the initial crisis had eased, we started looking at how the couple had gotten so far off track. Amy and Brian, both emotionally abandoned as children, had brought unresolved grief and disappointment to the marriage. We looked at how Amy had ached for a baby to fill the emptiness she felt—only to find that motherhood had cost her the closeness of her marriage; and how both Brian and Amy had floundered for months, each feeling alone and overwhelmed in the face of Katie's demands.

"This was important new information: Though they prided themselves on communication, Brian and Amy had unfairly expected the other to know their unspoken feelings and desires. Neither of them had learned in childhood how to share feelings, but they were both willing to work on this. I gave them exercises, like listening and then reflecting on what their partner had said without judgment, as in, 'I think I hear you saying . . .' The listener would ask the talker to elaborate—'Is there anything else?'—then validate the partner's feelings—'It must have been very hard for you when . . .' The two would take turns talking and listening, and they would call a timeout if they felt themselves become angry or defensive. This would help to keep them from acting out their frustrations in destructive ways. If she felt loved and understood, Amy would not have to seek an extramarital affair, as her mother had; Brian, too, would not need to follow in his father's footsteps, rejecting a child

and breaking his wife's heart by walking out.

"Brian admitted he had been rigid, making it hard for Amy to tell him how unhappy she was. Certainly their 'deal' that Amy would care for the baby alone had been unrealistic. Amy had been foolish to agree to it, and he had been wrong to ask.

"Fortunately, some things get better simply with the passage of time. Katie began sleeping for six hours at a stretch, which allowed Amy to get some rest—and begin to find real delight in her baby. Brian, however, was still on the outside. 'I change diapers,' he said, 'but it's like changing a tire—I feel no emotional involvement.' In response, I asked Brian to read a book on infant development, and then keep a journal in which he would note even tiny changes in Katie, like a slightly longer attention span, or a more alert look when the dog barked. Brian admitted, too, that he didn't know how to hold a baby, so I urged him to experiment with different ways of holding Katie to see what she liked. Part of what kept him on track was the fast results he got. For example, he took Katie to the park one Saturday, and found that he enjoyed her company as he strolled her along the shore, watching the waves and the surfers. The next morning, instead of going diving, he stayed in bed, watching his wife and daughter sleep. Suddenly, Katie opened her eyes, smiled, and held out her arms to him. He was enchanted.

"Both Brian and Amy were reassured by this milestone. 'I guess I didn't have to give up my dream so much as expand it for the three of us,' Brian mused in our last session. The challenge of melding two very different dreams can turn a promising marriage into a nightmare, but this couple truly used their crisis as a springboard. I feel confident that Brian and Amy—and Katie—are on their way to being a terrific family."

A TRUST CHECKUP

Trust is the expectation, often unspoken, that someone will be there for us. When trust is broken, we no longer feel safe—physically, emotionally, or spiritually. How much can you and your mate really trust each other? On the line next to each situation, rate whether it is (a) easy, (b) somewhat difficult, or (c) difficult for you to get help, support, or encouragement from your partner when:

1. _____ you feel indecisive.

2. _____ you're depressed.

3. _____ you feel exhausted.

4. _____ you feel guilty.

5. _____ you need encouragement.

6. _____ you need advice.

7. _____ you feel like a failure.

8. _____ you're in physical pain.

9. _____ you're in a money crisis.

10. _____ you feel humiliated.

Talk with each other about your responses. Then try this exercise as the next step in boosting the trust between you: Tell each other about one family or social situation when your partner has not been as helpful or supportive as he or she might have been. Maybe Thanksgiving dinner at your critical in-laws' is tough for you to sit through. Or perhaps your husband has difficulty socializing at school functions since he doesn't really know the other people all that well. Once you each identify the situation in which you would like support, work out a way to signal to your partner during that time. Your personal signal could be a light touch on the elbow or a raised eyebrow—any way that sends a personal SOS so your partner can respond. Once you do this, and see positive results, you strengthen the bonds of trust.

"My Husband Is Sleeping with My Best Friend"

Steve's infidelity shattered Chrissy's self-esteem. Can a marriage recover from a double breach of trust?

CHRISSY'S TURN

"What have I done wrong?" Chrissy, age thirty-two, sobbed. "Steve is sleeping with my best friend, Monica. I can't tell you how often Monica and I sat at my kitchen table having coffee and talking about everything under the sun. Her child just had a sleepover date with my son. Now I see that she was using me to get close to Steve. How could this be going on right under my nose?

"Of course, I suspected something. For the past few months, Steve has been aloof, impatient, and short-tempered with me and our three children—Kim, six; Timmy, four; and Ben, one. I tried to figure out why he seemed so unhappy, but he never reveals his feelings and I didn't want to push. We've been married seven years, and I've always been afraid that if I nag, he'll leave.

"I know I shouldn't have gone through his briefcase, but it was sitting open on the bedroom floor. . . . When I found the letters from Monica, I was stunned. That night, after the kids were in bed, I summoned every ounce of courage to ask him what was going on. He hemmed and hawed, then finally confessed that he's been sleeping with Monica for about three months.

"Now I see that Monica is just the type to steal someone's husband. She wears bikinis and high-heeled sandals to the town pool; her husband works twenty hours a day, so she hardly ever sees him.

"But what do I know about happy marriages? My father was in the military, and he and my mother divorced when I was eight. Even when Dad was stationed nearby, he never attended a single school event. When he did come to see me, we'd go for long walks and I'd feel special. But then he'd disappear again.

"My sister and I were basically raised by our grandmother. When Mom wasn't working, she was helpless and tearful most of the time. We learned not to expect much.

"I couldn't wait to get away from home. Enrolling at the state university was like a window opening for me. I realized for the first time that I was good at many things. I graduated with a degree in social work and found a job counseling adolescents at a residential treatment center near Atlanta.

"Steve was doing his pediatric residency and working part-time at the center. At first I wasn't interested in him, but he was persistent—as well as witty and kind and the most romantic man alive. He brought me flowers and wrote beautiful poems.

"We lived together for a year, then got married. Within the next year, Kim was born, and soon after, Timmy arrived. Steve was a staff physician at a clinic, and though he wasn't making a lot of money, we agreed that I'd stop working. I was determined to be the mom I never

had, and Steve was a great dad. But by the time Ben was born, we were slipping away from each other.

"My mother died when Ben was six weeks old. We had just moved into a new house, and I was overwhelmed caring for three small kids. Steve had been offered a part-time teaching position at the university, which we needed, because he'd just started his own practice. But at the last minute, the job fell through.

"That's when Steve really withdrew. He said it was my fault we spent so much on this new house. The truth is, we'd made the decision to be house-poor together. What infuriated me was that, at the same time, he went off and bought a shiny black Porsche, which is not exactly a family car.

"I never said anything. I didn't want Steve to resent me. I was already feeling insecure. He'd say things like, 'Chrissy, we're just not interested in the same things anymore,' and when I'd ask what he meant, he couldn't be specific.

"I must sound incredibly naive. Until I saw those letters, it never occurred to me he'd have an affair. I love this man, and I don't want a divorce. But I'm scared and lonely, and I have no one to count on."

STEVE'S TURN

"I don't know what's come over me in the last year or so," said Steve, thirty-two, a handsome man who spoke softly but in an oddly disconnected way. "I love Chrissy, and I can't believe I've hurt her so badly.

"Lately I feel like I'm going a hundred miles per hour and I can't slow down. Getting a practice going isn't easy, and though pediatricians make a very decent living, I'll never command the kind of salary a cardiologist does. Now I sound just like my parents. My dad was a psychiatrist, and my older brother is a neurosurgeon. In the medical world, those specialties garner greater respect than pediatrics. And status has always been very important to my parents.

"Mother, a homemaker who helped out with Dad's practice, was totally into appearances. I was a chubby kid, and she pushed me mercilessly to lose weight. For several years in my late teens I was bulimic—eating disorders in guys are not as unusual as most people think.

"I managed to stop the bulimia on my own, but the insecurities are still with me. Both Mom and Dad were goal-oriented and very controlling. Mother especially had a certain look whenever she was displeased, which was often. Though I was a success by anyone else's standards, I never felt as smart or as successful as my brothers.

"I always wanted to be a doctor, and since I loved working with kids, pediatrics was a natural choice, despite my parents' dismay. But money has been tight, and when the teaching position fell through, I came unglued. I also felt Chrissy was expecting certain things from me—a beautiful home, a certain salary—and that increased the pressure. But instead of talking about my fears, I pulled away. Of course, I see that only now.

"At that point, Monica, an administrator at the clinic where I'd worked, came into my office after the nurses had left and said flat out that she was not sexually satisfied in her marriage and was very attracted to me. I lost my head and forgot about everything I knew was right. It was stupid, it was hurtful, it was wrong. But I did it anyway.

"During the whole affair, I felt totally disconnected from what I was doing. I lied, I misled Chrissy, and I didn't care. I managed to put up a mental wall, to do what I felt like doing and ignore the consequences of my actions. I lived in a fantasy world—this incredibly sexy woman was coming on to me, and how could I say no?

"But when Chrissy confronted me, I was overcome with guilt and remorse. I have no excuse. I only wish I could make Chrissy stop blaming herself. She's always been like that—she criticizes herself constantly, doesn't think she's as pretty or as thin or as smart as her friends. It does make me a little nuts, but I'm not saying that's any reason for what I did. I want to stay married, and I only hope that somehow, someday, Chrissy will forgive me."

THE COUNSELOR'S TURN

"I believe strongly that just about any marriage can work as long as both people want it to," noted the counselor.

"Steve promised to end the affair immediately, and he accepted full responsibility for his actions, though Chrissy believed Steve's betrayal was somehow her fault.

"Having grown up with little emotional support, feeling unloved and abandoned by both parents, she never believed she could count on anyone. Though college had given her self-esteem a temporary boost, she remained haunted by self-doubt. For most of their marriage, Chrissy's priority was pleasing Steve. As long as she didn't make waves, she reasoned, he wouldn't abandon her.

"Despite his bravado, Steve was also lacking in confidence. He constantly pushed himself, yet received no acknowledgment of his efforts. More often than not, he was either criticized or compared unfavorably to his brothers. In Steve's home, appearances were everything, and every aspect of his life was choreographed; food was the only area in which he could gain some measure of control.

"Though Steve was unusually perceptive about his problems, he had no idea how to change; he hid his lack of confidence behind a facade of charm. When the multiple stresses of work, finances, and family became too much, Steve spun out of control. His wobbly ego needed the boost of an extramarital affair.

"My first goal was to get Chrissy to stop assuming that every problem was her fault. Discussing the similarities between her feelings of childhood abandonment and those she felt in her marriage sparked insight for her. I suggested that when she senses she is drifting into self-blame, she take a deep breath and ask herself: 'What's really going on here?' And, if she has any doubts, to bring them up with Steve before they mushroom. Once she was able to do this, we could move on to the next step—dealing with anger.

"Chrissy had been burying her resentment for years. She simply could not get angry. As long as she stayed in that posture, she would remain depressed and helpless—like her mother.

"Chrissy had confused confrontation with combat and assumed it should be avoided at all costs. But confrontation is the key to addressing problems as well as to determining whether your feelings are accurate. After talking about this for many weeks, Chrissy understood that by speaking up, she could short-circuit her self-deprecating thoughts and strengthen the communication between her and Steve.

27

"As Chrissy became increasingly aware of her rage at Steve's betrayal, frequent arguments erupted at home. She became upset over minor irritations—laundry left unfolded on the bed or the fact that Steve had said he'd give the children a bath that night and then got immersed in a basketball game on TV. Tension eased when I suggested that one of them immediately call a time-out when the atmosphere grew heated, write down what had started the fight and the direction it had taken, and then agree to table the issue until we could work it out in my office.

"For his part, Steve has worked hard to restore Chrissy's trust. He checks in during the day to ask how she is doing and to let her know what he's doing and where he's going. As their communication improved, Steve realized his self-worth was not linked to his net worth, and he no longer needs the external acknowledgment of his attractiveness from others, or to prove himself by buying expensive toys. He sold the Porsche and agreed not to make financial decisions before discussing them with his wife. He now shares things he kept secret before—the ups and downs of his work as well as his doubts about being a successful physician and father.

"Most important, Steve and Chrissy make a point of spending time alone together as a couple—they've hired a baby-sitter one night a week, and they plan one night away at least once a month. During one of these times they discussed finances, and Chrissy was able to reassure Steve that she didn't care how much money he made or what kind of house they lived in. 'Perhaps you're projecting your own expectations onto Chrissy,' I suggested, and Steve agreed.

"Chrissy, however, is still hurting and will be for some time. She and Steve have finished counseling, but they still come once a month to discuss personal issues. When I asked Chrissy if she'd forgiven Steve, she hesitated and said, 'Mostly. Each day is a test, but I believe we can get past that.' Indeed, I think this trauma has allowed Chrissy and Steve to get in touch with aspects of their personalities and their past with which they had never dealt, and to reveal themselves to each other in a much more intimate way."

FACING THE FEAR OF BEING CLOSE AGAIN

Trust in marriage means many things. To trust someone fully means to reveal yourself—your insecurities, weaknesses, and failures. Such vulnerability can be frightening, especially after a betrayal, and it's not uncommon to find those fears casting long shadows in the bedroom. It's hard to banish the ghost of your spouse's lover or stop dwelling on ways you believe you've failed ("I've never been a good enough lover" . . . "I haven't lost my pregnancy weight"). But the way to restore trust is to direct your emotional energies toward rebuilding intimacy.

Couples like Chrissy and Steve, who haven't made love for a long time, can't use their busy lives as an excuse for further lack of connection. Postponing intimacy until your stress level dissipates is a cop-out. You will always be busy and life is stressful. Instead, quit rationalizing and start thinking about what you can do right now to bring the two of you closer. What did you used to do when it was just the two of you? What do you miss most (reading by the fire, listening to jazz at a club downtown)? And how can you creatively weave those things back into your lives? Pick one idea—taking a coffee break on a busy Saturday afternoon, going for a walk to buy the Sunday papers, cooking a big dinner and choosing the wine—and just do it. Spending intimate time together outside the bedroom can translate into intimate time inside.

"He Placed a Personal Ad"

———◆———

Melissa was so wounded by Matt's betrayal, she refused to acknowledge the pain that had led him to it. How can two angry people break the cycle of blame and accusation?

MELISSA'S TURN

"I found this in Matt's briefcase," said Melissa, a twenty-eight-year-old financial analyst, waving a small piece of notepaper. "I was looking for his Palm Pilot to get the phone number of a restaurant, and right in plain sight was this draft for an ad that ran in the personals column of the paper: 'Successful banker seeks smart, sexy woman for fun and romance. Discretion a must.'

"All Matt could say was, 'I don't know what I was thinking. Please don't leave me.' So what do I do now? How do I know he hasn't gone out with women who responded to this ad—or even had sex with them? I feel so betrayed.

"Things haven't been right for a long time, though nothing even comes close to this. We're always snapping at each other, and little things quickly become major issues. Before we got married three years ago, we had a really good—and passionate—relationship. Now he's always the one who says 'Not tonight.' If he's so rarely in the mood, why is he looking for other women?

"Matt can be perfectly agreeable one minute, then lash out at me the next for something minor. And once he gets started, he doesn't stop. A few nights ago we had a huge fight about the built-in cabinets we're installing in our bedroom. He called me selfish because I wanted them

30

painted off-white. He preferred a gloomy dark walnut.

"Clearly, Matt thinks he's smarter than I am—and he doesn't hesitate to show it. He told our contractor not to bother explaining the details of his work to me because 'my wife wouldn't understand all that.' On our way to a wedding in New England last month, Matt cursed me out because I didn't give him directions quickly enough. He's hypocritical, too. He'll yell at me for spending too much money, then turn around and buy himself an expensive watch.

"I'm not used to being treated this way. My parents instilled in our family a sense of tradition, respect, and family values. Matt laughs at the idea of men opening doors for women, but little things like that were what counted in my house. My father owned a hardware store in Baltimore; my mom was a homemaker, and I had two much older brothers who were protective of their little sister. I can't deny that my family spoiled me.

"After getting my bachelor's degree, I moved to New York, hoping to launch a career in photography. Even though I majored in math, taking pictures has always been a passion of mine. I also wanted to be near Brent, the man I was seeing, who was attending law school. After a year of waitressing and only a handful of assignments, I lucked into an entry-level spot with an accounting firm, where I work to this day.

"Then, after nearly five years together, Brent told me he was in love with another woman. I was devastated. I didn't think I'd ever recover, until Matt came into my life. He lived in my neighborhood; I'd often see him at the deli or the dry cleaners, usually with a beautiful woman by his side. One night we ran into each other while we were getting Chinese takeout. This time Matt was alone, and he invited me to eat with him; that was our unofficial first date.

"I was still getting over Brent, and Matt was a sympathetic listener when I needed to talk about the breakup. When my father was dying of cancer, I took a leave of absence and went back to Maryland to help my mother care for him. Matt called me every day, came to visit several times, and attended the funeral. It was then that I realized how much I really cared about him.

"When I moved back to New York, I told Matt that I wanted to keep seeing him, but only if it would lead to something permanent. I didn't think I could handle another loss. A few months later, he proposed.

"But we certainly haven't lived happily ever after. The fact that we both work hellish hours doesn't help. If I leave the office at seven, I consider that a good night. Until I found Matt's ad, I was actually thinking about having a baby and leaving work to be an at-home-mother. But no child deserves to have parents who can't get along—or a father who's looking for a lover."

MATT'S TURN

"I'm mortified that Melissa found that scrap of paper," said Matt, a thirty-three-year-old investment banker. "The day I placed the ad, I was feeling as low as I've ever been in my life. I was still seething from the night before, when Melissa dismissed my suggestion about the finish on the bedroom cabinets with her typical what-a-moron attitude.

"While I was eating lunch at work, I flipped through the paper and spotted the personals column. Without thinking about the consequences, I scribbled an ad, phoned it in, stuffed the paper in my briefcase, and forgot about it. I got about a dozen responses, but I swear I never followed up on any of them. Did I fantasize about it? Absolutely. But I haven't had an affair.

"Even Melissa will admit that her parents catered to her. Whatever she wanted, she got, and she still thinks that's the way the world works. I don't know why it didn't bother me so much in the beginning. Maybe it was the lust factor. She's sexy and beautiful, and she was into the same things I enjoyed: skating, picnicking, going to the movies. Now she never seems to want to do anything with me.

"I'm tired of being the compromiser in this relationship. Melissa never lifts a finger around the house unless I ask her; instead, she gives me lists of things to do. She won't even feed our golden retriever, whom she adores. But she'll criticize me for a zillion little faults, like leaving my clothes on the bedroom chair. Or my new watch, which I paid for by selling my sports-card collection on eBay. Don't I have the right to choose what to do with my own money? Melissa also gets insulted about the silliest things, like not opening a door for her.

"For three years, I've put blinders on, figuring she'll never change. Melissa's a control freak, and you don't argue with her, because she goes ballistic. A discussion we had the other night about where to eat dinner suddenly ballooned into a major fight. I got enough of this kind of lousy treatment growing up.

"My childhood was less than idyllic, to put it mildly. My father was a pediatrician who, ironically, was considered an expert in his field. To his own children, he was emotionally and sometimes physically abusive. My mother couldn't stand up to him. Sometimes she'd secretly let us go out after he grounded us, but most of the time she was so worn down that she just parroted everything Dad said.

"I was your proverbial first child who pushed to be the best. I went to a good college and business school—

not that my father noticed. He wanted me to be a lawyer or judge, like his father, and was disappointed that I wasn't. So I put myself through business school, then moved to New York when I was offered a job.

"I didn't see myself getting married until I was at least thirty-five, but then Melissa gave me that ultimatum. I'd never been put on the spot like that, and I resented it. Still, I didn't want to lose her. I was crazy about her.

"But I never thought marriage would be such a one-way street. If I want to discuss the pressure at work or a difficult client, Melissa's not there for me. Ever. It's no wonder I pull away from her in bed.

"It doesn't help that we have a three-person relationship. I don't think there's been a day when Melissa hasn't mentioned her old boyfriend. His name invariably comes up when we're fighting. 'Brent never spoke to me the way you do,' she'll say.

"I know placing the ad was a big mistake. But I wonder if marrying Melissa was an even bigger one."

THE COUNSELOR'S TURN

"These two were so furious with each other that I had to keep calming them down," said the counselor. "Fighting had become the only way they could relate. While it's healthy to air gripes to your spouse, turning every squabble into a heated put-down match is not.

"I told them that the personal ad wasn't a sign that Matt didn't love Melissa, or that he wanted an affair. Rather, it was a cry for help. Matt was retaliating for Melissa's unacceptable behavior, much as his mother got even with his father by secretly reversing his punishments.

"Though Melissa was understandably hurt that her husband had placed the ad, she didn't recognize her role in the breakdown of her marriage. She insisted on keeping a firm control, issuing orders, making critical comments and playing the role of victim.

"I suspected Matt had been upset with Melissa for a long time, but couldn't bring himself to express his feelings. Instead, he buried them, only to blow up later. His rage also manifested itself in a low sex drive. Anger can be one of the main reasons couples stop making love.

"Slowly, as Melissa and Matt became aware of when and why they got angry, they were able to find ways to ease the tension and improve their communication. I told Matt he had to stop yelling and name-calling. Instead, I suggested he use the format, 'When you . . . then I,' as in 'When you bring Brent into the conversation, then I feel you're sorry you married me.' This allowed him to voice his feelings without finger-pointing.

"As Matt began to speak up more often, small concerns didn't have a chance to fester. Now, if a conversation starts to get out of control, he takes a time-out.

"As the tension at home lessened, and she saw that Matt was trying to prove that he cared, Melissa admitted that she had been unreasonable. 'I shouldn't be talking about Brent anymore,' she told Matt. 'It's you I love.'" Melissa also agreed to take on more responsibilities at home.

"I had Melissa practice repeating Matt's words back to him—a technique that forced her to really hear what he was trying to say. She now considers Matt's opinions instead of pushing her own agenda.

"Making an effort to reserve at least thirty minutes at night helped this couple reconnect. As they spent much-needed downtime together, their sexual relationship improved dramatically. Particularly important is that Melissa has genuinely forgiven Matt. 'I know he never meant to hurt me,' she said.

"Effective problem-solving takes patience and vigilance. By the time they ended counseling after seven months, Melissa and Matt had found a way to clear the emotional debris from their marriage."

OWNING UP TO THE PART YOU PLAY

Although you may still be smarting from the sting of infidelity, in order to fully heal, you need to figure out what part you might have played in the betrayal. Yes, you feel like a victim—angry, humiliated, hopeless. But in most cases each person shares some responsibility for what went wrong. This doesn't mean that anything you did justifies your partner's affair. It does mean that you may not be aware of the role you play in this domestic drama.

If you want to regain trust, you have to figure out what exactly that is. Consider: Are you close-minded and critical, like Melissa? Are you so easily angered that a partner may feel guilty or nervous bringing up his own concerns or feelings? Or, are you so needy or agreeable that people feel they can treat you like a doormat and walk right over you? To help you see yourself through your partner's eyes, reevaluate your expectations of the relationship, as well as how you act and what you say. Work to prevent small misunderstandings from snowballing into mistrust by vowing to resolve any issues when they first appear. The most important step you can take to protect yourself is to be direct and set limits for what you and your partner both need and deserve in the face of hurtful behavior.

"He Drinks Too Much"

———◆———

For a long time, unspoken marital trade-offs allowed Emma to tolerate Jay's drinking. But now that his job, his friends, and, most of all, his children were being hurt by his excesses, she had to stop pretending.

EMMA'S TURN

"When Jay walked into the school gym for our daughter's dance recital, I could tell he was smashed," said Emma, thirty-one, a part-time teacher's assistant. "Jay didn't do anything embarrassing, but he was unsteady on his feet and he cheered just a little too loudly. I think even Maddy, who's nine, could see that her dad had had one too many.

"Jay's drinking problem started long ago, but I didn't realize it then—or maybe I didn't want to. The first night of our honeymoon, he closed down the hotel bar, even though I had gone to bed hours earlier. I figured he needed to relax after the stress of the wedding, so I didn't chew him out.

"But by the time our son, Nick, was born six years ago, I couldn't ignore Jay's drinking any longer. True, he's not a sloppy, falling-down drunk; he can usually hold his liquor at restaurants or parties and, as far as I know, he's never been drunk at work. I'm also grateful that Jay has the good sense to take a cab home from the bars at night. But that doesn't mean he's got his drinking under control. It's begun to affect all of us, and it's got to stop. It's like having a third child.

"Jay's excuse is that he drinks only on weekends—but those weekends are getting longer and longer.

He's a broker, and he'll schedule client appointments for Friday afternoons so he can stay out drinking on Thursday night and come in late the next morning. We fight a lot about it—sometimes screaming matches, sometimes cold wars.

"I've begged Jay to go to Alcoholics Anonymous, but the one time he went, he told me that the meeting was full of 'real' drunks—naturally, that didn't include him—and he never went back. I've tried locking the front door so he can't get in after a binge. Once I actually called the police after listening to Jay bang on the door for an hour so hard that he hurt his hand. But the officers all know him, so they just cracked a few jokes and let him off with a warning.

"In fact, everybody knows Jay here. Both of us grew up in the resort community we live in now, and our families live close by. I have only happy childhood memories. My dad and his brother owned an appliance business in Manhattan; Mom was a full-time homemaker who did everything for everybody.

"Jay was friendly with my two older brothers, but I didn't get to know him until after high school, when he introduced himself to me at our beach club's huge Fourth of July party. He was five years older, which is a big deal when you're eighteen. I also liked his popularity; even today, people wave at him whenever he goes for a drive.

"We had a big wedding not long after I graduated from college. I taught first grade for two years, then quit after Maddy was born. I assumed that once we became parents, Jay would stop carousing and become more responsible. I was wrong. He continued to stay out late on Friday with his friends, then sleep in on Saturday and sometimes drink right up to Sunday night.

"Silently, I fumed, but I was busy with the kids and it was easier not to fight. The few times I tried to confront Jay, he'd say, 'I'm not an alcoholic! Stop nagging me!'

"So I focused on being a terrific mother. I love buying Maddy and Nick beautiful clothes, good books, and toys. Jay says I spoil them, but why shouldn't they have nice things if we can afford it?

"Recently, though, I've been getting on Jay's case a lot more—mainly because his drinking is affecting the kids. Nick has been getting into scrapes at school, and when he hears us fighting, he threatens to run away from home. Maddy's grades are slipping, and she's becoming a real watchdog, counting the number of drinks her dad has. If he has a glass of soda, Maddy will ask him for a sip just to make sure it's not spiked—and if it is, she tells me.

"Jay promises to stop drinking; I believe him, but then he goes right back to his old habits. I've gone to a few Al-Anon meetings, where everyone told me I should leave Jay until he sobers up. I don't want to break up our family. When he isn't drinking, Jay's the same wonderful guy I fell in love with—witty, considerate, romantic. And he adores our children. He's never missed a single soccer match, hockey game, or school play.

"I'm praying that counseling will work for us. I don't want Jay's drinking to doom our marriage."

JAY'S TURN

"I don't want to get divorced either," said Jay, thirty-six, a tall, handsome man who seemed ill at ease in the counselor's office. "I love Emma, and I don't want to hurt her or the kids. I can tell that they think I'm failing as a father. But Emma's got them so worked up it's like living with spies. Maddy's just as judgmental as her mother, and even Nick is dogging me. Last weekend we had some people over, and as I was getting a beer out of the fridge for one of my friends, Nick ran up and grabbed the bottle out of my hand.

"Despite what my wife may think, I'm not an alcoholic. My uncle was, and believe me, I know the difference. When I was growing up, our town had plenty of DUIs, car wrecks, kids who started on beer and vodka and went on to hard drugs. So I know what not to do. When I say I can handle this, I can.

"I'm the middle of five sons. Dad died when I was only twelve, and my two older brothers were already in college. I was devastated. But I promised myself I'd do everything I could to make Mom's life as easy as possible. She was overprotective of me, but that's understandable, since she had to do the job of two parents.

"I was a good athlete, but not much of a student. I took a year off after high school and worked as a local hockey coach. Then I enrolled in a business program at a city college, and discovered that I had a real flair for finance. By taking summer school and regular classes, I graduated in three years and was hired immediately by a reputable brokerage firm.

"Entertaining clients is part of my job, so I can't always come home early. And I don't appreciate being locked out of my own home. Emma does a lot of moaning about my hours, but it's funny how that griping stops when payday rolls around.

"I know our fighting has affected the kids, but you don't have the whole picture. Yes, Maddy's grades are slipping, but it's because she's so busy with her soccer games, dance classes, and play rehearsals that she doesn't have time to study. Nick's overbooked, too. He didn't want to try out for the swim team this year, but Emma insisted. She rarely considers my opinion when it comes to parenting. She never seemed to want my help, so I never had a reason to stop going out with my friends on Friday nights.

"Another sore point between us is Emma's spending. We both want to give the kids the best of everything, but she goes way overboard. Nick doesn't need another action figure every time a new kids' movie comes out. Emma doesn't stint on herself either. If she likes a turtleneck, she'll buy it in four different colors—without giving away any of her old clothes in exchange.

"This is crazy. At heart, we're good for each other, and I know Emma loves me. So why can't she stop hounding me about having a few drinks with my friends on weekends and going out for business dinners? I tried AA, but I had nothing in common with those people. They were all losers who'd bottomed out, and that's not me. I'm not sure what good therapy is going to do for our relationship either. I'm just afraid that I'll be painted as the bad guy, and then Emma will leave me."

THE COUNSELOR'S TURN

"Though Jay and Emma were angry and hurt," said the counselor, "they didn't see each other as the enemy. They were united by their deep love for each other and their children.

"Although Jay's alcohol use was a serious problem, it masked the other issues these two had—among them, an inability to negotiate solutions when it came to parenting, money, and household responsibilities.

"Emma, a micromanager like her mother, tried to do too much for too many. Whenever she felt problems were escalating, she sought more control over Jay. She also subtly encouraged some of his behavior by not confronting him directly. For instance, she assumed that once they had children, he would stop going out with his friends on Fridays. When he didn't, Emma was furious, but instead of saying so, she locked him out of the house.

"In their marriage, Emma had slipped into the mother role, with Jay as the son. This was a role he knew well, since his widowed mother had kept a tight rein on him. Drinking allowed him to escape.

"Though Jay denied it, he knew on some level that he had a drinking problem, and he felt so guilty about it that he rarely challenged his wife when it came to decisions about the children or the household.

"Jay was what's known as a 'functioning alcoholic.' He hadn't lost his job or his circle of friends, and up until recently, his marriage had appeared to be fine. But now Jay had to face up to reality. I urged Jay to go back to AA—for his family's sake if not his own. He went to a meeting that very night. Though it was far from easy, Jay quit drinking cold turkey. 'I still get tempted sometimes,' he admitted. 'But I've made my decision, and I'm sticking to it.'

"As Jay's drinking became less of a problem, he and Emma were able

HOW MUCH IS TOO MUCH?

Trust is an issue that comes up over and over again for those who have lived with or known someone suffering from an addiction—be it to alcohol, drugs, or gambling. Time and again they wonder: Can we count on him to be there, emotionally and physically? What's more, as Emma and Jay's case shows, once trust is shattered, it does take time to rebuild the relationship.

Although Jay did finally conquer his drinking problem, countless other couples are forced to deal with the difficult task of getting an addicted person to face his problem in the first place. Many of these victims deny their problems, to themselves as well as to their loved ones. Could you or your spouse be one of them? How can you judge how much is too much? The following questions can serve as a guide. Ask yourself honestly:

1. Are you drinking more, and stronger, drinks now than you used to?

2. Do you feel sorry or guilty about your drinking?

3. Do you find yourself unable to do something difficult unless you have a few drinks first? Does alcohol give you the boost of courage or energy you need to get going?

4. Do you insist to everyone, including yourself, that you are in control of your drinking?

The hardest step in overcoming an addiction is breaking through the denial. Once you can face the problem, you can reach out for help. You can talk to a clergyman, a doctor, or a therapist who is specially trained and knowledgeable about substance abuse or other addictions. You can also join one of the many self-help programs, such as Alcoholics Anonymous, or investigate in-patient treatment pro-grams at a hospital or, if you can afford it, a private clinic.

For more information, contact: Alcoholics Anonymous, PO Box 459, Grand Central Station, New York, NY 10163 (212-870-3400); www.alcoholic-anonymous.org; AAOnline.net; Al-Anon Family Group Headquarters, Inc., 1600 Corporate Landing Parkway, Virginia Beach, VA 23454; www.al-anon-alateen.org; 888-4AL-ANON; National Council on Alcoholism and Drug Dependence, 12 West 21st Street, New York, NY 10010 (212-206-6770); or consult your phone directory.

to focus on other issues. I suggested that Emma cut Jay some slack when it came to going out with clients. 'You don't want the responsibility of mothering your husband. That's no fun for either of you,' I said. 'Let him feel that he has control over his life.'

"It took a lot of effort for Emma to curb her anxieties enough to stop hovering over Jay, but she's worked at it. He became more responsible about coming home on time, and during business dinners, he stuck to soda and coffee. He eventually stopped going out with his drinking buddies in order to avoid temptation, and he faithfully attended his AA meetings.

"Once Emma felt she could trust Jay again, she was more receptive to listening to his concerns about the children. They agreed that Maddy and Nick needed to cut back on their after-school activities, and Emma promised to be less extravagant about buying toys. She also weeded out all the clothes she'd hung on to over the years.

"After the housecleaning was finished—in every sense of the word—Emma and Jay were able to end counseling after eight months."

"MY SECRET IS DESTROYING OUR MARRIAGE"

———•———

Humiliated by her secret past, Amanda blocked out her painful memories. But by not confiding in Bruce, she was hurting herself and depriving them both of the intimacy they deserved.

AMANDA'S TURN

"Something has got to change," sobbed Amanda, forty-four, her voice cracking. "I don't know what's wrong with me. I should be happy. Bruce's law practice is successful, and we have two beautiful sons—Jake is fourteen, and Jon is ten. But I feel overwhelmed and furious.

"For years now, often out of the blue, an overpowering rage wells up inside me, and I start lashing out at everyone. I can't explain it to myself, let alone to my husband. I feel controlled and overpowered by Bruce's needs, Bruce's desires.

"For the past four years, I've been working with Bruce in his law office. It was supposed to be temporary, but each time I try to leave, he pleads with me to stay.

"Bruce always gives me credit for my work. But we battle at the office and then we battle at home. In the last few months, Bruce has started to withdraw. The kids are suffering— Bruce is so impatient and harsh with them that Jake refuses to talk to him anymore, and Jon has become terribly overweight.

41

"Something has to change. I'm a physical mess: I have searing pains in my stomach, my head is pounding, and I'm exhausted all the time.

"My childhood was straight out of *Steel Magnolias*—at one point, my mother ran her own beauty shop in my bedroom. When I'd go to sleep, there were usually one or two women still waiting for a comb-out.

"Mom had a very traditional Southern upbringing, but she divorced my father, who was abusive to her, right after I was born. Shocked, her family cut her off and she had to support five kids on her wages as a hairdresser. When I was only a year old, she had to put us in a children's home run by the church. After two years, she brought my sister and me home, but it wasn't until I was eight, and Mom finally remarried—my stepfather was an engineer with the space program—that she was able to get my older brothers out. I'll never forget that day: We had moved into a small house in the suburbs, and I was bursting with happiness. We were a family at last.

"I was close to my siblings, since we spent a lot of time alone, with both of our parents working. We'd all have dinner together, though, when my parents got home.

"Our life wasn't *Father Knows Best,* of course. My parents fought a lot. I compensated by being the perfect child who always did her chores—and everyone else's, too.

"I idolized my brother Steve, who was two years older than I. We were inseparable; I knew that whenever I got into trouble, Steve would come to my rescue. In fact, even though we fought a lot, we were an affectionate family. But even though I was in the Honor Society and the debate club, was the head majorette and had a lot of boyfriends, I always felt I didn't deserve my achievements.

"There was no money for college, so after high school I moved to Denver and found a job as a secretary for a real estate company. Three years later, I was a regional manager. Yet even then, I felt like I didn't have the right to be there.

"I met Bruce through my brother Steve, who had also moved to Denver. I was immediately drawn to him. Quiet and thoughtful, Bruce had a gentleness about him and a wry sense of humor. Most of all he seemed interested in me because of my mind, not my body. We were friends before we were lovers—though our sexual relationship was marvelous from the beginning—and three years later we married. I kind of lost touch with Steve, though; I know he's not doing well—he'd been in Vietnam and he's had a long-standing drug problem.

"After the wedding, Bruce became an associate with a small law firm and I was a rising star in my company. I was the happiest I'd ever been. But when I got pregnant accidentally, all of a sudden Bruce decided he didn't want to be married or be a father. 'It's not in our plan,' he told me the day he moved out of our house.

"I was devastated, but determined to support myself and my child. Then, three weeks later, we reconciled, and Bruce moved back in. Of course, when Jake was born, Bruce fell head over heels in love with him. But the next few years were very hard. I quit my job to be home full-time, and Bruce still wasn't making much money. By the time Jon was born, I'd had several miscarriages and developed a host of medical symptoms ranging from gastroenteritis to erratic mood swings.

"Then Bruce suddenly lost his job. The guys who controlled the firm wanted him to do some shady deals. By mutual agreement, Bruce left. He was devastated, but he used this as a chance to open his own firm. I volunteered to help him get started, and we agreed that after four months, I'd leave.

"Four years later, I'm still there and he's still trying to control me at home as well as the office. The lectures never stop. The other day he was going on and on about how out of shape I've gotten and how Jon and I should join him on one of his marathon bike rides. Well, I don't care to, thank you very much. And I just wish he'd leave us alone.

"Look, I want—I need—to stop working. My insides are exploding. I need time for myself, and time to be with my children. But I'm really terrified that I'll never be able to break away. Maybe a professional counselor can help Bruce understand that I'm not rejecting him—and that he can survive if I'm not there every day."

"I have no idea what's wrong with Amanda," said Bruce, forty-nine, in a voice heavy with concern. "For a long time now she's been having these bursts of anger that seem to spring from nowhere. I get it in stereo—at home and at work—and I admit, I instinctively pull back. Her outbursts remind me of my mother's. But control her? Nonsense. She misinterprets everything.

"I feel like I'm skirting land mines—just like I did when I was growing up. My parents had nine kids. We lived outside of Chicago, and my father was a railroad mechanic whom I rarely saw because he was always working. Mother was a data processor. When she came home, she was too exhausted to pay much attention to any of us, except to rage at us. We all hated her. I never brought a friend home after school because I never knew when Mother would explode.

"I couldn't wait to get away from home. After college I was drafted and sent to Vietnam—I never thought I'd get out alive. When I did, I headed for Denver. In law school, I became friends with Amanda's brother Steve. You know, for years they were really close—I don't know why they hardly talk anymore. Steve recently sent Amanda a birthday card, and she left it on the hall table, unopened.

"Law school was a struggle, but meeting Amanda really helped me get through. The fact that someone so charming and so accomplished liked me made me feel great. I liked the fact that she was so independent, too. But even then, she'd have these out-of-the-blue rages. It was terrifying—that's the real reason I bailed out when I first found out she was pregnant. I didn't know if I could live with her.

"Of course, when Jake was born, I adored him and wanted a lot more kids. But considering Amanda's health problems, we're fortunate to have two healthy boys.

"When I had to leave my law firm, I was nervous, but I knew that I really wanted to work for myself. Amanda and I were a terrific team. My small firm—I hired one other lawyer as an associate—quickly became known as solid and responsible. Yet even at work, Amanda will lose it over the silliest details—if I point out that she put a comma in the wrong place in a subpoena, she'll start screaming at me.

"I have to say that the one thing that has never suffered is our sex life. Amanda is still, after sixteen years of marriage and two kids, the most incredibly sexy woman I've ever known. Maybe that's what's kept us together when everything else is falling apart."

THE COUNSELOR'S TURN

"Amanda and Bruce were in counseling with me, on and off, for several months," recalled the counselor. "They would come for a few sessions following a huge blow-up. Then, just when we were about to explore some tough issues, they'd abruptly end therapy.

"Finally, at the suggestion of her internist, who suspected a psychological component to her illnesses, Amanda asked to see me alone. Amanda's peculiar insistence that she was stuck in an untenable situation for the rest of her life suggested some deep-seated trauma. After discussing this with her physician, we agreed that her physical and emotional symptoms were typical of a victim of incest. I felt Amanda trusted me enough for me to ask her outright: 'Was there ever an incidence of incest in your life?' She nodded, stunned. The picture suddenly snapped into focus as Amanda told me what had happened."

AMANDA'S TURN

"One Saturday afternoon when I was about ten years old, my brother Steve, who'd gotten hold of a porn magazine, came into my room and convinced me to do some of those things with him. At first the episodes were mostly feel and touch, but after a few months we had intercourse. It was terrifying and painful. When I bled, I switched the sheets with my sister, who had already gotten her period. That way no one would suspect.

"I knew in my head that this was very wrong, so I blamed myself. Steve told me that if I ever told Mom, he'd never speak to me again.

"This continued for about two or three years. When Steve was fourteen, he had his first real girlfriend and he stopped being sexual with me. Though I was relieved, I also felt rejected.

"I don't know what to do. I can't tell Bruce. I'm afraid it will destroy our relationship. Steve is a very troubled man. I realized that having him in my life was destroying me, so I cut off all contact with him. Then, a few months ago, Steve's psychiatrist called me to ask about our childhood and the whole sordid story flooded me again."

THE COUNSELOR'S TURN

"Amanda's revelations gave me a new perspective on this couple's problems. Clearly, her life had been heavily colored by her relationship with Steve. Though she knew that what was happening was wrong, she, like many incest victims, felt she had no choice. She adored her brother and was desperate to keep this vital love connection in her life. Amanda couldn't go to her mother because she knew this revelation would not only shatter her mother but also destroy the illusion of a happy family life.

"In cases involving sibling incest, children have often been left home alone for long periods of time without an adult to set limits. I suspected that Steve had been a child with no sense of appropriate boundaries. Amanda, starved for affection, would do anything to make him happy.

"The legacy of an incestuous relationship is long and painful. Despite her many successes, Amanda grew up with an abiding sense of self-loathing. To soothe her guilt, she tried to please everyone all the time. By devoting herself to Bruce's success and serving his needs at the expense of her own, she was, without realizing it, making the same deal with Bruce that she had with Steve.

"I told Amanda firmly: 'You are not to go back to work—and you must tell Bruce this part of your story.' She was terrified, but over a series of sessions, we mapped out a plan: Once Amanda had become comfortable talking about the incest with me, she could then share her feelings with her husband. The next step would be to tell her siblings and her parents, and finally, to confront Steve.

"When she told Bruce, he sat for several moments in stunned silence. Then he rushed to hold her, saying over and over again, 'Why didn't you tell me? How awful this must have been for you.'" Once the forbidden had been spoken, Amanda and Bruce were able to begin putting back together the pieces of their marriage. Amanda no longer had to hide a terrible secret, and Bruce was finally able to see their relationship in clearer focus.

"Amanda's past experience exacerbated patterns already present in their marriage. For example, neither had grown up in a family where people spoke in a really collaborative, problem-solving way. As one of nine children of a passive father and an abusive mother, Bruce grew up feeling lost and devalued. Later, Amanda's total devotion to him boosted his self-confidence and made him feel safe. Though Bruce was certainly not an ogre, he didn't know how to speak in a caring and tactful way. He responded to Amanda's inexplicable rages in the same way

he responded to his mother's: by bailing out.

"Since Bruce now understands how his not listening triggers Amanda's old trauma, he has worked hard to stop tuning her out. He has slowed down the whole communication process, asking her to repeat something that's not clear, and listening without interruption.

"When arguments do occur, she and Bruce now stop, disengage, and then resume the discussion when they are both calmer. Most important, these two have carved out a new, more balanced relationship for themselves. They regularly make time for each other during the day to share their feelings. They've also made a point of doing things together, even if it's just a bike ride.

"I still see Amanda on a weekly basis as we work through how she is going to deal with her family members, including Steve. 'But I no longer feel that I have to keep everything bottled up inside,' she said. 'I'm not alone anymore.'"

THE TRAGEDY OF ABUSE

Amanda is not alone. Although precise figures are hard to come by, the Rape, Abuse, and Incest National Network (RAINN), the National Sexual Assault Hotline, estimates that 17 million women (one out of every six) have been sexually assaulted in their lifetime. Forty-four percent are under sixteen; one in six is under twelve. Boys as well as girls across all social and economic classes are victims of sexual assault. Ninety-three percent of the time, victims know their attackers. More shocking still is that most of these crimes are never reported because victims are either fearful of continued harassment from their attackers or too ashamed to ask for help.

Amanda's symptoms are also common. Incest is a betrayal of trust, and victims often find that feelings of overwhelming and unexplained anger linger years later. The horror of incest and other forms of abuse doesn't end when the abuse ends. Many victims suffer in silence, self-esteem shattered, afraid to speak up, afraid they made it up, ashamed they were unable to stop it, and guilty that they might have done something to provoke it. Their self-loathing makes them fearful of trusting themselves or others, and being intimate with another person may be impossible.

If you are the victim of abuse, talk to someone you trust about your experiences. Professional counseling can help you accept that the abuse was not your fault, and learn to trust your feelings and perceptions once again. For more information, contact RAINN, at 1-800-656-HOPE, or Survivors of Incest Anonymous, PO Box 190, Benson, MD 21018 (410-893-3322).

COMMUNICATE

Saying What You Mean, Meaning What You Say

O ver and over again, communication problems are targeted as the number-one cause of marital strife. "We're just not communicating" is a common lament. Every column since the inception of "Can This Marriage Be Saved?" describes at least one way (though usually more) in which husbands and wives either misread, or miss entirely, what their partner is saying. As a result, minor problems escalate into profound misunderstandings, layered with hostility, frustration, and blame.

In many cases, couples think they're communicating, but the messages aren't getting through. *Seven Secrets of a Happy Marriage* shows us that if husbands and wives can pinpoint why they're having trouble, they can sharpen their communication skills. In fact, in this conflict area more than any other, there are specific techniques and strategies for sharing ideas and feelings that couples can learn and practice—often initiating dramatic changes in the way they relate.

49

In many other cases, communication problems stem from differences in conversational styles between men and women, styles that can be traced right back to the playground, where little girls place a premium on talking and sharing secrets in order to make friends and be close, while little boys rely on displays of athletic prowess.

Early on, girls are schooled in the intricacies of intimate relationships. *Seven Secrets* shows us that when women grow up, they still put a premium on talking and sharing. Wives tend to be the emotional caretakers of the marriage. More attuned to their own feelings as well the shifting tides of their relationship, they notice and bring up problems more often than men do.

In interview upon interview, we meet women who yearn for their husbands to be a sounding board or to lend a sympathetic ear— to be someone with whom they can discuss their feelings and hash out problems. But men want action: Almost invariably, they'll interrupt a wife's recitation of a problem at work or with the children to jump in with a quick-fix solution. Moreover, once a man suggests an idea, he often considers the case closed. Given such disparate styles of communication, it's common to hear wives complain: "He doesn't care . . . he doesn't love me . . . he always tunes me out." Or for husbands to announce in frustration: "You want to know why I tune her out? Because she talks everything to death!"

Another common reason for communication foul-ups is what we call the mind-reader syndrome. Many couples—newlywed as well as long-married—fall victim. "If he really loved me, he would know what I want" is a typical complaint. So is: "She's not saying anything; she must be mad at me." Men are also much less likely than women to ask questions of a personal nature. They frequently think: "If she wants me to know, she'll tell me." Unfortunately, clinging to misconceptions about the way a partner ought to act often prevents couples from saying, honestly and directly, what they really feel and need.

Communication problems also occur when couples fail to state specifically what they really mean or want and, instead, couch those feelings in criticism of each other. Often, couples forget to use what marriage experts call "I" messages, which help each partner focus on his or her own feelings and take responsibility for them. Instead, they tend to launch conversations with "you" messages, which are hostile and blaming; unconsciously and almost automatically, they put a partner on the defensive.

How can a couple make sure they're communicating instead of criticizing? By beginning their conversations this way: "I feel hurt when . . . I worry that . . . I'm puzzled about . . ." instead of with "you" messages, such as "You're always late . . . You're just like your mother . . . You never call . . ." Of course, not every conversation that begins with "I" is appropriate or helpful in opening up blocked communication channels. When a partner says, "I'm sick of talking to you about this," or "I think you're a jerk," they're using what is called a "false I" message—one that's guaranteed to inflame rather than improve communication.

Timing can be equally crucial in getting your message across. The husband who wants to discuss a problem about the office when his exhausted wife yearns for sleep, or the wife who bombards a work-weary husband with a crisis the moment he walks in the door, fails to appreciate how important it is to pick the right time and place to initiate conversation.

Also important is the need to discuss one issue at a time—especially if it's a volatile topic. Many couples "kitchen-sink" their conversations: They start out talking about one problem and wind up arguing about another. Or one partner responds to a spouse's complaint by lobbing a nasty retort of his or her own; the arguments escalate as each launches old and new conversations, until neither can remember what they were talking about in the first place.

Couples chronicled in *Seven Secrets* also discover that there are other ways we communicate besides talking. Most of us don't realize that how we say something—our body language, facial expressions, and tone of voice—is as important as what we say. A curl of the lip, a roll of the eyes, arms tightly folded across the chest, or a false smile says contempt loud and clear. A glazed look or monosyllabic answers to a spouse's question says, "I'm fed up . . . I don't care about what's important to you."

Communication problems also occur at the listening as well as the speaking end—and once again, some of them may be linked to gender differences. Linguistics studies reveal that men tend to listen silently. They rarely nod in agreement or give their partner a verbal signal ("mm-hmm") that they've heard. On the other hand, women punctuate their listening by nodding their heads or saying mm-hmm at regular intervals. Because of this, wives may feel their husband is ignoring them. Husbands may interpret a wife's nodding to mean, Sure, I agree with you, only to be dumbfounded when she tells him later that she doesn't.

Couples who communicate well are empathic listeners. That means they listen for intent, not just content, and try to hear the feelings behind their partner's words: Is she or he tense? Worried? Happy? Listening empathically is hard work and doesn't come nearly as naturally as most people assume, even if they love each other very much. To be empathic listeners, people must put their own egos, feelings, comments, and judgments on hold. And they must look at each other when they talk, not at the newspaper, a cookbook, or out the window. One point *Seven Secrets* makes clear is that many people think they're listening, but what they're really doing is trying to figure out their own response. They lie in wait for the conversation to slow down so they can jump in with their own observations, opinions, or arguments.

As the following case histories illustrate, many people don't realize they aren't saying what they mean, or meaning what they say. Recognizing how each partner contributes to communication problems is the first step in changing old patterns and reconnecting in new, more loving, more empathic ways.

"He Criticizes Everything I Do"

When "Can This Marriage Be Saved?" debuted in January 1953, couples were actually facing many of the same problems they are today. In this, the very first column, newlyweds Diana and Guy had no idea how to talk to each other and resolve their differences. Under the constant barrage of criticism, trivial skirmishes soon escalated into all-out war.

DIANA'S TURN

"I have no home, no children, and no peace," said Diana, a pretty twenty-two-year-old. "I have no husband and no love as I think of it. Guy never kisses me except when I'm frantically busy at some household task, and then his kisses are rough and hurt me. For six years my husband has made love to me as a matter of routine, like taking in a bottle of milk—something to be done in a hurry. And he picks the time; I don't.

"My secretarial job is as hard as Guy's job, but Guy refuses to so much as dry a dish. He throws a newspaper on the floor for me to pick up, and then complains our apartment looks like a pigsty. When dinner is five minutes late, he flies into a fury, but he won't even help me with the shopping. We own an automobile, but Guy won't allow me to drive it. When we drive anywhere, it's where he wants to go.

"My savings are supposed to be set aside so we can buy a house, but in fact they're always being frittered away on his car. Guy says that we're too young to own a house and I wouldn't know how to keep it anyway. I want my babies while I'm young, but my husband seems determined to postpone having a family until he's an old man. He tells me I would make a rotten mother.

"Guy criticizes everything about me: my tastes in clothes, my hairdo, even my Saturday art classes—one of my few pleasures. Other people—my boss, the girls and young men I work with—find things to admire about me, but from Guy I receive only nasty comments, never a word of affection or praise.

"I knew Guy just six weeks when we eloped. I was barely sixteen and had just begun dating and dancing and having fun. I thought marriage would be wonderful. I think I fell in love with Guy because he was nineteen and seemed like an older man to me. And he was so gentle and kind . . .

"My family was really poor, but one place we lived, just a shack really, had a backyard with a big tree and a swing. There were nine of us kids and it was hard to be alone, but often at night I would slip out of bed and go to the tree. I would swing and swing, higher and higher, to see if I could reach a star with my toe. The night I married Guy—this may sound crazy and corny, but it's true—I felt as though I'd touched a star. Something in me wished and believed the lovely, peaceful feeling would last forever.

"The feeling didn't last. Even our honeymoon was awful. We ran off to Las Vegas in a car Guy borrowed from a friend; the car broke down and the repairs took all his money and mine, too. I had a job, of course; I've always worked. When we got back here to Los Angeles, with only ten cents between us, we had to go and stay with Guy's family. His mother was furious over the marriage—she hated to lose Guy's earnings and didn't mind saying so—and she was dreadful to me. His father wasn't so bad, but he drinks too much and doesn't work half the time so is forever cadging loans from Guy.

"After I took all the abuse I could stand from his mother, we moved in with my family. Two of my sisters doubled up with my little brothers so we had a room to ourselves, but Guy criticized my whole family.

"Finally, we took our own apartment; in six years we lived in seven different places—the landlady asked us to move out of the last one because we quarreled so much—but none of our places has been a home. Clearly, we're unsuited to each other in every way.

"My back isn't strong, and sometimes it pains so much I can hardly bear it. The doctor says the pain is caused by worry and nerves. Sometimes I cry for hours; I have horrible nightmares and even cry in my sleep. I'm trying so hard to please Guy and I'm always and forever failing. For six years I've been a failure in everything.

"The lawyer I went to for the divorce suggested I come to you for advice and that's why I'm here. I want a divorce, a new life, a new start. I'm young. Surely I'm entitled to a home and children and a husband who loves me. I don't see how you can help me and Guy make anything of our marriage, but if you can, I suppose I'm willing to try."

GUY'S TURN

"Sometimes when Diana is crying the way she does," said the twenty-five-year-old Guy, "I think I'll go crazy. I'm back listening to my mother crying over imaginary aches and ills and making me take care of the twins and put supper on the stove, while she lies on the bed jawing about my dad being no good. Diana thinks her back and her nerves are all my fault, like everything else that goes wrong. She's just like my mother, always whining and complaining and crying for sympathy or compliments.

"My wife wears tight sweaters and skirts to the office, and then comes home and tells me how cute her boss says she is. Then she has another crying spell unless I tell her she's beautiful, when her boss—that big shot—has already said it, and said it better, as she doesn't hesitate to tell me. I'm just a dumb mechanic, and these days my wife is too high-toned to be interested in machinery.

"Maybe she should have married a big shot like her boss, or an art professor like the one whose classes she goes to on Saturday mornings, or some movie star like Clark Gable who'd hand her lines of mush all the time. She'd probably condescend to dress up and primp for Gable the way she primps for the office. You ought to see what she wears at home for me! Any old thing will do.

"I've done everything on earth to please my wife, but Diana is a girl you can't please. We've moved seven times in six years to find a place she likes, and now she's insisting that we buy a house we can't afford. Sure, I'd like my own home someday, and some children, too, but what's the hurry? Why can't we wait?

"Diana thinks I'm a dope, but I think she's the one who's completely childish, thinking of nobody except herself. Our meals are always two hours late and then the food isn't fit to eat. You can hardly get in our kitchen for the dirty dishes. One thing I always wanted when I married was a clean, peaceful place to go to when I finished my day's work, the kind of place my dad never had with my mother. Living with Diana, I sure haven't gotten it.

"When I was a boy and would think about finding a wife, I'd picture someone docile and pretty and sweet, not necessarily brainy and with a lot of ideas, but someone who would keep a nice clean house and look after me the way nobody ever had. Diana at first seemed that way to me—shy and sweet and kind of scared, not a know-it-all like most girls. You should have heard her say how wonderful I was to be so smart about mechanical things. Boy, did she change in a hurry! Now she's forever nagging to drive our car, and she doesn't know beans about how to treat a car. She wrecked the one I borrowed for our honeymoon and ruined our trip, so we had to go to my home to stay. My mother kicked up one of her rows and Diana couldn't handle what I'd been taking all my life. She'd have left me then if I hadn't agreed to stay with her family. Let me tell you, my family is no bargain, but hers is worse.

"Diana and I haven't had a peaceful day since we married. If she wants to go ahead and get a divorce, it's all right with me. A new shake might be better for both of us. I'm sick of things the way they are. But if you can help change things and improve Diana, I'll do my part."

THE COUNSELOR'S TURN

"**D**iana and Guy got off to a wretched start," said the counselor. "Both were unready for marriage, both were selfish and immature, ignorant of themselves and of each other and of the differing family backgrounds and experience that had shaped their personalities. In short, they knew nothing of the meaning of marriage.

"For instance, their sexual relations were disappointing. Diana was a romantic, chronically resentful that marriage didn't provide the thrills and fun she missed in her teens. On the other hand, Guy was contemptuous of tender lovemaking in marriage, which he considered 'unmanly.' During our sessions it became clear that his contempt and the 'roughness' during lovemaking of which Diana complained were based on ignorance: This young husband was actually unaware that sexual satisfaction for women existed. Several good books on the subject enlightened him, and once he learned to show tenderness and consideration for Diana, this couple's sexual maladjustment was solved.

"When Diana stopped reporting office compliments to her husband and bought a few pretty dresses for home use exclusively, she soon received from Guy the compliments and praise she had been tactlessly demanding. By the same token, Guy's vanity was soothed by the extra attention, and his jealous belief that Diana was forever comparing him disadvantageously with other men was changed into pride that he had such a beautiful wife.

"Diana and Guy saved their marriage not only by changing their attitudes and behavior, but also by applying thought instead of emotions to their problems. A new marriage would have solved nothing for either of them, since their basic trouble lay within themselves. For six wasted years, both honestly believed they were trying to please and understand each other when, in truth, they were merely indulging in harmful criticism. They promised instead to eliminate mutual criticism as far as was humanly possible; and they endeavored to understand themselves and each other and to communicate their needs honestly. As a logical result of this gradual reeducation, they began to give each other that loving help and attention that is marriage.

"Diana's poor housekeeping stemmed from a weak, inefficient mother and a slovenly girlhood home. Similarly, Guy's unrealistic dream of perfect meals served in a clean, well-run home, with himself doing nothing to assist, represented a rebellion against a dominating mother who overloaded him with housework when he was young and made him the butt of jokes by male friends. Once this couple realized the origin of their combative attitudes, they became more tolerant of each other and found their own solution: Guy, who was a better cook than Diana, began helping her plan the menus and thus was painlessly led into carrying his fair share. He enjoyed teaching Diana how to cook, and she enjoyed learning. Incidentally, shortly after the meals prepared by both started reaching the table on time, Guy voluntarily offered to teach Diana how to drive a car and they began sharing the use of the automobile.

"The questions of home ownership and children, both legitimate desires of Diana's, were tougher to solve. Guy shrank from assuming additional financial responsibility and, again after several sessions, the reason became apparent: Guy had seen his amiable but weak father, to whom he was devoted, crushed by the excessive demands of his dominating mother. Diana, insistently clamoring for a home and children as her right, had given no thought to her husband's desires and fear of running into debt.

"When the two started driving around on Sunday to inspect housing developments, they told themselves they were merely looking. But here again, Diana discovered a fact about her husband she hadn't learned in six years of quarreling. Indifferent to home ownership, Guy was extremely interested in rare California plants and flowers, which dated from the time when he worked as a yard boy on a big estate. In the end, they purchased a small house with a big backyard and Guy has a garden. Diana and Guy now garden enthusiastically together, their first common interest. As an outgrowth of Diana's genuine interest in his gardening, Guy became interested in her love of painting and joined the weekend class he had previously jeered at. Two pictures hang in their living room—a landscape by Diana, a seascape by Guy. She considers his painting far better than hers, and is quick to call it to the attention of visitors. The two have changed the pattern of destructive criticism into constructive mutual praise and approval. Their in-law problems have also been solved: since they now understand the 'why' of their elders' failings and virtues, they can calmly discuss their shortcomings.

"A year ago Diana gave up her job—'little Guy' was wanted by both. Diana is now awaiting the birth of a second child. She no longer needs to demand assistance from Guy because he gives it freely, anticipating her wants because of his pride and joy in his wife, child, and home. The two frequently inform us they are supremely happy—since they've realized they have to work at marriage, they have earned a good successful union."

STANDING UP TO PUT-DOWNS

Many husbands and wives feel unfairly criticized by their spouses, yet find themselves powerless to defend themselves. If you have a similar problem, these steps can help you rebuild your self-esteem and regain your footing:

1. Remind yourselves that you are entitled to your feelings and have every right to speak up and say: "I feel offended by what you just said," or "That was inconsiderate." If the insulting behavior continues, try to control yourself and not lash out wildly in defense. Instead, walk away. You'll be sending a far more powerful message.

2. Choose your words with care to avoid fanning the flames. Speak firmly, but in a way that doesn't demean your partner.

3. Try not to respond to criticism by hurling criticism of your own. This escalates the argument and deepens the power struggle. If you think you can't respond reasonably, say so: "I'm too angry to talk about this right now. After I've had a chance to calm down, we'll continue." Agree to talk about a more neutral topic.

4. Ask yourself if there might be even a shred of truth in what your partner is saying. If there is, can you negotiate a compromise? Sometimes your partner really does have a point, but he's blowing it way out of proportion. Think about what he says and decide if there are changes you can make that might ease the tension.

"My Perfect Husband Wants Out"

Howard and Gail had a model marriage until the day Howard suddenly packed his bags. Why would a man run from the family he's loved for twenty years?

GAIL'S TURN

"This is a nightmare, and soon I'm going to wake up," said Gail, a trim forty-year-old with perfectly coiffed blond hair, classic clothes, and tears in her eyes. "Night before last, we finished dinner, the boys went up to their rooms, and Howard and I sat down in the family room to have our coffee. But instead of bringing up something about the office or the church, Howard said in this calm voice, 'Gail, I'm leaving you.' Like a bolt out of the blue. I couldn't speak. My friends always told me my marriage was too good to be true; I'm beginning to think they were right.

"Howard and I met when I was in junior high and he was a senior in high school. He worked after school at Friendly's, and my girlfriends and I used to go there, order sodas, and flirt with him. I couldn't believe it when he asked me out. My parents said I was too young to date, but finally, when I was in the tenth grade, they invited him for dinner, and after that they let me go out with him.

"By then, Howard was a sophomore at MIT, and they were so impressed with him. I mean, he's incredible—sensitive, hardworking, brilliant, and good-looking, too.

"Anyway, we got married when I was nineteen and a sophomore at Tufts. Howard already had a good job at an engineering firm, the first step to owning his own company. "My parents gave us a beautiful wedding, although Howard's parents weren't exactly thrilled that it was a Methodist ceremony. They're an old Boston family, High Church Episcopalians. He wanted to do whatever made me happy, and since I had always been involved in my church, Howard agreed to become a Methodist and raise our children as Methodists. This does not qualify as an interfaith marriage in my opinion, but his mother was really uppity about it.

"This never bothered Howard; he doesn't have a warm relationship with his mother at all. It's cordial but cool. She's what I would call an alcoholic, but Howard calls her a lady drunk. She never takes a drink until after dinner, and then she drinks herself to sleep every night. As far as I can tell, she's always been too hungover to do much mothering. Howard and his two brothers brought themselves up with the help of a sweet old housekeeper whom they adore.

"Howard's father is a nice enough man, but aside from earning a lot of money—he's a corporate executive—he was indifferent. I'm the oldest of five, three girls and two boys, and my mother has devoted her life to us. My father spent a lot of time at his job with an electronics firm, but he was always home for dinner, and he helped us with our homework, took us on camping trips, things like that.

"I told Howard right from the start, I wanted my own kids to have the same kind of childhood. Howard never objected, and he was making enough so we could afford a four-bedroom house in a good school district. Our first son, Scott, was born while I was still in college and the second, David, just after my graduation. My mom helped with Scott so I could stay in school, but I couldn't wait to graduate and become a full-time mother.

"I did want Howard to be a very involved father and he certainly went along—happily, it seemed—with everything I suggested, starting with being my labor coach and moving right along to being on the board of directors at the nursery school, coaching the soccer team, even chairing the board for the Methodist summer camp where the boys and I go every summer. I work as a counselor there and Howard comes up on weekends. He likes the time alone during the week to read and go to plays and things. It all worked out.

"At least I thought it did. Oh, I suppose there were signs of trouble over the last few years, now that I look back. For one thing, our sex life is, well, pretty nonexistent. I figured it was some kind of midlife thing and maybe he just lost interest, so I never said anything to Howard; I didn't want to embarrass him. To be honest, the last time we made love was a year ago. I'm sure there isn't another woman, though.

"What's wrong? The boy's behavior for starters. Scott and David are now sixteen and fifteen and the teenage years have been hard on Howard. He hates rock music, the needless phone calls, and the general state of chaos the house is always in. Howard is a neatness nut and has always done his share of the housework. Now that I have a part-time administrative job at a boarding school nearby, plus all my usual volunteer work, I've fallen down on my end of the job at home. The boys' clothes and things are all over the place. But is this such a big deal? Look, they don't do drugs, and they get pretty good grades. What Howard sees as problems are just normal growing pains, if you ask me.

"So all right, Howard has complained about the boys and the house, and we haven't been making love. But was that supposed to prepare me for his announcement? He only agreed to come here on the grounds that we consider it divorce counseling. Howard has no intention of trying to save our marriage, but I really can't imagine life without him. How can I change his mind?"

HOWARD'S TURN

"Do you know what it's like to wake up one day and realize that all the time and energy you've devoted to your family has been a complete waste?" asked Howard, a distinguished-looking forty-four-year-old with graying temples.

"When I married Gail, she said her dream was to bring up kids in the same good family atmosphere she had enjoyed as a child. That appealed to me. From what I could tell, her parents had done a great job. My mother is very proper and reserved and she spends her evenings drinking alone in her room. My father is a pleasant guy, but he never had much time for us either.

"I never minded all this, really. I'm naturally self-sufficient and don't remember having any particular highs or lows as a kid. I was good in school and I knew I wanted to get into a good college and have a career. Actually, I guess I'm kind of a loner. But Gail, she's the joiner. I pretty much had to get on this board or that committee or I never would have seen her. But I also believed she knew what she was doing. She said we had to be involved parents, she pushed religion, and I went along with everything—even the church camp, which was a great experience for Gail and the boys, but it made a summer bachelor out of me.

"Of course, even if they'd all been home during those months, I still wouldn't have had any time with Gail. From the minute Scott was born, motherhood has been Gail's priority. Certainly our sex life took a backseat, though I don't think Gail ever noticed. Or cared. And she has let me know in no uncertain terms that as the father of two boys I have a responsibility to be their role model. I was also supposed to be a modern husband and do housework and cooking.

"In case you think I never complained, I did. Not very often and not in an angry way, but I did tell her how I felt. Gail just never paid any attention.

"The funny thing is, if I thought the boys were turning out okay, I would have continued to live her way. But frankly, none of this attention has had any effect on my sons. Don't get me wrong—I love them, but I don't believe that boys who wear earrings are normal teenagers. Why a healthy American male would want to spike his hair with green gel and wear jewelry is beyond me. They do their homework, but they're not getting top grades, and they have no ambition that I can ascertain. They talk back, they throw their stuff all over the place—I've had it.

"Look, I'm a conservative New Englander. I had a job after school from the eighth grade on. I think they're spoiled rotten.

"But does it matter what I think? Gail is always right. Well, fine. She can watch them squander the most important years of their lives. I don't want any part of it. I don't care if I live in a furnished room somewhere, as long as there's peace and quiet. I'm not worried about being lonely. I'm alone as it is. And no, there is no other woman. I don't think I'll trust myself to get involved again.

"Don't try to talk me out of leaving. Just give us some advice about how to have a civilized divorce. For once in my life, I'm not going to say yes when I know I should say no."

THE COUNSELOR'S TURN

"This is one of the most difficult cases I've ever handled," said the counselor. "Howard had spent a lifetime keeping the peace, first by steering clear of his alcoholic mother, who was never emotionally available for him, then by complying with Gail's every wish and command to create a storybook family. As he pointed out, he was a yes-man, and when he admitted that nothing was working out the way he had imagined, it was as if a dam had burst. In his mind he had rejected marriage and family life, and by the time he had told Gail, his decision seemed irrevocable.

"At first, I went along with Howard's phrase, 'divorce counseling.' I was humoring him to gain his confidence. I saw the two of them separately for some time until I felt that a joint visit would be fruitful. I would have lost Howard early on if he thought I was forcing him to participate in a reconciliation.

"During her first session, Gail was frightened and puzzled, and one could certainly sympathize with her. Still, as we worked together, she started to see how she had taken advantage of Howard's compliance, a coping style he had learned as a child. She also admitted that Howard, in his own polite way, had indeed given her warning of his dissatisfaction—warnings she had ignored. Finally, Gail learned to face the fact that there had been too much focus on the children and that some measure of discipline was in order.

"Meanwhile, in separate sessions with Howard, I encouraged him to consider what his life would be like in that furnished room or, for that matter, to consider if he really wanted to be alone for the rest of his life. Gradually, he realized it might be worth trying to save the marriage.

"The first joint session was not very successful, since Gail dominated the conversation and Howard sat stone-faced, saying only that he had known this would be useless. However, subsequent sessions went much better; Howard began to exercise a newfound ability to express negative feelings, and Gail, in the therapeutic setting of my office, found it easier to listen. I advised them to make a point of taking turns talking every evening at home. In preparation, I saw Howard privately again, to help him get in touch with his physical response—such as a knot in the stomach—whenever Gail said something to which he objected, and then express his opposition.

"It was during this time that a great many changes were decided upon: Howard dropped several boards and committees that didn't interest him; the boys were given house rules and chores; Gail cut back on her vol-unteer work to have more time with Howard and more time to do her share of the housework. And, most important, Gail and the boys agreed not to attend the church camp that summer. Instead, the boys found summer jobs, and at one point, Gail's mother came for two weeks while Gail and Howard took a trip to the Bahamas.

"Those weeks proved to be just what this couple needed. Without the usual distractions, Howard and Gail focused on each other for the first time in years, and fell in love all over again.

"In the year since they finished counseling, I've been in touch several times. The oldest boy, Scott, is now eighteen and a freshman at Boston University, with plans to go to law school. He has adopted a much more conservative look and has a steady girlfriend whom Howard and Gail approve of. David, while still into punk styles, will enter Juilliard next fall, where he plans to major in music. Howard and David will never be close, but at least they coexist peacefully.

"Howard in particular looks forward to the empty-nest years, which are closer than he had realized. Gail still has her part-time job and some of her volunteer work, but she now accompanies Howard to the theater, and they have joined a literary discussion group. Clearly, what had looked to all the world like a perfect marriage was certainly not, but the marriage that Howard and Gail now have, though not perfect, is loving and certain to endure."

LEARNING TO TALK—AND REALLY LISTEN

Throughout most of their marriage, Gail and Howard had been running on parallel tracks. Like many couples, they communicated about the mundane, superficial aspects of their lives—Who was going to drive the boys to soccer practice? What time is the school board meeting?—but forgot about sharing their hopes and dreams, their fears and uncertainties. Gail, in fact, was so caught up in her daily activities that she never heard many of the things her soft-spoken husband had been trying to tell her. Like these two, many couples are afraid to rock the proverbial boat, so they talk about their relationship only when they're arguing. Experts assure us, however, that the best time to really communicate is when things are going well.

Do you, like Howard, feel that your partner either doesn't listen or misinterprets what you're saying? The counselor who helped this couple communicate on a deeper level coached them in a classic therapeutic technique called reflective listening. Here's how it works:

Set aside at least half an hour, perhaps after the children are asleep. Make a pot of tea or coffee, or share a glass of wine, and let the answering machine handle all calls. This time is for you. Take turns being the sharer of information or the listener. The sharer has ten minutes to speak freely about anything that's on his or her mind. You could talk about a funny incident that happened at the office, what you look forward to doing on vacation or something one of your kids did. (Initially, it's best to avoid potentially volatile subjects until you both feel emotionally safe enough to do so.) The listener must look directly at the speaker, and refrain from interrupting, judging, or rushing in with a comment. After ten minutes—use a kitchen timer if you like—the listener must recap not only what the sharer said, but also the feeling behind the words. The sharer then says, "Yes, that's right," or "No, that's not what I meant," and if necessary, repeats the comments. This way, the sharer knows that his or her feelings and thoughts are truly being heard and valued.

Like most people, Howard and Gail felt that this exercise was awkward and artificial at first. However, the structure and format of this exercise can be just what chronic noncommunicators need to get in the habit of sharing their feelings and their lives.

"We Have Nothing in Common Anymore"

After twenty-five years of marriage, Mark and Carrie were convinced that their differences far outweighed their similarities. What happens when two people who love each other drift apart?

CARRIE'S TURN

"Who is this man I'm married to?" demanded Carrie, fifty, a tall, slender woman with a tense, unhappy face. "Mark and I have just celebrated our silver wedding anniversary and I still feel as if I don't know him. I am equally certain he doesn't know me.

"On the one hand, my husband can be jovial and happy-go-lucky, always out for laughs and a good time. He has a million friends and every one of them thinks I'm so fortunate to be married to such a fun-loving guy. But let Mark have a few drinks and a different side of him emerges. He will turn on me in a rage and pour out a hate-filled diatribe of cruel and vicious insults.

"I don't mean to imply that Mark is an alcoholic. He doesn't drink often, but when he does take a drink or two, usually at a party, I brace myself for what will follow. The moment we've left the group, Mr. Nice Guy disappears. Mark goes into a tirade, accusing me of being penny-pinching, nagging, bitchy— every hideous adjective he can come up with. When we get home, I bury my face in my pillow and cry my eyes out. I feel so worthless. But in the morning, Mark reverts to his sunny self, spilling over with apologies for having had a few too many. When I try to discuss the previous night he refuses to acknowledge that any scene occurred.

"I fell in love with Mark because of his exuberant approach to life. I had been raised in a family that put duty before pleasure. My father, a German immigrant who never went to high school, had educated himself by taking correspondence courses. He worked as a self-employed building contractor and supported us so well that Mother never had to work outside the home. Dad doled out money to her to run the house and I don't think she ever knew what they had in the bank. Both my parents were strict disciplinarians and my sister and I were always on our best behavior.

"I don't know much about my parents' personal relationship. I now think there may have been some problems, but they didn't let it show. They lived apart for three years while I was a teenager, but that was supposedly because my father had to be away on business. Dad and Mama never argued. I can remember only one fight, during dinner one night, when Mother got up, walked around the table, and slapped my father. I will never forget the shock of seeing her do something so incredibly out of character.

"My high school years were pleasant. I made good grades and enjoyed sports, although I didn't date much. After I graduated I went to college, but soon dropped out to take an office job. I had no particular career goal. All I really wanted was to be a housewife and mother.

"When I was nineteen, I married Frank, my girlfriend's brother. It was a foolish thing to do—I was in love with love, not with Frank. Although I soon realized I had made a mistake, I hoped that once we had children life would be better. When three years passed and I still had not become pregnant, my mother-in-law casually mentioned that Frank was sterile. He had known all along and had never told me. After that, there just didn't seem to be any reason to stay married.

"Mark came into my life two years after my divorce. He was a salesman for the company I worked for and I was immediately attracted to him. But Mark was married, and although he and his wife were separated, I still didn't feel we should go out together. I encouraged him to give their relationship one final chance, but the effort was not successful. Once Mark was legally free, we were married.

"I can't put into words what I actually expected from the marriage. I know I hoped it would be more than it is. When I look back over the past twenty-five years, I feel as though we have been treading water. Except for having raised two children, now on their own, we have nothing to show for all our time together.

"Not that I ever expected to be rich. I knew Mark had an obligation to the three children from his former marriage, and I never quarreled over the portion of his income that went to them. What I have resented is his inability to adjust his lifestyle to compensate for that expense.

"Although Mark won't admit it, we live hand-to-mouth. He works on commission and his earnings have never been consistent. It's true that many of his career problems have not been his fault. He started a promising business and that didn't work; his partner was unreliable. I don't blame him, but his stubborn refusal to accept our situation makes me furious. How can he take afternoons off to play golf when we need every penny? How can he expect us to eat out with friends several nights a week when I'm going crazy figuring out how to put food on the table?

"I went back to work several years ago to help make ends meet. My job consists of dull, boring, unrewarding office work, but that's all I feel qualified to handle. Mark uses my earnings to subsidize his membership in the country club. He's the only one who uses the facilities—I'm too tired after work and housekeeping to even think of going there. But Mark shows no appreciation of my efforts. Many nights he doesn't show up for the dinner I've fixed, and he doesn't even call to tell me he's not coming home. Then, hours later, when he finally walks in, he can't understand why I'm not in the mood to make love.

"I don't feel that our relationship has any meaning for Mark. I'd like us to spend time alone together to discuss what matters to each of us. But Mark wants to be out socializing every evening. When I attempt to talk to him about the problems in our marriage, he acts as though I'm speaking a foreign language.

"I don't want a divorce. Mark and I have invested too much of our lives in each other to split up now. But the thought of going on as we have been for another twenty-five years is more than I can face. It was different when the kids were home. I felt confident and secure in the role of mother. Now that it's just Mark and me, I feel so unfulfilled and empty. Our relationship is all I have left—and it isn't enough."

MARK'S TURN

"I don't know what I'm doing at a counseling service," said Mark, fifty-six, a handsome, white-haired man with an affable grin. "I'm a fun-loving guy who takes life as it comes. The last thing I want is for some cockeyed therapist to change me.

"My dad was the same sort of person. All the youngsters in the neighborhood loved him. He'd take us all fishing, build a bonfire, tell us scary stories—he was like one of the kids. My mother was the one who always played the heavy.

"My father was a dredge operator who worked at dam construction and every six to eight months he'd be transferred to a new location. I had attended twenty-four schools by the time Mom finally put her foot down and announced she was sick of moving. From then on, my brothers and I saw Dad only on weekends and our mother took over control of the family.

"As a kid, I had one big dream— to become a doctor. When I graduated from high school I was drafted into the Navy, where I trained to become an operating-room technician. I served as a surgical assistant during the Korean War and was more competent than a lot of the doctors. After my discharge I entered college on the GI Bill, fully intending to go to medical school. That plan fell through and I have no one to blame but myself.

"I got married, which was crazy for a young man in my position, and then my wife, Sheila, immediately became pregnant and had to stop working. I held all sorts of odd jobs in the evenings and on weekends, and we borrowed money from our parents, but the bills kept mounting. Sheila nagged me to leave school and get a full-time job.

"My grades kept dropping. I blamed that on financial pressure, but to tell the truth, that was only part of the problem. During my

years in the service, I'd forgotten how to study. When I flunked out of college in my junior year, I was actually relieved. Finally, I could go to work and support my family.

"I found a job selling office supplies, and I was good at it. Our finances improved, but our marriage didn't. Sheila was on my back constantly and I could hardly bear to come home at night. Two more babies arrived, which added to the chaos. We were both miserable and decided on a trial separation.

"That's when I met Carrie. She was tall and stately, lovely to look at and as soothing to be with as Sheila was overbearing. At Carrie's urging, I returned to Sheila to give our relationship one last chance. The reconciliation was a farce; my heart and mind were totally focused on Carrie. Although the divorce was at my request, it was painful. I have always felt guilty about leaving Sheila with three children.

"Carrie insists that we have nothing to show for our twenty-five years together. What does she want, a twenty-room mansion? We have two fine kids, lots of friends, fun times to remember, and good health.

"Having been through eight hellish years of bickering with my first wife, I resolved that things would be different this time. I'm proud of the fact that I've kept my oath. Carrie isn't the easiest person to live with, but I've tried to ignore the negative and focus on the positive. When she gives me the cold shoulder sexually, I grin and bear it. If she doesn't want to go out partying, I go without her. Carrie is a martyr. When she starts pulling her 'poor me' act, I just close my ears.

"Carrie's big complaint is that I sometimes get rowdy after partying and pop out with things that might have been better left unsaid. I occasionally do that, but I always apologize. A guy can't be held accountable for every remark he makes when he's had one beer too many, now, can he?"

THE COUNSELOR'S TURN

"When this couple walked into my office, my initial reaction was an echo of Mark's," said the counselor. "What in the world, I asked myself, are these two people doing here?

"Within a few minutes, however, it became obvious that there was a tremendous difference in their personalities. He was a ride on a roller coaster that had no end, while she was a gentle canoe trip on a rippleless lake. Despite the fact that they had shared their lives for twenty-five years, neither had developed any tolerance for the other's individuality. Carrie felt Mark's social behavior was extravagant; he felt she was cold and a party pooper. Although there were certain areas in which they were compatible (they had no friction, for

instance, over raising their children), they were in total disagreement about the use of their money and leisure time.

"Most important, and hardest to deal with, was that each had perfected a facade that prevented sharing and self-exposure. In Mark's case, the facade was a clown mask, fashioned after the personality of his genial but weak-natured father. 'Keep laughing and you won't notice what hurts you' was his motto. Mark was filled with bottled-up emotions—hostility toward his nagging first wife and resentment toward Carrie when she exhibited any of her annoying traits. He also felt guilty about what he saw as his life's failures—his unsuccessful first marriage, his aborted dream of becoming a doctor, and his ineffectual business ventures. Because his Mr. Nice Guy image was so important to him, he successfully repressed these feelings most of the time. When his control was loosened by alcohol, however, they came bursting to the surface. Mark did not have a drinking problem per se; he drank very occasionally and then in moderation. But he used liquor as a scapegoat when his frustration level became too high.

"Carrie played the role of martyr. Her father had been the sole provider and authority figure and she viewed Mark's easygoing approach to life as a sign of irresponsibility. Sensing that his extravagances were his subtle way of spiting her, she retaliated by denying herself any pleasures.

"Their behavior was so deeply ingrained that for a while I was afraid counseling would not be productive. Each wanted the other one to be fixed up, but was resistant to any idea of changing themselves. The turning point came when Carrie admitted she was partially responsible for their problems. Mark was then able to face up to his own contribution to Carrie's unhappiness.

"As Carrie recognized, this couple's problems were compounded by a breakdown in communication. Mark bottled things up and Carrie spoke generalities. 'Mark does not understand my needs,' she would say accusingly, defying her husband to figure out what these needs were. Mark, understandably frustrated by this game-playing, shrugged off the challenge and went his own way. In counseling, Carrie learned to be more specific about what she wanted. One assignment I gave her was to come up with a list of things that would give her pleasure. Amazingly, she was unable to do this. She had sunk so far into her martyr role that she could not be the least bit self-indulgent. Finally, with reluctance, she revealed that she would like to be able to soak in a hot bath for an hour after work. The idea that she had been depriving herself of such a simple luxury was so ludicrous that even Carrie laughed.

"Soon Mark and Carrie began to air their feelings and to develop an appreciation for each other as individuals. By sharing his past with his wife, Mark was able to confront his negative emotions and understand where they came from. He learned to express his feelings on a daily basis, instead of letting them build.

"Carrie and Mark have learned to make compromises and now spend leisure time in activities they both enjoy. Carrie joins Mark for tennis and golf on weekends and is more open to home entertaining. Mark, though still gregarious, spends many more evenings at home, and if he does decide to have dinner at the country club, he phones Carrie to ask her to join him.

"Now that she, too, is enjoying the club facilities, Carrie no longer complains about the cost of membership. A contributing reason for this is an increase in family income. Carrie recently received a surprise promotion at work: She was made office manager—a direct result, I believe, of her new, positive approach to life.

"Three months after this couple terminated counseling, I phoned Carrie. 'There's not much news,' she told me, then added, 'except that I've fallen in love with my husband.'"

LEARNING TO ACCEPT—AND APPRECIATE— YOUR DIFFERENCES

Despite the fact these two have shared their lives for twenty-five years, neither had developed a tolerance for the other's individuality. Like Mark and Carrie, many couples mistakenly believe that, in a good marriage, partners must think and feel exactly the same way. In any close relationship, differences in opinions and priorities, as well as in the way each partner handles anxiety and stress, are bound to develop. Although Carrie and Mark didn't notice these differences when they were caught up in childrearing, once the nest was empty the disparity appeared glaring—a communication gap had grown so wide that it affected every aspect of their relationship.

If you and your partner are struggling with similar issues, break the stalemate by keeping the following points in mind:

- Acknowledge the part you both play in any problems you may be having. Carrie and Mark automatically assumed the fault lay with their partner.

- State your needs and feelings as specifically as you can without being accusatory.

- Be willing to compromise. If Carrie stops playing the martyr and joins Mark on the tennis court once in a while, she will realize how much fun she can have and he will be more open to quiet evenings at home.

- Develop an appreciation for each other's individuality and perspective. Stop trying to be right. Instead, adopt the motto "I could be wrong."

- Remember that no matter how well-matched you may be, there will be times when you and your partner will clash. So keep in mind that "different" is just that—it's not a moral judgment. Sometimes we become so rigid in our approach to things that we forget that there is usually no right or wrong. For example, you may have certain rules for bedtime that help you get the kids to sleep on time. Your spouse, coming home late from the office, may march in and start playing with them just before lights out. While a good night's sleep is important, so is playtime with Dad. So as long as this doesn't happen every night, ask yourself if it's better to go to the mat on this one or better to send the message that there are two ways of looking at an issue?

"HE ALWAYS TUNES ME OUT"

*B*arb can't understand what happened to the caring, thoughtful man she married. Gabe can't understand why his wife is so upset. Instead of trying to find out, she screams and he withdraws, preferring not to listen to what he doesn't want to hear.

BARBARA'S TURN

"I don't even know where to begin," said Barbara, thirty-four, a short, dark-haired woman in a pink jogging suit. "Gabe has things worked out just the way he wants them, with no thought to my wants or my needs.

"I thought we were going to have the perfect marriage. Gabe and I were best friends for two years before we became lovers.

"But we've been married four years now and Gabe has taken a 180-degree turn. There are no more jogs in the park or breakfasts out. No romantic dinners. Gabe used to take the initiative. Now all he does is stay home and watch a baseball game or read some esoteric German philosopher.

"So we lead separate lives. We have no family life and he doesn't seem to care. The more I explain that he's just not there for me and our daughter—Callie is thirteen months old—the more he withdraws.

"Some days I can't bear to get up in the morning. I go to the office—I'm a personnel director at a computer company, but I've worked only three days a week since Callie was born. I race home from the office to watch Callie so Gabe can work. We both decided when I got pregnant that we didn't want to hire a baby-sitter, so he's been Mr. Mom for the past year. Since Gabe

72

works at home—he also has a carpentry business and does fine cabinetry—we thought that would work.

"When I get home, I barely have time to change my clothes before I'm on duty until Callie goes to bed. By then, I'm catatonic. I have no energy left to talk to my friends anymore.

"Another reason I've lost touch is that no one seems to be good enough for Gabe. He used to be gracious about doing things with my friends and family. But now he calls my friends boring airheads.

"Weekends are worse. I feel like a single mom. Gabe says this is the only time he can get any work done, so I'm in the park all by myself, pushing Callie on the swings. I see all these moms and dads together and my heart breaks. What kind of life is this? We never make love anymore either. Gabe literally pushes me away.

"And he feels totally put upon if I ask him to do anything. Everything with him is a big deal. My mother was coming for a visit last month and I asked him to install a simple window fan in the bedroom so she'd be comfortable. He never did.

"Then he gets on me about spending money. Gabe's needs are maybe four new T-shirts every year, so compared with that, naturally my needs seem excessive. Well, I'm the one who's working. Don't I have a right to buy my daughter something if I want to? I don't buy anything for myself. I buy toys, for heaven's sake, or something for the house. Recently we had a huge fight because I bought a lamp for the bedroom. I'm tired of living with hand-me-downs from our parents. But when I explain that, he gives me a dirty look, arches one eyebrow, and walks out of the room. Or he explodes, just like my father. I could never deal with Dad's outbursts—they seemed so illogical, just like Gabe's.

"I'm the youngest of three. My dad was the manager at a paper-processing plant and my mother was a stay-at-home mom until I was in college, when she went back to work at a gift shop.

"Everyone in my house was sort of closed off. I remember having dinner at a friend's house when I was in junior high and it was a revelation to discover that people actually talked to each other at the dinner table.

"I thought that if I did well in school, Mom and Dad would be pleased, but even though I got good grades, they didn't seem to notice. I'd often spend the night at a friend's house; I loved chatting with someone else's mother.

"I couldn't wait to go to college to get away. I attended a small Midwestern church-affiliated school that had offered me a scholarship. After graduation, I lived at home until I found an entry-level job as a secretary. Finally, I had enough money to rent an apartment—which brings me to how I met Gabe.

"Gabe's parents, who are wealthy, bought this small, run-down apartment house for Gabe to fix up, manage, and live in rent-free. That was very generous, but I think they did it because they were afraid their son would never be able to support himself. Anyway, I rented an apartment in Gabe's building and we quickly became friends. After about two years, we realized that our relationship was shifting. We were married a few months later.

"At first, Gabe was really tuned in to what I needed. Now he's living on another planet. Recently, I'd been out shopping all day with Callie. I came in loaded down with bags. I desperately wanted Gabe to take the baby, give her a snack, and help me put away the groceries. Anybody could see I was wiped out. But not my husband. He strolls into the kitchen, says hi, gets a soda, and goes back to his workshop.

"On top of that, when I get home from the office, so excited to see my daughter, she runs to her daddy. I think Gabe encourages that, too. We've been having rip-roaring fights all the time. Both of us have terrible tempers and we dig in our heels. In the past, if a relationship didn't work out, I always thought it was my fault. This time, I know it's not."

GABE'S TURN

"I married my mother," said Gabe, thirty-five, a sandy-haired man in a work shirt and frayed jeans. "We used to call my mother 'the little general.' Well, Barbara has turned into such a critical, overbearing person, I often get this déjà vu feeling: I'm twelve years old again and my mother is shouting orders. My philosophy then was—and still is—to keep out of sight.

"I'm from St. Louis. My family still lives there and they can't understand why I don't. Mother always complained that my father wasn't involved enough in the family; she wanted him to be the boss, to help her manage all of us. My father would give anything for me to come home and join him in his real estate firm; both of my younger brothers are now full partners. They all have these huge homes and fancy cars. That's not who I am.

"My parents always seemed to find time for the things they wanted me to do, but never for what I wanted. I'd spend hours reading in my room or puttering in my workshop—my father did buy me some equipment most kids would kill for. Throughout high school, I had a sense that nothing I did got a response from my parents—positive or negative.

"As soon as I graduated from college, I headed for New York. I didn't know anyone there or what I wanted to do; I just had to get as far away from Missouri as I could. I did odd jobs, tending bar, working in a hardware store. When my father finally realized I was never going to come home, he bought this building for me to manage.

"I wanted to go out with Barb the minute I saw her, but she can close off and look very aloof, so I figured she was involved with someone. Barbara thinks the relationship has changed dramatically from the way it was when we were dating. I don't think it's all that different. Maybe I do want to stay home. What's the point of going out for the sake of going out?

"As far as socializing with her friends, well, unless I can really feel that I'm learning something from people, I see no point in having a relationship. I'm not interested in neurotic, superficial people.

"Okay, so maybe I don't have an official job like Barb, but I resent her implication that I'm a freeloader in this relationship. I manage the building where we live, renovate all the apartments, paint them when necessary, collect the rent, and do whatever maintenance work a superintendent in an apartment building does. I don't think Barb has the slightest idea how much effort that takes.

"Plus, I'm trying to establish myself as a master carpenter. I love the creative effort involved in choosing the woods, designing a piece that is aesthetically beautiful yet functional, too. Right now, my work is my focus. Finally, it all seems to be coming together. Yet I sacrifice three workdays a week to care for Callie. The problem is, I need structured time to finish a piece of furniture. I need more than just a half hour here or there.

"Barb doesn't appreciate what I do or what I need to do it. She'll barge into the workshop and say a fan needs to be installed or the air conditioners have to be cleaned. If I don't drop everything right that minute, I'm screwing up.

"Then there are the times when I'm supposed to have these supernatural powers to read her mind. The other day with the groceries is typical. I didn't realize she wanted me to help. I came in to say hi and I got my head blown off.

"I also don't like being told that I'm rejecting her in bed. She's the one who doesn't want to make love. You can tell when someone is just going through the motions.

"But I adore my daughter; I'm a terrific father, and Callie and I have a special relationship. Barb is jealous. When she comes home, if Callie doesn't rush into her arms, Barb thinks she's being rejected. Of course Callie loves her. But she's only thirteen months old. It's only natural that since she's spent the day with me, she'd take a little time to warm up to Barb.

"As far as the weekends go, what can I say? I don't love going to the playground. I go there with the baby during the week and weekends are two days when I can grab some uninterrupted work time.

"Money is a real issue for us. The furniture we have is just fine. In fact, I think Barbara spends entirely too much on things we don't need. Callie's playroom looks like Toys 'R' Us.

"Look, I'm here because Barbara insisted. And although I know you're not supposed to take sides, I'm sure you're going to label me the bad guy in all this."

THE COUNSELOR'S TURN

"I've never seen a client as angry as Barbara was," said the counselor. "At our first session, she shouted nonstop, berating Gabe for not caring and not being involved. She believed that Gabe had set up their life exactly the way he wanted it and that she was the drone who shouldered most of the financial and household responsibilities. As she saw it, her options were few.

"Gabe couldn't figure out what was going on. From his point of view, he was giving much to the relationship. It was essential for Barbara and Gabe to understand why the other reacted the way they did. I believed that once Barbara understood that Gabe withdrew because he was frustrated and not because he didn't love her, she'd feel less alone and more eager to find constructive ways of working together. In turn, if Gabe could become aware of when and why he was ignoring her, he'd be able to change. For this marriage to work, both of them needed to negotiate solutions instead of ignoring the other person or screaming.

"One of the most important things I did for Barbara and Gabe was to provide them with an impartial sounding board. They are both intelligent people who really do love each other, but they were so burdened by the responsibilities of parenthood that they were unable to think clearly.

"A vivacious, strong-willed woman, Barbara grew up in a home where nothing she did seemed to have much impact. Her mother was emotionally needy and her father was a passive man who had little interaction with the family except when he blew up in fits of anger for no apparent reason.

"Gabe came from a traditional, wealthy Midwestern family. His father was undemonstrative and wrapped up in his business dealings. His mother was domineering and critical. Everyone in the family learned that the only way to get along with her was to tune her out. Neither parent bothered to take Gabe's interests into account. To cope with disappointments, Gabe learned to turn a switch in his head, to withdraw and disengage. He also learned that the only way he was going to do what he wanted was to pursue it single-mindedly. Gabe never knew what it meant to be in a reciprocal relationship; nor did he believe there was any point in cooperating or talking things over.

"There was also the problem of different social styles. Gabe was a loner who prided himself on his off-beat ways. Barbara was sociable and liked to go out.

"Before we could get any work done, however, I had to help Barbara calm down. This wasn't easy. I told her that although she did have the right to get upset with Gabe, the intensity of her anger was out of proportion to the 'crime.' In time, she began to ease up.

"Barbara's number-one complaint was that Gabe had arranged their lives the way he wanted and that she had no options. Since I wanted her to be more self-determining, I said, 'Forget about Gabe; let's talk about you. What in your world would you like to change?' Barbara was able to see there were many things she was pleased with. She was making a good salary working three days a week—most women do not have that option. Furthermore, she enjoyed her work.

"At this point I said, 'So what can you do to change the things you're not happy with?' While their decision not to hire a sitter seemed like a good one at first, it was not working. I suggested that hiring someone to care for Callie would give Barbara time for herself after work, and Gabe time to work during the day, freeing both of them to enjoy family time.

"I wanted to make sure Barbara understood that Gabe's contribution to the family was as important and as valid as hers was. Giving him an established, uninterrupted time to work and telling him she appreciated his efforts allowed Gabe to be more responsive to some of the other things she was saying.

"Together, we settled on a plan: Barbara agreed to make a list of the things she'd like Gabe to do each week. This way, they could discuss the timetable and Gabe could say, 'Yes, I can put the fan in this afternoon, but I won't get to the air conditioners until Wednesday.' Although Barbara might want the job done sooner, she felt better knowing it would at least get done.

"Barbara also had to learn that she could not expect Gabe to read her mind. If she needed help putting away groceries, she had to say so. She has become better at voicing her needs simply and clearly and Gabe has been more willing to help her. Barbara also admitted that perhaps she was so jealous of Gabe's closeness to Callie that she bought her all those toys to try to make up for her time away. Now that she feels better about herself and her relationship with her daughter, Barbara has stopped spending so much on toys. In turn, Gabe has agreed to spend a little to fix up the house.

"Reaching a compromise when it came to their social life was trickier. As Callie gets older, I told them, they will most likely make new friends through her whom they both like. Already, since they've been spending much more time together, they have become friends with two other families they see in the park.

"In the past, Barbara and Gabe were so angry that neither had felt very loving. As tensions eased, their sex life improved. Barbara and Gabe ended therapy after a year, pleased with their progress and confident that they could negotiate solutions as problems arose."

CURING THE MIND-READER SYNDROME

Although they don't realize it, many couples are victims of the mind-reader syndrome. This can happen if one person has difficulty getting in touch with his or her own feelings, much less communicating them to a spouse. Such people believe that their partner will magically know how they feel. A wife may assume that, because her husband loves her, he'll automatically know she needs transition time after grocery shopping or work to unwind. That's just too much to expect from any person.

Could this be happening in your marriage? Perhaps you are not explaining your needs or expressing your thoughts as clearly as you think you are. Use this short personal checklist to focus your feelings and specify what you'd like to change instead of complaining or criticizing.

When a disagreement surfaces, ask yourself:

- What exactly am I thinking and feeling right now?

- What do I want my spouse to know right now that he or she may not realize?

- What am I assuming my partner knows that he or she may not have thought of?

- What is my partner thinking I mean?

- Am I acting in childish or petty ways that I thought I had outgrown? Do my tone of voice or actions say something that I'm not saying directly? Could he be misinterpreting what I really mean?

Taking the time to do this will help you clarify your own needs so you lessen or avoid problems entirely.

"He's Ashamed of Me"

Adrienne was convinced that Bob did not think she was as attractive or sexy as his co-workers. What happens when qualities and traits you admire and love begin to irritate and annoy?

Adrienne's Turn

"Bob is embarrassed to be seen with me," said Adrienne, thirty-seven. "A few weeks ago, we were getting ready to run errands. I was wearing an old blue jogging suit, and when Bob saw me, he snapped, 'You look like somebody's fat grandmother. Don't you have anything nicer?' I didn't have the energy to argue, so I changed into a sweater and jeans.

"In the two years since Bob became the head of his department at the advertising agency he works for, the gulf between us had widened. I know he thinks I'm not as pretty as the pencil-thin women in his office. Well, I gained twenty pounds with each of our two sons, and no amount of dieting will make it go away. Bob can't deal with it. When we have dinner with friends, he always makes a nasty remark about what I order. He'll even grab a cookie or doughnut out of my hand.

"I feel as if I'm in constant competition with Bob's female colleagues. They're cool, while I'm the dumpy suburban mom juggling orthodontist appointments and soccer matches. It's not that I want to be like them; I just don't understand why Bob thinks such superficial things are so important. He used to love me for me. Now he expects me to change into somebody else.

79

"Everyone in his office is quite close—too close, if you ask me. They're always hugging and air-kissing. The company encourages it by hosting picnics and parties, with no spouses invited. I don't think it's smart for Bob to be so chummy with his associates.

"I'm dying to know more about Bob's business, but he hardly ever tells me about it. One night, he was complaining about staffers making too many personal calls. When I tried to explain how we handled the issue at the office where I used to work, he just gave me a cold stare and walked away. I felt so alone—but that's nothing new for me.

"I grew up in a suburb of Cincinnati with my three younger brothers. To the outside world, we were the perfect family; in reality we were miserable. My parents fought constantly, and I became the pawn in their battles. Mother would do nothing for hours, then fly into a rage. She used to hit me—with anything she could grab—and tell me I was stupid, fat, or totally incompetent.

"I met Bob during my sopho-more year in high school. He was my first and only boyfriend, and the one person who really listened to me. We were the couple everyone knew would live happily ever after.

"Thanks to Bob, we carefully planned our lives. He's much more organized than I am, and I love the way he always knows what he wants

and goes after it. I'm much more laid-back about things, whether it's the housework or choosing living room furniture.

"I quit my copywriting job after Matt was born ten years ago. Tommy was born years later. I adored them but being a full-time mother wasn't as wonderful as I thought it would be. Those early years were exhausting, and I missed the energy of the office.

"The other thing I missed was the equality in our marriage. The minute I stopped working, Bob expected me to handle all the chores and child care. Now, if I dare ask him to pick up a quart of milk on the way home, he'll bellow, 'Why can't you remember to do that?' If I'm sick and can't make a school meeting, Bob won't take my place. His career comes first.

"Sometimes I feel like I'm drowning in housework, and unless I do everything precisely the way Bob wants it done, I'm a failure. He'll complain about the toys in the living room or that the countertops don't sparkle. He even expects me to drive downtown to pick up his pay-check and deposit it in the bank—even though there's a branch about six blocks from his office. He says that's part of 'my job.'

"I can't remember the last time we made love, and the closeness we used to have is gone. That was glar-ingly obvious last New Year's Eve. We always invite our extended family over, but this time, Bob insisted on including the people from his office. He spent the whole night with his co-workers and barely acknowledged the rest of us.

"After midnight, I was in the kitchen making coffee when I overheard voices in the next room—Bob was with Claudia, a married co-worker. He was saying, 'It feels so good to share my feelings with someone.' That was it. I confronted him right after the party. Bob swears he's not involved with Claudia, and I believe him, but it's still devastating to realize that my husband would rather confide in her than me.

"Bob insists that these are all my problems and my issues. Maybe they are. Or maybe we've both changed so much that there's no hope for us."

BOB'S TURN

"I don't know what's gone so wrong with Adrienne and me," said Bob, thirty-nine, a tall, thin man. "She makes me sound like the most horrible, abusive husband. Well, I'm hurt and angry, too. We used to be so close, and we hardly ever fought. I thought everything was perfect.

"I don't think I've changed. I think she has. Adrienne has gained a lot of weight, and yes, I care about what she looks like. Call me superficial, but I'd be lying if I didn't admit it. Maybe it's because of my job. There's an edge to the way the

women at work dress, and I guess I'd like my wife to be a little more hip.

"But Adrienne's attitude bothers me more than her appearance. I don't talk to her about work because she dissects everything I say or do. Maybe I just want to have someone listen to me ramble, instead of telling me how much I screwed up and what I need to fix.

"I guess we had different ideas about how our life would work. When Adrienne said she wanted to be with the kids, I assumed that meant she'd also handle things at home. As the sole breadwinner, I have to pour all my energies into my job. I work in a highly competitive field—I'm talking sixty- or seventy-hour weeks—and it's frustrating to get home late to a messy house, dinner that's half-cooked, and a pouty wife.

"Don't misunderstand; I'm not a male chauvinist. I don't expect Adrienne to drop everything and get my slippers and pipe. But I do feel that if I'm busting my butt all day, she should be taking care of the details around the house. I want to be able to relax and enjoy her company when I'm home.

"I know that I'm a perfectionist. I suppose that can be hard to live with, though it's a quality that serves me well at work: I push myself and everyone else to be their best. I get it from my mother, a housewife who would have put June Cleaver to shame. Our house was always immaculate—underwear ironed and folded, toys neatly stacked in color-coordinated bins in my bedroom.

"Actually, my childhood was the opposite of Adrienne's. My father, a lawyer, did have a drinking problem, but he wasn't abusive, and we were all very close, loving, and supportive. I always loved art, and my parents and teachers nurtured my talent.

"I was smitten with Adrienne the moment I saw her. She was so cheerful, so kind, such a good listener. When I learned how awful her mother was, I wanted to swoop in and take her away. I knew that if we stuck together, we were unbeatable.

"Now I find out that Adrienne has been unhappy for a long time. I don't get it. I thought this was the life she wanted. She always said she planned to quit work when she had kids and be the kind of mother she never had herself. Of course, I wanted that, too, even though it meant putting the financial burden on me.

"Instead of appreciating the work I do, Adrienne is negative about me and our life together. It scares me to see my wife turn into a shrew, like her mother. I think Adrienne looks for things to be upset about; sometimes she'll yell about an incident that I barely remember.

"I'm so confused. We had a life plan, and somewhere along the way we got lost."

"Bob and Adrienne's problems developed slowly," said the counselor. "Qualities and traits they once loved and admired in each other transformed over time into triggers for rage.

"Adrienne was hurt and brittle, convinced that Bob was ashamed of her. She wasn't especially happy with herself either. Shy and tentative, she was afraid of making mistakes and acutely sensitive to criticism—not surprising, considering her painful childhood.

"Missing the stimulation of a workplace, she was desperate to connect with Bob the minute he got home—only to be crushed by his cold reaction. Naturally she was hurt, but she tended to stifle her resentment and then burst out in a tantrum later.

"But Bob felt equally justified in his anger. They had established a 'life plan' early on, and Bob thought everything would be fine so long as they stuck to it. He didn't realize how hard it was for Adrienne to keep the house immaculate, stay in shape and care for two children. Because life in an alcoholic household can be unpredictable, Bob craved order and structure, which included having a spotless house.

"Adrienne was used to being a problem-solver, so she flooded her husband with suggestions and opinions when he brought up issues at work. Now, Adrienne listens for the emotion behind Bob's words and then asks appropriate questions.

"As the tensions between them began to lift, the couple stopped criticizing each other. At one point, Bob said, 'Would I like it if Adrienne lost a few pounds? Sure. Does it matter? Not anymore.'

"We talked, too, about the balance of power in their relationship. Many of Bob's demands—such as making her cash his paycheck—went beyond what he could reasonably ask of her.

"For her part, Adrienne had to learn to say no nicely instead of bending to meet everyone's expectations and then resenting it. She now tells Bob what's bothering her, so they can come up with solutions together.

"They had an opportunity to test out their compromising skills recently. Adrienne enrolled in a Wednesday-night art class. When Bob's boss dumped a last-minute project on his desk late one Wednesday afternoon, he assured Adrienne that he would find a baby-sitter. 'In the past, he would have told me: "This is your problem; you deal with it,"' she said. 'In fact, Bob now pitches in a lot more with everything.'

"Once Adrienne felt loved and appreciated again, her self-esteem rose. 'I'm eating right, and I've started losing weight,' she reported happily. 'Maybe I'll even throw out that old sweat suit—it is getting pretty ratty.'"

HOW TO BRING UP TOUGH TOPICS WITHOUT MAKING THEM WORSE

Adrienne was her own worst enemy. Instead of speaking up and telling Bob how she felt, she swallowed the hurts until she exploded in a rage that often seemed far out of proportion to the "crime" committed. A better plan:

1. Admit there's a problem. Sounds obvious, but too often we ignore, rationalize, or excuse the things that bother us. Sometimes we do this so regularly, we don't even realize we're doing it. But the stress of not handling issues that are important to you has a way of slipping out sideways: You may simmer with resentment, bristle with irritation, snap at others when you don't mean to. If you recognize these signs in yourself, try to pinpoint the source of your anger by thinking back to a specific time when your partner, or behavior on his or her part, upset you.

2. Name, don't blame. Focus on the issue, or what you think your partner is doing wrong. When we're upset, criticizing and blaming comes easily. So does dramatic exaggeration (as in, "If you don't help me with the kids tonight instead of disappearing into the den, I will have a breakdown!"). Instead of attacking your partner, which will only make him defensive, you'll make more progress if you focus your concern on one problem and one solution. Work with the basic formula, "I feel ____ when

you ____." For instance: "I feel stressed when you don't help get the kids started on their homework or ready for bed." This way, you communicate your emotional experience without putting your partner in the penalty box.

3. Pay attention to what you say. Stick to the facts and skip the provocative attacks and ultimatums. Also, acknowledge your differences with respect and make clear your willingness to brainstorm a solution: "I know you need a break after a work, but I do, too. Maybe if we talk about it, we can find a compromise that works for both of us."

4. Think of changes you can make that will speed a solution. If you say, "I could pick up a barbecued chicken on my way home from the office so I don't feel the pressure to cook every night," your partner may say, "And I'll get the kids bathed and into bed before I turn on the basketball game." Behavioral changes we make on our own are more enduring than those forced upon us. They keep lines of communication open, comfortable, and fair.

"HE EXPECTS ME TO GIVE UP MY LIFE"

John wanted to relocate, but Stephanie refused to pull up her roots. Did loving him mean losing what was most important to her?

STEPHANIE'S TURN

"They say opposites attract, and I suppose they do," said Stephanie, forty-one, a tall blond in an ankle-skimming floral skirt who works part-time at a community arts center. "But maybe they can't live together.

"I found John's gentleness and solidity unbelievably attractive when we first met, but after ten years of marriage, I think we're slowly driving each other crazy. And now that it looks like his company might be moving to northern California—he's an industrial engineer—I don't know what to do. A move would be difficult for me even if our marriage were idyllic. But since things have not been so great lately, I feel I have to decide whether this can work.

"I feel rooted here. John makes it sound so trivial when I tell him I don't want to give up my friends, my book clubs, my art classes. Maybe for him home is anywhere he can hang his hat, but at this point in my life I can't just pick up and start all over again.

"These days I don't understand John at all. He insists he loves me, but when I poke my head into the den while he's working on something and say, in a perfectly friendly voice, 'Do you want a cup of coffee?' he'll bark at me to leave him alone.

"When he treats me like that and tells me how I should feel or what I should do, I feel, well, stupid.

"I met John on a ski-club trip to Utah eleven years ago. We laughed easily and talked for hours about everything—his two children from

85

his first marriage, who were living with their mother; how his wife of fifteen years had betrayed him by having an affair. Even though I had just met him, I felt I'd known him for ages.

"Of course, our backgrounds couldn't be more different. I was raised in southern California and my parents were wealthy—my father was a self-made man, very charismatic but opinionated and domineering. He came to this country from Europe when he was fifteen and made a fortune in the import/export business. I adored him, though I saw very little of him, and I hated my mother. She was, and still is, a very interfering woman who always insisted she knew what was best for me and constantly criticized me. I wasn't particularly smart or pretty—things that were important to Mother.

"I wasn't an unhappy kid, but I was pretty unfocused. After high school, Dad wanted me to go to college near home. I dropped out during my sophomore year—the one rebellious thing I ever did—with no idea what I wanted to do. My older brother lived in San Diego, and he suggested I move there. Much to everyone's surprise, I managed to support myself. I always seemed to fall into some kind of interesting work, though nothing held me for long. Still, I was happy, and I had a great group of friends.

"When I met John, I was ready to settle down, even though I wasn't

too crazy about his kids. His daughter, who's twenty-one now, thinks the world revolves around her; his son, who's twenty-two, is just plain rude and ungracious. He'll bring his new wife over for dinner and never lift a finger to help, never say thank you. Why John doesn't say something to them, as well as to his ex-wife, who is forever saying horrible things about John to the kids, is beyond me.

"But all we really do lately is argue about stupid things—like the fact that he's a neatness nut and I don't notice clutter. Last week he had a fit because I didn't rewind the garden hose.

"I'm also very social. I enjoy people and love having a house full of friends. But big parties are an ordeal for John. He's happy as a clam sitting in the den poring over his engineering journals or fiddling with the computer.

"Frankly, our love life is not that great either. As far as John is concerned, romance is a three-letter word: S-E-X. John is totally unromantic. I wish he was more, well, erotic. It would be nice to have him surprise me with some grand, exciting gesture. That would mean the world to me. I'd love to have a candlelight dinner and make love on the rug in front of the fire. But in a million years, John would never think of doing anything like that.

"I realize that our problems don't sound earth-shattering by most people's standards. But this business about moving has brought everything to a head. If I lose my roots and don't even have a marriage, then where will I be?

"I know jobs are tight, but people like John are much in demand. I'm not sure what I want or expect, but I'm afraid a move now will be the final blow for our marriage."

JOHN'S TURN

"This is typical," said John, forty-nine, in a quiet, measured voice. "Stephanie is so emotional. She blows everything way out of proportion, in that highly dramatic way.

"The way she carries on, you'd think I was telling her we're moving to Iceland. Stephanie is going to love San Francisco. Besides, it's not like she doesn't know anyone. My brother lives there. The trouble is, we can't have a simple, rational conversation about this move.

"That happens all the time. Talk to Stephanie about one problem and before you realize it, she's thrown everything into the mix. I wish she'd stick to the subject.

"I suppose I'm just not used to people like Stephanie. I'm the oldest of three—my father owned an auto-parts store and Mother was a homemaker. We were a close family, but communication was not our strong point. I was always a serious kid. My parents weren't able to finish college, so they were set on my going to a good school. I focused my energies on my studies and was accepted at Stanford University. After graduation I started working for the company where I've been ever since, and I married my college girlfriend.

"I met Stephanie about two months after I separated from my first wife. Talking to her felt so comfortable. She's a real free spirit.

"Maybe that's the problem. I like to think things through and apply some logic to a problem. Stephie is all emotion, and she jumps to all sorts of conclusions about what I'm thinking. Just because I'm focusing hard on a project doesn't mean I don't love her.

"Stephanie takes pride in her creativity, and I do, too. I've tried hard to encourage her artistic pursuits. But creativity has its limits. I don't think we should be creative with our checkbook, for instance. I like to know down to the penny what we have, and it drives me nuts the way Stephanie never remembers to record the checks she's written.

"And, yes, it does irritate me that she's such a slob. Can I help it if I like the house to be neat? I'm not saying spotless, just orderly. Stephanie leaves things all over the place. Recently, we got into a ridiculous argument about the garden hose, which she had left looped all over the lawn. Now it sounds so dumb, but it really made me mad.

I've asked her a million times to wind it up properly.

"We also get into plenty of battles over my children. Stephie thinks my kids take advantage of me. She wants me to have it out with them. That's not my style. I know Barry was deeply hurt by my divorce. That's no excuse to be rude, but it is a reason for his behavior. Same with Kim. When I'm ready to talk to her, I'll talk—in my own time and my own way.

"But as for my ex-wife, what can I do if she bad-mouths me? Janet is out of my life, and I don't want to see her or speak to her unless I have to. My life is with Stephie now; can't she let things be?

"This upcoming move has both of us on edge. I know how rooted Stephanie is here, but if my company is consolidating, I don't see what choice we have. I love Stephanie more than I've loved anyone, and I don't want to fight with her. Maybe talking with you can help us figure out how to get past this stalemate."

THE COUNSELOR'S TURN

"Stephanie and John had serious communication problems, exacerbated by the fact that they were so different in so many ways," said the counselor. "Nevertheless, I could tell they were motivated to make their marriage work. During a session, John would often place his hand on Stephanie's knee; she'd give him a loving smile.

"The key to resolving their problems was, first, to help them understand the source of their difficulties, and then to help them shift their attitudes and expectations so they could be more respectful, compassionate, and loving.

"John is focused, logical, and orderly. When he's involved in a project, he is one hundred percent immersed in it. Any interruption breaks his concentration, and it takes him a while to get back on track.

"On the other hand, Stephanie is emotional, intuitive, creative, spontaneous, and extroverted. It's easy for people like her to juggle multiple tasks at once. However, her life was chaotic in many ways, and the possible relocation was the last straw for a woman struggling with issues of self-confidence and direction. Her overbearing parents had made most of her decisions for her. As a result, she was so used to turning to those around her to determine what she should do and feel that when she had to make any sort of decision on her own, she was lost. John had always been Stephanie's Rock of Gibraltar, the voice of authority she depended on to make decisions and keep her centered.

"Stephanie made John happy, too. She could drag him away from his solitary pursuits and make him laugh. One of the qualities that in the beginning endeared her to John is that she says everything that's on her mind. John is much more reticent; he speaks in deliberate, steady tones, and thinks carefully about what he wants to say and when he wants to say it.

"In the beginning, this balance of opposites worked well for both of them. In time, however, these qualities seemed much less charming. 'Each of you brings things to this relationship that the other can learn from,' I explained at one of our first sessions, 'but if you want to be really happy together, you must accept each other's limitations as well.'

"That meant Stephanie had to stop jumping to conclusions about John's behavior. Now, when he's engaged in any task, she consciously reminds herself that it would be best if she either slipped him a note or, better yet, waited to ask even the most innocuous question. Stephanie also realized that taking more care to neaten the house and being more diligent about properly recording checks were little things from her perspective, but they loomed large for John. He, in turn, had to learn to count to ten before responding to Stephanie when he was in the middle of something.

"The differences between them also showed up in the way they handled other people. Stephanie is a confronter, but confrontation scares John, and he prefers to wait and see whether problems can straighten themselves out. 'You have to let him solve the issues with his children his own way,' I told Stephanie.

"As for their problems in the bedroom, I explained to Stephanie that it wasn't that John didn't find her sexually arousing; it's just not in his nature to court her like a hero from a romance novel. Stephanie's attempts to push him in that direction inevitably led to hurt feelings, bickering, and unhappiness for both of them.

"'Take responsibility for your own sensuousness,' I advised her. 'Buy your own sexy lingerie or bath oils.' I introduced her to sex therapist Lonnie Barback's tastefully written but erotic stories, which helped her get in the mood for lovemaking. 'How you feel about yourself sexually is not your husband's responsibility. It's yours,' I told her. More aware of his wife's concerns and wanting to make her happy, John made a strong effort to turn his lovemaking into a more intensely erotic experience.

"At this point, I believed both of them were ready to discuss the move to San Francisco. With Stephanie, it helped to break down her overwhelming fears into specific, practical issues. 'What are you doing here that you can't do there?' I asked. 'How exactly did you meet people when you first moved to San Diego? Why couldn't you do the same up north? What prevents you from starting a book club in your new community?' By giving time and thought to each point, Stephanie realized that she did have the where-withal to relocate her life.

"During these sessions, I often encouraged John to think about the move in emotional terms. He made lists of people and activities he enjoyed in San Diego and brought them to the session. Tuning into his feelings in this way helped him to be more patient and compassionate with his wife when she needed to talk. And his compassion made Stephanie realize that she really did want to be with John.

"This couple was in counseling for nine months. By the time John heard that the move was definite, Stephanie was no longer terrified at the prospect. Through her sister-in-law, she got in touch with the director of a YMCA in the San Francisco area and is hoping to use her talents to teach art to preschool-ers. They plan to visit San Diego regularly and have friends come north. Most important, they both feel renewed excitement about the marriage and their ability to work through any problems that arise."

LEARNING TO THINK POSITIVELY

When arguments percolate and tensions rise, it can be difficult, if not impossible, to remember what it was you liked about your partner in the first place. Yet experts report that when you can hone a positive, rather than a negative perspective about your partner, it can help you weather more easily the tough marital moments. To do that, we sometimes need a little reminder. Try jotting down five things you like and admire about each other. Maybe it's your partner's ability to make you laugh when life takes a downturn, or the way he focuses his attention on the kids when they're talking. When you are not together, take this list out, memorize it, and think of it often.

"HE'S SO IRRESPONSIBLE"

F*rustrated, frantic, and furious, Maggie can no longer live with a man who promises to do things but never follows through. What happens when one partner's anxiety overwhelms a marriage?*

"I love Tim more than I've ever loved anyone, but I can't live with him one more day," sobbed Maggie, twenty-eight, her blue eyes red from crying. "We've been married four years and we've been on an emotional roller coaster almost all that time.

"Tim and I both grew up as Navy brats. I come from a family of five kids and Tim has two brothers. We left the States when I was five and lived all over the world until my last year in high school, when we moved to Norfolk, Virginia.

"My parents have been married for thirty-five years, and they have a solid marriage. They've always been very affectionate, but it couldn't have been easy for Mom, raising all of us and moving so many times. Sometimes Dad would drink too much and I know that bothered her.

"Mom was the practical parent; Dad was impulsive, emotional, and indulgent. He's a great entertainer and everyone loves him. When we were little, we were very poor. Dad owned a small string of grocery stores before he joined the Navy, but each one had failed. Every time my father got a new posting, the move would be wrenching, but I always landed on my feet. I made friends easily, and I was a model child and a good student. I was constantly worried about how Mom was feeling, though. I was the family peacemaker, and Mom knew that she could count on me.

91

"So did the girls in my freshman dorm. I went to a small women's college two hours from home, and there, too, everyone came to me for advice—they put a sign on my door that said 'mental-health clinic.'

"After college, I shared an apartment with my brother Matt and started working for a Head Start program. Matt introduced me to Tim. They'd been childhood friends.

"One night Matt and I went to a political rally, which was absolutely uneventful, but we ran into Tim and ended up arguing politics until one in the morning.

"I thought Tim was adorable and very smart. The following week, he called and asked me to dinner. We had a lovely meal—but when the check came, he didn't have enough money. I told him not to worry, but he was so embarrassed. And that, I must say, foreshadowed a lot of the problems we're having now.

"After a week of seeing each other practically day and night, Tim was telling me how much he loved me. After less than a year, we had a huge wedding with a terrific jazz band, and we all danced through the night. But things just haven't been right since. We can't get in sync. I'm detail-oriented; he's the opposite. Tim says I'm crazy to get worked up about things, but he doesn't understand that he never does anything that he promises to do. Bills have to be paid, but I don't trust him for a second to pay them on time.

He borrows library books and never returns them. We have seventy dollars worth of library fines right now. And parking tickets! I can't think about how many he has!

"Even more embarrassing, we'll meet friends for dinner, and he never has enough money to pay the check. Now, that was cute on our first date, but it's not cute anymore. Unless I nag, nothing changes. I hate having to remind him that he's going to miss an exit on the expressway, but if I don't, he'll drive right past it.

"But it's more than his being irresponsible about little things. Tim never wants to be with me anymore. Maybe some of it's my fault. I have a wonderful but demanding job as director of community educational programs for underprivileged kids, and until a few months ago I was going to night school. For two years, we hardly saw each other.

"Now there's no fun or romance left. I try to kiss Tim or reach for his hand and he pulls away. When I ask what's wrong, he either says 'Nothing' or marches into his office.

"I know Tim's work is very important to him. Last year he finally quit his radio job and decided to try freelance writing. We figured in six months we'd know if he could make it. He worked at home and did well.

"Unfortunately, he's become this incredible workaholic. And since his office is in a corner of the bedroom, he never seems to be able to distance himself from work. I'll be in the kitchen, telling him about something that's really upsetting me at work, and he'll just tune out. He even takes work-related phone calls at any time of the day or night.

"I hate the fact that he never listens to me anymore. He pretends to, but I can see his eyes glaze over.

"Lately we've been having terrible fights. Out of the blue, he'll start kicking a chair for no apparent reason. Often he's upset about things that happened ages ago. So I cry my eyes out and try to drag out of him what's wrong.

"These battles are so draining that last week I told Tim I have to move out for a while. I'm just so furious and frustrated, and I need some space to think about things."

TIM'S TURN

"I can't believe she wants to leave," said Tim, twenty-nine, a handsome man in cutoff jeans and a T-shirt. "But Maggie's right; I hate the way things are between us, too, and I don't know what to do about it. I've tried to be the kind of husband she wants, but half the time I have no idea what's bothering her. She gets so emotional it scares me.

"I'm not used to this kind of constant crying. No one in my family ever acted this way. Like Maggie said, my father was also in the military and we moved a lot when I was

younger. But my parents never seemed to fight. Everything in my family was kept on an even level.

"My parents were affectionate, although nowhere near as touchy-feely as Maggie's family. I had a temper and I'd pop off about a lot of things; part of it was typical teenage rebelliousness, but there were other things, too. I'd felt established in junior high school, then we moved abroad. Those were unhappy years for me. I hated the Vietnam War, I was very cynical about my parents' generation and didn't know what I wanted to accomplish in life—but I never felt comfortable talking to my parents about anything remotely personal. My father died of a heart attack when he was fifty. Oh, he was drinking and smoking far too much, but I also think he was miserable about his work and he held it all in.

"In college, I decided to become a journalist. I snagged a job on a small paper in Oklahoma and was back visiting my family for Easter when I met Maggie. I purposely took a job back home so we could be together.

"As Maggie said, I hated that job and finally quit to freelance. That was scary. I worked like a demon, but since Maggie was at school most nights that was fine.

"So here I am, working my tail off, and Maggie's on my case about how I don't love her and I'm not connected enough. She hangs all over me and wants to make love all the time. I don't know how to react when she climbs into my lap when I want a quiet minute to sit and read the newspaper. I feel smothered.

"She also accuses me of not listening to her. Believe me, I pay attention, but when you hear something twenty times, you can't digest it anymore. Maggie always beats a problem to death.

"But I should also say I love my work and it's hard for me to break away from it. I'm finally doing something I love and people are recognizing that I'm good at it. Why can't my wife see that?

"Anyway, she's right about how we go in cycles. Things are better for a while, then before I know it she's berating me for being irresponsible. I'm fed up. She's not my mother, and I don't want to be henpecked about paying the bills, going to the bank, returning library books. I don't want her keeping schedules for me and reminding me to buy a present for my brother, whose birthday is three months away. And Maggie is the worst backseat driver you ever met. If the light turns green and I don't go that second, she jumps all over me.

"Most of the time I never bother to tell her how I feel. Why should I? I rarely win arguments. She's much better at expressing herself and I wind up looking like the bad guy.

"So maybe I'm just not able to have an emotional relationship. I feel inadequate and I know you're going to come down like a ton of bricks on me. But I can't deal with Maggie any more than she can deal with me."

THE COUNSELOR'S TURN

"When this couple came to see me, Maggie was sobbing and desperate," said the counselor. "She was afraid of Tim's waning sexual interest and frustrated by his irresponsible attitude.

"Tim was confused. On the one hand, he felt helpless in the face of his wife's outbursts and genuinely puzzled as to why she perceived him as disconnected when he thought he was a loving husband. But Tim also felt smothered by Maggie's demands for attention and affection and besieged by her constant nagging.

"After listening to Maggie for a while, I told her gently but firmly to stop crying and speak slowly so that we could start to sort out what was troubling her.

"As Maggie began to tell me about her family history, it became clear that while there was undoubtedly a tremendous amount of love, affection, and devotion in her family, there was also a history of alcoholism and depression. While Maggie hadn't experienced her father's alcoholism as anything terrible—he was not an abusive alcoholic who disappeared for days at a time but rather the drinker whom everyone indulged—his illness affected her nonetheless. Highly sensitive, Maggie's role model was her mother, herself a superresponsible woman who tried to do everything for everybody.

"Even as an adult, Maggie never felt she could stop worrying and relax for a minute. She continued her do-everything-for-everybody role in college, at work, and in her marriage. Maggie took Tim on, much as she would any project—she agonized about him constantly, trying to prevent or forestall any problems.

"Tim was passively aggressive in response to Maggie's pressuring. He was angry at his wife for smothering him, but since he came from a family where no one ever said how they really felt or what they needed, he wasn't used to expressing his anger. Instead, his irritation took the form of forgetfulness, distractedness, and lack of interest in sex. The more Maggie pushed for attention, the more Tim would pull away, which, of course, made her even more anxious.

"Tim, like his father, was congenial and outgoing, but he'd picked up the family trait of not recognizing his own needs as well as tuning out those of other people, especially to avoid conflict. In the process of numbing himself to Maggie's demands, he numbed himself to responsibility—hence the parking tickets and overdue books. My work with Tim was to get him in touch with his feelings and then to prompt him to speak up.

"One of my recommendations to Maggie was that she see a colleague of mine, a psychiatrist trained in psychopharmacology—the use of medication to help in the therapy process. I felt strongly that there was a biochemical basis for Maggie's difficulty in focusing on her worries without feeling overwhelmed. My colleague confirmed my opinion, but Maggie didn't want to take an antidepressant. So, with the psychiatrist, she worked out a program to strictly monitor her diet, sleep, and exercise habits to see if there was a connection between her lifestyle and her mood swings.

"By keeping a meticulous daily log of her activities we saw that as little as one half hour of sleep each night could affect the way Maggie acted at her job as well as with her husband. Whether she exercised or drank coffee also influenced her, as did her menstrual cycle. The link was so clear that Maggie resolved to take an aerobics class three times a week and aim for eight hours' sleep a night. She switched to herbal tea at work instead of coffee and now rarely drinks alcohol.

"These simple changes showed Maggie that she was capable of self-control, and once she became conscious of this, she was able to stop smothering Tim with demands for affection. Simply backing off for a little bit got immediate results, which, in turn, was strong positive reinforcement for her. 'It's like magic,' Maggie reported. 'If I give him space, he reaches out to me.'

"Maggie also learned not to get furious if she sensed that Tim wasn't listening to her. 'If I see his eyes glaze over, it's a signal to me to stop and ask myself if I've said this a hundred times already,' said Maggie.

"Tim was tremendously relieved when he realized I wasn't going to put the full responsibility for change on his shoulders. I did suggest, however, that he join one of my weekly therapy groups, and this proved a real catalyst for him. In the beginning, Tim was characteristically late for the group sessions or would forget about them completely. Yet each week, several other people challenged his forgetfulness, often echoing what Maggie had been telling him all along. This finally helped him realize that he, too, had changes to make.

"To help Tim separate himself from his work, they decided to rent a small office for him downtown. 'So now I really can leave my work at the office,' Tim said. He also takes the initiative in planning activities for them to do together on a regular basis.

"I suggested that Maggie let Tim see the consequences of his inactions. Maggie had reached the point where she was assuming her husband wouldn't do something before the situation even arose, and she had to stop running interference for him.

"'If he has no money the next time you go to dinner, what could you do?' I asked. 'Well, I could go to the ladies' room and let him figure it out, instead of handing him the money,' she replied. Having a reasonable option made her feel better. Since bill paying was also a big issue, Tim made a commitment to pay them every month and Maggie vowed not to nag him. While he didn't pay them as quickly as Maggie would have liked, they did get paid, and the couple's credit rating remained strong. Similarly, Maggie stopped nagging about the parking tickets, and Tim found he was unable to renew his license unless he went downtown to the motor vehicle bureau and settled his fines in person.

"But most important for Tim, instead of withdrawing, he has learned to tell Maggie how he feels in a straightforward way and not store up hurts only to explode in anger later. Since Tim has been so sincere in his efforts to change in other ways, Maggie can accept his criticism without feeling threatened.

"Maggie and Tim ended couples counseling after a year, but both continued in groups—Tim for two years and Maggie for three. 'I realized there was more about me that I wanted to change,' she explained. 'And since we'd made so much progress in such a short time, I was inspired to continue on my own.'"

DEPRESSION:
A Symptom and a Cause

Sometimes, what appears to be a marital issue really stems from a problem that "belongs" to one spouse. When real marital difficulties emerge, they cannot be dealt with, let alone resolved, until the root of the problem is uncovered. As Maggie and Tim discovered, you can't end an argument with your spouse if you're not talking to each other. That's why treating Maggie's depression became a priority.

The National Institute of Mental Health reports that more than 11 million Americans (one in ten) suffer from some form of clinical depression, but twice as many women as men. Maggie suffers from dysthymia, a low-level depression that can wax and wane. Unlike more severe forms of depression that can put its victims out of commission, dysthymia allows its sufferers to function, though not well or happily. Clinical depression is more than the blues, more than a lousy day, more than the pain you feel when you lose a job or grieve the death of a loved one. A depressed person can't simply will herself to feel better, or snap out of it. Depression, though not untreatable, is a real illness that can seriously disrupt a person's life. Doctors in this field have learned ways to alleviate the effects of depression through medication and counseling. The first step in getting help is recognizing these common but often overlooked symptoms:

1. Marked changes in sleeping and eating patterns.

2. Withdrawal from family and friends.

3. Lack of interest in activities or events that once gave pleasure, including sex.

4. General irritability.

5. Difficulty concentrating or making decisions.

6. Inability to find pleasure in any aspect of life.

7. Talk or thoughts of a despairing or suicidal nature ("It's no use" . . . "Things will never get better" . . . "It's all my fault"), which can lead to self-destructive behavior.

Remember, too, that depression can also be a symptom of physical problems—thyroid disease, nutritional problems, diabetes, or cancer—so a complete physical examination in order to identify any and all causes is essential. With proper treatment, most cases of depression can be helped, even cured. For more information, contact the National Institute of Mental Health (800-969-6642), the American Psychiatric Association (202-682-6000), or the American Psychological Association (800-373-3120).

"OUR BABY WAS STILLBORN"

When tragedy struck, Olivia and Scott retreated to opposite emotional corners. How can two people move on without jeopardizing their future together?

OLIVIA'S TURN

"Three months ago, our baby was stillborn," said Liv, thirty-two, a stunning brunette who spoke in a monotone and clasped her hands tightly in her lap. "I was thirty-six weeks pregnant and until a month or so before, I'd had a perfect pregnancy.

"Now I think I'm going crazy. One minute I'm sobbing, the next I'm numb. I can't sleep. I can't work. I'm a translator for a large company that handles a variety of clients from government agencies, to book publishers and game manufacturers. But I can barely talk to friends, let alone hold a job. Every Sunday, I relive my baby's death, minute by minute. I can't stop blaming myself either. I should have known something was wrong; I should never have listened to my doctor.

"Around my sixth month, I started to get severe lower abdominal pains. I don't like to complain, but it was so bad, I couldn't walk, stand, or even sit. There was no position that was comfortable for me. My doctor told us not to worry; he said it was probably the baby pressing on the sciatic nerve. But the pain continued even though the sonogram and other tests showed nothing wrong.

"We knew it was a boy—we'd named him Daniel—and though I was a little nervous about buying baby things, I did have two showers—one was a surprise from my girlfriends, the other was a brunch for couples at a restaurant. It was during that brunch that I suddenly noticed the baby wasn't moving. I had a tall glass of orange juice to see if that would make a difference, but it didn't. I called the doctor immediately; he told me, 'The baby's probably settled in the birth canal. It's normal. If he doesn't move in four or five hours, go to the hospital.' I was upset by his cavalier tone; he sounded as if he didn't want to be bothered!

"After about two hours, the baby still hadn't moved, so I insisted on going to the emergency room. The next few hours were surreal. I know I was hooked up for a sonogram and they couldn't find a heartbeat. I panicked and started screaming and thrashing around. Then, my contractions started. Scott was crying and in shock, too. It's hard to talk about what it's like to go through labor and delivery when you know your baby is already dead. To this day, I remember perfectly what that room looked like—every picture on the wall, the color of the curtains. The delivery took seven hours. Although we granted permission for a routine autopsy, the doctors never found out why our baby died.

"One of the nurses told me that I should be sure to hold my baby. At first, I thought, 'How bizarre! Why would I ever want to do that? But I am profoundly grateful that I did. The nurses took two Polaroids,

prints of his feet, and gave me a lock of his hair—that's all I have left. The next morning, I checked out of the hospital. Everyone asks if we are going to sue the doctor, but we have checked with several lawyers who all told us that, in New York, there are no grounds for malpractice because an unborn child is not considered a human being. If the baby had lived even a few minutes, it would have been different. Now we have no recourse whatsoever. My blood boils every time I think of that man. I've since learned that a good doctor would never have dismissed my complaints like that.

"We decided to have a short service at the funeral home and a private burial, though some people just let the hospital take care of everything. At first the tragedy made me and Scott closer. As wonderful as my friends and family were, no one else knew what we were going through. And though everyone meant well, sometimes they said truly insensitive things, like 'Oh, you'll have another baby' or 'You're still young.'

"But as close as we were at first, we're miles apart now. Scott, who's a stockbroker, went back to work a few days after the funeral. I'm sure that took his mind off things, at least for a while. I'm happy that he found some distraction, but I can't help thinking he just doesn't care as much as I do. He makes some suggestion that he thinks will solve all my problems, then announces he doesn't want to talk anymore.

"Unfortunately, this isn't the only thing we have to deal with. Scott was in the throes of a messy divorce long before we even met. Now, we spend countless hours every week preparing papers for his upcoming custody hearing. Scott's ex-wife does everything possible to destroy Scott's relationship with his two daughters and make our life miserable. We'll make plans to pick the girls up at her house to spend the weekend, and they won't be there. She'll break dates and change schedules whenever it suits her. Worse, she makes up lies about us, telling them we really don't enjoy having them spend time with us. In spite of this, I've always had a wonderful relationship with his girls—at least until recently. It's very hard for me to be with anyone's kids, even my own stepchildren.

"Then there are the financial issues. Five months ago, the firm where Scott's worked for fifteen years was taken over and, suddenly, he was out of a job. While he tried to figure out what to do next, we started bickering about things that never used to bother us. Every conversation became a fight. Often, he'd cut me off with a curt, 'Not another argument.' Well, I wasn't arguing, I was talking. Can't he see the difference? His attitude made me furious. Just yesterday, we had another clash—the never-ending fight about my parents coming to visit. Scott truly dislikes

them and he no longer even makes an effort to be nice. I know they can be very domineering—they're very old-world—but they are getting on in life and I want to spend more time with them. I don't want to have to defend my feelings every time.

"I was born in Mexico and moved here when I was twelve. My parents emigrated to New York two years earlier to start a better life, leaving me with relatives I didn't really know and who didn't pay a whole lot of attention to me. I didn't hear from my parents for months and I was lonely and terrified that I might never see them again. When I finally joined them, it was very difficult. I didn't speak a word of English and though people were very friendly, I always felt like an outsider. It didn't help that my parents were incredibly strict. They thought all my American friends were sex and drug fiends. Even though I was a straight-A student and adored school, they frowned on college. In their minds, universities were hubs of radical thinking and they wanted me to get married. When I was nineteen, I did. It was basically an arranged marriage, which I agreed to just to get out of the house. The marriage lasted nine years. One of my biggest regrets is that I never actually graduated from college, though I've taken more courses than most people who have Ph.D.s.

"After my divorce, I took several intensive language courses—I was already fluent in four—and found work as a translator in a new firm headquartered in the same building as Scott's brokerage office. We kept bumping into each other in the elevator, he asked me to lunch and, after only a few months, I knew this was the man I wanted to spend my life with. Scott is smart and charming and magnetic. He has this aura about him that somehow demands respect.

"It took a long time for me to get pregnant, and we were both thrilled when it happened. Now, I feel lifeless. One day I want to try for another baby right away; the next I vow to never have a child. For so long, I was proud of the fact that I could fend for myself. Now I know I'm not going to make it unless I get some help."

SCOTT'S TURN

"Imagine coming home from work to find your wife sobbing inconsolably on the bathroom floor, rocking a folded towel in her arms as if it were our baby," said Scott, forty, a stockbroker, his voice filled with resignation. "My heart is broken for her, but nothing I say or do seems to make one bit of difference. She's in a place I can't reach and I'm worried that I'm losing her. I make a suggestion—let's go to dinner and a movie, let's take a walk—and she screams at me like I'm some kind of moron for not understanding.

The day the baby died, "Liv lost her faith in God, and in herself. I do know what she's going through, but don't you reach a point when you have to say, 'Okay, we'll find a way to move on?' Why does she obsess about what happened, and what she should have done differently?

"I'm under a huge amount of stress—the baby, my job, my ex-wife. I know that all of that is bound to have an effect on a marriage, but my relationship with Liv has changed in ways that I never expected. She's overly critical and demanding—she complains that I haven't put the groceries away properly or that I should have known to get the air conditioners checked. And arguments about her parents get totally out of hand. I've never gotten along with them—I find them both, her mother especially, unbelievably intrusive. And I will never understand how her parents could have left her alone for so long when she was such a little kid. She basically fended for herself. Liv used to make room for my feelings. Now, she just gets furious and calls me selfish.

"When we first met, I was in the middle of a bad divorce. As soon as my ex-wife found out about Liv, she really tightened the screws on me, cutting back on my visitation time with our kids and brainwashing them into believing I no longer wanted to see them. She's turned both of them against me. It's been awful. I love my kids, and I feel terrible that the breakup of my marriage has prevented me from being the dad I have always wanted to be. I know I wasn't the most attentive father to them. I'd hoped that this time, with Liv, I'd have a second chance.

"Losing my job has been a bigger shock than I imagined. One day I was making six figures, the next they confiscated by my ID and told me to clear out my office by five P.M. I don't want to make my situation sound any worse than what many other people were going through, but still, it was humiliating—and frightening. I found a new position after about seven months, but it pays less. For the first time in my life, I'm worried about money. There's child support and future college tuition to think about. I probably wasn't as attentive to Liv as I should have been in the last few months, but I've always tried my best to be there for her.

"Liv is a brilliant, fascinating woman who can do anything she sets her mind to. I miss talking with her. I've always relied on her wisdom, whether I'm bouncing business ideas off of her, or asking for advice about my kids. She always knew what to do, how to handle any situation. But now she's not interested or available in any way.

"I have a Xerox of our baby's footprints in a frame on my desk and I think about him all the time. I've never said this, but sometimes I feel I have to prove to Liv how much I'm hurting. Even though we will never know why he died, I think Liv blames me to some degree for his death. I guess I blame myself, too. Because of my divorce and my job situation, she was under a ton of stress at a time when she should have been more relaxed. I should have questioned the doctors more, but after they assured us that she was fine, and the tests revealed nothing wrong, I tried not to dwell on it. I'd been through two pregnancies, and I know that when a woman is pregnant she has a million different anxieties. I tried to help Liv put hers into perspective.

"But the truth is, I can't talk about the same things over and over again the way she does. She's incredibly analytical and our conversations never end. I can't just listen to problems; I need to find solutions. So now I try to prevent those kinds of conversations from getting started in the first place. I don't know why I can't give her what she needs. Maybe it's because we run at a completely different pace.

"My family never dwelled on problems. I grew up outside of Philadelphia in an Italian-American family with two older sisters, so that made me king. At least in my mother's eyes, I could do no wrong. It was a fairly traditional childhood—my dad, a factory worker, was the disciplinarian. Mom, a homemaker, was the softie. They had problems, like every couple, but I think they had a happy marriage. Stuff happened, but we dealt with it. No big deal. I was a happy kid—I did well in school, played quarterback on the football team, and always knew I wanted to go into business. One of my older cousins was working on Wall Street, so, after graduating with a degree in economics, I headed there. I made a lot of money quickly and invested it well. My first marriage, to my college girlfriend, was unhappy almost from the start but at least I have two terrific daughters.

"Right now, I feel paralyzed. People call me all the time to ask how Liv is doing. No one ever wants to know how I'm doing. I'm not feeling sorry for myself. The world focuses on the mother, I know that. But it's hard to always be strong for her when I need someone to be strong for me, too."

THE COUNSELOR'S TURN

"When I first saw Liv and Scott, they were struggling with the incongruent grief so common in couples who have been through a catastrophic loss," says the counselor. "The discrepancy between the intensity of her grief and his, as well as their different coping styles, was beginning to tear them apart. My first goal was to assure them that what they were experiencing was normal. At the same time, I had to educate them about what to expect of themselves and each other so they could mourn and move forward instead of retreating into opposite emotional corners.

"In the first few weeks after their son's death, Liv and Scott had turned to each other for solace and support. However, by the time they walked into my office, their initial closeness had been shredded by arguments large and small. Marital tensions were further exacerbated by the stress of Scott's job loss and bitter divorce. Liv, an intelligent, insightful woman, who had always managed every aspect of life quite well, was simply not functioning. After such an unexpected loss, some women experience symptoms similar to those of posttraumatic stress disorder, and Liv's experience, while intense, is not uncommon. Her inconsolable crying, flashbacks, and waves of rage and guilt made me suspect that disorder. She desperately needed to talk about her pain, over and over again. Mistakenly, she assumed that because her husband didn't, he wasn't hurting as much as she was. 'Lean into your emotions,' I advised her. 'You're entitled to what you feel. But understand that Scott's feelings, though different from yours, are equally legitimate.'

"A Type-A personality, Scott was used to solving problems, and he was baffled by his wife's deepening despondency. He was trying to heal

103

in the only way he knew how—by throwing himself into his work. But increasingly, he saw his role not only as breadwinner but also as caretaker, a part for which he felt ill-prepared. So he tried another tactic—not talking about their baby. In truth, after the first few months, there had been less and less room for Scott's expression of pain. Colleagues, friends, and even family members often forget that a man suffers as much as a woman.

"By talking again and again about the various ways that people grieve, Liv started to understand that Scott's reticence didn't mean he didn't care about her or the baby. Scott was reassured to know that he would indeed get his wife back, though it might take longer than he'd imagined. However, for both of their recoveries, it was essential to set limits so that the grief didn't swallow up their entire life.

"'Dwelling on what you both could or should have done is not only useless, it's unfair,' I told them. Instead, I suggested that they set aside fifteen or twenty minutes every day to talk about what they were feeling and how they were coping. Scott tried hard to listen to whatever Liv needed to say without jumping in with a solution or suggestion. At the end of the designated time, they would back-burner the conversation until the following day.

Similar boundaries were established for discussions about his ex-wife and their divorce issues, which were also consuming their time and emotional life. The lawyers were able to hammer out a joint custody agreement and Scott is beginning to rebuild his relationship with his daughters. The girls know about the stillbirth and in their own ways have tried to show Liv how much they care. I told Liv that she should join them only when she feels up to it—and not berate herself if she doesn't. 'The girls have been astonishingly helpful in my healing,' she reported. 'They've made me beautiful cards and when they come over they always run to snuggle in my lap. I love them so much and that gives me hope that I can feel good about my life again.' To further ease stress, I made a relaxation tape of deep breathing and visualization exercises, which they both use once a day to de-stress.

"Because Liv had lost faith in herself and her own body, we spent several sessions discussing ways in which she could reclaim some sense of control over her life. Her rage against her old doctor was also sapping her strength. Although she had no legal recourse, she wrote a detailed letter to the hospital as well as the state medical review board, outlining her experience. While their muted response was expected, the letter-writing exercise provided a sense of closure for her on this issue.

"Deciding to find another obstetrician was another hurdle to leap in reclaiming control. 'I need a doctor I can trust,' she said, 'but I'm worried that a new physician won't be as sympathetic of what we'd been through.' Again, I assured her that her fears were common. After interviewing several ob-gyns, Liv and Scott found a physician specializing in high-risk pregnancies with whom they both feel confident. 'I can say anything to this man, no matter how silly, and call him at any time during the night, without feeling guilty that I'm disturbing him,' she reports.

"Participating in seminars and support groups at the pregnancy loss center further helped this couple see that they were not alone in their ordeal or in the marital problems they were suffering. 'Meeting so many people who had survived and emerged intact showed us that some day we could, too,' Liv said.

"The first year following any tragedy is the hardest. But healing can take several years, or a lifetime. Couples should expect that the intensity of their pain may last well into the second year. Equally essential is the need to prepare for significant anniversaries—the date they conceived, the baby's due date—as well as holidays, since these dates can trigger feelings of sadness.

On Mother's Day, Liv and Scott visited their son's grave and planted flowers. However, as the second anniversary of the baby's death approached, they both noticed that the sadness and rage had quieted down. 'It will never go away—I don't want it to,' Liv said. 'But I feel that I've turned a corner.'

"At this point she began to think about trying to get pregnant again. For almost a full year, she had had no interest in sex, which I also assured her was normal, and they had begun making love slowly and tentatively. 'But in the last few months, I've found myself starting to think about another baby,' she told me.

"Three years after Liv lost her son, she gave birth to a healthy baby girl. I suggested that they might find further peace if they could incorporate the child they lost into their lives. Liv is finally able to talk calmly about her son, and to tell those who ask how many children she has: 'I have one living daughter, and a son who died,' she responds. What's more, they've become regular volunteers at the Pregnancy Loss Support Group, talking on the phone to other grieving parents and moderating seminars. 'Helping others is part of the legacy we want to leave for our son,' she explained.

WHEN THE GRIEF
IS MORE THAN YOU CAN BEAR

According to the latest statistics from the National Institutes of Health, there are 800 stillbirths in this country every year and 900,000 early miscarriages. In 50 percent of the cases, the cause of death is never known. Parents struggling to deal with such a terrible loss often feel alone and adrift—unable to explain to others who haven't seen or felt the baby that a real member of the family has died. Bereaved parents often gain insight and help through counseling organizations such as SHARE Pregnancy & Infant Loss Support, based in St. Louis, Montana (www.nationalshareoffice.com), as well as the Pregnancy Loss Support Group of the National Council of Jewish Women (212-687-5030), a nonsectarian organization open to anyone in need.

FIGHT FAIR

Working for,
not against, Your Marriage

——————

nger is inevitable in marriage. If two people are living together, they are bound to disagree about small, seemingly petty things ("Whose turn is it to walk the dog?" "Why am I always doing the laundry?") as well as larger, more significant issues ("How should we handle out two-year-old's tantrums?" "Why don't you ever back me up when your mother criticizes me?"). Yet anger itself is not the real problem. It's how couples handle and deal with anger that separates a healthy relationship from one at risk.

People manage their anger in different ways. Some deny it, thinking that in the short run, it's easier and less painful than admitting the anger and dealing with the potential repercussions. Such people bury their resentments—however legitimate they may be—deep inside. And in the heat of an argument, they either crumble or explode as soon as a spouse gets defensive or, worse, counterattacks.

Women in particular have a difficult time dealing with anger because they are often made to feel guilty about feeling anger in the first place—witness the countless wives interviewed for the column who wonder "Do I have a right to be angry?" or "Besides, what good will it do?" Our culture teaches that men who speak their minds are assertive and strong. Women who do so are bitchy and shrill.

The problem is, unexpressed anger doesn't just disappear. Years of denial can eat away at self-esteem, as well as trigger migraines, ulcers, and a host of other stress-related ailments. It also saps energy—physically and emotionally—and, as medical studies report, may be a leading culprit in heart disease. Anger that is not dealt with appropriately seethes beneath the surface, only to erupt in a volcano of rage (often toward the wrong person) over a seemingly innocuous comment or action. The woman who is furious at her boss or her mother-in-law, but who does not dare to express her true feelings, may lash out at her children or her spouse.

While many husbands and wives deny that they're angry, others nurse their anger. Holding on to grudges and hurts gives them a sense of power they wouldn't otherwise possess. Since they may believe they're incapable of coping with any type of open confrontation, keeping their anger simmering on a low flame provides a protective shield that makes them feel less vulnerable. Those who nurse their grudges are often mistrustful and mad at the world. And it's hard to knock that chip off their shoulders.

Still other people vent their anger, often in the mistaken belief that "getting it off my chest" is healthy and clears the air. Sadly, explosive tirades only push a partner further away and give them more reasons to continue doing exactly what provoked their spouse in the first place.

Yet the most pernicious way of handling anger in marriage is not to handle it at all. This is when anger becomes self-perpetuating, locking husbands and wives in a vicious cycle of blame and hostility. Stuck in repetitive arguments that go nowhere, some couples dig in their heels in a vain attempt to prove themselves right and their partners wrong. Every conversation becomes a confrontation and the slightest provocation sends tempers flaring as each person falls into old, hurtful patterns. It's not uncommon for these warriors to drag a third party—usually a child—into the arguments to bolster their respective positions. In time, the only way such couples relate is through their anger and bickering.

Some couples are aware that their self-perpetuating fights are useless, yet neither partner can figure out how to break the stalemate. *Seven Secrets of a Happy Marriage* shows that it's possible to direct anger constructively to improve a marriage rather than destroy it. A key step is for each person to recognize the part he or she plays in provoking and sustaining the anger. Another is to learn to recognize the feeling of anger immediately—not an easy task if a couple have been suppressing negative feelings for a long time.

In this chapter we watch as each spouse learns to tune in to the body's individual reaction to anger. These anger signals—when the stomach churns, the heart races, the muscles tighten in the temples, neck, or back—are too often dismissed. When heeded, however, they can serve as warning signs that buried anger and resentment need to be addressed and resolved. Once husbands and wives learn to express their needs effectively, they can disagree constructively—brainstorming, negotiating, and, when appropriate, compromising. In this way, both partners maintain self-esteem—and reinforce their marriage, too.

"My Husband Is So Moody"

Life with Peter was an emotional roller coaster. How could Andrea stay with a man who was so out of control?

ANDREA'S TURN

"I can't believe that this is happening again," said Andrea, thirty-two, a soft-spoken woman in a gray knit tunic and matching skirt. "Everything was going so well, but then Peter's cycles of depression and anger reappeared. He won't talk to me. He snaps at Jimmy, our two-year-old son, and whenever I ask what's wrong, he gets furious and shuts me out.

"Peter's mood swings have been happening on and off since we were married, six years ago. On top of all this, he doesn't lift a finger around the house and I'm getting tired of doing all the work.

"My own parents fought constantly, mostly over money. They're still fighting over the same things to this day, so I assure you, I have no illusions about living happily ever after. But I swore I would never have a marriage like theirs, and look what's happened: This is my second, and now it's falling apart.

"Soon after I married my first husband, I realized I didn't really love him; I had just been desperate to get out of the house. I was also so afraid of arguments that I let him make all the decisions. Finally we were divorced and I moved back to my parents' house, but nothing had changed there. That's when I decided to make a clean break, so I packed up and moved to California.

"About five years after I moved here, I met Peter. I was working at a large hotel downtown and he came in to reserve a banquet room. We started talking, and when he asked for my phone number I was really excited.

"We hit it off right from the start. Peter was a social worker counseling kids at a local juvenile center; we had so much in common. Like me, Peter had been married once before and was determined to make his next relationship work.

"A month after we met, Peter moved into my apartment, and four months later we were married. Almost as soon as we were married, our relationship seemed to change. For one thing, I was fired from my job because my boss didn't want anyone who wasn't willing to be on call twenty-four hours a day, and now that I had Peter I certainly wasn't. For six months I looked for a new job, and by the time I found a spot in an insurance office, we were pretty broke.

"Just about this time, Peter decided that working at the juvenile center was too emotionally draining. He was burned out, he said, and he was going to try working as a salesman for a computer software company. He worked on commission and he was quite good at selling, but in the beginning money was tight.

"Still, there were blessings: We had fallen in love with a little house and scraped together every penny we could for a down payment. And we decided to start a family. Life was stressful, but we thought that once we bought our house everything would fall into place.

"Unfortunately, it didn't. For one thing, we'd been buying everything on credit so we could save all our cash. After we moved into the house, we realized how financially strapped we were and how much we owed. On top of that, I had to have surgery for infertility—there was scar tissue on my fallopian tubes, and if I had an operation, perhaps then I could conceive. Of course, I had the operation, but I was out of work for six weeks, and though my medical bills were covered, I didn't get a paycheck.

"Well, that just about put us under. I was upset, but Peter became terribly depressed. That was the first time I witnessed one of his moods. But it certainly wasn't the last—they occurred frequently after that. Sometimes they lasted ten minutes, sometimes ten days. He'd withdraw from me completely, refusing to talk and refusing to make love. He'd mope around, expecting me to wait on him hand and foot. The more I asked what was wrong, what I could do to help, the angrier he became. I didn't know what was happening and I started to think I was to blame.

"The worst part was when Peter's depression turned to rage. Just like his father, the least thing would set him off. You see, although his family always pretended nothing was wrong, Peter's father, who died ten years ago, was an alcoholic. Whenever he drank, he was especially hard on Peter, his only child, criticizing him about everything. If Peter ever tried to talk to his father about it, he was either yelled at or ignored. His mother, a shy, quiet woman, was apparently unwilling or unable to stand up to her husband, and Peter had to handle all of it himself. Peter doesn't drink, but he's like his father in other ways.

"Usually Peter calmed down after these explosions. In fact, for almost two years things did seem better and we became very close again. I even became pregnant! It was a difficult nine months, and then I had to have a cesarean, but Peter couldn't have been more supportive. I thought our dark days were over.

"Needless to say, I was wrong. A few months ago, Peter started having problems at work. He and his boss can't seem to get along and it looks as if Peter will have to change jobs. I've tried to get him to talk, but he ignores me. Once again he's moping around the house. Just last week we got into a huge fight because it takes him four days to carry the trash cans from the curb to the backyard. I'm not a slave, for heaven's sake. I'm a nervous wreck again; I eat to calm myself down, so my weight is zooming up. And our sex life? It's nonexistent.

"I love Peter, but his anger and depression are leaving no room for our marriage. I've been thinking about a divorce. If he doesn't change soon, I don't see that I have a choice."

PETER'S TURN

"Andrea is fed up and I don't blame her," said Peter, thirty-four, a pleasant-looking man in a tan business suit. "I know my moods can be scary, but I would never hurt her or Jimmy.

"I don't mean to yell, but Andrea has a way of pushing my buttons. Whenever I feel low, she nags me constantly. And when Andrea tries to get under my skin like that, it really makes me mad.

"I wasn't very happy growing up. My relationship with my father was lousy. He would call me stupid whether I came home with a low grade on a test or accidentally burned the toast. He humiliated me in front of my friends.

"I think my father was a very unhappy man, so he sought relief in the bottle. I first remember him drinking heavily when I was thirteen. I hated his drinking, but any discussion on my part was impossible.

"By the time I went away to college, the drinking was so bad we never knew if he'd be coming home that night. And he was always a belligerent drunk, going out of his way to irritate people and to humiliate me in particular. I guess I learned early on to put up a wall so that he couldn't get to me. Andrea thinks these moods are new and her fault, but she's wrong; I remember getting depressed like this back in junior high.

"Anyway, I thought going away to school would help, and it did—for a while. I met my first wife during my senior year. That marriage lasted only three years, and it probably worked for less than two.

"About a year after my divorce was final I met Andrea, and I was immediately struck by her independence and strength. Our relationship progressed quickly; before I knew it we were planning a wedding. The problem was, I didn't think I was ready to be married again. I wanted to postpone the wedding until I had worked out my problems, but I didn't have the guts to tell her. I was afraid I'd lose her.

"Shortly after we were married, I decided to quit the counseling center and start my sales career. My father had always told me I could never be a salesman—he didn't think I had the personality or the wherewithal to do it—but that only made me more determined.

"I really liked selling, and I was doing well, although I see now that Andrea and I bit off more than we could chew by buying the house. We were also trying to have a baby, but we couldn't. It was all too much and my moods began again.

"Now when I get depressed I just want to be left alone. It's not that I don't want to help out; I simply can't. But no matter how bad I feel, eventually I get over it. Although I have tried to explain this to Andrea, she either starts to cry or insists on bugging me. That makes me angrier, and before I realize what's happening, I'm yelling and knocking over chairs.

"Lately it seems my depressions are more frequent. The pressure at work is mounting—I have a new supervisor and he and I don't see eye to eye. I want very much to quit, maybe even start my own small firm, but I have a family to support; I'm too old to start over.

"I love Andrea, and I give her a lot of credit for hanging in there. Maybe I'm not cut out to be anyone's husband. I'll take the blame for our problems, but can't she understand that there are times when I need to be alone?"

THE COUNSELOR'S TURN

"At first, this couple's problem seemed one-sided," said the counselor. "But though it was true that Peter's periods of depression and rage were a major source of conflict, Andrea shared responsibility for the trouble this marriage was in. A key issue for this couple was their inability to communicate what they wanted and needed from each other.

"Like many children of alcoholic parents, Peter came to this relationship carrying some heavy emotional baggage from the past. When a child is growing up, he needs to be able to trust his parents. But an alcoholic parent can't always be trusted. Peter never knew when his father would lash out at him, much less come home at all. He never learned the importance of sharing his feelings with others and was left instead with a great deal of unexpressed rage.

"As an adult, whenever anything bothered him, Peter coped by withdrawing, and he viewed any attempts to help him as an invasion of privacy. He reasoned that telling Andrea how he was feeling would make him vulnerable, as he had been as a child.

"Peter continued this pattern over the years; as soon as something shook his self-confidence—financial problems or a crisis at work—he reacted by internalizing the problem and blaming himself. Ironically, Peter's perception of his own problem was not off the mark. He simply needed help marshaling his many good qualities to overcome his negative behavioral patterns.

"Andrea's childhood experiences, although not nearly as difficult as her husband's, had also failed to teach her how to communicate effectively. Since her parents fought constantly over the same problems, she never learned how a couple can work through problems and solve them. Desperate for a 'nice' marriage, she deferred to her first husband's every wish, which made her unhappy.

"In her relationship with Peter, she shifted gears and became all-controlling. When Peter was depressed, she probed relentlessly for the cause of his mood. When she was unable to find out what was wrong—when, in fact, Peter pushed her away—she dealt with her frustration by overeating and then blaming her husband.

"In our first session, I outlined three goals for this couple. The first was for them to make a firm commitment to make this marriage work. I pointed out that because of their inability to connect on an emotional level, much of their marriage was based not on intimacy but on accomplishments—saving for a house, trying to have a child, and so on. I also referred Peter to a colleague of mine, a psychiatrist, to see if medication, perhaps an antidepressant, would be helpful. For the time being, we've decided to see if other avenues prove fruitful.

"The second goal was for each to take a share of the responsibility for their problems. For a long time, only Peter was willing to do this. Andrea persisted in seeing herself as the blameless victim of Peter's moods. It was essential, then, for them to decide who was responsible for what.

"We began with the practical aspects of their life—deciding, for instance, which chores were appropriate for each partner to do. Once Andrea saw that these basics were being taken care, of she began to relax and soften her adamant stance against Peter.

"At the same time, I urged Peter to take at least twenty minutes a day to relax, either by practicing deep-breathing techniques or by meditating or doing yoga. Although many people dismiss such simple measures, recent studies have proved that depressed people like Peter show remarkable progress when they implement relaxation techniques to combat stress. And although Peter agreed that he could not always withdraw from the family—that is, have the luxury of being the 'sick' one—I instructed Andrea that when he wanted to be alone, she must respect his wishes.

"The third and most difficult goal was for them to learn to share their feelings. We worked on a simple exercise: Each was to pick one upsetting incident and say, 'When you do this, I feel this way.' Just learning to recognize a feeling and expressing it in a nonthreatening way was a big step.

"When I discovered that Andrea and Peter had spent virtually no time away from home together since their marriage, I suggested that they arrange for a baby-sitter on a regular basis so they could get out of the house and into a neutral environment away from chores that needed to be done. The time alone reinforced their deep feelings for each other and gave them more practice in communicating.

"And the more they communicated, the more they realized how good their marriage really was. Peter has learned that he needn't be afraid to express his fears to Andrea, and this trust has given him a renewed sense of confidence. Rather than become immobilized over a possible job change, he has been setting up interviews with executive placement firms.

"Peter's openness has had a positive effect on Andrea. Although she will probably always worry about problems until they are solved, Andrea has learned to keep her anxieties at a manageable level, and she has acknowledged that overeating is the way she copes with stress and not something that is Peter's fault.

"Although this couple terminated joint counseling two months ago, we agreed that Peter would continue to see me for a while longer; he still feels the need to talk about ways to handle his moods when they do shift. However, as the couple find out more about themselves, they know that any problems that crop up will be ones they can tackle together."

THE BLAME GAME

While Peter acknowledged his problems, Andrea acted like a martyr and refused to believe that she played a part either in triggering or exacerbating their difficulties. This happens in many marriages. And though it may be difficult, couples can break the impasse and interrupt the cycle of blame—when both partners stop insisting that their ideas and opinions are infallible, take responsibility for their individual behavior, and make healing the relationship the top priority. This exercise will help those trapped in a cycle of self-righteous blaming to take constructive steps to work on the real issues dividing them:

1. Think of an issue that's currently causing pain in your relationship.

2. In three sentences, write down your position on that issue.

3. Pretend to be your partner and describe how he or she sees that issue. Be fair.

4. Now ask yourself: What would have to change inside for me to see the issue from my spouse's point of view? Are these changes ones I'm comfortable with? If so, why am I not making them? Why are they difficult for me? Again, be as honest as you can.

"He Says I'm Pushing Him Away"

Laura and Stewart were having a hard time adjusting to parenthood. What happens when every discussion snowballs into a long, ugly battle?

"This is supposed to be the happiest time of my life," said Laura, thirty-eight, a pretty, petite woman who barely took a breath between thoughts, "but I'm miserable.

"I have a beautiful child—Max will be two next week—and a wonderful job, but my marriage is falling apart. Stewart and I fight constantly, usually about stupid things at first, but it soon escalates into all-out war.

"One of our biggest fights is about sex. Or, rather, the lack of it. Before Max, our sex life was great. But to be honest, the thought of sex rarely enters my mind these days. Either I'm thinking about the baby or I'm too exhausted. I'd like to have another child, but Stewart complains I'm just using him as a baby manufacturer.

"Stewart was different from anyone I'd ever dated. We met through friends and married nine months after our first date. It was a fabulous wedding at a very elegant restaurant in the city, then we went to Bermuda for ten days. I went back to work— I'm vice-president in charge of planning and development for a large hospital—but since I was thirty-five, we wanted to start a family.

"Finally, I got pregnant. That was a fabulous time for us. I felt terrific, and even though I gained forty-six pounds, I remember this as the most idyllic time of my life. We traveled, made plans, had great sex.

117

"I worked up until a week before I was due, then planned to take a two-month maternity leave. But my delivery was horrendous. After seventeen hours, the doctor decided to do a C-section.

"My recovery was awful, too. All that maternal bonding . . . well, it wasn't happening. I felt none of that instant love—only out of control and panicky.

"Most of all, I was, and still am, scared that my child will grow up to dislike me the way I dislike my own mother. But while I was a basket case, my husband turned out to be a natural father.

"I don't know when we started bickering; we both have tempers. I'm a yeller—my mother is, too—and Stewart can be as sarcastic as she is. But what really gets me is when he starts to tell me something, then clams up and walks out of the room.

"Ignoring me is the worst thing you can do; it was another of Mother's tactics. Mother and I had a very acrimonious relationship—she clearly favored my sister, Judy, whom I'm still not close to. Judy did everything Mother told her to. I was bratty, 'the selfish one,' and jealous of the attention Mother paid her.

"I was Daddy's girl, though now my father practically worships Stewart. They're best buddies. Like my father, Stewart works in his family's business—they manufacture handbags and small leather goods.

Frankly, I've never liked my in-laws. Stewart's father is a tyrant. I know Stewart is unhappy and stressed out, but he idolizes his dad and keeps trying to prove himself.

"The problem is, I'm always left doing everything—the grocery shopping, making Max's appointments with the pediatrician, checking to see if he needs new sneakers, . . . Must I also remind Stewart to do the few things he promises he'll do?

"Sometimes I don't know why I bother. When Stewart tries to help, he gets everything wrong. He takes Max to the park but forgets to take his hat or bottle of milk. He offers to watch him so I can lie down, but if Max cries, Stewart gives him juice even though it's right before dinner. Then he's not hungry when he's scheduled to eat. I keep telling him that kids like routine, but he doesn't get it. I clip articles on child care, but he never reads them.

"Then, last month, he announced that he wanted to start his own company. Let's be realistic. This is the kind of thing you do when you're younger; it will take years to turn a profit. Am I supposed to support all three of us?"

STEWART'S TURN

"Will she ever shut up?" asked Stewart, thirty-nine, an athletic-looking man whose voice was heavy with resignation.

"Laura's constant anxiety, her panic over the littlest thing . . . I can't stand it. Life according to Laura is so hard, you'd think this was *The Grapes of Wrath*. She never stops reminding me how much she does and how little I do. If I forget to call the plumber within the time frame she deems acceptable, she hits the ceiling: 'Well, did you call? Why didn't you call? You know, Stewart, I do this and I do that. . . .'

"I was treated like that growing up—in fact, my parents still treat me like a twelve-year-old. Both my parents were first-generation immigrants, very Old World. I was never close to them or to my sister, Marcy.

"Despite all that I achieved—I was the first kid in my family to graduate from high school, not to mention an Ivy League college—I know my parents thought of me as the black sheep of the family; Marcy was the good kid, I was the bad kid.

"No one ever laughed in our house, or rarely. That's one of the things that attracted me to my wife: She had spunk. I idolized my father and dreamed about working with him. Growing up, I expected to take over the business after he retired. During vacations and over the summer, I would work in the factories and warehouses . . . I traveled with him to the Far East, learned four languages—I loved it.

"But things aren't working out. I know I have to leave. I'm not enjoying my work anymore, but I'm confused and, I guess, scared. And I'm not a kid anymore. I have a family to think about. It would be nice if my wife could support me a little. I can't talk about it with Laura, though. She gets panic-stricken.

"Laura is a perfectionist. There's no room for anyone else's opinion, and certainly not mine. I try to help, but with Laura I can never win. Well, guess what? I'm not going to try anymore. Period. I don't need to read an article from some magazine about how to give my kid a bath. Listen, I've gone to every single pediatrician's appointment Max has had, so don't tell me I'm not a full partner. She takes me for granted, and I'm sick of it. So I forgot Max's hat. Big deal. The kid had a hood on his sweatshirt. He'll live. So I give him a little juice. If he eats at seven o'clock instead of six, Laura has a fit.

"And you wouldn't believe the things that come out of her mouth. To be blunt, she's a bitch, hurling four-letter words, telling me she hates me.

"I agree that we fight about stupid things. The other night, I got so mad, I put my fist through a door. Then she demands that I tell her I'm sorry. When someone says that to me, I see red. That is something my parents always said. Sorry for what?

"She used to be my best friend. But now she doesn't have the slightest idea what's really bugging me. We never make love; I try to be affectionate, but she brushes me off, so lately I've stopped trying. I expected this right after the baby, but it's been going on too long now. She's pushing me away. You know, one day I really am going to leave, and when I do I won't come back."

THE COUNSELOR'S TURN

"What happened to Laura and Stewart happens to many couples when the pattern of their relationship is disrupted," says the counselor. "Neither one really wanted to admit how much their lives had changed after they'd had a child.

"However, these two brought a higher than usual degree of competition and resistance to change in their marriage. Instead of recognizing what they were doing and learning to compromise, each refused to bend until the other did first. Such competition is common, particularly in couples who are still dealing with unresolved sibling issues or who have come from homes where parents favored, or appeared to favor, one child over another. Laura and Stewart often tried to one-up each other: Who's the better parent? The better lover? Who initiated sex last time? Who will apologize first?

"My goal was not to make the problems go away, but rather to help Laura and Stewart lessen their duration and better deal with them. While the intensity of their conflicts was great, I sensed that, deep down, these two really loved each other.

"High-strung Laura was a perfectionist who thrived on organization and control. She had always been a success, yet motherhood presented her with a host of unpredictable situations over which she had little control. Her new-mother anxiety was fueled by her desperation not to make the same mistakes her mother had made.

"When she became anxious, Laura fell into a pattern of thinking solely of herself. When I first met her, she was angry and jealous that her husband was so comfortable with Max, while she felt so unsteady and unsure. She had convinced herself that she wasn't a good mother, and although Stewart tried to reassure her, she couldn't hear him.

"Compounding their communication problem was the fact that Laura presented her worries in such a way that Stewart perceived it as nagging and frequently responded to her with a patronizing 'It's so easy; if you can't do it, I will' attitude. This invalidated her concerns and made her feel out of control.

"I told Laura she had to change the way she communicated her fears to Stewart. In time, she was able to speak in a nonanxious way so he didn't automatically tune her out. He, in turn, had to listen to the feelings behind her words. To do that, he had to promise to set aside everything that he wanted to say, all his defenses and comments, and simply hear her out. This technique is called reflective listening, and in many cases the therapy process in general can serve as a model of behavior for each partner. During a session, I listen empathetically to each person in turn. By hearing me encourage Laura to talk about her feelings, Stewart learned how to do the same at home.

"But more than speaking in a less anxious way, Laura had to develop confidence in herself as a mother. I pointed out that because of her perfectionism, Laura had a list of 'shoulds' that few people would ever attain. 'Take a look at your son,' I told her. 'He's thriving, he's happy. You must be doing something right!'

"Another factor dividing this couple was Laura's desire for her husband to help with the baby, although she was unwilling to relinquish any decision-making. I explained that while Stewart's way of handling Max was different from hers, it was no less correct. If Stewart is going to take Max to the shopping center, let him decide if he wants to take along a bottle of milk. 'Cross that off your list, Laura,' I told her. 'You don't have to worry about everything all the time.'

"As Laura's anxiety about her mothering began to lessen, I pointed out that the distance between her and Stewart had grown because they each had different ways of dealing with problems, ways that were often

in conflict. Laura obsessed; Stewart denied. As a result, everything became a power struggle.

"When I first met Stewart, he was depressed. He needed to talk about the possibility of his leaving the family business. This would ease his fears about making the break and not being able to support his family. But rather than talk with Laura, Stewart's inclination was to tell her one or two things, then cut short the conversation. 'That's not a discussion,' I told him. 'Share your anxieties with Laura and engage her in listening to you.'

"At the same time, however, Laura had to overcome her resentment about being the breadwinner if Stewart went off on his own. Laura had an I-want-to-have-my-cake-and-eat-it-too attitude toward Stewart's plans. For a long time, she was unwilling to admit that one of the reasons she was so upset at the thought of Stewart's going off on his own was the fact that this was in some way an abrogation of the contract they had made with each other when they got married. Yes, of course she would work, but her salary would be gravy. 'Many women are like this,' I told her, 'but things change. You made a commitment to each other, and if it means you have to shoulder most of the financial responsibility until his business gets going, then so be it.'

"'When Stewart starts a discussion about his work and plans for the future,' I continued, 'you must listen carefully to what he is saying and not pepper him with questions and let your own fears silence him.' 'You're right,' Laura said. 'It doesn't matter who makes the money. It's our money.' Stewart did leave his father's business at the end of last year and started a competing firm.

"As the tension eased between them, as they learned to control their hair-trigger tempers, they started to laugh again and enjoy being together. Since each was waiting for the other to make the first move sexually, I also gave them the assignment of taking turns seducing each other. This wasn't as easy as it sounded, since the power struggles between these two were long-standing, and they were both too proud to say, 'I need you; I want you.' Once they did, Laura realized how much she enjoyed sex with Stewart and how much she had missed it.

"As Laura gained more confidence in her mothering abilities, she became less rigid about schedules and stopped insisting things be done only her way. 'I was trying so hard to surround us with perfection,' she said when we ended counseling after a year and a half. 'I've learned that if I just ease up on myself and everyone else, things have a way of working out.'"

HOW TO END AN ARGUMENT— SO YOU'RE BOTH HAPPY

1. Stop trying to win. In most arguments, each person is a little right and a little wrong.

2. Schedule a time and place to resolve conflict. Timing is everything. Don't bring up important issues when you are too tired or too rushed to resolve them.

3. Be clear and specific. Discuss one issue at a time and stay focused on the point you are trying to make. Try to be as neutral as you can in presenting your point of view.

4. Make suggestions for resolutions, brainstorm ideas, and pick one to try that seems to satisfy both of you the most. If that doesn't work, don't despair. Pick another. Comments such as "Let's try to find a common ground" or "Where do we more or less agree?" show that you're serious about negotiation.

5. Call a time-out when either of you is so white-hot you will soon say or do something you regret. Remove yourself, temporarily, from the situation. You can say "I'm feeling very angry and I'm beginning to lose it now. I want to take a time-out." Or "I see you're very angry right now. Let's discuss this tonight, after the kids are in bed." Make a definite time and place to continue the conversation. Then, leave the room and do something physical— walk, jog, clean the garage—anything to defuse angry energy. When you're calm, ask your partner if he's ready to resume the conversation. (If he says he's still too angry, respect his feelings and wait.)

6. Promise each other you won't be nasty, sarcastic, or personally critical.

7. Don't insist on the last word. You may win the battle but lose the war by building resentment.

"HE'S NEVER THERE FOR ME"

Stressed to the limit, Candace and Jack were unable to enjoy their children, their jobs, let alone their marriage. Can two people who have so many individual responsibilities ever find time for each other?

CANDACE'S TURN

"I'm so angry, I don't even know where to begin," said Candace, forty, an architect and mother of two boys, eight and ten. "Our world is brimming with stress. Neither of us is happy. We're both so busy doing what we have to do there's no time to do what we want to do.

"Jack is not pulling his weight in this marriage; I can't rely on him to do anything he promises to do and we're fighting all the time because of it. I'm talking about big things and little things. He yeses me to death one day, then forgets what he says the next. My kids could go on for hours about how Daddy doesn't listen. He acts like he is, but then it dawns on you that he isn't paying one bit of attention to anything you're saying.

"I'm frantic. I work from eight-thirty to six-thirty as an architect at a small firm, then race home to my other full-time job. I'm the one who keeps this family running. Jack is an incredible father and he's always there for the boys, to the point that he'll leave work to coach their soccer team or make sure their class gets to see the new exhibit at the science museum. But I'm the one arranging the car pools, making the doctors' appointments. Though I've hired a cleaning service once a week, I still do everything else around the house:

I take out trash, mow the lawn, shovel the walks, and do the grocery shopping and laundry because, while I ask Jack to help me, he never does. I pay the bills and each month must remind him to deposit money so checks don't bounce.

"The stuff we've fought about, and never resolved, is endless. If we've discussed once we've discussed a hundred times that he'll help me get Zach, our ten-year-old, into bed by nine-thirty. Now, you can't wait until nine-twenty-five to do this, since it can take Zach forty-five minutes to get undressed if you don't monitor him each step of the way. Am I the only one in this house who can tell time? Why am I always the drill sergeant? Other times I'll calmly say, 'I'm having my book club over here in an hour, could you please take your laptop and files out of the den?' Jack responds: 'Sure,' in a very sweet voice, but when the doorbell rings, and twelve women march in, do I have to tell you what's still spread all over the place?

"Last weekend Jack asked me if he could help me with the chores. I said I'd be grateful if he switched the laundry from the washer to the dryer while I ran to the grocery store. Well, when I came back, I found him reading with Oliver, our eight-year-old on the couch. I went ballistic. And of course my children and my husband thought I was a maniac. I cringed when he took them aside and consoled them: 'This has nothing to do with you guys,' he said, 'Mommy's just in a bad mood.' It's so undermining.' Then he runs around the house closing all the windows because he thinks the neighbors can hear me. I knew I was out of control and I felt horrible yelling like that. After all, he was doing this wonderful fatherly thing. But the bottom line was, someone had to do that laundry and it was going to be me!

"When stuff like that happens, Jack gets all quiet and pouty and says, 'Oh, I forgot.' Well, that's not good enough anymore. Why can't he change? Why am I the one who must take all the blame for what's wrong here? Why am I the controlling demanding witch? He's putting me between a rock and a hard place—and then he says it's all my fault. Last Sunday was another typical example: He said he'd make dinner, but as it got closer and closer to six o'clock, he still couldn't make up his mind. He kept asking me, 'What should we have for dinner?' You know, if he says he's going to do it, then he needs to decide and do it. I don't want any part of it! I just want to go to the kitchen, sit down, and see food on my plate. I don't care if it's home-cooked or Chinese or Kentucky Fried Chicken. Just please, let someone else take care of it!

"I'm tired of asking, tired of reminding, tired of begging. I hate myself for losing my temper, especially at my kids. Sometimes, I can't believe how angry I get. Oliver, in particular, hates when we fight. He's the peacemaker, very sensitive. But it's my husband pushing me over the edge. If Jack showed one ounce of concern for me, or some sense that he bears a little responsibility for our problems, things would be totally different. I would love a hug, but Jack would never do that. So as a result, we really have no relationship at all. We're so mad at each other, we can barely tolerate being in the same room. In that sense, I suppose it's not all that much different from the family I grew up in. I don't think my parents were particularly happy either.

"I'm from Denver, one of seven. There were three older kids, a gap of about four years, then three younger ones. I was the oldest of the younger group, kind of a mother hen, but frequently lost in the shuffle. It seemed like the older ones or the younger ones were always needing attention and I was frequently left to fend for myself. My dad, who was a purchasing agent for a small business, ruled with an iron fist. He hated his job but stuck with it until retirement, complaining his whole life and taking it out on us. The worst thing Mother could say was 'Wait till your father gets home.' We were spanked, we were whipped, and there was never any discussion about it.

"You can imagine the scene: seven kids with seven opinions, lots of anger, and plenty of slammed doors. We yelled at each other all the time. I was fairly close to my mother but she wasn't really able to stand up to my dad. It's so ironic to see my parents as grandparents; they're incredibly loving to my kids, but I certainly never had that kind of relationship with them. As parents, Jack and I probably go overboard trying to accommodate our lives to our children's needs.

"I did well in school but it was college, when I took a class with a world-renowned architect and art historian, that I decided to study design and architecture. Since I had a lot of advanced placement credits I was able to complete college in three years, then went on to graduate school. Jack, who's an investment banker now, was in business school at the same university; he'd graduated several years before me, worked for a few years, and had recently gone back for an M.B.A. So even though he's older than me, we both got our graduate degrees at the same time.

"I thought he was gorgeous but I'd sworn off dating his type. He seemed too suave, too cool for me. But after I got to know him, my resistance melted. We got serious pretty quickly and, six months after I graduated, we moved back to Denver. I didn't want to stay in the east.

"I went to work for the same company I'm with today. The hours were long and I loved it, and when I got pregnant they were flexible and allowed me to arrange a part-time schedule when my kids were small. Two years ago, though, the firm expanded and they started pressuring me to come back. It was clear that I either had to be full time or find something else. That's when I started to feel overwhelmed.

"When we moved to Denver, Jack took a job with a hugely respected businessman-cum-philanthropist. Though semi-retired, he became a mentor of sorts, and Jack ended up working for him for several years.

"But I don't think Jack has ever been truly happy with his career choices. I think Jack measures success by money and he's always vacillated between wanting to make money and wanting to make the world better. He's so wracked by his inability to find the right balance in his life that he can't let himself be happy. Now, fifteen years later, he's still dealing with the same issues.

"Jack's led a charmed life: His father was a self-made millionaire, who unfortunately lost most of it over the years. But Jack went the prep-school-to-Harvard route and his friends are the guys you see on the cover of *Fortune* magazine. Before he moved to Denver, Jack worked in Washington and I know he loved the excitement of being in the center of things; though he's never said it, maybe he regrets leaving that life. He's extremely well-respected, and he does seem to love it here. But financially, he will never match old friends and I can't help but wonder if deep down that's why he can never make a decision about his work.

"Whatever the reason, his indecision about his career has caused countless arguments in our marriage. In the fifteen years that we've been married, he's never been satisfied. He's switched jobs several times—same field, different firms. Over the years, all that jumping around meant a loss of income for us that's really caused me to worry. At one point, we had to take out a second mortgage on our house. But even when Jack was with a company for a long stretch, he was constantly churning: Big firm? Small firm? Do I like these guys or don't I? Do I want to specialize or generalize? Do I want to work long hours, or would I rather spend more time with my kids? I've always been supportive. Time and again, I'm told him, 'Do whatever you want to do. Just do it.' But he's like a broken record. It's hard to explain this, but he literally goes around in circles when he talks. I know he's depressed, even though he won't admit it to me. I just don't have the patience to listen to him obsess anymore. I'm worn out. It's amazing that we're even here—two months ago he promised to call and make an appointment, but each time he never managed to do it. It figures."

"Candace is Type A, forceful and opinionated. And while I was immediately attracted to that when we first met, now I'm fed up," admitted Jack, forty-five, a George Clooney look-alike who has a somewhat self-deprecating tone to his voice. "I'm always dodging bullets. My wife's outbursts are out of control and so out of proportion to the so-called crime committed, I can't deal with her anymore. It makes me anxious and angry. I can't reach out to her, I certainly can't give her a hug. I just want to run out of the house.

"I especially hate the way she talks to the kids. When she's calm, she's a loving, engaging mom. But when she erupts like a volcano, she scares them. I don't think a day goes by when she doesn't fly into a rage about something. Usually, it's something I haven't done or failed to do to her standards. Like dinner the other night. I didn't want to make something she didn't want. As always, I wanted her to be happy. But if I made steak, and she was in the mood for Chinese, well, who knows what kind of explosion that would have set off?

"Maybe it's because we come from such totally different backgrounds. Candy was raised in a strict, conservative home where you did what you were told and never asked questions. My parents were much looser in the discipline department. Still, I don't have warm and fuzzy memories of my childhood. I was raised in Greenwich, Connecticut. My older sister was the academic in the family, and my parent's favorite. Though I always did well in school, I was labeled the family jokester and rarely taken seriously. Candy says I had a charmed life; compared to her childhood, I guess I did. But I spent more time at my friends' homes than I did at mine. Dad was always working—he made his fortune in the photographic-supply business. All he did was make money. He never took much of an interest in me. I think he showed up for one lacrosse game during my whole high school career, and he never bothered to learn the game even though I was team captain. My parents divorced when I was fifteen, after several very bitter years.

"So maybe I don't watch the clock like Candy wants me to because I don't think ten or fifteen minutes one way or another is all that important. What's important to me is that I'm lying on the floor with my sons, talking about the hockey game or why the Giants' defense was so bad in the Super Bowl. Though it might not be within her time frame, Zach will get to bed, just like the counter will get wiped, and the dishes put away. If I have two hours of available time, I'm going to prioritize, and doing the laundry won't be at the top of my list. Candy can't stand that. She's so compulsive, she'll get up an hour early to do it. I refuse to live that way and I don't understand why she does.

"She's right about the papers the night of her book club. I should have moved them, I don't know why I don't remember to do what she asks. Sometimes I tune her out. I'm so wrapped up in my own worries about work, I can't think about anything else.

"I wish I had Candy's ability to be so sure that I'm making the right decisions. She tells me, 'Make a choice, deal with it.' She's able to see the world in black and white, but I always see eighteen shades of gray and stall out. If a decision doesn't feel completely right to me, I can't make it. My dad was notoriously indecisive, too, but I don't know how to break the pattern.

"But the truth is, I have no direction for where I want to go with my life. I don't want to be like my dad; I want to do some good in the world, to help the underdog. But I've learned that you can only do good in the world when you have the luxury of money. I like the excitement of investment banking, but I'd like to be able to do that kind of work for start-up companies, perhaps in inner cities or minority businesses. It's not that we're scraping by—we live nicely—but I did have to take out that second mortgage and it's also time to start thinking about the boys' education. Since I'm only working about thirty or forty hours a week, my salary is nowhere near what other people in my profession make. I've consciously put myself on the Daddy track. I want to be the available parent, if they forget their lunch or need to go somewhere, they know they can reach me on my cell phone anytime. Besides, if I worked the typical hours of an investment banker, Candy would be even more overloaded. Can you imagine what our home life would be like then? And I can't shake the thought that when it comes to my accomplishments, I might have peaked when I was twenty-seven.

"You see, when I finished my undergraduate work, I volunteered on a whim to work on the Democratic presidential campaign. Think *Primary Colors* and *The West Wing*. The next thing I knew I was working in the White House and I loved it. But when the Republicans swept into office, I was out of work, so I decided to get my M.B.A. and find a way to combine business with helping people. Nothing I've done since has matched the excitement of what I did in my twenties. But I certainly don't miss D.C. or regret staying in Denver—why does she think that? I love this city and I've met some terrific people here. It's just that some piece, somewhere, is missing and I can't put my finger on it.

"Right now, I feel pretty discouraged, like an athlete who can't get motivated. Sometimes it's hard to push myself out of bed in the morning. Once I get going, I'm okay. But lately, getting out of that starting block is impossible.

"It's hard to believe there was actually a time when Candy and I lived another way. In college, when we first got married, she was full of life, sassy, outdoorsy, unafraid to speak her mind. I loved her sense of freedom and adventure. Now I can't find that woman in her anywhere. More than anything I want us to have time together, time with our kids. I know I spend a lot of time worrying about how to please Candy—will she be mad if I do this or don't do that? At this point, I'm only staying for the kids. We're not really living our lives."

THE COUNSELOR'S TURN

"Candace and Jack had been riding a merry-go-round of resentment, blame, and anger so long, they'd lost the ability to communicate effectively about their individual and mutual concerns," noted the counselor. "Years of tension caused every conversation to automatically disintegrate into finger-pointing, rage, and withdrawal. Both of them assumed they knew what the other was thinking and what prompted their behavior, and neither took the time to verify their often-wrong assumptions. In such a climate, misconceptions flourished

and decisions, large or small, became impossible to make.

"Anxious, brittle, and exhausted, Candace did everything thoroughly and well and expected the same perfection in others. Although aware of this tendency, she was so dominated by the "shoulds" in her life, she found it difficult to cut herself, or her husband, any slack. Such doggedness and perfectionism most likely stemmed from childhood: Candace's hypercritical father had stayed in a job he hated because his family relied on him to do so, and Candace had, to some extent, internalized the fear that she might not be able to rely on her own husband. Considering the depression, and anger that such doggedness had triggered in her father, it was clearly a destructive mind-set for her to fall into. However, those negative episodes with her father were balanced by her close relationship with her mother and younger siblings. As a result, when she was rested and calm, her loving, nurturing side blossomed.

"Unfortunately, the cumulative effects of Candace's anger were taking their toll on both Candace and Jack—a common scenario in many marriages. As small stresses pile up, anger builds. When it does, powerful chemicals such as epinephrine and norephrenine pour into the bloodstream, causing blood pressure and heart rate to soar. You may not feel the effects of one stressor.

However, if you experience another equally minor irritant in quick succession, you receive a double dose of anger chemicals, and your psychological reaction is likely to be disproportionate to the importance of the issue.

"Over the years, Candace was so demoralized by Jack's failure to keep his promises that she'd lost the ability to differentiate between trivial and important disappointments. Depositing money in the bank, failing to share discipline duties, or obsessing over his career path loomed as large as his failure to make dinner or fold the laundry. And they were all evidence, as well as justification, for her fury.

"Jack's family life may have seemed charmed to outsiders, but it was not a happy environment. He sensed that his parents favored his older sister, that while they showered her with love, they dismissed, ignored, and sometimes mocked his comments and feelings. When you grow up believing no one ever listens to you, you learn not to listen to others. You also learn to distrust your own judgment and perceptions. Throughout his life, Jack had been afraid that every decision he made would provoke criticism. So he asked himself myriad questions—often the wrong ones, which merely added to his confusion—and took the path of least resistance. Desperate to appease his quick-to-anger wife, he figured that ignoring her was

better than putting forth the effort only to be lectured anyway. However, Jack's failure to follow through was fueling Candace's anger; he needed to acknowledge this and find ways to change.

"My first goal was to help Candace manage her anger—and for Jack to understand it. 'Try to get underneath her outbursts,' I told him, 'so you can see that they are based on fear and exhaustion. Then you can better figure out how you can lessen them.' Initially, Candace, like many clients, was reluctant to consult a psychiatrist about medication. 'I don't want this to be a case of 'Let's medicate Candace and let Jack off the hook,' she told me.

"Her fear is common. Many people confuse the word 'medicated' with 'sedated.' Rather, medicated generally means filling in the missing biochemical pieces so that a person can function normally—much like a diabetic does with insulin. Medications generally do not cause sedation—rather, they produce normalized functioning to replace the overwhelming irritation, moodiness, or rage. Once these chemical imbalances were corrected, Candace was able to react more calmly to life's bumps with reasonable resilience. She also improved her ability to think through what she wanted to say and do.

"'Medication alone isn't generally enough,' I told them. "Couples therapy can help you build understanding

131

and skills that will enable you to put your lives back on track.' I told Candace to think of these medications as emotional normalizers rather than antidepression drugs. They reduce a person's quickness to flare up in the face of criticism and blame, as well as mitigate excessive self-blame and negativity.

"Candace met several criteria that indicated that medication might be helpful: She had a genetic predisposition to depression—I suspected that her hypercritical father was also depressed. Her persistent painful emotional states were preventing her from functioning normally. Although she was able to concentrate and work well at her job, at home, in spite of her best intentions, she often found herself in out-of-control rages at her children and husband. She also suffered sleep difficulties.

"It took one month for the medication's side effects—edginess and fatigue—to wear off, but by then Candace was more in control of her reactions. Their conversations took a much more productive turn and we were able to work on specific tasks to lessen the antagonism between them. For example, couples often think that in a good relationship, partners help each other. I disagree. The 'helping' mind-set makes for muddied clarity about who's responsible for what. In a smooth-running household, each person has separate functions. That doesn't mean that some tasks aren't defined as joint: both may opt to do the dishes together as a chance to spend time together after meals. But that's very different from: 'I do the dishes and you are supposed to help me.' The latter case fit Candace's profile: everything was on her list, and when it became too much, she felt obliged to ask for her husband's assistance. He, in turn, often struggled to find his role. It was a recipe for disaster since Candace was always furious that Jack never asked or volunteered.

"Over several sessions, I had them hammer out a list of roles and chores. For all their arguing over the years, they had never specifically done this, and as a result, Jack was often guessing what Candace wanted, or reacting to her orders or rebukes. To eliminate the ambush factor, we also designated a specific time each week when they could both voice their concerns about how things were going. 'Consider this your administrative meeting,' I told them. 'That's when you talk about what's working and what isn't. But only then. At all other times, if it's on his list, you let him handle it his way.' For example, Candace agreed to do the cooking and grocery shopping; Jack took over laundry and bill paying. Whenever new tasks crop up, they designate one person to be in charge. By clarifying who does what at home, Candace no longer feels she's overseeing what Jack does, and she's stopped criticizing when and how he does it. They've also streamlined the boys' routines so that they now pack their own lunches and are responsible for remembering their homework as well as doing more chores around the house. 'I was tethered to that cell phone, running to school for forgotten items, and it was eroding my effectiveness,' Jack agreed. 'Now they call me for emergencies only, and we've redefined what that really means.'

"Whereas Jack's ineffective personal and joint decision-making is also typical of people who experience depression, but in his case we were able to treat his symptoms without medication. Once he was able to identify the patterns he fell into, as well as pinpoint the areas in his life that triggered the most despair, Jack learned new ways to think through and talk about problems and make better decisions. As his home life became calmer, Jack found the emotional energy to focus on his career. Instead of asking myriad questions, confusing himself and then tossing out each piece of the puzzle, I suggested he learn a new paradigm for decision-making that he could use in all areas of his life: 'Instead of trying to figure out the 'smart' thing to do, consider what you really want to do.' Listing the pros and cons isn't always effective, because you wind up tossing out some good ideas with the ones that don't work. Instead, consider all your concerns, then find a job situation that best matches them. Jack wanted a position that offered a higher income yet still allowed him to be a flexible parent, work with people he respected, and become involved with challenging cases. We spent several sessions analyzing how each of these parameters could fit into different scenarios until he settled on an offer from a small firm near his home, where he would be in a semi-partnership arrangement with like-minded colleagues.

"Jack switched jobs three months ago and is 'radically happier,' he reported. 'He's not obsessing anymore,' Candace agreed. 'I really can't believe I'm saying this, because six months ago, we couldn't tolerate each other. But now, we are really very good friends. We're paying attention to our marriage, consciously making time for ourselves. If we hadn't worked so hard to get here, I'd say it was a miracle."

GETTING A HANDLE ON ANGER

You can learn to manage your anger even if you haven't had much control in the past. It won't be easy and it won't be quick, but by carefully monitoring your feelings and responses to different people and situations, you can better understand your reactions and change them. Here's what you can do:

1. First, give yourself permission to be angry. Not all the time, and not for any old reason, but understand that feeling anger is a normal, expected, and acceptable emotion. You are not a bad person for getting angry, so don't drown yourself in guilt.

2. Monitor your behavior for one week. Who did you get angry at and why? Can you identify any "hot buttons" that are guaranteed to set your temper flaring? What results did your anger produce?

3. Recognize your body's reactions to anger and don't ignore these messages. When your hot buttons are pressed, does your stomach churn or your heart race? Do you feel a tightening in your temples, neck, or back? Tuning in to the messages your body is sending can help you handle anger. Many times we are unaware that we are being hostile to our mates. Getting in touch with your anger responses will help defuse arguments before they rage out of control.

4. Learn to state what you feel when you feel it. Without being hostile, demeaning, or blaming, talk to your partner so he not only hears you but is motivated to change. Be as specific as you can about what is upsetting you as well as what your partner can do to make the situation better.

134

"HE'S ALWAYS ANGRY"

R*oss never hit Sara, but she still felt battered by his heated outbursts. Would he ever understand that his hurtful words were as damaging as physical blows?*

"I don't think I can live with this man another day," said Sara, thirty-seven, a soft-spoken homemaker who came to see me by herself the first few times. I'm terrified of Ross's temper. Not that I think he would ever physically hurt me or the kids—Andrew is thirteen, and Haley is nine—but there's no question in my mind that the verbal abuse has gone on long enough.

"The children are afraid of him, too. I tell him that, but he doesn't hear it. He says I'm trying to turn them against him, that I'm always siding with them. Recently, we stopped at the drive-in window of McDonald's on the way home from a soccer game. The woman in the car ahead of us was smoking, and for some reason Ross went into a tirade about it. The kids were in the backseat, and they were dumbfounded, too. The woman was nowhere near us, and we didn't even know who she was.

"But that's the point: Everything, large or small, irritates him. Instead of handling it rationally, Ross screams, slams doors, and becomes positively obsessed. How can he get so upset about something like misplacing his keys, for heaven's sake?

"His fury is totally unpredictable. The other day he came home and couldn't find a pencil next to the phone where he likes it, and he became enraged. Ross is a blamer: Whatever goes wrong, there has to be someone to blame, usually me. If I kept the house more orderly, then we wouldn't have this or that problem. If I disciplined the kids more firmly, they wouldn't mess up his downstairs office. Always, it comes down to

135

something lacking in me. He calls me lazy and stupid. Ross is a workaholic; the man doesn't know the meaning of the word 'relax.' So maybe, to a person like him, I'm lazy. To any other person in the world, I'm not.

"We've been married almost fifteen years, and I've rarely told him how I feel. What's the point? For the first few years, I think I didn't realize that the way he was treating me was all that bad. My mother had taken a lot of grief in her marriage; the way my husband treated me seemed normal. I simply tried to do better. I bent over backward for him. But it's never good enough.

"Though I was born in Alabama, I spent my first five years in California, where we moved because of my dad's job. He was an executive with a paper-goods company, and he traveled a lot. I never really knew him. Even when he was home, he never paid much attention to me. My mother and I were extremely close, though.

"When I was fifteen, we moved to Alabama. That was wrenching, even though I had spent nearly every summer vacation there and was close to all my cousins. The South, especially then, was a very different place from San Francisco. I vividly remember some kids making fun of me during one of my summer visits because I took a drink from a water fountain that was marked "colored." There seemed to be unwritten, unspoken social rules that everybody knew except me.

"I was shy and never expressed a lot of opinions. One time I had an opportunity to choose which public high school I wanted to go to, and, instead of choosing the one my father wanted me to go to, I chose the other one. Dad was incensed. The same thing happened when I decided to go to a small liberal arts college instead of my father's alma mater.

"But I went and that's where I met Ross. We started dating freshman year, and I think we knew right away we'd always be together.

"We got engaged senior year, married the following summer, and moved to Indiana, where Ross was stationed for three months to fulfill his ROTC obligation. After that term was up, he chose to leave the Army and join the reserves, and we moved to Atlanta to start a family. Ross found a job as a salesman with a major computer company—at which he has been very successful. Now he's regional accounts manager. He works out of an office downstairs in our home and travels much of the week.

"I suppose if I had been more aware, I could have noticed the problems earlier. Ross and I used to be able to talk about anything. We had the same values, the same goals. When it was only the two of us, I could handle his temper. But when he gets on the kids, it's too much.

"Ross has always been particularly hard on Andrew, and it's gotten a lot worse now that he's a teenager. When Andy was little, Ross would take him out to kick around a soccer ball or play catch. Andy always came home in tears because Ross would say that he wasn't trying or something. That upset me so much. How could I not intervene? It's gotten to the point where I can look at his face and anticipate when he is going to pick on them.

"Weekends are especially hard. Ross gets up early and starts giving the kids orders: Do this, do that. Mow the lawn, clean the garage. Then he goes through the house, opening the drawers and closets to find things wrong. You haven't done this or that, he'll yell. And then he'll call them stupid and lazy.

"I know he worries about work. But Ross's expectations, for himself and the rest of us, are impossible. Our sex life is nonexistent. I mean, I can't give myself to him when he's like this. Something has to change, or I'm going to have to leave."

ROSS'S TURN

"I don't think I am anywhere near as bad as Sara says," says Ross, thirty-seven, a handsome man with a firm voice and easy handshake who came to see me a month after Sara.

"I absolutely do not understand why she is so upset. That incident at McDonald's she mentioned—I don't know what she's talking about. I wasn't that angry at all. But I do agree that we need help.

"I'm not happy. There isn't a lot of pleasure in our lives right now. I am odd man out in my own home. I'm sick of Sara jumping in and defending the kids. I love these children, and I'm trying to be a good dad. But I feel like it's me against them. She makes me sound like the devil himself.

"Sure, they're good kids, but they are spoiled. I don't care if an extra wrestling practice is scheduled for Saturday; for three weeks, Andrew has promised to help me clear the yard after the last storm, and I'm tired of hearing excuses. I ask both of them to clean their rooms and take out the trash, and do they do it? No.

"The toughest thing for me is when they come into my office and turn things upside down. It's more than borrowing staples or a pencil. They've left the computer or copy machine on, so the motor burns out. They move things around on the desk so I can't find them. Listen, this is not a simple home office. I don't just sit and pay the bills there. I travel most of the time, and when I'm home, this is headquarters. I want my children to stop being so cavalier about going down there. I've told them to leave my office things alone; I've told Sara I can't take it anymore. Why don't they listen?

"I do so much for these kids, and they don't appreciate it. When I was growing up, I didn't have it easy. I was the third of four kids. Dad worked at the hardware store in town and we never had a lot of money; we never did things normal kids did. I couldn't even go the county fair because my father thought that was much too extravagant.

"My father met my mother in England during World War II. She was quiet and let my father rule with a strict hand. I know she loved us, but she never stood up to him. We learned to abide by Dad's rules, and, let me tell you, with four kids and one bathroom, life was strictly regulated. I remember wanting to try out for Little League and Dad saying, 'No, we don't have time for that.' He didn't believe in extracurriculars unless they were connected to the church or the Boy Scouts. Free time was meant for studying or chores.

"I don't think my dad had any idea what it was like to be a kid. To some extent, I found a way to get around my father's orders, usually by watching my older brothers and figuring out what I could and couldn't do. In junior high, I was desperate to have a pair of penny loafers. I know it sounds superficial now, but to a kid, it means the world to be like the others. Dad said I couldn't have them. So I went out and got odd jobs mowing lawns and painting houses. It took me six months, but I saved up enough to buy those loafers.

"Going to college was like starting over for me. I met Sara at a party, and though we dated other people, we kept close tabs on each other. She was so smart and easy to be with. I related to her very well. There are parts of our marriage that really were so good; I don't know now things got so bad. I'm under a lot of stress at work—pressure to sell more and meet quotas. But I'll never let my wife and kids get into the position that my family was in.

"I used to be able to talk to my wife about business, and she was supportive and insightful. But we never talk anymore. In fact, she seems to avoid me completely. I want to make love, and she's always in the bedroom lying down, telling me she doesn't feel well. I'm glad Sara got me here to talk to you. We need help, but we don't even know where to begin."

THE COUNSELOR'S TURN

"Though Sara had initially come in on her own, I told her it was essential for Ross to join us if we were going to accomplish anything," said the counselor. "For several weeks, she insisted Ross would never come. I told her, 'Until you ask him, you'll never know.' Finally she did, and he came—willingly, in fact.

"I also saw Ross alone for several sessions, as I always do when I have a prior relationship with one spouse, so the other won't feel disenfranchised. During these sessions I was shocked at the depth of his pain: He felt alone, unappreciated, and left out of his family. Though it may seem hard to believe, he was genuinely unaware of how harsh and unpredictable his tirades were. A kind man, he wanted to be a loving husband and father, but he was so out of touch with his feelings and actions that I knew this would be a difficult case. However, since both Ross and Sara told me how much they loved each other and were motivated to change, I felt optimistic that they could.

"Most of the first few weeks were spent discussing their families and how their respective childhoods had influenced their attitudes and actions now. Neither was aware how profoundly his or her current feelings had been affected by the families they grew up in.

"As a child, Sara had never had her father's love or approval, something she desperately wanted and continued to search for in her marriage. An only child, she had also never experienced the normal sibling rivalries. Having never fought for her fair share with a brother or sister, she had never learned to stand up for herself or express her feelings. She needed to understand that she was allowed to have opinions, then learn to trust those feelings and express them in a way her husband could hear.

"Ross was an emotional cripple. He had been so unhappy as a child that if he focused on his feelings, he couldn't make it through the day. As a result, he pushed his feelings so deep inside that he simply wasn't aware that he had any. It was a struggle for him to tap in to them now.

"Ross had no idea of the depth of the problems for his family. Cool and competent in his work, he repressed much of that stress and frustration. What's more, with an office in the home, he had no transition between his business mode and his personal mode. If someone called with a work problem at nine P.M., he'd calmly handle the call, but when he returned to the family, he was so tense that a minor interruption seemed like an earthquake. In fact, anytime he's under stress, that early anger flares up.

"The first goal for Ross was to help him understand the history and pattern of his anger—that is, that his rage was rooted in the past and had little to do with the incident at hand. This way, he could nip it in the bud, and perhaps, in time, avoid it entirely.

"Much of Ross's anger was centered on what the children, especially his thirteen-year-old son, did or didn't do. I asked that Andrew and Haley join us for four sessions, and that proved to be a real turning point. When Ross heard the pain in his children's voices, heard them say that they were, indeed, scared of him, it proved to be a catalyst for real change.

"I pointed out that in many cases, the children's behavior was normal and age-appropriate. While I wasn't condoning the messy room or the poor follow-through with chores, it helped Ross to understand that Andrew was not doing this to get back at him or purposely disobey him. Ross had a harder time with this concept than other parents because his own father had ruled with an iron fist, and there had never been any discussion or negotiation. Ross had no model for what a healthy family life could be.

"Another anger pattern that Ross had to be aware of was the impact of work-related stress. I told him; 'Your mind is working overtime. You are putting so much effort into business that you have no energy left over for the joy of personal relationships.' Ross heard me and has tried hard to change. He's learned to stop and ask himself: What am I really upset about? When my kids don't listen, how does that make me feel? When did I have that feeling before? This process helped him cool down and back off.

"I also taught Sara how to help her husband recognize when his anger was out of control. She learned to offer sympathetic understanding, but then to disengage from him. For instance, instead of saying, 'You're ridiculous,' and leaping in to defend the children, she now tells Ross, 'I know why you're angry. I agree that the kids should be punished, but you're too angry right now.' This helps Ross realize that she is on his side and that together they can work out a way to handle it.

"In counseling, Sara also gained the confidence to express her feelings and not feel guilty about it. Hearing the reasons for her husband's anger, however, also helped her to be more sympathetic to what he had to struggle against. Together, they've learned to talk to the kids about why Ross gets so angry, something parents should always do when they lose control. Ross says, 'I make a point of telling them why I got so mad, if it was a problem at work that had upset me. It doesn't justify the way I act, but at least they know it's not their fault.'

"Now there is much more communication between Sara and Ross. More aware of what's happening inside, Ross is now willing to talk about his feelings when he feels stressed out. Their sex life has improved now that Sara sees the changes Ross has made.

"Ross has also started jogging and lifting weights to reduce stress. And he's trying hard to lighten up on the weekends, too, though this is complicated by the fact that his office is in the basement. 'I hear the fax machine or the telephone and I don't feel I'm allowed to sit and read the paper,' he told me. He's been better lately at putting on the answering machine and not returning calls until business hours the next day.

"Since Ross still has trouble figuring out what would give him pleasure, Sara and the kids try to schedule fun family activities outside the house—going to the movies, a potluck dinner with friends—which Ross finds more relaxing. Since Haley is in a soccer league, they've also been going regularly to games and have enjoyed socializing with the families afterward.

"'We have a way to go,' Ross said with a laugh, 'but now I know I have my family behind me all the way. That makes all the difference.'"

DEALING WITH A SPOUSE'S ANGER

While Ross needs help in dealing with his anger, it's essential for Sara to know what to do in the face of her husband's outbursts. Verbal abuse is as damaging to the psyche as physical abuse is to the body, and it's imperative that both partners recognize this fact.

Therapists recommend the following ideas to help partners remain strong when a spouse loses control. Find out which ones work for you.

1. Learn to really listen to a partner's anger. It's not easy to do when faced with a barrage of insults; most of us react quickly with angry accusations of our own. This is especially true when your mate pushes your "hot buttons," such as bringing up old issues or comparing you to your mother. However, take a deep breath and hear your partner out.

2. If your partner insists that you don't understand, assure him you're trying to. Ask for specific examples to make the situation clearer to you. Questions such as, "What exactly do you mean?" or "What about my tone of voice is so hurtful?" will move the discussion in a positive direction.

3. Validate his angry feelings. Telling someone he has no right to be angry or that he "shouldn't feel that way" fuels anger. You can't pass judgment on how someone feels.

4. Take responsibility for your behavior in triggering the anger. You may be provoking (albeit unconsciously) a spouse's fury. What steps can you take to change your behavior?

5. Think of a way to short-circuit a spouse's anger. You might agree on a code word that one of you can say when tempers seem to be getting out of control. One couple purposely chose a comical word, "rutabaga." as their anger signal. Whenever they say it, they usually laugh, and that breaks the tension.

6. Call a time-out if a partner is losing control, just as you do when a child throws a tantrum. Tell him you refuse to be spoken to in such an angry, humiliating, or abusive way. Leave the room, but make it clear you'll be available to talk once he calms down.

"We Fight All the Time"

Whenever Valerie launched her litany of complaints, Mike fired back with his own. What happens to a marriage when partners keep one-upping each other in the misery department?

VALERIE'S TURN

"We can't talk for five minutes without yelling at each other," says forty-year-old Valerie, the former director of a community outreach program. "Half the time I can't remember what we're arguing about; one fight blends into another.

"Mike and I decided I'd stop working after our first child was born. I thought I'd enjoy the time with the kids—Jenna is four, and our second daughter, Caitlin, was born nine months ago. I adore them, but I wasn't prepared for how completely my life would change. I'm afraid I made the wrong decision.

"I was totally dedicated to my job. When I had Jenna, suddenly I was isolated. I was nursing around the clock, doing laundry, cooking, and barely getting out of my bathrobe by the afternoon. I was exhausted and weepy, and my husband was completely unsympathetic. He thought I was crazy, and didn't hesitate to tell me. I was better prepared with Caitlin, but he still has no clue what it's like to be home all day.

"Last month, I started to tell Mike again how I feel the world is passing me by, he immediately countered, 'You think you have it hard? Try running a business in this cutthroat real estate market.' I know he works hard. I simply want him to listen to me, to acknowledge how difficult this is.

142

"The stupidest stuff is ammunition for a battle royal. If we're in the car and I ask him to slow down, he snaps that if I'm not happy, I can drive. We're not strapped finacially, but still, Mike nickel-and-dimes me about everything. When I wanted to buy a new coffeepot, I got a lecture that the old one is fine. He even has a fit if I buy Jenna a blueberry muffin on the way to preschool.

"Mike also thinks I spend too much time on the phone with my friends after the kids are asleep. But that's the only way I can stay in touch with the people who offer me emotional support.

"We've been married for five years. In the beginning we were always on the same wavelength. We met on a blind date and talked for hours. I was struck by the way he approached the world so rationally. Little did I know that would come back to haunt me. He was also very romantic. He'd send me roses at work for no reason at all. Now, talking is like picking our way through a minefield. Mike is quick to take offense and insists that I'm criticizing him when I'm not.

"It took me a long time to find the right man. My parents' marriage was a disaster and I had no intention of falling into the same trap. My father, a lawyer, was a cocaine addict, an alcoholic, and a philanderer—your basic catastrophe of the seventies. Chaos was always just around the corner: I never knew when my parents would start screaming and throwing things. Then Dad would leave town for a few weeks with one of his girlfriends. My mother, a housewife, was constantly on the phone, pouring her heart out to her friends. I was fifteen when they divorced, and my father died of a drug overdose when I was in my twenties. Later Mom remarried and moved to Oregon.

"We became serious pretty quickly. We weren't kids—he'd been married before for five years. When Mike wanted to settle down right away, I thought that was great; I was tired of commitment-phobic guys.

"We were married a year later in a small outdoor ceremony. I threw away my birth control pills, but we never imagined I'd get pregnant immediately. I had an awful time— my hormones were completely out of whack, and I sobbed uncontrollably for months. Mike didn't know what to do with me.

"The night Jenna was born is symbolic of all our problems. My water broke at two A.M., a month early. It took forever for the doctor to get back to me, and my husband refused to get out of bed. He told me in this very condescending voice to calm down, then rolled over and went back to sleep. Of course, he has a rational explanation for his selfishness. He says he knew we'd have a long day ahead, so he figured he was helping both of us by getting a good night's rest. He has a way of intellectualizing everything and making me feel small in the process.

"Then there's Mike's mother, the most overbearing woman on the planet. I have tremendous respect and sympathy for what she's gone through—she survived the Holocaust, then lost her husband and raised two children alone. But that doesn't give her license to take over our lives. When I was nursing, she insisted that the baby needed water. Even though I told her no a hundred times, the second my back was turned, she'd pop the water bottle in Jenna's mouth. Mike can't understand why I don't want to spend every Sunday with her.

"Mike also complains about our social life and our sex life. I don't like to leave my children with just anyone, and, frankly, a good night's sleep sometimes sounds a lot more exciting than dinner or a movie. As far as sex goes, when I'm nursing, it's always felt funny to have Mike touch my breasts.

"I'm tired of fighting and trying to make it work. I'm lonely. If it weren't for our kids, we wouldn't have anything in common."

MIKE'S TURN

"Why does Valerie think she's the only one working on this relationship?" asks Mike, forty-one, who co-owns a small real estate development company. "She's not exactly easy to live with. Anything and everything can make my wife come unglued.

"I don't think she has any idea what she sounds like. I don't appreciate her negativity and her sarcasm. In her book, I'm not contributing enough, and when I do, I get it wrong. If I go shopping, I have to brace for the inquisition afterward. 'Why did you buy this brand of macaroni and cheese?' 'Jenna doesn't like that kind of peanut butter.'

"Also, it would be nice if once in a while she saw things from my point of view. I have a thing about waste, for instance. If the coffeepot works, why buy a new one? And I think it's ridiculous to spend a fortune on a muffin that Jenna takes two bites out of.

"Valerie is never content to stick to the problem at hand; before I realize it, I'm defending myself for something I did a year ago. She's an obsessive worrier. When she spouts her anxieties and complaints, I have to get out of there fast. She's my mother all over again.

"My parents were both in a concentration camp in Germany, and emigrated right after the war. My dad died of cancer when I was only ten, so I don't have a lot of memories of him. For my mother, daily life has always been a huge burden. I know she's been through hell, but she was always crying when I was kid. I know she loved me and my sister, but she was never there for us. I was dying to join Little League, but she said she had no way to get me to practice. She could have called a friend or the coach, but she never made the effort.

144

"If I misbehaved, Mom would take it personally. 'Why are you doing this to me?' she'd sob. When I got older, I became the man of the house—I'd pay the bills, do the chores, and try to mediate between my older sister and my mother. Believe me, I know how difficult my mother can be, but I feel a huge obligation to include her in our lives. Valerie is being selfish about our Sunday afternoons.

"I met my first wife in college. I was crushed when she left, but it made me determined to make my next relationship work. I fell in love with Valerie the minute I saw her. She's gorgeous, she laughed at my jokes, and we could talk for hours. Now, we fight all the time, but I still believe we're meant for each other.

"She's right when she links our problems to her first pregnancy. Valerie was a maniac, and I just tried to hold on until the baby was born, I still don't think I acted inappropriately when her water broke with Jenna. There was nothing I could do for her until the contractions started; at least one of us needed to get a decent night's sleep.

"Valerie's anxieties get worse and worse. I try to be helpful, but she goes on like a broken record. She tells me I'm not there for her; I feel the same way about her. She's got plenty of time to talk to her friends at night, but no time to talk to me, no time for sex, no time even to go out for dinner. Valerie has to stop blaming me for everything, or I'm out of this marriage."

THE COUNSELOR'S TURN

"I could hear Valerie and Mike bickering in my waiting room," said the counselor. "Theirs is a classic example of how unresolved arguments can fuel a bitterness that festers and destroys intimacy. Valerie's and Mike's constant anger pushed aside any positive feelings they had for each other and erased their joy in their children and in their relationship.

"Ironically, Valerie and Mike had similar complaints. Articulate and outspoken, they both felt ignored and unloved. They desperately needed to learn how to listen, how to express anger without blame, and how to really be a couple. To protect herself from the destructive environment in which she had grown up, Valerie developed a tough outer shell. She demanded constant support from Mike, and when she felt she wasn't getting it, she became anxious and even more demanding. Like her mother, Valerie used the phone as a lifeline to her friends. She was totally unaware of the impression she had on her husband. She didn't hear the sarcasm or criticism in her voice and failed to understand that she was making no room in her life for her husband.

"When Valerie brooded or became panicky, Mike would try to pressure her into his solution. When she resisted, he retreated. This was how he had reacted to his mother's helplessness and hysteria. Mike needed to develop empathy for Valerie and to accept the fact that her approach differed from his. Until he did this, their problem-solving would be stalled by power struggles.

"After they spent several sessions blaming each other, I tried to break the stalemate. 'You have a choice,' I said. 'You can continue to squabble, or you can try to see things from the other's point of view. Until you both emotionally commit to this marriage, I can't help you.'

"Although you can't scold people into acting lovingly, Valerie and Mike truly wanted to preserve their marriage. My challenge was the push they needed to start improving communication.

"'When we left last week,' Mike said at our next session, 'Valerie and I walked home holding hands. I can't tell you how long it's been since we did something simple and tender like that.'

"The next few months proved fruitful. Valerie worked on learning to calm herself before she speaks. I asked her to think about specific physical sensations she feels when she gets anxious. She said she noticed a tightening in the back of her neck, and has learned to take deep breaths or leave the room for a few minutes to compose herself. I told Mike to point it out—nicely—as soon as she speaks in that hammering, blaming tone.

"I taught both of them the reflective listening technique; sitting quietly while one party expresses feelings, then reflecting those feelings back without judgment. Like many women, Valerie needed her husband to pay attention but not necessarily offer a solution. He became more responsive when she asked him to just listen for a few minutes. Since she can now talk to her husband, Valerie no longer needs so much time on the telephone.

"As the bickering ceased, it became easier for Mike and Valerie to compromise. Mike agreed to pay more attention when his mother tries to steamroll her ideas over Valerie—though now that Valerie feels more attended to, her mother-in-law's visits are less an issue. In addition, Valerie realized that she really missed her career. After discussing it with Mike, she has made plans to resume work after Caitlin's second birthday.

"Valerie's fear that she and Mike had little in common has also eased since she found a college student to baby-sit. Last month, on the spur of the moment, Valerie called Mike at work and said, 'I just read that airfares to Paris are the lowest in years. Go buy two tickets for a five-day trip—before I chicken out.'

"'Paris proved we still enjoy each other's company.' Valerie reported. 'If we work hard to make sure both of us get our needs met, we have faith that we won't lose ourselves in the process.'"

RULES FOR A FAIR FIGHT

Before any couple can even begin to solve their problems they have to learn how to use their anger constructively. How can anger be constructive? Use it to explore the underlying causes of your disagreements, and you'll find ways to address both of your needs.

If bickering punctuates your days; if arguments escalate quickly until you're both shouting things you later regret; or if you too often smile through gritted teeth while your stomach is roiling like an ocean in a hurricane, the following rules can help you defuse the rage and focus your energies on practical strategies for change. Make a promise to:

1. Remind yourself that it is okay to be angry, and don't feel guilty about having those angry feelings. Women, especially, grow up believing that it is unladylike and bitchy to express any negative feelings. Better to suppress anger, they're taught, than express it. But there are times when anger is legitimate and those occasions must be recognized and addressed. Once you do that, you'll be in a stronger position to say how you honestly feel and find a path for change.

2. Understand that although you disagree, you are not enemies. No matter how much people love each other, differences will eventually trigger conflict. Fighting fair means you will not attack each other— physically or verbally. Name-calling, cursing, screaming, or blaming are verboten. So, is threatening separation or divorce.

3. Never use something that has been previously told to you in confidence as a weapon in an argument. When you do, you betray the trust your spouse has placed in you, and make it harder for your partner to feel emotionally safe in the marriage.

4. Never walk out of the room until you either both agree that an argument is over or have decided to table the problem and chosen a specific time to bring it up again.

5. Acknowledge each other's feelings and perceptions, without judgment or criticism. There's no "right" way to feel, and there will be times in every marriage that you simply will not agree. But you should always make the effort to unravel what is troubling your partner and show genuine caring for and awareness of his or her emotional experience. Phrases such as "I never thought of that," "Tell me more about what you're thinking" will help you break out of an anger stalemate.

"HE HIT ME"

———— •❦• ————

Nina had vowed to stand by her husband, until the day his violence got out of control. What happens when deep-seated rage threatens to derail a marriage?

"Last week I had my husband arrested," said Nina, twenty-eight, a kindergarten teacher and mother of two-year-old Kelly. "What other choice did I have? He grabbed the back of my sweater as I was walking upstairs, dragged me down three steps, and smashed my face into the wall. Thank God my daughter was at my mother's house and didn't see any of this, though she's certainly been living in a household filled with rage for a long time now. Kelly hears us screaming at each other, and she'll run over from wherever she is crying and push us apart.

"That night, I ran across the lawn to my neighbor's house and called the police from there. I was sobbing hysterically and the side of my face was all swollen. When the police came, they handcuffed John and he spent the night in jail.

"The judge issued an order of protection, but it didn't really mean very much. All it said was that he was not to antagonize or intimidate me. A lot of good that was going to do me! They did demand that John attend a six-week class for men that teaches them to control their anger. But where does that leave us? We have so many problems, I doubt the class will have much impact.

"The only positive thing is that John has at least agreed to come for counseling. Clearly, we need a lot of help. We've been married for three years, and we lived together for three years before that. It's never been easy. This wasn't the first time John hit me, though it was certainly the worst. We argue incessantly about everything; when I took Kelly to McDonald's for dinner a few weeks ago, he lit into me and practically accused me of poisoning her. He's in the food business, you see, and he thinks that fast food is a sin. I don't do it every night, for goodness sake, but once in a while, when I'm rushed and hassled, what's the big deal?

"I'm worn out. John expects me to do everything around the house—all the cleaning and cleaning up, all the errands. John is a slob and though he helps with Kelly—I know he adores her and is a very good, sometimes too-indulgent father—he leaves so many things undone or half-done, I might as well do it myself. The other night he gave Kelly a bath, which I appreciate, but then he leaves the bathroom a mess, with a puddle of water on the floor and dripping towels in the sink. This is not a help. In fact, it's the last thing I need after working all day teaching twenty-five kindergartners, not to mention the several extra hours a week I spend at the bookkeeping job that I've taken on to bring in extra money.

"Even still, we can barely make ends meet and I'm frantic about how we're going to manage. Every month, we're one step ahead of the bill collector. Is it any wonder I don't want to make love? And that's another battle royal we have all the time. Why would I want to sleep with someone who treats me the way he does? We'll have a huge blow-up,

then John wants to kiss and make up. I just can't let go. I feel that at any moment I'm going to boil over with rage.

"For some reason, we bring out the worst in each other, though in the beginning, I thought we both loved each other very much.

"I didn't have a very happy childhood. My parents divorced when I was a toddler, and I haven't seen my father since. When I was five, my mother remarried a man who was verbally and physically abusive to her and verbally abusive to me. I can't explain what it was like to grow up in that home. My mother tried to protect me as much as she could, and to keep my life as normal as possible, but how could it be? Never a day went by that I wasn't scared that Tony, her husband, would hurt her. I still have a vivid picture in my mind of Tony sitting on top of my mother as she lay on the floor, and he was pounding her head on the kitchen floor. On top of that, Mother had diabetes, and was very weak. I was scared she was going to die. I grew up fast—recently, one of my childhood friends told me that I was the most mature six-year-old she had ever known.

"Mother and I are very close and I adore her. As miserable as her life was, she was always there to listen to me and guide me. If I had a problem at school or with friends, she would never tell me what to do but, somehow, she gave me the strength to know that I could figure things out on my own. Whenever my life gets really messed up and crazy, I try to hold on to that feeling, though it's getting harder and harder to do that.

"I met John at a party at my aunt's house and I was immediately attracted to him. He's very handsome and charming, and we spent most of the afternoon laughing and talking in the den. One of his friends was the gym coach at the school where I worked, and we just seemed to have a lot in common. When he asked me to dinner the following week, I was really excited. I was dating a few guys at the time, but once John appeared on the scene, I had no desire to be with another man.

"We never had much money to do anything special, but we always seemed to have fun. Living together seemed like the natural thing to do. After three years, we decided to get married. I knew it wasn't perfect—what relationship is?—but I really hoped that I had finally found the happiness that had eluded my mother for so long. She liked John and was really happy for us.

"But after we married, and especially after Kelly was born—she wasn't planned, by the way—the fighting really started in force. I'd say something, he'd argue back, and before I knew it we were pushing and shoving each other. At my daughter's christening, I had a black eye, thanks to John. I was so worried about how I was going to explain this to all our relatives, but I decided to tell them the truth. My family was very angry; they wanted me to leave him. But his family had the most unbelievable reaction: His mother actually told me, 'If my son did that to you, you must have deserved it.' That tells you a little bit about what I'm up against. I can barely stand to be around members of John's family. They are so condescending, always implying that I'm a bad mother and that they, far better than I, know how to handle every child-related problem from an earache to a temper tantrum.

"What happened at Thanksgiving put me over the edge. John called from work to say that he had to stay even later than usual and wouldn't be home until after seven. We were expected at my mother's house at five. Now, last Thanksgiving John worked late. The guys are supposed to alternate holidays. Yet my husband is always the one to volunteer and agree to extra hours. I'm tired of being the last priority on his list. So we got into an argument on the phone, I took Kelly to Mother's, and John didn't show up until after nine P.M.—and I could smell liquor on his breath. I was livid.

"When we got home that night, we continued the argument and I'll admit we both lost control. I told John that I was going to call the police because he had obviously been driving while he was drunk. I started up the stairs, and the next thing I knew, he had yanked me backward and started pounding my head into the wall.

"Right now, I'm not sure there is any hope for our marriage, but if there's any chance at all, I owe it to Kelly to try. If I felt that I could support myself, I would leave John today, but my teaching salary prohibits that. As disgusted as I am, I don't want my daughter to grow up in a single-parent household, or to have the same kind of life I had. That's the only reason I'm here."

JOHN'S TURN

"**M**y love for Kelly is the only reason I'm here, too," says John, thirty, a muscular man with black curly hair. "Nina always threatens to take the baby away from me, and I know I couldn't bear that. She's the only good thing that has ever happened to me.

"I was the youngest of four kids. My father was fifty when I was born—I was definitely an accident—and he retired from the police force when I was nine. That meant he was home a lot more than when my older brothers were little. Dad was an old-fashioned Old World kind of guy and he thought I was out of control, rude, and defiant. Look, I was certainly no Boy Scout, but I was no worse than my brothers were. Dad used to bellow, 'The others were never like this,' and my mother would always insist, 'Yes they were; you didn't see it because you were at work.'

"To be honest, my father was a brute and I was scared of him. He was always screaming at me and my mother, and when he was really angry, he'd come after me with a stick or a belt. By the time I was a teenager, we were warring constantly and he was always on my back for one thing after another. Though I managed to get decent grades, I never once remember getting his approval or thinking that he was proud of me. Mostly, he complained that I was hanging out with kids he didn't like.

"My mother was very sweet but pretty helpless when it came to dealing with my father. She tried to defend me from his outbursts, and that created a lot of problems between the two of them. As soon as I graduated from high school, I got a job at the local grocery store, and moved into an apartment with one of my older brothers. I never took another penny from my father again. He died five years ago and I can't say I was sorry. My mother and I are still close, though.

"I dated a lot of women but no one I ever considered marrying until I met Nina. The first time I saw her she was in the middle of a group of people at a party, laughing. That's what I remember most about the times when we started dating, that beautiful laugh. I had never felt so

151

comfortable with another person. It's hard to even remember the way we used to be—that our lives could have disintegrated like this.

"I know I'm not an easy guy to live with and I've always been too physical, but Nina is no angel. She gives as good as she gets. She baits me. Maybe I don't help as much around the house as I should, but I feel she overlooks the things I do. Her complaints ring in my ears from the moment she walks in the door—pick up your clothes, clean the fish tank, stop tracking dirt in the house. She's like a broken record. I can feel my teeth clenching and my ears getting hot when she calls me names that would make you blush.

"She also mimics me and then screams at me to get out of the house. That pushes all the same buttons my dad used to. I took crap from my father my whole life, I'm not going to take it from anyone else ever again, certainly not my wife.

Thanksgiving is a perfect example of how Nina takes a small incident and lights a match to it. Now I didn't want to work on the holiday any more than she wanted me to, but, hey, it's my job. I'm the manager of a gourmet grocery store and when the owner asks me to pitch in, I feel it's my responsibility to do it. I'm going to get paid for the overtime, which we could use, and besides, these guys are my friends. Why create waves when I have to work twelve hours a day with these

people? If I make a stink, it only generates ill will.

"Well, Nina went ballistic. She called me at work and started screaming so loudly I had to hold the phone a foot from my ear. It was embarrassing. Everyone in the store heard me getting scolded; she told me not to bother coming home.

"After we closed that night, my friend Will suggested I have a beer with him and cool down before going home. That's what I had—one beer—but as soon as I got to her mother's house, Nina accused me of getting drunk.

"We continued the argument at home. She smacked me across the face, started hammering me with her fists, and then said she was going to call the police and have me locked up for driving under the influence. That's when I lost it.

"Yes, spending the night in jail knocked some sense into my head. I have no excuses for my behavior. I was wrong and I want to change. But we can't have a marriage unless she changes, too."

THE COUNSELOR'S TURN

"There's no question that some marriages cannot, and should not, be saved," said the counselor. "When there is abuse of any kind in a relationship, that must stop before any marital counselor, or the partners themselves, can begin to address the underlying issues that prevent a couple from relating to each other in a healthy way.

"In many abuse cases, counselors will see the husband and wife separately. However, for several reasons, I wanted to work with Nina and John as a couple. First, unlike some abusive men, John was aware of his actions, sorry for them, and deeply motivated to change. He had also just completed a court-ordered anger management class, which, though only six sessions, had at least given him some insight into the reasons for his actions and how he could begin to temper his outbursts.

"What's more, my sense as a clinician was that John was not a hard-bitten abuser. Rather, this was a young family so weighed down by financial and emotional pressures, and so lacking in the basic marital skills needed to handle the myriad stresses in their lives, that they were on the verge of becoming another statistic. I believed I could help them, though I was emphatic when I told John: "If you hit her again, the marriage is over. But if you want to make a real change in your lives and that of your daughter, we can work together to achieve that goal."

"When I first met with Nina and John, I believed it was important for them to listen as they each described the sadness, loneliness, and violence that permeated their respective childhoods. Hearing each other detail their lives also helped them

both understand how their present actions often inflamed old wounds.

"One of my first goals in counseling was to simply instruct them in some basic information about violence in the home. I pointed out that they both grew up in families where anger raged out of control and where the abused spouse not only continued to accept the unacceptable but felt that she had somehow deserved to be treated that way.

"'You're both victims,' I told them, 'and you shouldn't be victimizing each other.' Countless studies have also drawn a direct link between violence that is witnessed as a child and abusive actions later on. What's more, I added, women who are raised in violent homes are more likely to marry men who will abuse them. This last fact was pivotal in convincing John he must drastically change his ways. 'I don't want my daughter to marry a man like me,' he said with tears in his eyes.

"Then it was time to explain how their childhood experiences had influenced their current attitudes and actions. The overriding influence in John's life had been his relationship with his hostile father—though he was forever trying to avoid him, they inevitably locked horns. John's mother tried her best to keep the peace, and while she indulged young John out of sight of her husband, she never had the strength to actually stand up to her husband. Unfortunately, violence seemed like such an ordinary, inevitable part of life that she continued to excuse her son's behavior toward Nina.

"Though he's smart, John never received any support for his studies or encouragement to continue his education. He also has no idea how to properly express his anger or, for that matter, how to be a kind, supportive husband.

"Nina had spent a lifetime caring for others and, though she was unaware of it, she was actually furious that while she was doing for and giving to others, she was getting little in return. She buried a lot of her rage—against her father, stepfather, even her mother—but it came spewing forth against John. Feeling frustrated and unloved, her fuse was short and any issue, large or small, set off the same hostile reaction in her. Although she understood in a calm moment that a dripping wet towel on the bathroom floor was not as important as the fact that her husband might have been drinking and driving, each had the power to put her over the edge. She always felt 'on duty' and stressed out. Unable to rein in her anxiety, she would lash out in the only way she knew could infuriate him—with hurtful words and mimicry.

"Nina's barrage of insults often provoked John to use physical force. This is not to excuse or justify his actions in any way, but it was essential for Nina to understand the part she played in the marital dynamic.

Once she was able to separate her past anger from present anger, she learned to react more appropriately to what was happening in her life today. Instead of overreacting and leaping to global accusations, she has learned to take a step back and ask herself: 'How important is this issue right now? What are my priorities?' While John is trying to heed his wife's desire that he be more helpful around the house, she's working on putting those desires in perspective. For instance, which is more helpful—the fact that John bathed the baby and got her to bed on time, or the fact that the bathroom is untidy?

"To build Nina's self-esteem and confidence in her own abilities, we focused on what she had already achieved despite great odds: putting herself through college, working at a demanding full-time job, mothering a young child. Though finances were clearly a serious issue for this couple, Nina decided to give up her bookkeeping job and, instead, work in the evenings toward a masters in special education. When she completes her degree, she is most likely assured of a higher paying job.

"My work with John zeroed in on reinforcing his efforts to manage his anger so that disagreements didn't explode into full-blown arguments. He's learned to recognize when he's getting angry, and literally call a time-out to cool down. They've both learned to short-circuit misunderstandings by asking each other,

'What do you hear me saying?' and then immediately clarifying any misconceptions. What's more, after an argument is resolved, they have both come to appreciate the healing power of a simple apology to clear the air and look toward the future.

"It was important for Nina to see that John could support her and stand up to his family when they either criticized her or implied that they knew more about raising a child then she did. 'Even if you think she's being too sensitive,' I told him, 'let her see you're on her side.'

"When Nina saw some real changes in John she felt some of her old affection returning. They desperately needed to carve out some couple time, but with their work schedules and Nina's classes, that was not going to be easy. Right now, Monday nights are their only time alone together. To make the most of these evenings, they try to get Kelly in bed by seven-thirty so they at least have a quiet evening together. Nina feels more loving toward John and no longer withholds sex. I told her: 'Remember, he doesn't have to be perfect, he just has to try.'"

FINDING THE STRENGTH TO FIGHT BACK

Although the figures are by no means complete, almost one-third of American women report that they have been physically or sexually abused by a partner. Among these women, too many blame themselves for the emotional or physical abuse they endure. They may think: "I deserve it." "I'm just not good enough for him." "It must be something I'm doing wrong." Or, lacking self-esteem and confidence, they believe that the abuse is simply something they must shoulder, their sorry lot in life. These women don't know what to do to break out of the cycle, or even what's really wrong in their relationships.

A woman may not be able to change her partner, but she can make changes in her own life. The first step is to seek help. There are shelters and self-help programs across the country for abused women. If a shelter or recovery program tells you they cannot help you, ask for a referral. Call these numbers for additional information and guidance:

The National Domestic Violence 1-800-799-SAFE; www.ndvh.org; the National Coalition Against Domestic Violence, 303-839-1852; the National Clearinghouse for the Defense of Battered Women, 215-351-0010, or the National Council on Child Abuse & Family Violence 202-429-6659 or 1-800-222-2000. Many states also have toll-free hotlines for domestic violence. Check your telephone directory.

If you are a victim of abuse, it's critical to speak to someone who will believe your story, support you in your desire for protection, and respect your privacy. Confiding in the wrong person, someone who reinforces your belief that you are to blame for the violence or minimizes the offending behavior, can be harmful. Seek out professional counselors, legal advisers, medical doctors, or community groups that have experience in dealing with abused women and can explain your legal rights, especially related to child support and custody.

Build a support system. Controlling partners often try to isolate a spouse from friends and family—all the more reason to keep those relationships intact. Stay in touch with friends, other mothers, co-workers, and people you meet in self-help groups.

. . . AND A WORD ABOUT THE MARRIAGES THAT SHOULDN'T BE SAVED

It is often difficult for an outsider to understand why a woman would remain in a relationship where any kind of abuse is the norm. Psychologists explain that when a person rides a roller coaster of abuse for years, she is so beaten down, emotionally and physically, that she becomes numb. She can't leave because she sees no way out. Many times finances can handcuff a woman to an abusive relationship. It can be hard to leave when you're worried about being able to support yourself and your kids.

If you're in a marriage that is marred by violence, physical or verbal, how do you know when enough is enough? No one can answer that question for you, but you should start thinking about your options if you answer yes to any of these questions:

- Are you agitated, anxious, or easily intimidated when you're around your spouse?

- Are you isolated from family and friends? Does he make it difficult for you to maintain relationships with others?

- Did you grow up in a home where someone was abused?

- Do you believe that you will be able to change an abusive partner's behavior?

- Do you think that he is treating you harshly because of something you have or haven't done—in other words, that his behavior is your fault? Does he blame you for his behavior?

- Do you often find yourself rationalizing or making excuses for a spouse's verbal or physical abuse, telling yourself that he didn't really mean it, time and again?

- Does he make you account for every minute of your time?

Often, a woman will be lured back into a destructive relationship by a spouse's promises to change. How can you tell if he really means it? That's a tough question, too, and there are no hard-and-fast answers. Consider: Has the abuser accepted responsibility for his actions? Does he understand the impact his violence has on your children, or does he still minimize what he has done? Has his coercive control over all areas of your life ended? Are you in charge of what you do, who you see, what you think? Most important, do you feel that you have your life back? Because only when you gain control of your own thoughts and actions can you begin to work toward rebuilding trust and faith in your marriage.

"HE'S JEALOUS OF MY SUCCESS"

———◆———

Sharon expected Derek to handle responsibilities at home, since she spent so much time at work. What can be done when arguments over who does what begin to destroy the very foundation of a marriage?

"Some days I wake up filled with this overwhelming sadness," sighed Sharon, forty-two, the mother of Michaela, ten, and Tyler, four, who works full-time as an executive in a national food-service company. I'm exhausted, drained, and angry. Derek and I have been married for twelve years. Three years ago we agreed that I'd be the primary breadwinner and he'd handle most of the home and child-care responsibilities, since the small electrical-supply business he inherited from his uncle went bankrupt and the computer-servicing company he set up in our spare room wasn't bringing in enough money. At the time, it made sense, though we did think it would only be temporary. But it simply isn't working. Derek is still trying to build a client base, so he bills only about twenty hours a week. The rest of the time he's supposed to be doing everything else. But too often, the jobs I assumed he'd take care of are left for me.

"We're arguing all the time—and I'm convinced it's because Derek can't handle the fact that I'm making more money than he is. It's never bothered me that by conventional standards I'm more successful than he is. But last year, when we went to have our taxes done, this stupid clerk looked at our forms and burst out laughing. 'Well, look at this,' he said. 'Your wife makes more money than you do.' I wanted to smack him. Derek was mortified, although he didn't say anything.

"I leave the house at seven-thirty every morning, and some nights I don't get home until nine-thirty if I have to take clients to dinner. All I want to do is take a shower and fall into bed. I don't appreciate finding a sulky husband who is too busy watching the TV news to make a proper dinner for himself and the children. Is it so difficult to broil some hamburgers? If I don't specifically spell out what to feed everybody, they wind up eating dry cereal or pizza. Last Saturday, when I had to finish some spreadsheets for work, I asked him to keep the kids occupied for the afternoon. I had hoped he'd take them to the children's museum or even roller-skating. But his idea of quality time was making popcorn and renting a video. Well, I lost it. I said things that I shouldn't have, but if I can't count on my husband, who can I count on?

Derek used to work for the same company I do. It was easy to fall in love with him. First of all, he's gorgeous. But he also has a sweetness and sensitivity about him that is positively endearing. Everyone used to say we were the perfect couple. But even though I loved him very much, I knew we were different.

I'm outgoing and upfront. I say what's on my mind. Derek is quiet and shy, almost timid. Trying to get him to talk about how he feels has never been easy. I like to get things out in the open, tackle a problem head-on, and get it resolved. Derek ignores issues, hoping they'll disappear.

"Anyway, the company doesn't allow spouses to work together. So Derek decided to take over his uncle's business to see if he could make a go of it. I soon found my niche and started getting promoted. But while I was moving up the ladder, things weren't working out so well for Derek. Thank goodness we had my salary to fall back on.

"I enjoy my work; I'm now manager of sales, and I coordinate a team of over one hundred people. Ever since I was a little girl, I knew I wanted to make a lot of money and be a success. My mother was my role model—she's a very strong, loving woman who virtually raised six kids on her salary as loan officer at a bank. My father, who passed away five years ago, was a lifer in the army. He was also an alcoholic—and an abusive one at that—who spent his pension on drink. He was totally unreliable, and Mother shouldn't have stayed married to him. They fought constantly and bitterly.

"Now I'm afraid my marriage is beginning to fall into the same pattern. No, Derek isn't drinking; it's just that I feel the whole burden of providing for this family is on my shoulders. Busy as I am, I've tried hard to stay involved in as many of the kids' activities as I can. But I'd be lying if I said I didn't have plenty of regrets. Derek may fall down in the chores department, but in terms of being there emotionally for the kids, he's great. I know they feel closer to their father than to me—and, yes, I suppose I am jealous about that. It hurts when Tyler and Michaela run to him with their problems, or when I have to miss things like Michaela's school play.

"It doesn't help when Derek grumbles that I'm spending too much time at work. Doesn't he understand the commitments I have? If I don't work hard, I'll never get ahead, and then where will we be financially?

"The truth is, we have no relationship anymore. You know, Derek initially refused to come for counseling. I had to give him an ultimatum, because I can't imagine living this kind of life for the next twenty years. We're not friends, we're not lovers, and we never talk anymore. It's hard even to remember why we got married in the first place."

DEREK'S TURN

"Sharon calls herself up-front, but I think most people would call her pushy, bossy, and demanding," said Derek, forty-three, a handsome man with an athletic build. "She's always in my face, like a dragon breathing fire.

I don't appreciate being dressed down because I haven't done something exactly the way she wants me to, or in the time limit she deems appropriate.

"I get furious when Sharon assumes that her way is better. I'm sick of being the bad guy around here, and I can't stand the way she talks to me. So when she pushes me to the wall, I blow up and we end up in another fight.

"It's certainly news to me that she thinks I'm a good father. You'd never know it from the way she treats me. It's not easy living with Sharon. I fell in love with her energy and feistiness; now I feel like those qualities have turned negative.

"There's no question in my mind that Sharon's work takes up way too much time. Sure, I understand she has to go the extra mile in order to advance, but she's eaten dinner with the family just twice in the last month. She has no regard for the rest of us. When she promises to be home, she inevitably shows up late. Weekends are often more chaotic than the rest of the week. Look, I know she enjoys her work, but the truth is, we hardly have any time alone together anymore—and she doesn't spend much time with the kids. If that's the way it's going to be, fine, but where does she come off criticizing what I feed them, what I do with them on weekends?

"I didn't mean to sound like a complainer, but I don't think my wife, or anyone else for that matter, appreciates all that I do. When I used to take Tyler to gym classes, everyone looked at me like I was some kind of freak. I'd go to a school meeting—they call the parent-teacher association at Michaela's school 'The Mother's Club'—and everyone automatically assumed I was unemployed. That bothered me a lot. Still does. I don't like having to explain why I'm there and their mother isn't. Even our pediatrician was less than sympathetic: When I'd take the kids for a checkup, he'd give me instructions to pass along to my wife, as if I were too incompetent to handle things on my own.

"Like Sharon said, soon after we got married, I tried to resuscitate this half-dead electrical-supply company I inherited from my uncle. When that went bust, I started a computer-servicing company out of my home. It wasn't growing as fast I had hoped, so, as my wife's job became more demanding, we sort of fell into our current arrangement. I don't think either of us expected it to last this long.

"Sharon does all she can to make me feel worthless. Many times she talks out of both sides of her mouth: She says she needs and wants me to be involved with the kids, but then she second-guesses me. I'm Mr. Mom, with all this responsibility, but she treats me more like an assistant than an equal partner. She still makes all the decisions.

"Yes, it's true, Sharon had to drag me here, but maybe counseling will help after all. We certainly haven't been able to figure out how to reach a truce on our own."

THE COUNSELOR'S TURN

"When they first came to see me, Sharon and Derek were like two snarling lions. What they had initially seen as a temporary role reversal had become permanent, triggering major upheavals.

"Torn between wanting to move ahead in her career and being the perfect mom, Sharon was depressed and guilt-ridden that she wasn't spending enough time with her kids and her husband. Though she enjoyed her work, because of these conflicts she was unable to reap the satisfaction from her job that would have helped compensate for what she was giving up. What's more, she turned her guilt inside out, insisting that the reason for their battles was Derek's jealousy of her success. Blaming her husband for her own doubts created a cycle of resentment that only exacerbated their problems.

"These two had been arguing for so long, they rarely spoke civilly to each other. Also, though they were struggling with division-of-labor issues that confront all working parents, they had never actually sat down and tried to hammer out a solution that would work for both of them.

"Before we could even begin to talk about the practical issues, Sharon and Derek had to learn to control their anger, so that every conversation didn't deteriorate into a shouting match. Sharon reacted much like her father, whose chronic rage had often erupted into verbal and physical attacks. While she prided herself on being in touch with her feelings, the only way she knew to express those feelings was by blaming and criticizing Derek.

"I told Sharon that it was imperative that she view issues from her husband's perspective instead of marching into the house like a drill sergeant issuing orders. Though Sharon thought she was handling the discrepancy in their income in a caring fashion, the reality was that many times she treated Derek like a second-class citizen. She had to learn to curb her hurtful outbursts.

"Sharon was a get-it-off-your-chest kind of person, while Derek held on to his hurts. Instead of making his own needs and concerns clear, Derek spent most of the time defending himself against Sharon's criticism. Shy and lacking in self-confidence, he nevertheless had an inner resilience that neither he nor his wife appreciated.

"Like many men today, Derek found great joy in fatherhood, but he also felt overwhelmed and, at times, trapped. For all the talk about the new, involved father, there are few role models for stay-at-home dads. As Derek discovered, it didn't help that men receive mixed, occasionally hostile messages about their changing roles.

"In therapy, I worked with Derek to shore up his sense of self-worth and develop confidence in the decisions he was making. It helped when I pointed out to them that many men would have been swamped by the business failure that Derek had managed to use as a springboard for a new and rewarding life.

"Once Sharon and Derek broke the cycle of criticizing and defending, I was able to help them find ways to turn their arguments into opportunities for cooperative decision-making. To do this, they had to learn to rephrase their complaints, fears, or desires in terms of what they want and need instead of what their partner is, or isn't, doing (using softer 'I' statements rather than the blaming 'you' statements). Sharon, for example, learned to say, 'I'm concerned that the kids aren't eating well-balanced meals. Can we talk about it?' instead of lambasting Derek for allowing them to have pizza or cereal for dinner. They also had to learn not to react defensively to each other.

"Once these two were able to speak honestly with each other, they could focus on the scheduling and chore-war issues that fed their anger and triggered so many battles.

"For this couple, talk and time were the real healing factors. Bit by bit, the general level of tension dissipated, and they realized that many of the issues that had loomed large a few months ago weren't so critical after all. As Derek grew more confident and happier in his parenting role, Sharon relaxed her rigid standards. She realized she didn't have to do it all, and if she allowed Derek to handle things, he could manage more than adequately. To ensure that they stay on top of things, they now sit down each Sunday night with a pencil and paper and jointly plan who does what in the upcoming week.

"For her part, Sharon admitted that she needed to prioritize tasks at work so she could leave at a reasonable hour. And as Derek noted during one of our last sessions, she hasn't worked weekends in two months. Sharon will probably always feel ambivalent about not being the primary parent, 'but my working-mom guilt feelings have lessened considerably,' she reported. They've learned to laugh and enjoy each other's company once again, too. 'I think we both feel more in control of our lives,' says Derek. 'We're making decisions about the family together.'"

MARRIAGE BURNOUT

Heated arguments outside the bedroom can so seriously affect what happens inside that the marriage itself can be in danger of burnout. A mere simmering bitterness can also significantly erode intimacy. Think about reinforcing your own marriage and read the following five misconceptions to which many people still subscribe. Are any of them causing your relationship to burn out?

1. "I have so much more to do than he does."
Competition for who's doing more, and who's more exhausted, creates resentment in many relationships. Or conversely, do you (the stay-at-home mom, or the career woman whose income is lower than her husband) feel less deserving because you don't bring in as much money? Marriage is not a marathon. You both deserve and need a break, so work on finding ways to support and nurture each other.

2. "It's no big deal if I get up early in the morning to do my work, or do it on the weekend."
Well, that depends. Once in a while, working overtime at home isn't a problem. But if you find that you or your spouse is doing this on a regular basis, chances are you are (a) tired, and (b) short-changing yourself and your family by not spending time together.

3. "If I'm upset with my partner I tell him so, right away."
Again, it's what you say and how you say it. We teach our kids to count to ten before saying something in anger—it's worth holding your thoughts in much the same way. Ask yourself: How big a deal is this to me? When you're feeling stressed, the tendency is to blurt out your anxiety. But usually that anxiety is over something small that, in the grand scheme of your relationship, isn't worth bickering about. Instead of flipping out, try to put life's bumps into perspective.

4. "If he (or she) would just do more, I wouldn't be so overloaded."
Nope. When you're feeling swamped, it's usually because you're putting too much on your plate. While it's natural to assume that a partner will be there to help out—and in a good marriage, he or she usually is—a large chunk of the stress is your own doing. You need to take care of yourself, prioritize, and focus not on what you wish your partner would do differently, but on what you can do differently.

5. "I just can't help it—that's way I am."
Old dogs can learn new tricks. It won't be easy, and it takes practice, but just because you always were messy or always ran late (or because your parents were or did) doesn't mean you can't change now. Blaming our past or our parents for our actions today is a cop-out. Find new strategies that work for both of you now.

DEFUSE POWER STRUGGLES

Respecting, and Accepting, Differences

—◆—

Marriage should be a partnership of equals— but sometimes, that's not the case. Power struggles—some obvious, others subtle—permeate every relationship. And while we most often think of power in terms of who controls the checkbook or who's the boss in the bedroom, the battle for control is fought in many other arenas. Whether the issue is which movie to see on Saturday night, how to discipline the children, where to spend Christmas, or which friends to socialize with, countless husbands and wives jockey for power and control every day.

Traditionally, the scales of power were tipped in favor of the financial heavyweight. Whoever made the most money controlled the pursestrings—and the marriage. Roles, tasks, and responsibilities

165

were clearly defined and divided according to gender. But as women entered the workforce in increasing numbers, the power pendulum swung in the opposite direction—and took stay-at-home wives as well as those who work outside the home with it. In the last three decades, women interviewed for the *Ladies' Home Journal* column "Can This Marriage Be Saved?" have consistently demanded a larger role in family decision-making, no matter the size of their paycheck or whether they received one at all.

While many husbands clearly respect a wife who wants an equal voice in marital decisions, some feel threatened. It follows, then, that one of the most wrenching marital dilemmas facing couples in recent years has been learning how to renegotiate roles and expectations without triggering a power dispute.

There are many ways to wield power in a marriage. Some are blatant: The partner who barks orders, insists on having things a certain way, or even resorts to violence is clearly pushing for control. Frequent criticism and fault-finding—as well as being disrespectful, sarcastic, or humiliating to a spouse in front of others—are also ways of exerting power and proving who's the boss.

But no less controlling is the quiet manipulator who sulks, cries, plays the martyr, or dismisses a partner's actions, ideas, or opinions as unimportant or ridiculous: "How would you know? I'm the one who understands kids," a wife may insist when arguing with her husband about how to discipline the children. Instead of discussing the situation, explaining her views, and listening to his, she asserts her power and implies that his way is the wrong way. Similarly, the husband who tunes out and pretends to listen to his wife's problems, when he's usually reading a newspaper or watching a football game, registers high on the power and control scale, too.

Another more subtle type of power struggle is set in motion when one person insists on his or her version of the truth: Whether recalling an incident, describing a family vacation, or even voicing an opinion about a new movie, these people are convinced that the way they think is the way everyone should think. Does a mate view the situation differently? She must be wrong.

Perhaps the most common, though frequently unrecognized, power struggle is when partners treat each other in what marital therapists term a passive-aggressive manner. This occurs when partners undermine each other by pretending to cooperate; instead, they either ignore what a partner has said, or promise to do something with no intention of actually following through. The result: a cycle of nagging and ignoring that frustrates everyone and triggers frequent skirmishes in the ongoing battle for control.

Being able to recognize marital power struggles is a key step in defusing them, but equally important is understanding why a partner is so desperate for total control. Some spouses set up a power struggle out of a deep-seated need to protect themselves emotionally. Perhaps they grew up in a home punctuated with bickering, fighting, or uncertainty—we see this often when a father or mother was alcoholic. To feel safe, calmer, more in control, they want to make every decision themselves.

Other people control out of fear. They think: "If I trust someone else to be in charge, if I put down my guard for an instant, I'll leave myself wide open to pain and hurt. I'll be vulnerable." Still others have such low self-esteem that the only way they can feel good about themselves is by belittling others—and those closest to them are the most likely targets. Sadly, while the ego boost is only temporary, the damage to the marriage is often long term.

Whenever one partner feels powerless, manipulated, threatened, or demeaned, resentment brews. Instead of acting together as a team, each interaction becomes a competition, a game of one-upmanship focused on who's winning and who's giving in. In such marriages, any criticism or disagreement is taken as a personal rejection. Slights and aggravations are duly noted—and the stakes are high.

Ultimately, the only lasting way to defuse a power struggle is to learn to accept each other fully, without competing, criticizing, or blaming. It doesn't mean being, thinking, or feeling the same as your partner. In any close relationship, differences in opinions, priorities, habits—even in the way stress, anxiety, disappointment, and anger are handled—are bound to develop (and are actually healthy). Yet time and again we meet couples who, instead of being empathic, attempt to coerce their partner into doing or feeling exactly the way they do. Instead of being encouraging of a partner's goals and interests, they feel threatened and so disparage them.

Seven Secrets of a Happy Marriage makes it clear that in order to avoid power struggles, couples must learn to express feelings and ideas clearly in the face of criticism or disagreement, without resorting to accusations or criticisms of their own. They listen empathically to a partner's ideas and feelings, acknowledging his or her strengths and supporting his or her weaknesses. As we shall see in the next two chapters, "Be Money Smart" and "Make Love," they are flexible enough (even in areas where power struggles are the most destructive) to negotiate changes and cooperate. In that way they are free to concentrate on what they share rather than on what divides them.

"He Won't Do His Share"

———•———

Carol was tired of doing it all, but Tony felt that nothing he did was enough. Can two people resolve their differences when each feels the other isn't pulling enough weight?

"Sometimes I wonder if he will ever grow up" snapped Carol, thirty-five, a tall blonde five months pregnant with her second child. "You won't believe this. Two weeks ago, we were on our way to visit my mother when we pulled into a rest stop so Sam, our four-year-old, could go to the bathroom. The whole way we'd been arguing about the renovation we're in the middle of—like why Tony hasn't managed to install shelves in

Sam's room like he promised, and the fact that the plumber he hired has disappeared with twelve hundred dollars of our money. So you know what he did? While I was in the bathroom with Sam, he left the restaurant and walked home.

"At first, I was frantic, then furious. After looking all over the rest area for him, it dawned on me that this was just the kind of obnoxious, immature thing Tony would do to get back at me.

"Tony and I have been married for almost six years. When we met, he had a small contracting business, but his real passion is his painting. My husband is a gifted artist, and it's been hard for him to put his dreams on the back burner while we pour every penny and all our time into renovating our house.

"I guess I'd been seeing such a series of creeps, I couldn't believe that Tony could be so sweet. When I was sick with the flu, he came over

169

with chicken soup. We also had many interests in common and seemed to balance each other. My only problem was that he didn't talk very much. Tony says he doesn't like to fill the air with unnecessary chatter, but it's hard to know what he's thinking if he doesn't tell me.

"We married within a year. When I found out I was pregnant, we agreed it made more sense financially for me to continue working—I'm in charge of the photo lab at a major advertising agency—and for Tony to stay home with the baby and do whatever odd jobs he could get on the side.

"Three years ago, when we bought this very run-down, six-floor brownstone, it made sense for Tony to handle the renovations. We moved into the ground-floor apartment, and planned one day to rent out the top three floors. For once, he'd have his own art studio, too.

"But if you came by, you'd wonder what he's been doing for three years. His perfectionism is beginning to make my hair stand on end. It takes forever for him to complete something. Sam is in school most of the day now, so I don't see why this is taking so long.

"Since I'm earning the money, I don't think it's expecting too much to ask Tony to do a little comparison shopping. I want to know if it costs less to buy Sheetrock at the hardware superstore than at the lumber store around the corner. Tony doesn't even bother to check out things like that.

"What probably makes me the most furious, though, is the way Tony says he's going to do something and never does. Tony said he'd take Sam and go look for a new car—ours is a mess. Did this ever happen? No. Did he ever apply for the auto loan as he said he would? No again. Well, you know what? I can't handle everything all by myself.

"I suppose I never thought my father measured up either. I grew up in Massachusetts. Dad was a Harvard business school graduate and had his own business, but, frankly, he never did all that well. But I do have memories of a happy childhood. We'd all go sailing off Cape Cod in the summer and skiing in Vermont in the winter. Then, when I was about fifteen, my parents divorced and Dad married his secretary.

"I adored both my parents, though I knew I was a constant disappointment to them. My beautiful, peppy, extroverted mother, the former captain of the high school cheerleading squad, couldn't accept her shy, ugly-duckling little girl. I didn't do especially well in school either—another disappointment to Mother, who was a teacher.

"But my high school art teacher saw I had talent and became my mentor. She encouraged me to study fine arts in college, and after graduation, she helped me find a job as a photography assistant in a large advertising agency.

"Look, I know I agreed to this arrangement, but I'm overwhelmed. I work long hours, and I still have to pay the bills and do the taxes. Tony doesn't understand the first thing about our finances and doesn't care to learn. I think he's jealous of the fact that I make the money.

"The bottom line is, I love Tony very much, and I know both of us want this marriage to work. But we're at each other all the time. I can't live this way."

TONY'S TURN

"Carol doesn't have the slightest idea what I do all day," said Tony, thirty-six, his jaw clenched in anger as he slumped on the couch. "Nothing is ever good enough. She's nitpicky and downright petty. If I forget to do something, or don't do it as perfectly as she wants, she blows up. I finally installed the closets and cabinets in Sam's room, and now she says it's the wrong kind of wood. Here's another example: Recently, after two burglaries in the neighborhood, she wanted me to change the locks on the doors, that very night. It was the middle of January, it was too late, too cold, and I was too tired. But Carol was relentless, so I finally did it.

"Carol never used to snap at me this way for stupid things. But now, if I'm in line at the supermarket, get preoccupied reading a newspaper, and don't empty the shopping cart

fast enough, she makes some nasty crack. I'm sick of being treated like a four-year-old.

"Let me make this clear: I do not resent Carol's salary. I'm grateful for it. What I deeply resent is hearing her talk about how I'm spending 'her money.' We're married—isn't whatever we bring in 'our money'? Doesn't she realize we're saving thousands of dollars by my doing all the general contracting, carpentry, and painting for the renovation? When she moans about having to write all the checks and apply for the car loan, she forgets that I'm the one entertaining Sam.

"I want to have this place finished by the time the new baby is born as much as she does. That's why I'm not about to run all over the city comparison shopping. I know how much Sheetrock should cost, for Pete's sake. She's just going to have to stop second-guessing everything.

"Our recent problem with the plumber is a perfect example of how I get blamed for everything. I've called him day and night and even driven to his house to speak with his neighbors, but no one has seen him. Does she want me to get a posse and lasso him?

"Her lack of patience, especially about inconsequential things, sets off my anger. That's what happened when we were at the highway rest stop; we were only two miles from our house, so I walked home. We end up yelling—loudly, I admit—in front of Sam. I hate losing my temper. My father did that and it scared the hell out of me.

I'm from a small town in Pennsylvania. Mother was a housewife, and Dad worked at the steel mill. My parents are still together after forty years, so I guess it was as happy as any marriage. But my father had an explosive temper that intimidated all of us. His style of discipline was to yell and spank me and my brothers hard. With Dad, you just couldn't make a mistake. I think he was frustrated that he was working in a steel mill because, for financial reasons, he was never able to finish college.

"I knew at an early age that I wanted to be an artist. I drew all the time, and my parents encouraged it. I graduated with a degree in fine arts, but I don't have to tell you how hard it is to make a living painting. It's frustrating to accept the reality that I can't support a family on the few sales I do make. For years, I made ends meet by doing carpentry work.

"The first thing I noticed about Carol were her eyes; they're so expressive and caring. Being with her came easy and felt right. It ticks me off when she still complains that I don't talk enough. Anything I need to say, I bring up immediately. I don't like to invent something to say just to fill space.

"I love being home with Sam, and I'm not the least bit ashamed of what I do. How many fathers get to spend this much time with their kids? I'm looking forward to doing it with our second child—if I ever get this damn house finished. But I hate the tension and fighting between Carol and me."

THE COUNSELOR'S TURN

"Carol and Tony's marriage was a true nineties role reversal," said the counselor. "Though they professed to like their nontraditional roles and responsibilities, each had plenty of complaints. First, they needed guidance in learning to resolve conflicts so the tension between them didn't become unbearable.

"Despite her forceful manner, Carol had little self-confidence. Her mother had consistently undermined her self-esteem, and Carol replayed this scenario with Tony: Her high expectations and her almost rote criticism of him undermined her husband's self-confidence in much the same way.

"Carol's way of expressing her disappointment was particularly corrosive for the marriage. Whenever she was anxious or frustrated, she unwittingly hammered away at what she saw as her husband's incompetence and lack of support.

"Low-key and sensitive to criticism, Tony was not one to waste words. His comment that his father came down harshly on him if he made a mistake was telling. He was a perfectionist, and Carol's remarks about how he was messing up everything from the renovation to the finances was like pouring salt in those old wounds.

"Tony's response to his wife's negativity was also classic: He simply withdrew until he exploded. This is a very common dynamic in marriage. The more one partner pushes to get her way, the more the other digs in his heels.

"Consequently, Tony and Carol fought loudly and often. Arguments never ended as they countered accusations with harsh remarks, and failed to listen to the frustration behind their partner's words.

"One of Carol's concerns was that Tony didn't open up to her. I told her that she would have to accept that to a certain extent this was the way he was. Nevertheless, if she stopped interrupting him so much, there would be more opportunity for him to talk. I taped some of their conversations in my office and played them back so Carol could hear how she was railroading Tony out of the conversation. She was amazed and quite chagrined.

"As Carol began to react differently, Tony did, too. He learned to set limits so he felt less harangued. Instead of acting out his anger or withdrawing, he'll now say directly: 'I don't appreciate that comment,' or 'Carol, you're doing it again.' Also, instead of automatically saying yes to Carol's demands, he has learned to tell her honestly how he feels. In addition, at my urging, the two

made a budget, and Tony now takes care of certain bills. I believe it's not a good idea for one spouse to be ignorant of the family finances. But along with Tony getting more involved, I wanted Carol to see that she wasn't valuing her husband's contribution sufficiently. I asked her to go home and calculate what it would cost to have a caregiver for Sam as well as a contractor and carpenter for the house. She did, and she began to show more respect for what her husband was doing.

"Tony had to acknowledge that controlling his anger was his responsibility. Because of his father's frequent rages, Tony felt that all anger is bad. I explained that anger is natural and sometimes appropriate, but it shouldn't be expressed the way his father had—or by walking away from your wife and child at a rest stop. 'The excuse that Carol provoked you doesn't fly,' I told him.

"I suggested that if a problem was escalating to a point where they felt unable to contain their anger, they should acknowledge each other's feelings but table further discussion for an hour. Afterward, if they found they still couldn't deal with it, we'd hash it out in my office. Soon, Tony and Carol were able to work out differences before they became divisive.

"After eight months of therapy, these two are true partners again. And even with time off for the birth of their daughter, the house is just about finished.

REAL MEN CAN DO HOUSEWORK . . .

But in the real world, they often don't. While studies from the Institute for Social Research at the University of Michigan confirm that this generation of couples do half the amount of housework their parents did, most of those chores are still shouldered by women. Is there a way to prevent everyday skirmishes over home front responsibilities from escalating into full-scale wars—and still get him to put the dishes in the dishwasher? Let's look at both sides of the problem.

Her side:

- "I'm tired of doing all of it all the time."
- "It's the psychic energy that's so draining. I have to be responsible for things even if I'm not in charge of them."
- "How come he can fix a car engine but can't figure out how to put the toilet paper on the roll?"

His side:

- "When I do the grocery shopping, she says I buy the wrong tomato sauce."
- "She'll find one spot of food on a pot and yell, 'Is this what you call clean?'"
- "The fact that I can't remember to put my socks in the hamper is not a personal attack against her. I just . . . forget."

Even the best counselors don't have a foolproof recipe for success on this one. But here are a few suggestions. Try them; you never know . . .

1. Figure out exactly what needs to be done and who's doing it. Keep a log of everything for a week down to the minute details: Who walked the dog, who did the laundry, who folded, who took the car in for repair, and so on. It could well be that a spouse is doing more than you gave him or her credit for. In that case, make a point of appreciating each other's efforts. By not taking the chores, large or small, for granted, you create a spiral of appreciation that, in time, can erase resentment.

2. Talk about how things were done when you were growing up and what role models you had for sharing the work at home. If Mom did all the cooking, you may both hold the expectation that planning and cooking meals is only a woman's job. Some women also feel that if their husbands earn more than they do, they don't have a right to ask for help at home, even if they work, too. But as gender roles shift, and more women as well as men move in and out of the workforce, those expectations must change, as well. Talking about what you each expect and want is essential to balancing the scales.

3. Consider various plans for a fair division of labor. Maybe you go with a scenario based on expertise: Who excelled in math? Put that person in charge of the checkbook. Depersonalize the process, as if you're tackling something with a colleague. What's one way to solve the problem? What are five other possibilities? Who else could help with this problem? Perhaps hiring a neighborhood teenager to handle some chores, errands, or child care would lighten the load for both of you.

4. Let go. Sometimes, when it comes to housework and children, women are their own worst enemies. You asked Daddy to dress the baby and the kid comes out with a top and bottom that don't match? So what? You wanted him to do the shopping? Then let him do it his way. The principle here is simple: If you give up responsibility for a chore, you have to give up control over it, too. Besides, some things just aren't worth quibbling about.

5. When all else fails, go on strike. It has been duly noted that some women have simply stopped doing domestic duty to make a point. Laundry? Wash and dry only yours. Kids need something bought or signed? Tell them to ask their dad. As long as things keep getting done, he may not realize how much, and in what detail, you actually do. Only when you stop will he get the hint.

6. Train your kids. Instead of fostering helplessness in the next generation, make sure your children, boys as well as girls, grow up believing that sharing the physical as well as the emotional chores at home is just what considerate people do.

"My Husband Wants a Perfect Housewife"

Carl said he supported Hannah's career, but he still wanted her to be the model corporate wife. What happens when one partner expects too much?

HANNAH'S TURN

"Okay, so there were dog hairs all over the seat of the car," said Hannah, thirty-five, sinking her lean, nearly six-foot frame into a chair. "Is that enough to trigger a rampage?

"I am not kidding. When Carl pulled into the garage the night before last, he purposely looked inside my car and then stormed into the house, raving like a madman about dog hairs. Look, I'm not a world-class housekeeper, but I also do not have time to run a household the way Carl's mother did.

"On the day of the dog-hair incident, I had driven our daughter, Sharon, to school so her science project wouldn't get wrecked on the bus. This made me late for work—I have a three-day-a-week job as music editor of a regional magazine—so I was rushing all morning to catch up. Then I used my lunch hour to take the dog to the vet. And, as usual, I dashed home so Sharon, who's ten, wouldn't be alone after school. I picked up around the house a little, did some work on a book I'm writing about music appreciation for kids, and started making dinner. The idea of vacuuming the car never entered my mind.

"So in comes Carl, carrying on about how he knew I'd leave the car a mess after the vet appointment. I have never been one to engage in shouting matches, so I just stood there. Before long, he was on a roll, bringing up everything that bothered him . . .

like, I'm not tough enough on Sharon, who is going to become a slob like me . . . I don't go to the functions that wives of his colleagues go to . . . I waste time and money on yoga classes and writing my book. He hit me with a whole litany of offenses, then marched out of the room. I stood there crying, unable to think of a single word to say back.

"Now, this isn't the first time Carl has criticized me so vehemently. He's been treating me like this for years, but I guess this last time pushed me over the edge. I insisted we find professional help.

"Actually, I think it's already hopeless, even with your help. Maybe we're just too different to stay married. Carl comes from a large, boisterous, upper-middle-class family. He grew up in an exclusive Chicago suburb; his mother was your typical clubwoman, his father a very successful businessman.

"My family is the opposite. Both my parents are artists and I'm their only child. We never had a lot of money, but I had a childhood filled with trips to museums and the ballet. We lived in a loft in Greenwich Village, and you could never tell where the studio ended and the living quarters began.

"I never had much of a social life, though. I was always so tall, and the kids at school weren't into the arts, so I was a loner. Even when I was a scholarship student at Juilliard, I never found my niche socially. Carl

was the first person besides my parents who ever made me feel loved. And I do still love him—that's what's so terrible about this.

"Our first meeting was so romantic. I was a member of a string quartet, and when we played in Chicago in December, Carl came to the stage door with a dozen roses for me. He said he had been in the audience the night before and that I was the most beautiful woman he had ever seen. Do you believe that? I could tell he meant it, and the fact that I was three inches taller than he didn't seem to matter.

"We had a whirlwind courtship because I went back to New York and he went back to Philadelphia, to finish his M.B.A. at Wharton. Still, he did the most romantic things, like surprise me with a visit on Valentine's Day. Carl still does romantic things every now and then, although I know it's just because he feels guilty for being so hard on me.

"We were married in May of that year, eleven years ago, and moved to Virginia. Carl had landed a good job with a manufacturing firm and he had to begin right away. It seems our trouble started the minute he carried me over the threshold. All of a sudden, my romantic suitor turned into a neatness fanatic.

"Although I was very busy working full-time at the magazine plus playing with the local orchestra during the season, I was expected to do all the housework, too. Carl helped, but he always implied that he was doing it because I hadn't done a good enough job.

"When I got pregnant, Carl felt it was important for me to cut back on my activities and be home more. I knew I would have to drop out of the orchestra, but I was able to arrange a part-time job at the magazine.

"I've tried hard to keep up all my interests, but Carl has never supported me. Would it have killed him to stay with Sharon some nights so I could continue to play my cello?

"No, I never said anything to him. It was clear Carl just didn't care. So I tried to work on myself a bit. I signed up for a yoga class at night. Carl agreed grudgingly to stay home with Sharon, but I could tell he didn't approve.

"Then something happened that made me wonder about this marriage. I called after yoga to say that a few of us and the instructor were going for coffee so I'd be a little late. Carl blew up. He accused me of having a crush on the instructor! On the one hand, I should have just laughed it off. But on the other, it proved that our relationship has dissolved into a lack of trust."

CARL'S TURN

"I do love Hannah," said Carl, thirty-seven, a sandy-haired man with a vibrant manner. "The trouble is, the things that drew me to her are the things that cause problems.

"Hannah is a dreamer. That's great, but there are times you have to discipline yourself to get on with the business at hand, especially when you have a family.

"Take this book she's writing. She could have had it finished months ago if she had only worked at it systematically. But no, she dawdles, she leaves manuscript pages all over the house, she wastes time staring out the window. Meanwhile, the house is filthy and she's ordering in pizza.

"I am not exaggerating. I will concede that my standards for housekeeping are pretty high, but Hannah is truly impossible. When she goes into her creative mode, she's in another world. She doesn't see dirt. She leaves dishes in the sink and uses paper plates.

"Okay, I probably got a little carried away the other night, but that business with the dog was the straw that broke the camel's back.

"Still, it's not just the housework. Hannah is simply not there for me. Oh, I don't expect her to attend every company dinner. But I would like her to participate a little bit in my company's social plans. All the wives do. What gets me is that she not only won't join me, she's smug about it. She says she's not that kind of wife.

"So what kind is she, then? Certainly not a very demonstrative one. I'm not referring to our sex life, which has always been fine. She doesn't make me feel like she loves me, I guess.

"Listen, I like to think of myself as a bit of a romantic. And when I do something romantic, I'd like her to reciprocate once in a while or be appreciative. I've slacked off with the corny gestures since they're not getting me anywhere, but every now and then, I look at her and I have to go splurge on flowers. Since I first laid eyes on her, I thought of her as a Modigliani painting, with that mesmerizing beauty, so pensive and ethereal. She still affects me that way. I give her the flowers and—nothing. Just a cold thank-you.

"I wish I knew when and where things went wrong. We didn't spend much time together before we were married, but we did talk about the future. And we both decided she would drop out of the orchestra when the baby was born. So why am I the bad guy?

"Okay, this yoga business really does drive me nuts. I'm home alone with Sharon, and Hannah's off doing some Eastern thing and going out afterward with cute young guys. Couldn't she be spending that time with me?

"I don't think Hannah wants this marriage to work. I think she's deliberately or subconsciously provoking me. It would break my heart if I lost her and Sharon, but what can I do?"

The Counselor's Turn

"After only one session with this couple, I knew that the first step had to be the hiring of a cleaning woman. No amount of counseling would do as much for them.

"Naturally, they protested, since they were paying my fee, plus a baby-sitter in the afternoon, but I made them realize that in their case, household help was not a luxury but a necessity: It was needed to defuse the present tension. Hannah found someone who could come every other week, and as I predicted, the level of tension between them dropped dramatically.

"Now we were free to move on to the problem of Carl's constant criticism of Hannah. Because of his resentment over her messiness, Carl had unconsciously gotten into the habit of belittling his wife. When I pointed this out, Carl vowed that he would change. He made a conscious effort to focus on the ways Hannah was a wonderful mother and to compliment her in that regard. She's very involved in her daughter's life and takes her to numerous cultural events. She also treats her daughter with deep respect. These are all qualities that Carl had always admired but never mentioned before.

"Of course, Hannah's housekeeping standards are not the same as Carl's, but our third task was to get her to realize that even her laissez-faire upbringing did not excuse total disregard for order in the house. During one session, Hannah admitted to being provocative on this issue.

"'I guess I'm just angry,' she said at one point, 'angry that Carl doesn't appreciate what I do, angry that he made me give up things I really love, like playing the cello.'

"That's when Carl spoke up. 'Look,' he said, 'until now, you never mentioned all this. I can't read your mind.' Carl explained that he thought he had been communicative and that they had reached a mutually acceptable decision about Hannah's leaving the orchestra.

"At this point, I reminded them of Carl's comment that Hannah had distanced herself from him. As she had said, she was not the type to engage in shouting matches, but in fact, she had long had a problem responding to Carl on any level. Shy and insecure with her peers as a child, she still found it difficult to open up, which Carl, understandably, interpreted as coldness.

"I gave Carl and Hannah a simple assignment. They were to concentrate on the little things they could do to show tenderness and love, whether it was a good-bye hug in the morning or a quick phone call during the day to say I love you. Long-married people, I noted, often forget that the simple romantic gesture can help cement a relationship.

"I also instructed Carl to curtail his verbal barrages and to make sure he gave Hannah time to respond. If he was upset about dog hairs in the car, he was to mention it, then wait for her to respond instead of marching out of the room. When we play-acted this scenario in my office, Hannah said, 'The next time I feel I have too much to do, can I ask you to take Sharon to school or take the dog to the vet?' This was a breakthrough: Carl saw her point, congratulated her for speaking up, and agreed to take on more chores.

"This was the beginning of a pattern of compromises for this couple that helped steer their marriage back on course. Hannah has gotten more involved in functions having to do with Carl's work, and now that she's met more of the other wives, she is not as uncomfortable with them as she thought she would be. She's learned to respond appreciatively to Carl's romantic gestures, and they've made an effort to go out more.

"Hannah finished her book and decided not to embark on another project for a while but rather to resume playing with a local string quartet. Now that Hannah gives so much more of herself to him, Carl is not troubled by the fact that she wants to take an occasional yoga class. He has begun to appreciate this time alone with his daughter. 'And it's become a family joke that Daddy takes the dog to the vet,' he told me during one of our last sessions.

"Carl and Hannah ended counseling several months ago, confident that they had overcome their major problems and had the tools to solve any others that may come up in the course of their relationship."

UNMASKING THE REAL ISSUES

These two aren't really fighting about dog hairs or dishes. For Carl and Hannah, as well as for many couples, battles over housework are often red herrings. Unwittingly they have fallen into a power struggle that gets played and replayed whenever hot buttons get pushed.

If you and your partner often argue about the same, seemingly trivial issues, that may be a warning signal: Perhaps the surface arguments are masking a deeper, more troubling, problem you need to discuss. It's helpful if you can take a step back and try to observe your interactions with an impartial eye and ask yourselves: What are we really fighting about here? When have I felt like this before? Did we ever see anyone else, perhaps one of our parents, acting this way? Tracing behavioral patterns to the past can help you rechoreograph your actions now.

In this case, Carl's resentment of his wife's messiness blinded him to her many wonderful qualities. He fell into the habit of belittling her. Hiring a housekeeper to come in twice a week was a turning point. Now that the housework was no longer a kindling issue, they could focus on the real issues—for instance, Hannah's anger that Carl doesn't appreciate her interests, as well as her inability to express her feelings in the face of frequent criticism. In order to bypass the blame and criticism, she tried: "What are you really trying to tell me?" and "When you criticize me, I don't feel like trying to please you." Once Hannah expressed herself, Carl made an effort to get out of his attack mode and, if he did have something to say, to at least wait for her to respond before marching out of the room in a huff.

They were then able to negotiate compromises and eliminate their constant bickering. For her part, Hannah is much more willing to join Carl for his business obligations—happily, in fact.

"He's a Child, Not a Husband"

Sally tried to be a good wife, but Gary still expected more and more. What happens when your best is never enough?

SALLY'S TURN

"What does he want from me?" asked Sally, thirty-three, as she dropped her briefcase on the floor and settled into a chair. "I'm trying to be a good wife, but as far as Gary is concerned, it's not enough. 'You don't care. . . . You don't love me as much as I love you. . . . You never listen.' I'm worn out from his litany of complaints!

"I have a full-time job—I'm in computer sales and it's a tough, competitive job. Even though I leave the office at seven, sometimes seven-thirty, at night, I still cook dinner for my husband. I'm so exhausted some nights I can't even see straight. Yet he'll burst through the door and launch immediately into some heavy discussion, telling me about his problems at work or wanting to know everything that happened to me that day. I feel ambushed. But if I don't give him my undivided attention, he goes berserk.

"I know, I know. You're thinking I'm horrible and ungrateful, but please hear me out. Gary is devoted, kind, loving, generous to the point of extravagance. Most women would give their right arm for a man like this, but sometimes he's just too much for me. He tells me how much he needs me and I feel as if I'm going to jump out of my skin.

"With Gary, every conversation has to be deep and involved. Do I have to listen to him analyze every action from every angle? Last month he called me at work; I had four people in my office and I couldn't talk. I could tell he was hurt, but I wasn't about to sweet-talk him out of it with all those people listening. He didn't speak to me the whole night.

"That is typical. If I'm short with him, or I say something he takes the wrong way—usually something so minor I'm totally unaware he's offended—he'll remember it for days and get back at me, either by not talking or by refusing to make love. Most times, our love life is fabulous, except when he feels slighted and punishes me by depriving me of sex.

"Other times Gary gets furious, just as my father used to. I'm drained by his outbursts. I never knew how to calm my father down either. I grew up in a traditional home; we were the only professional family in our blue-collar suburb. My father was a commercial banker, my mother a housewife. I was Daddy's girl and he was my role model—since there was no son in the family I was brought up to be the tough super-achiever. Thinking back, I realize my father was interested only in how well I did in school. If I told him I got ninety-five on a math test, he'd ask why I didn't get one hundred. Every once in a while, when he was angry, he'd explode, kicking over a wastebasket or slamming doors. There would be days when he didn't speak to me or look at me.

"I was a goody-goody. I studied hard and I'm proud that I always had a job after school and paid for all my own clothes and gifts. I had lots of friends and tons of boyfriends, but never anyone serious. I was determined to be successful in my career before I got married. I didn't want to be dependent on anyone.

"When I was a freshman in college, my parents' marriage fell apart. Mother discovered that Dad had had a mistress for ten years. She tried to kill herself by swallowing barbiturates and we had to put her in a hospital for four months. I transferred to a school near home so I could nurse my mother and talk some sense into my father, but it finally dawned on me that I couldn't fix things. Dad is now married to that woman and my mother is very bitter. She calls me all the time, weepy or despondent.

"Of course, that explains the distance I sensed but couldn't figure out as a child. You see, outwardly we were the happy family, but behind the facade, there was little emotion.

"This is the total opposite of my life now. Gary is all emotion. We met at work. Gary had been with the company for ten years; five months after I started, he was promoted to head my department.

"My first impression: He was gorgeous—I mean movie-star gorgeous. Every woman in the office had a crush on Gary, but I honestly didn't consider him a dating prospect. First of all, I had a strict rule about not dating anyone from work, let alone my boss. It was more than unprofessional; it was stupid.

Besides, Gary was fourteen years older than I; he'd been married before and had a son, who's now in college.

"We were just real good buddies for about eight years. In fact, he was more like a confidant. If I had a problem with the guy I was dating, Gary would help me work it out. There was always a lot of energy and special chemistry between us. Our relationship changed the night a colleague got married. We were both invited to the wedding, but since neither of us was dating anyone at the time, we decided to go together. It was a magical evening, and Gary ended up sleeping over.

"That blew my mind. I told myself this had better work out, because if it didn't, we were in big trouble. I was so nervous when I saw Gary at work the next day that I spilled coffee on my new suit. When he stopped by my apartment that evening, we had a long talk and decided it wasn't going to work. We desperately tried to avoid each other. It sounds so corny to say that passion got the better of us, but it did. I was torn; I knew I wanted to be with Gary more than I'd ever wanted another man in my life, and I knew the feeling was mutual.

"For over a year, we lived this crazy life, bending over backward to avoid any evidence of impropriety. After about six months, Gary decided to quit his job and start his own consulting business. That meant we could finally make our relationship public. We were married at a small hotel on Long Island—and as it turned out, people had known about us all along but didn't care.

"But things haven't gone very smoothly. I'm nervous about Gary's career change. Right now, I'm pretty much supporting us, since it takes a long time to build up a profitable business. Gary wanted to fly to L.A. to make a presentation to a possible client. I pointed out that it was an expensive trip, and since there were perhaps twenty others making a pitch for this client, maybe it wasn't worth it. He hit the ceiling and said I had no confidence in him. Also, we had talked about having a baby— I'm going to be thirty-four in May and Gary is forty-eight. I wanted to take time off after the baby, but how can I do that if his income is so low?

"Look, I'm embarrassed about being in counseling, but Gary insisted I come. He wants me to change, but I am what I am. Why can't he accept that?"

GARY'S TURN

"She doesn't get it. She just doesn't get it," said Gary, forty-eight, a tall, handsome man in jeans and a sweater. "What's the matter with her? Most women would die for a husband to treat them the way I treat her. You see how she's rolling her eyes now? That's the way she acts with me most of the time. I try to get her to talk, to tell me about her day and how she's feeling, but she interrupts me.

"And she doesn't listen when I talk either. She's totally closed off, even in bed. We'll be making love and I can sense that her body may be there but her mind is a million miles away. She's a cold fish; I know she's thinking about everything but what she should be thinking about. I tell this woman how much I adore her and she gets silly. Like it's a big joke. As soon as our lovemaking is over, she practically leaps out of bed. It makes me crazy. This rage just comes over me.

"I've always been an emotional kind of guy. We were very poor when I was growing up—my mother cleaned other people's houses and I slept on a roll-out cot in the living room—but I was tough. My mother and I were very close—she was president of my fan club and incredibly supportive. She never put any limits on my dreams. It wasn't that way with my father; there was always a real distance between us.

"Dad was a postal clerk, hard-working but undemonstrative. He loved me, but he never said it and never showed it. Would you believe I have no memories of him ever hugging me? He would often do what Sally does: I'd be very excited about something and he'd make fun of that enthusiasm.

"When I was about seven, my mother got very sick. I think she had

some kind of nervous breakdown and she was in a sanitarium for about two years. My dad joined the Navy and I went to live with my aunt until my mother was well enough to come home. That was a terrible time. Not that my aunt wasn't kind or loving, but I was terrified that my mother was going to die. When she came back, she was never the same, and I was always worried that something would happen to her.

"I knew that I'd have to pay for my own college education, so I did. I earned a four-year swimming scholarship, and then, since I wanted to work with underprivileged kids, I also went for a master's in psychology. During vacations, I found a job at a large computer company and they offered me a full-time position when I graduated. It was too much for a poor kid to turn down, so that's how I got into sales management.

"I think my psyche background and my ability to make people feel comfortable and motivate them have served me well. That doesn't mean I don't need confidence-boosting myself, however. I'm more than a little scared about making this move professionally. It's not easy to head off in a new direction at my age. Many people in the business thought I was nuts to give up a prestigious job with a solid company at a time like this. But one morning I looked in the mirror and said, 'Gary, you gotta make a change.' I was dissatisfied. So I made my move.

"I thought Sally would be more supportive. When I first met her, I was completely blown away. I don't think Sally knows what a powerful sexual energy she has. I also had so much respect for her and the way she did business. She's smart and savvy. It kills me that Sally doesn't think I can make my consulting firm work. But I don't think I can tell her how frightened I am about starting a new career. She'd flip out. She's not a risk-taker.

"We had a really big disagreement about a trip I wanted to take to L.A. last month. Sure it was a gamble, but you're not going to get ahead if you're not willing to stick your neck out. Sally looks at life with a glass-is-half-empty attitude; I look at the same thing and see a glass half full. By the way, I made that trip and I won the account. However, since I spend most of my time trying to drum up new clients, I'm hit with a hell of a lot of rejection. When I get home, I don't want to be treated like a delivery man dropping off a package."

THE COUNSELOR'S TURN

"Sally and Gary were atypical of most couples I see," said the counselor. "Usually, the wife complains that the husband doesn't listen, doesn't talk, and is unemotional. In this case, the reverse was true. I could tell immediately that in this relationship,

Sally was the doer; Gary was the be-er. She intellectualized; he emoted. Unfortunately, Gary interpreted his wife's behavior to mean that she didn't love or care about him.

"Serious, guarded, businesslike, and pragmatic, Sally had great difficulty getting in touch with her feelings and expressing them. The first child of unemotional, undemonstrative parents, she grew up in a home where love was conditional: If she performed well, she was praised. The message from her parents, especially her father, was: Try harder; if you push a little bit more, you'll win Daddy's love.

"Sally grew up to be ambitious and driven, a woman who was the opposite of her helpless, dependent mother. If there was a problem, she learned to zero in on what was wrong and fix it.

"As a child, however, when she tried to soothe her moody father's unpredictable temper or win his admiration, she was confronted with icy silences and rejection. Gary's outbursts left her similarly frustrated.

"Although she refused to admit it for a long time, Sally had been devastated by her father's affair and her parents' divorce. She had adored her father, modeled herself after him, and her image of this perfect man was shattered. The experience left her with a deep lack of trust for men in general. At the same time, she felt weighted down by her mother's almost total dependence on her.

When Gary demanded her total attention, it reminded her of her mother and she felt smothered.

"Bright and articulate, Gary was a passionate man who looked you right in the eye and leaned toward you as he spoke. But he was also an angry man with a chip on his shoulder, a sad look on his face, and pain in his voice. When he first came to see me, he was furious and spoke in a harsh, accusatory way. Pointing a finger at his wife, he would say over and over again, 'You don't get it, do you? You just don't get it!' When he did this, Sally would start to cry; she really didn't get it.

"Gary grew up in a poor home. When his mother took ill, she remained hospitalized for two years. His father left him in the custody of his aunt and Gary felt unloved and rejected, terrified he'd be out on the street. After his mother finally came home, Gary became highly solicitous of her every need. Although the family was reunited, Gary still felt his position was precarious. He put pressure on himself to be the perfect little boy.

"Much of Gary's rage, however, was directed toward his father, who was unable to provide for his family and was emotionally remote. Now, in his relationship with Sally, he felt he was again giving emotionally and getting little in return.

"In the most basic terms, Sally had to learn to give and Gary had to learn to pull back. But the process was a slow one. I don't think Sally understood how skittish she was about revealing herself to men as well as to me. I suggested that she come for individual counseling, and for several months she came one week alone and the next week with Gary.

"Initially, every time our conversation veered toward a discussion of how Sally felt about something, she would change the subject yet continue to deny that she was afraid to talk about her feelings. This is what she did with Gary at home and in bed. In time, my constant reassurances gave her courage to open up. Once she learned to take a risk with her emotions, she discovered that Gary didn't turn away.

"This process was helped when Gary learned to curb his angry outbursts, which he did once he understood that he was trying to see how far he could push her. When he was feeling upset, I suggested he count to ten or go out for a jog.

"At the same time, Sally had to learn to respond positively to Gary. Instead of making jokes or rolling her eyes, she owed it to him to listen and be more sensitive, although she didn't have to put up with his rages. When he acts like that, I told her, 'Don't cajole him. Clear out.' One weekend when they were visiting friends in the country, Gary again felt she wasn't paying enough attention to him and started to lose his temper. Sally told him she was going to leave if he didn't calm down, which she had in the past threatened to do. When he didn't, she got in the car and drove home. Gary took the train back to the city, and by the time he got in the door, he realized he had overreacted and apologized.

"However, Sally had to acknowledge that there were times when she wasn't listening to Gary at all. Gary had a right to feel nervous about his new business venture. 'He is facing rejection every day,' I told her, 'and he needs to talk about it.'

"As Gary pulled back, Sally had more room to move toward him. However, I told Gary that while I didn't think he expected too much in general, he did expect too much of Sally. 'Perhaps another woman wouldn't feel pressured the way she does, but you chose Sally. You love her and you want to make this work. Sally has her limits, and you haven't been respectful of those limits.'

"This couple stopped coming to therapy after two years, although I still occasionally see them separately. Gary's firm is doing surprisingly well, considering the sluggish economy. Sally, who has been unable to get pregnant, is now considering artificial insemination. They just returned from a long weekend in Florida. 'I truly feel that Sally loves me,' Gary says. 'After all, who else would put up with a guy like me?'"

THIRTY MINUTES
THAT CAN SAVE YOUR MARRIAGE

To feel loved and nurtured, we must believe deep down that our partner is really there for us. That sounds simple, but it's far more complicated than most couples realize. Although Sally and Gary insisted that they were being attentive, they had difficulty being emphatic. That's significant: Marital researchers have found that couples who help each other weather stressful situations outside the marriage have stronger, happier relationships than those who can't.

The key is empathy. Empathy isn't the same as sympathy or pity. It means being able to put yourself in another's position, to feel what they feel and see what they see, without losing yourself in the process. And it means you do all that even though you may disagree with a partner's perception, opinions, or feelings. Take thirty minutes a day, at a time that works best for both of you, to empathize with the stresses and strains you are each experiencing in other areas of your life. It can make a difference between a marriage that succeeds and one that fails. Consider:

Empathy Don'ts:

Don't stonewall (ignore what a partner is saying).

Don't minimize a spouse's concerns: "What's the big deal?" "You're always so sensitive!"

Don't rush to fix the problem: "Well, if I were you I'd . . ." or "You should have. . . ." Many people mistakenly believe that downplaying worries or offering advice is helpful. In fact, pat reassurances often magnify negative feelings, since they force a person to try even harder to feel acknowledged. Women especially resent a partner's interruption with solutions, preferring instead to simply vent and know that someone is really listening.

Empathy Dos:

Do pay attention. Set aside the newspaper or catalog and turn off the TV when your partner is talking. An occasional uh-huh or nod of the head indicates you haven't zoned out.

Do validate feelings. "He gave that special assignment to the new recruit? I can see why you're annoyed."

Do ask questions with genuine interest. Make sure your partner knows you heard what he or she has said. "So how did you respond to him?"

Do respond with affection, understanding, and support: "I'm really sorry you have to put up with that." "Oh, sweetheart, that could happen to anyone. Don't be so hard on yourself."

Do show support. Take your spouse's side. "I think your boss went a little overboard, too," is appropriate. "Well, you shouldn't have been late in the first place" isn't.

"My Husband Is a Perfectionist"

Nothing was good enough for the supercritical Jake and, after fifteen years, Kylie no longer cared to meet the high standards he set—for himself and for everyone else.

KYLIE'S TURN

"Unless Jake—my husband is a brilliant architect— moves his office out of our home, and quick, he can have all ten rooms to himself," said thirty-eight-year-old Kylie, mother of four, in a voice as fiery as her bright-red hair.

"Fortunately, when I finished art school, I inherited a modest trust fund. so I'm now in a position to establish a separate residence, provide my son and daughters with a little peace and quiet, and try to preserve my own sanity.

"Jake complains bitterly about everything. He was upset because Ellen, who is seventeen months old, dribbled milk down her chin and dropped applesauce on the floor. That domestic sight interfered with his 'creativity.' I'm an artist myself, but I'm smart enough to realize that children and messes go together. But Ellen's soppy dress, Jake said, was typical of my bad management as a mother.

"That evening at dinner he jumped on twelve-year-old Billy and his sisters because they hadn't greeted him with cries of delight when they came in from school (as an at-home Dad, his presence is hardly a surprise to any of us) and because they squabbled at the table. He accused all three of being undisciplined, although seven-year-old Janey is a perfect little lady and just as sensitive as Jake himself. She burst

190

into tears. Billy took Janey's side and sassed his father. Jake then ordered the three children to leave the table and go outside and practice self-control; he wanted them to pick three bouquets of flowers—can you imagine making such an idiotic proposal to hungry youngsters!? I told the children to stay put and continue the meal. Jake ate by himself in the kitchen, again.

"My husband has enormous talent and many lovable qualities. However, his sulkiness, finickiness, and procrastination have become intolerable.

"Jake and I have been married fifteen years and have owned our present home for eleven. It is nowhere near furnished. Downstairs we have no window shades. Upstairs we have fantastically expensive draperies, woven in Andalusia to Jake's specifications. There is no sofa in our living room. Our guests sit on a lumpy contraption concocted from two beat-up daybeds, covered with Navajo blankets that Jake admires and I despise. I have dragged him to furniture stores but have yet to find a sofa with lines, fabric, and construction that please him.

"Jake is the only man I have ever loved. I met him at sixteen, soon after I entered art school. He was teaching an occasional class in draftsmanship. I signed up for every class he taught, but he ignored me. Through family friends I wangled an introduction.

"We dated, off and on, for years. Jake and I went to art shows, museums, concerts, the theater. On my twenty-third birthday, after seven years, I decided I had waited long enough and should forget about marriage. My father offered to send me abroad for a year of painting, and I accepted.

"On our next date, I explained my plans to Jake and to my astonishment, he proposed to me that same night. Two weeks later we were married.

"For two years, we were divinely happy, even though my parents' marriage fell apart during that period. Jake was a tower of strength to both my mother and father, to my brothers, and to me. In those days he and I had no sex problems, no money problems, no in-law problems, no design problems, no problem of his incessant meddling and bossiness. Our first home was a small rented apartment. He worked afternoons and evenings in the one tiny bedroom. In the morning he worked in the office of an older architect. He left me every day at eight A.M. and was gone until noon. I missed him badly those four hours. That now seems incredible.

"Now Jake's office is the original maid's room in our home, which directly adjoins my kitchen. In theory his door is supposed to be closed from nine o'clock until five. In fact, he bobs in and out dozens of times a day and is always breathing down my neck. When he does receive his clients, he hollers for me to be less noisy or to bring in coffee and cake. When he steps outside for a leisurely stroll in search of inspiration, I'm under orders to take his business calls, act as his secretary, and send out his bills, because he won't hire a typist.

"When I bring in groceries, Jake instantly rushes out of his office and criticizes my purchases. I can't keep a cleaning woman; he pushes them around until they quit. He revises my menus, alters the arrangement of my pots and pans. Nothing is ever permanent, and few things tarry long in the places where I put them. Jake uses my kitchen as a laboratory, where he tests out every new product or material that comes on the market and catches his fancy. In eleven years, I've had five new sinks and more color schemes than I can remember. Last week he even rearranged things in my studio.

"I can't stand it anymore. If Jake doesn't move his office, I intend to move the rest of us out."

JAKE'S TURN

"It is unfair to ask me to separate my work life from my home life, my emotional life," said forty-two-year-old Jake, a tall, blond man with dazzling blue eyes. "The genuine creators, the innovators, the men I admire and venerate—men like Frank Lloyd Wright, produced and flourished while working from their homes. My home is a means of self-expression, my card of introduction.

"Most of my work has been done with churches. Almost all the church building committees I've dealt with were inexperienced people, doubtful of their own judgment, and skeptical of me and my ability. Once they entered our house, however, they quickly responded to the cheerful informality of the living room and almost visibly relaxed. Consequently, we could concentrate on the job without wasting time. Modern commercial buildings are sterile and cold.

"Besides, creativity doesn't just switch itself on at nine A.M. and off at five P.M. like an electric light bulb. Just recently an idea struck me in the middle of the night. I rushed downstairs to my drawing board and in fifteen minutes had the solution to a nagging problem that had perplexed me for a week. It would surely have escaped my mind by morning.

"Kylie has been sleeping on the living room couch, despite the lumpiness she incessantly complains of, to punish me for differences aired earlier in the day. At lunch, she cooked hamburger and beans for the fourth time that week. She allowed Ellen to smear her high chair and face with applesauce, rather than locate a bib for her. Kylie is hopelessly disorganized and lets our kids get away with murder. It is futile for me to enforce decent standards of behavior, to teach our youngsters the joy and beauty of discipline and order.

"Dinner that evening was worse than lunch. When I told my son and older daughters to wash their hands, Kylie said their hands were clean enough. They mocked me openly, shoved each other, and turned the meal into chaos. I ordered all three to go outside and calm down by arranging bouquets of flowers, a task I've seen accomplish miracles with Japanese children. Kylie contradicted my orders and the youngsters became even more obstreperous.

"Although Kylie may not realize it, she constantly destroys my dignity and undermines my authority with our children. She jeers at my opinions in their presence, screams at me, slams doors, and threatens divorce. This is damaging the kids: Billy is doing badly at school; Janey has a poor appetite and is argumentative and pigheaded; Sue is nervous, bites her nails, and has begun to stutter. Before I proposed to Kylie, she promised that we would share the whole of our lives. She now speaks of my home, my kitchen, my money, and even my children as though they had no father.

"Unlike me, Kylie is an impulsive buyer. I am willing to take the time to acquire something rare or, with luck, unique. Why choose a sofa with offensive lines or fabric merely to possess a sofa? What's the

rush? The daybeds in our living room are honest and unpretentious; the blankets covering them are beautiful.

"I've heard Kylie and her mother discussing all this on the telephone many times. Every morning she hops to the telephone and broadcasts our intimate affairs to everyone in both families. Why can't she see any of this from my point of view?"

THE COUNSELOR'S TURN

"These two artistic people were making an inartistic hash of their marriage," the counselor said. "Both were exceedingly strong-willed, but Jake was the more obstinate of the two, as well as the more impractical and self-centered.

"Not that Kylie was entirely blameless. She damaged her relationship with Jake and prejudiced the children when she contradicted him in their presence. It didn't help for her to confide intimate affairs to friends and family and appeal to them for backing.

"Under the circumstances, however, her remarks and behavior were understandable. In the power struggle of their marriage, she was fighting to survive as an individual.

"Jake was acutely sensitive to color, structure, form, design, and his own reactions and feelings. However, he was insensitive to Kylie's feelings, oblivious to her wishes and rights as a wife. He endeavored to rule the entire household. Since he was always on the scene, Kylie and the children were under observation day and night.

"It wasn't until Jake invaded every corner of Kylie's realm as a wife, a mother, and an artist that she rebelled. When she taunted him with the fact of her financial independence and threatened to pack up the children and move out, she was desperate.

"The real danger to this marriage, and, for that matter, the primary flaw in Jake's personality, was his overwhelming drive for perfection. His expectation of a forever serene household was ridiculous. I told him so. I also told him that his complaints that outside distractions interfered with his inspiration were nonsense. The main obstacle to his work lay in his own personality. Jake himself wasted time and energy and delayed his labors at the drawing board. He continually dissipated his creativity and interrupted the flow of his talent by thrusting himself into what should have been Kylie's sphere. He did not allow himself the freedom of an uncluttered mind so he could carry out his commissions promptly (he was tardy in nearly all his projects), and he hardly gave Kylie room to breathe.

"It wasn't easy for a man as opinionated and articulate as Jake to acknowledge that he and Kylie could and should divide the areas of decision-making in their marriage. However, he was extremely anxious to avoid a separation and, eventually, he and Kylie were able to reach a number of compromises.

"They discussed money at great length. Although it seemed impractical at first for the family to live solely on his earnings and bank Kylie's income from her trust fund, she agreed to give this a trial. Jake realized this would mean Kylie must sacrifice the social value of her service to the P.T.A., her work with charities, her volunteer work in the Head Start program. He then agreed that the value of her contribution to the community outweighed the artificial soothing of his vanity. Kylie now pays the sitters and cleaning women from her income without protest from Jake, and he tries not to interfere with their efficiency.

"After our first interview, and with Jake's permission, Kylie went furniture shopping. She selected three sofas in different styles and periods for him to choose from, as well as three sets of dining room chairs and so on. Within these parameters, he picked out the pieces he liked the most or, perhaps, disliked the least. Within a month, the house was completely furnished.

"It is six months since I have seen Kylie and Jake, but they send me bulletins from time to time. Jake is now established in a roomy office in a midtown professional building and his clients, a little to his chagrin, do not seem to miss the charm of his 'at home' atmosphere. Indeed, his clients have multiplied and he has broadened his architectural horizons, entering the field of low-cost housing. He still keeps a drawing board at home, where he may work if inspiration dynamites him in the middle of the night.

"Children mirror the tensions of their parents; so with tensions lessened by the daytime absence of a temperamental father, Billy and his sisters have become less unruly. Jake is surprised and pleased to have them greet him affectionately when he comes home. The marriage of artists is seldom calm, but essentially they pursue the same objectives and have the same goals. Kylie and Jake belong together—and now they know it."

5 THINGS YOU SHOULD NEVER SAY IN AN ARGUMENT

Every couple fights. The problem is not that you argue, but how you argue can make one partner feel put down all the time and your marriage like a constant competition. When tempers flare, however, it can be hard to step on the verbal brakes. The following phrases, or ones similar to them, should have no place in your disagreements if you hope to resolve conflicts lovingly:

1. "This is just like the time last year when you . . ." Resolving conflicts with love and acceptance means you don't get hysterical—or historical. Reeling off a laundry list of your partner's past transgressions proves that you never forget, or forgive.

2. "My mother always said you'd never amount to anything." Did he marry you or your mother? Third-party criticism is inflammatory and destructive to any peace process.

3. "And you're a lousy lover, too." Demeaning, hostile, or sarcastic remarks, teasing, or poking fun at someone's vulnerabilities is beside the point and will cast a shadow on your relationship long after an argument winds down.

4. "Well, if you can, I can, too." Tit-for-tat arguing is kid stuff. Leave it in the playground.

5. "I want a separation [or divorce]." This is one of the most hurtful things partners can say to each other. Threatening to abandon the marriage tells your mate that you don't think he or the marriage is important. Why should he try to resolve an argument if that's the way you really feel?

"HE NEEDS ME TOO MUCH"

Doug had always been the strong one until illness robbed him of his ability to walk. Could Lisa find enough strength for the two of them?

LISA'S TURN

"How do you plan your life when you have no idea what you'll be planning for?" wondered Lisa, a thirty-two-year-old newspaper reporter. "In six months, Doug could be in a wheelchair. The uncertainty is terrible. I have no idea how people like Michael J. Fox and his wife cope with a debilitating illness.

"Until recently, I thought our life couldn't get much better. Then last spring, Doug was on a business trip. He called me one night and mentioned that he'd felt a funny sensation in his leg earlier that day when he'd gone for his morning jog. 'I'm not in any pain, but I can't push off on my foot,' he told me. At first, we thought it might be a muscle spasm or a sprained ankle, so we didn't think much of it. A few weeks later, however, he felt that weakness again and decided to get it checked out. We were totally unprepared for the diagnosis.

"Doug has a mysterious neurological condition that is gradually robbing him of the use of his legs. The condition is not fatal. We were extremely relieved to hear that, but it's still a crushing blow to Doug and to me.

"Doctors have no clue as to what caused this illness, which is very frustrating. Right now, there's no treatment, let alone a cure. His doctors said there was nothing we could do except watch Doug grow weaker and more helpless.

196

"Well, I refused to accept that. I've spent hours on the phone with specialists, and even more time on the computer doing Internet research. I've tried to convince Doug to consider alternative medicine, but he's so stubborn. We've had terrible fights just because I want him to see an acupuncturist. Why is he acting this way?

"Of course, Doug is bullheaded about a lot of things, and we're having intense arguments about such stupid stuff as our opinions of movies. Otherwise, I talk and Doug pulls back and doesn't say a word. I'm not like that; I don't have it in me to be quiet if there's something weighing on my mind.

"I'm overwhelmed with worries. Our five-year-old son, Max, has been great; kids are so resilient and sweet. But how is he going to feel once he realizes that his dad can't play baseball or soccer with him? What if this condition leaves Doug unable to make love? We've always had a great sex life. Are we going to have to move to a single-level house so he won't have to climb any stairs, or totally remodel the house to accommodate a wheelchair? Doug is a broker for small businesses, helping people who want to sell their companies. He can do his job from anywhere with a computer, fax, and PalmPilot. But what if he becomes too disabled to work? My salary at the newspaper isn't enough to support the three of us.

"At this point, only our family and close friends know about Doug's illness. To look at him, you wouldn't notice right away that there was something wrong. Doug isn't in pain. He can still walk short distances on his own, though sometimes he loses his balance, and he's taken some bad falls. But his condition is steadily getting worse. At first he could still ski and mountain bike, but now he can't. That's very difficult for a guy who's used to skiing double black diamond slopes, and his mood swings from anger to despair and back again. How do I help him? Doctors predict that the paralysis will affect only his legs, but what if they're wrong?

"I was raised to deal with problems head-on. I was a happy kid, the younger of two girls. We grew up in a suburb of Atlanta; my mother was a high school teacher and my father was a lawyer. They're one of the happiest couples I know, and they instilled in me the belief that you control your own destiny.

"I majored in journalism in college, and found a job as a reporter for a paper after graduation. Around the same time I met Doug, and we became fast friends. By the following winter, I realized I was in love with him. We're such soul mates that we can finish each other's sentences. Though Doug was reluctant to commit again—he had been married before and still had bitter feelings about the relationship—he finally agreed, and we had a lovely wedding on the beach where we met.

"I got pregnant before long. After Max was born, we moved to Denver. We wanted to raise our child in wide-open spaces and indulge our love for the outdoors. Everything about our lives was perfect until this happened.

"Though Doug has never come out and said so, I know he's afraid I'll leave him. I'll never do that; I love him with all my heart. But it's hard to keep from worrying obsessively. Suppose he becomes totally dependent on me in a few years? And what if I can't deal with that?"

DOUG'S TURN

"I don't want to ruin Lisa's life," said Doug, thirty-nine, choking back tears. "She shouldn't stay with me simply because she feels sorry for me.

"I suppose I'm in a state of shock. It's not easy coming to terms with being sick. I don't know where to turn for answers, or even what questions to ask. Lisa pressures me relentlessly to try all these alternative treatments, but I don't want to go that route. Some of our arguments get pretty heated, and Lisa's always had a tendency to talk on and on about things that are bothering her. Maybe I do retreat into my shell when she rambles, but I can't help it. She needs to let me handle this in my own way.

"I admit that there are nights when I lie awake, wondering if I'll die or become so helpless that I'll barely have a life at all. Not to brag, but I was always a very good athlete. Last winter, I was skiing the most challenging slopes. Now I can't even stand upright on skis, and that's a terrible blow. To lose that is to lose a part of who I am.

"Getting around the house is a struggle, too. I can't climb stairs easily or run around the yard with my son. Not long ago, Max started to chase after a neighbor's dog, and I got very upset because he turned a corner and I couldn't catch him. Just the week before, I'd been able to keep up, and it scared me to see how quickly I was losing my strength.

"I sense that the few people who know about my situation don't know what to say or do, and that makes it awkward for me. I'm not into self-pity, and I'd rather not broadcast my problem to the world. It's mine to deal with, and I will. That's how I was raised by my hardworking parents. Pop, who had a house-painting business, was strict, very much of the old school when it came to parenting. There were five of us boys, so Ma had her hands full.

"I got married right out of college, which was a big mistake. The only good thing to come out of that relationship was my beautiful daughter, Lena. She lives three thousand miles away now, but I see her whenever I can, and she's been very supportive of me through all this.

"Those were difficult times; in addition to my crumbling marriage, my two older brothers were killed in a freak car accident. It took me a while to work through all those devastating losses. Then I met Lisa. She is a special woman: smart, fun, beautiful, spiritual. I was filled with such hope for the future. Then I get hit with this new curveball. It's just not fair.

"Now I'm terrified for myself, for Lisa, and for Max. What will our lives be like next year? In five years? Am I going to end up an invalid, relying on other people to feed and dress me? Just when I've begun to accept the fact that I can't do some activity, another part of me fails. How do you live with so many question marks?

THE COUNSELOR'S TURN

"Dealing with a chronic illness can send even the most stable person into an emotional tailspin," said the counselor. "Strong as Lisa and Doug's marriage was, their inability to express their feelings clearly and resolve conflicts made it difficult for them to face the challenges of Doug's disability, much less reclaim their joy and intimacy.

"For example, Lisa was always a go-getter who faced problems by shifting into high gear and searching for solutions. In the face of Doug's illness, however, she was beginning to feel helpless. Perhaps because she had a strong sense of fairness, she was prone to anger when she felt she wasn't being heard or understood. We worked to pinpoint the causes of her anger, such as the times when Doug resisted her suggestions about treatment. Being more aware of these personal triggers helped Lisa recognize them and calm down before she went out of control.

"Doug had faced his brothers' deaths by cutting himself off from his emotions. But with this new setback, he needed a different set of skills in order to cope with his illness and keep his marriage thriving. 'You must be more flexible,' I told Doug. 'Learn to assess when to accept your disability and when to look for other solutions. You must also allow your wife and family to be there for you. They want to help.' It was hard for Doug, but he started sharing his fears with his loved ones and drawing strength from them.

"Lisa and Doug needed to understand that it was okay for them to deal with the situation in their own different ways. Doing research on the Web and interviewing doctors made Lisa feel more in control. I told Doug, 'Giving in to your wife a little—for instance, trying meditation or massage—may help your relationship in the long run.'

"At the same time, I advised Lisa to be respectful of the fact

HOLDING ON TO "YOU" WITHOUT LOSING "US"

There are difficult times in every marriage, with or without a serious illness. Some are predictable—a child's adolescence, an elderly parent's death—others aren't. One of the qualities that separates a strong marriage from a failing one is each partner's ability to make the other feel respected and cherished even in crisis. When all energies are focused simply on coping, that's a tough task. Many people suppress their feelings while operating on a kind of emotional autopilot. After all, how can hope be nourished when they're not sure how the story will end? Well, no one can predict the future, and while you may not have it all, you can still appreciate what you've got. A grateful spirit brightens mood, boosts energy, and infuses daily life with a sense of abundance that will inevitably spread to those around you. Hard as it is, try to:

1. Register the good things. How often do you find yourself dwelling on the negative, cataloging all the troubles you have, the mean things people have done to you, the things they failed to do? Instead, train yourself to notice good things, large and small, in your life. Store up kindnesses that have come your way—a colleague's helpfulness, a friend's encouragement—and when sorrow fills your heart and mind, guide your thoughts toward them.

2. Don't ignore the needs of the healthy while you attend to the needs of the ill. Reconnect with friends and family and engage in the activities that bring you joy. Totally denying your own needs won't help a loved one heal faster. Don't hesitate to seek professional counseling for children and adolescents; they may need help

sorting through their feelings. You could also try writing down your feelings: What has been the most painful part of this experience? What did I need the most and was unable to receive? Discussing your responses can deepen understanding of each other's experiences.

3. Comfort and nurture equally. Like actors in a small theater ensemble group, you need to work hard to support each other's happiness. Everyone needs a cheerleader—someone who rejoices at our victories, scowls at our adversaries, and encourages us to keep going when all we feel like doing is crawling into bed for a good cry. To do that, you must be able to carefully observe the subtleties of a partner's body language and words—to hear, in essence, what may not be said. Can you distinguish when a spouse is really angry, or just blowing off steam? Between everyday tiredness and sheer exhaustion? Between sadness and despair? Between a bad day and real depression? By replenishing emotional reserves, you restore self-esteem and confidence for yourself, your partner, and your future together.

4. Stay psychologically open to new possibilities. With or without a crisis, a marriage is always changing. A willingness to reshape your relationship at each crossroad is essential if the marriage is to endure. When you approach change as a positive rather than a negative factor, you widen your view of the future and prevent yourself from settling for second best.

5. Reminisce about the good times and return to the luminous memories you have—your first date, the first time you made love. Music often helps rekindle happy moments, so play a tape you both enjoy; if possible, revisit places where good times were had—a favorite restaurant, the theater, a cottage in the mountains.

6. Nurture a vision for which you can both be thankful. In marriages that last, couples invariably talk regularly about where they see themselves in five, ten, twenty years. Not that they cement every detail; rather, they create a sense that "we are here for the long haul . . . this marriage has a history—and a future." From time to time, ask each other: What do you want to do when you retire? If you won the lottery, what would you buy? How do you feel about having grandchildren?

that Doug's physical condition and emotional state were constantly changing. 'Tune in to his moods, and be accepting of the times when he doesn't want to talk. He needs time to grieve and to reassess his abilities,' I told her. As Lisa gave Doug more room, he became more responsive to her suggestions. He went for an acupuncture session; though it didn't seem to work for him, he's not ruling out other alternative remedies.

"During one session, when Doug seemed particularly sad, I said: 'You may have trouble walking, but you still have control over your upper body, as well as other, more important strengths like your mind and feelings. You're a wonderful husband and father. You manage your business brilliantly. You can still go to the theater, to concerts. You have a rich, full life ahead.'

"Then I challenged him: 'If you love skiing so much, why did you quit? Colorado has an excellent program for disabled skiers, but you've never looked into it.' Doug agreed to meet the head of the program for lessons in the new mono-ski for disabled athletes, a sledlike device with special poles. 'I was so scared,' Doug said, his voice breaking. 'But somehow I did it.'

"Doug and Lisa are learning how to manage day-to-day living. Max is starting to ask questions about his father, which they're answering honestly, and they are looking into support groups for persons with disabilities and their spouses. Said Lisa, 'We know we have more issues ahead. We'll probably either have to move or do major renovations on the house to make it wheelchair-accessible. But we won't worry about that until the stairs become a real problem.'

"These two don't have the luxury of being able to plan for the future. 'Nobody really knows what will happen to them,' Lisa said. 'We're focusing on living in the moment.' Doug added, 'I'm not ready to give up our life. It's just a matter of finding ways to do the things we love for as long as we can.'"

"HE'S NEVER HOME"

Sean traveled constantly for his job, only to criticize Cecelia as soon as he was home. Can a couple learn to live with—and without—each other?

"Here we go again, fighting about Christmas," said Cecilia, thirty-five, an at-home mother of two. "Sean has always disliked the holidays because his family, who was very poor, rarely celebrated anything. He doesn't share my excitement about putting up the tree, decorating the house and baking cookies. And if I don't consult him before buying gifts for the kids, he accuses me of spending too much.

"Well, what am I supposed to do? As an officer in the merchant marine, Sean is at sea four months out of the year, and if he isn't home by early December, I have to do all the shopping. That's fine with me, but I can't stand being criticized and second-guessed for every choice I make.

"I've always been very responsible. I grew up in the Midwest, the oldest of four. My mother left my abusive father when I was five, and we never saw him again. Mom was incredibly independent and self-sacrificing, and I learned a lot from her. Still, I missed not having a dad.

"In my junior year of college, I fell in love with a classmate and unexpectedly became pregnant with my son, Charlie. I married my boyfriend, but it didn't last long. I managed to finish my teaching degree though, and taught elementary school for several years.

"I had no intention of getting into another relationship until I met Sean at a friend's wedding. Every day after that for three months, he called to ask me out until he finally wore me down. I was pleasantly surprised; he was charming, gentle, funny, and down-to-earth. We married, and Sean adopted Charlie, who's now fifteen. After I had Christina nine years ago, I quit teaching and opened a home-based gift-basket business.

"I was determined not to let us become another failed military marriage. Before the wedding, Sean and I even went for a few counseling sessions at church to talk about the problems we might face. Honestly, I wasn't concerned about Sean's traveling, though it is hard not being able to speak to each other for months. Even when his ship is in port, it's expensive for him to call collect from places like Kenya or Thailand, and the time differences are always difficult. At night, I'm so tired I don't always feel like writing long letters. But Sean gets upset and says I'm hiding things from him if I send a short note.

"The first few days after Sean gets back are like a honeymoon. Then the trouble starts. He expects time to stand still while he's away and gets upset when he realizes it hasn't. When he comes down hard on Charlie and Christina for minor matters, then says 'Let's go fishing' half an hour later, they're not going to forget everything and rush off with their dad like they did when they were younger. So Sean feels hurt.

"I'm forever playing mediator between my husband and the children. Sean doesn't understand that kids act up every once in a while, or that it's normal for them to leave their rooms a mess or forget to turn off the lights no matter how much

you nag. I've learned to pick my battles, but Sean fights the kids on every front and tells me I'm too easy on them.

"Our biggest arguments by far, though, are about money. I try to keep to a budget, but Sean accuses me of wasting his paycheck. I hate having to defend every little thing I buy, from grape jelly to Christina's soccer gear. The public schools here aren't the greatest, so Charlie, who's very bright, wants to transfer to a private high school next year and take the advanced courses he needs to get into an Ivy League college. We can afford the tuition if we budget carefully, but Sean won't hear of it.

"I admit I've made mistakes with money. When I was starting my business, I ran up five thousand dollars on my credit card. For a long time, I kept it a secret from Sean, but I finally confessed, and we're paying it off. He was understanding at first, but now whenever a financial problem crops up, he flings that old debt back in my face.

"Sex is a huge issue, too. Sean wants it all the time. Well, I'm not going to drop everything just because my husband happens to be home and in the mood. Not long ago, he asked me to tell him what I like in bed. That's not really my thing, but I made a suggestion about something I wanted to try, and he accused me of having an affair! 'You didn't learn that from me,' he said. So I'm damned if I do and damned if

I don't. The other night, I refused to sleep with Sean, and he hasn't spoken to me since. Not that he really cares what I think. He talks, I listen, and if I open my mouth, he says I'm wrong.

"I want our loving relationship back. But if something doesn't change soon, I may have to leave."

"I don't understand my wife at all," sighed Sean, forty-two. "Cecilia knows the holidays always stress me out, and that I worry about money. So why does she have to go crazy buying gifts? Can't we give Charlie and Christina one nice present each and be done with it?

"I'm tired of feeling out of place in my own family. When I'm at sea, I miss Cecilia like you wouldn't believe, but she doesn't seem happy to see me when I return home. I feel as if I'm intruding in this special world she's created. I don't get any affection or sex from Cecilia, or any respect from her or the kids. She's also stopped writing the long letters I used to look forward to receiving. We don't have Internet access on my ship, so mail is the only way I can keep up with home life. Is that too much to ask?

"Everyone is on their best behavior for maybe a week when I'm around, and then it all falls apart. My kids ignore me and refuse to do the simplest things, like turn off the TV when they leave the room. When I try to lecture or punish them, Cecilia won't back me up. The other day I asked Charlie to help me stack some firewood. He moved one log, and then wandered off. Why should I pay several thousand dollars to send him to a fancy private school when he can't muster any courtesy for his father?

"I think I have a perfect right to question my wife's judgment, especially when it comes to money. I don't understand where it all goes, Cecilia rarely bothers to balance the checkbook. Then there's that huge debt of hers, which took me completely by surprise. I hate feeling that unpleasant things are going on behind my back. I had enough of that when I was growing up.

"I wasn't the happiest kid. Cecilia is right when she says I don't have pleasant memories of the holidays. I was raised on a farm in Pennsylvania by parents who were constantly fighting; only when I was older did I find out that my dad was drinking away his paycheck and sleeping around. I was the only boy, and in my dad's eyes, I couldn't do anything right. He always said I'd never amount to anything. My mom was tense about money because we never had any, and she taught me how to be thrifty, which I think is a virtue.

"I had no direction when I graduated from high school. I worked odd jobs and spent several years in the Marines. I joined the merchant marine in my late twenties because I love the sea and traveling, and it seemed like a good opportunity. Still, it's not easy being away from my family for so long.

"You know, I never mean to tear Cecilia down. I love her, and I'm doing everything I can to keep this marriage together. If we could just figure out a way to stop butting heads, we'd be fine."

THE COUNSELOR'S TURN

"Sean and Cecilia's issues are similar to the ones couples face when one spouse works long hours or travels often, only to come home and feel like a stranger," said the counselor. "It's also easy for the spouse at home to establish a routine where she's no longer dependent, emotionally or physically, on her partner. But it is precisely interdependence that deepens intimacy and allows a marriage to flourish.

"Sean was desperate for the love and attention he lacked when he was at sea. Feeling unappreciated and craving a connection, he badgered Cecilia to have sex with him and to include him in the family decision-making. As the son of an alcoholic, philandering father, Sean had grown up wary and mistrustful of others.

"His neediness, suspicion, and second-guessing, however, robbed Cecilia of her confidence. Competent at handling things on her own, she found it hard to switch gears to bring Sean into household decisions when he was home. The more he criticized her and urged her to talk, the more she pulled away, which Sean took to mean that she didn't love him.

"At our first meeting, we established a commitment to work on the marriage. I also told Sean that while his anger over his wife's credit-card bill was justified, it was time to set that matter to rest and stop rehashing past mistakes in order for both of them to move on.

"We discussed some basic communication skills. Their first assignment was to write a letter to each other every week addressing five issues: what made them angry, what made them sad, what they were afraid of, what they regretted, and what they wanted to happen. This not only helped Sean express what he wanted, but also showed him how negatively he came across at times.

"Talking about their letters helped Sean understand Cecilia's need for space, so he tries not to pester her. Feeling less hounded, Cecilia now has a better understanding of his need for affection and reassurance, which he lacked growing up. Once their anger and resentment dissipated, the emotional and physical intimacy both of them yearned for was restored.

"Cecilia had work to do, as well. She admitted that she wasn't the most efficient bookkeeper; so she balanced the checkbook and looked for ways to handle their budget as effectively as she ran her business. This reassured Sean that she wasn't squandering their money and made it easier for them to agree on how to spend it. For instance, they agreed that Charlie would benefit from going to private school, so Sean enrolled him in the winter semester.

"It was also true that Cecilia was subtly undermining Sean's authority as a parent. I encouraged her to involve him in choosing family activities, and to be more consistent about disciplining the children, instead of letting Dad be the bad guy. As he learned how to control his temper, Sean also learned not to get upset over every little annoying thing the children did, which made a big difference.

"Sean and Cecilia now make a concerted effort to set aside time each week when he's home to discuss what's working for them and what's not. They also go out on dates without the kids so they can talk and simply be together. Knowing it's important to stay in touch while Sean is away, Cecilia is more conscientious about writing. Keeping a diary helps her remember important details to include in her letters.

"Although there are times when these two slip back into their old patterns, the difference is that they're now aware of when they're doing it and know how to stop. They're looking forward to spending the holidays as a family this year. Sean doesn't worry about Cecilia's Christmas shopping anymore. In fact, he even suggested they could go to the mall together to pick up a few last-minute stocking stuffers for the kids."

WHEN NOTHING YOU DO IS GOOD ENOUGH

Power struggles often flare when one partner tries to help but finds his or her suggestions consistently rebuffed, or when one partner feels criticized and ignored despite myriad attempts to please or be heard. If your marriage feels like a tug-of-war over issues large and small, break the cycle by:

1. Reminding yourself that you are entitled to your feelings and opinions and have every right to speak up: "I feel offended by what you just said," or "That was inconsiderate." If insulting behavior continues, try to control yourself and not lash out wildly in defense. Instead, walk away. You'll send a far more powerful message.

2. Choosing your words with care, to avoid fanning the flames. Speak firmly, but in a way that doesn't demean your partner. Stick to what therapists call the "When you . . . I feel" model introduced in the previous chapter. For instance, Cecilia might say, "When you overrule what I've told the kids, I feel hurt. I feel that you're saying my ideas and opinions don't count."

3. Not responding to criticism by being critical. This only escalates the argument and deepens the power struggle.

4. Not playing Freud. Just because you may be savvier about the psychological nuances of your partner's behavior doesn't mean he or she wants you to share your knowledge. Leave the psychoanalysis to the marriage counselor and instead, focus your insight on how to be empathic and really listen to what a spouse is trying to share. If you don't think you can respond civilly, say so: "I'm too angry to talk about this right now. After I've had a chance to calm down, let's talk again."

5. Considering whether there might be some validity to what your partner is saying. If there is, can you do something differently? Comments become criticism when they're exaggerated and off-base. However, many times, if we allow ourselves to admit it, there just may be a kernel of truth in what a spouse is saying. Think: Is there something you could do that would make your interactions with your mate smoother and happier? Then just do it.

"My In-Laws Are Driving Me Crazy"

Ever since Don's parents moved in, Leslie insists, their marriage has disintegrated. How can she make him understand she feels like a stranger in her own home?

LESLIE'S TURN

"I want a divorce," said Leslie, a thirty-year-old petite blonde. "Our five-year marriage is hopeless and I don't want Don to talk me out of ending it.

"The thought of going it alone with an infant daughter is pretty scary, but I feel so alone already, it can't be much different. Since Don's parents moved in with us, he's turned into a different person. We never talk anymore. We just scream.

"Actually, it was my idea to move my in-laws here. They had retired and moved to California, but they were very unhappy there. They had health problems, too, so I thought that if they lived with us, we'd be in a better position to help them if they needed it. Pooling our financial assets to buy a nice house made sense, too.

"Don had reservations about my idea, but I convinced him. Actually, I had never met his parents—they couldn't come to our wedding because his mom had been hospitalized with heart problems and didn't want to make the long trip. But we had talked on the phone and got along great. I was so naive!

"An only child, I grew up in a very small town—there were six people in my high school graduating class. My dad came from a wealthy family, but when I was ten, he was cheated out of his hardware business by a dishonest partner. We lost everything. My parents sued the man, and the only thing that kept my parents going was the hope that justice would prevail. We ultimately lost the court case, however. After the decision, my parents were devastated and they divorced a short time later. I never see my father and speak to my mother only rarely.

"When I was nineteen, I moved to San Antonio, the nearest big city, and found a job as a clerk in a department store. You can't imagine what a culture shock that was. But after five years I had settled into a quiet life. I think I fell in love with Don the first moment I saw him. I had gone to a club with my girlfriend, something I had never done before, and there he was in his Army uniform. We danced a few times and then he asked me out. Part of me was terrified; he was from Boston and my small-town upbringing made me wary of big-city types.

"Don was wearing a suit and tie when he picked me up for our first date and he brought me yellow roses, too. We went to an elegant restaurant, another first for me.

"Don had been married and had two small children. His wife had left him for another man—his best friend, no less—and my heart went out to him. But everything seemed to be perfect between us. Don was making plans for a wedding as well as for the rest of our lives, which was fine with me. He had everything under control.

"I suppose I was so blinded by love I didn't realize how wrapped up Don was in his military career. This man lives and breathes his job. Don

is a medical lab technician and he signs on for every committee at work; to him, that's part of being a 'good soldier.' So, even though we were married, I wasn't seeing very much of him at all.

"On top of that, his children— Caitlin was five at the time, and Jeremy was three—came to visit every other weekend. After an hour of token fatherhood, he'd inevitably have to go to work. I'd be left to entertain his kids.

"But I never said anything. I just didn't know how to bring it up and thought I would sound selfish if I did. Instead, I decided to surprise Don by joining the military myself shortly after we married. My clerk's job had no future and I wanted to share Don's life more. I hoped it would bring us closer.

"Don was furious; he resents any decision that's not his. But he came around after he went with me to the recruiter and helped set me up in the computer training program.

"His parents arrived just before I came back home after my basic training. I walked in the door of our tiny apartment to find the whole thing rearranged. There was even a sign hanging on the refrigerator saying 'Alice's Kitchen'—that's Don's mother's name. She did ask if I minded and, of course, I said no, but it really broke my heart.

"I'll never forget our first Thanksgiving morning together. Don's mother and I were getting dinner ready. In my mind, I had imagined it would be wonderful, the two of us in the kitchen talking and cooking. That morning, I was peeling potatoes and left a little skin on one. Don's mother didn't want to ruffle my feathers, so instead, she told Don to tell me. He came in and whispered in my ear, 'Be sure to get all the skin off.' I could have died.

"But that's now typical of our family life. My mother-in-law complains to Don about everything I do. She puts me down when he's not around. Don will say things like, 'Mom, you'll have to teach Leslie how to make a pot roast like this.' He doesn't realize that every time I try to help her with anything, she informs me that her son has never eaten anything like that and never will.

"On top of this, Don and his mother argue all the time, yelling and swearing at each other. I'm not used to that. Don's father pretends he doesn't even hear them, hiding behind his newspaper. Whenever I try to talk to Don about how I feel, he tells me I'm being too sensitive.

"I soon realized I'd become the outsider in my own home." All the spontaneity had gone out of our marriage. No more romantic things, like tossing a blanket in the back-seat of the car and heading to the woods for an impromptu picnic.

"Despite the distance between us, Don and I were determined to have a baby. At the time Lindsey was born, she was the only bright spot in my life. We had been married almost four years. I put Lindsey in day care—my mother-in-law couldn't handle the responsibility of a baby—and returned to work when she was six weeks old. Don was working crazy hours and I was left to deal with his mother. Don and I were hardly speaking. I know I shouldn't have, but I began bringing the baby into our bed to sleep. I admit it was my way of telling Don it was hands off. I was so mad.

"When Lindsey was two months old, we found a house we all agreed on. I was so relieved, thinking, again naively, that once we had a bigger place, my mother-in-law and I would stop getting on each other's nerves. But things got worse.

"I've had it. I have to face the fact that Don and I are strangers. The worst part is that Don has become compulsive just like his mother. The other day he had a fit because I had the coasters for drinks on the coffee table instead of the table where they used to be.

"I love Don, but our marriage is in a shambles and the only way I can survive is to get out. You've got to help me convince him that divorce is best for everyone concerned."

DON'S TURN

"This is just like Leslie," said Don, thirty-seven, a tall, serious man with a precise, disciplined manner. "She

211

wants a divorce, and I'm the last one to know about it.

"Leslie operates entirely on emotion and impulse. Like when she joined the military. Without one word to me, she quit her job and enlisted. Most wives would discuss a career change with their husbands, but Leslie had to 'surprise' me. I found out from a message on the answering machine. I don't enjoy surprises. My first wife surprised me by running off with my best friend.

"I love Leslie and I love our daughter. I won't deny we've had major problems, but I did try to warn her about having my parents move in with us. She was determined we'd be this big happy family, and now that the reality doesn't match her fantasy, she's ready to pack her bags and quit.

"There's also no doubt that I come from a vocal family. Yelling and swearing were commonplace when I was growing up. It doesn't mean anything, and I can't understand why Leslie goes into such a tailspin. My father was always, well, complacent, so I guess I expected Leslie to tune it out like he did.

"I should tell you that my father is a recovered alcoholic, but before he joined Alcoholics Anonymous, it was sort of Mom and me against the world—my two sisters are seven and ten years older than I am. We never knew from one day to the next what he would be like when he got home from work. I think yelling allowed us to let off steam over the frustration and anger we were feeling about Dad. We always knew there was love underneath.

"I moved out when I went to college, which went over like a lead balloon with my mother; she had depended on me for so long. I loved my independence, but I wasn't especially excited about college. Some Vietnam veterans in my classes got me interested in the military, though, so I decided to drop out and enlist in the Army.

"Except for a couple of low moments, I even loved basic training. I'd had twelve years of parochial schooling, so the discipline wasn't anything new to me. The rest of the guys were in shock from being yelled at all the time, but again, that wasn't new for me either. Once I got over the shock of Leslie's enlistment, I was proud that she wanted to serve in the Army, too.

"Leslie was so easy to love, so sincere and refreshing. When I met her, I had just gotten divorced and I felt shy and awkward dating again. I didn't think she'd go out with me; she didn't know I was just as excited and nervous as she was. I think I fell in love with her that night, too.

"Then, immediately after we married, Leslie started campaigning to have my parents move in with us. I tried to tell her that my mother is the kind of person who is happy being unhappy, but she wouldn't listen. I loved Leslie's compassion.

Besides, splitting the cost with them was the only way we could afford a house, which we both wanted.

"Right away, I felt the pressure. I was working long hours in the lab; the research we were involved with at the time was critical. I was stressed to the breaking point, and suddenly I had to deal with a new bride, my parents, and disputes over potato peelings.

"You know, Leslie never told me how much it bothered her that my mother rearranged the furniture. And she never told me that my mother criticized her cooking. I thought Leslie was relieved that Mother was there to cook and clean since she had a new full-time job.

"Look, I know my mother can be difficult. But it's easier to placate her than to fight her. I've been doing that all my life. Why can't Leslie? Her remark about token fatherhood hurts. She was the one who wanted to be close to my kids. I thought she wanted the time to develop her own relationship with them.

"Lately, I feel my world is closing in on me: a stressful job, a crushing mortgage, a new baby, an ex-wife, and two kids. And I feel guilty because I can't make peace between my wife and my parents.

"Leslie says I've changed. Well, I think she's the one who's changed. She is no longer interested in being close and makes it clear she doesn't want to have sex, since she has been bringing Lindsey into bed with us.

"No, I don't want a divorce. I'm as sad as my wife that our family is torn apart."

THE COUNSELOR'S TURN

"These two were struggling with so many pressures that even a couple who communicated well would be under stress," said the counselor. "Leslie and Don had such serious communication problems, I wasn't surprised that they were in turmoil. Although it was clear that the arrangement with Don's parents was not working, both Leslie and Don continued to feel guilty about it. Neither was able to discuss the subject without exploding. These two weren't in charge of their marriage—Don's parents held the reins. But before they could find a way to make their own decision they had to believe they had a right to.

"Don and Leslie are sincere, likable people, and both of them had known considerable pain. They also shared a genuine compassion for the needs of others. Unfortunately, from the beginning of their relationship, they had put everything and everyone ahead of themselves. And they never had the chance to establish themselves as a couple before Don's parents moved in.

"Like many children of alcoholics, Don yearned for stability and order. His idealized vision of military life and responsibility gave him a convenient excuse to ignore the problems in his marriage. Leslie had also been raised in an unpredictable, emotionally barren home. On a life-long quest for the happy family life she had lost at an early age, she desperately hoped her in-laws would fill the void.

"When they met, Leslie and Don each perceived the other as having the missing piece they needed to make their life complete. Leslie was attracted by Don's big-city background; he was the sophisticated man who would be decisive and educate her in the ways of the world. However, Leslie gave him far more credit in this department than he deserved. Having attended an all-male high school, Don's experience with the opposite sex was limited: Shy, demure Leslie seemed ideal compared to his wayward first wife and domineering mother.

"Don's assessment of their basic personalities was correct. He operated on logic; Leslie operated on emotion. This combination of 'feeler' and 'thinker' can be very effective in a marriage when they complement each other. Unfortunately, by the time I saw these two, the qualities that had attracted them to each other had become intimidating and irritating. My goal was to build on their genuine love and concern for each other's welfare.

"During our first few sessions, Don and Leslie tended to talk more to me than to each other. But in time, and with my guidance, they grew more comfortable expressing their feelings to each other. During one session, they discovered that they both yearned for time alone together but had never made it a priority. Now they've agreed to hire a baby-sitter every other Saturday night so they can go out alone. They'll reserve every other Sunday for a family outing with all three children. They've also promised to discuss any new plans or extra projects with each other before committing to do them. Leslie also realized that bringing their daughter into bed was a childish way of getting back at her husband and she's agreed not to do it.

"Because of their poor communication skills, this couple ran into problems whenever conflict arose. I pointed out that Leslie's stoic refusal to vent her anger and frustration was just as damaging to the peaceful home they both wanted as Don's yelling was. Don was honestly baffled at his wife's unhappiness because she never expressed her feelings to him. Once he was aware of how hurt she had been, he was much more conscious of making comments about his mother's cooking and less willing to play middleman between them. Instead of placating Mom, he tried hard to support his wife. Instead of tuning out when his mother spoke to Leslie, he came to his wife's defense whenever his mother made a cutting remark.

"At this point, I outlined some fair-fighting strategies for them: Whenever tempers started to flare, I told them, they had to agree to stick to one subject at a time. What's more, they had to give each other a chance to say everything they had to say, without criticizing, judging, or interrupting. If they couldn't resolve a dispute, they learned to set a time limit of no more than one-half hour for discussion, at which point they would table the discussion but set another time and place to resume the conversation.

"This structured discussion enabled Don and Leslie to face some hard decisions about his parents and take control of their lives. They decided to put their house on the market and look for a smaller one so that their mortgage payments would be more manageable. They were lucky and got back what they paid for the house. They've asked Don's parents to move to an apartment complex for senior citizens a few miles away, where they will be safe, cared for, and able to meet people their own age.

"As the tension eased at home, as Leslie saw her husband stand up to his mother and support her, these two began to feel much closer. Although Don will probably always be more conscious of neatness and order than Leslie is, they have both learned to laugh at his idiosyncrasy rather than argue about it.

"'We've had our own basic training in marriage,' Don said at one of our last sessions. Leslie agreed: 'I think we feel much more capable of handling problems.'"

HOW TO MAKE PEACE WITH YOUR IN-LAWS

Even if in-laws don't live with you, or even near you, power struggles that one or both of you may have with them can cast a long shadow over your marriage. As more young couples move back in with their parents, and as parents live longer and move in with adult children, the predictable problems are inevitable. While it may never be possible to develop a deep love for your in-laws, learning to tolerate their attitudes and behaviors and minimize their ability to interfere with your relationship is definitely doable. Here's how:

1. Try to maintain personal and direct contact with in-laws if possible, instead of relying on a spouse as a go-between. Don't expect instant love and affection; expect, instead, to build a relationship as you would with any person you meet. Also, by establishing an open, honest, and direct relationship in the beginning, you may well be able to avoid common divide-and-conquer in-law problems later on.

2. Try to think of your in-laws as people, separate and apart from the role they play in your life. What are their interests and strengths? Get them to share them and their enthusiasm instead of only focusing on family issues and problems when you get together.

3. Ask for in-laws' advice and opinions once in a while. Everyone likes to feel needed. While you should make it clear that you're confident you can make your own decisions, give their opinions the same consideration you would those of a friend or other adviser.

4. When problems loom, take immediate steps to talk candidly about your feelings and perspective on the issues. Use the same nonaccusatory, nonjudgmental communication skills discussed in Secret #2, "Communicate."

5. Don't routinely or offhandedly blame an in-law for problems you're having with your spouse. Your mother-in-law is an easy target, but it may not be her fault that her son isn't listening to a thing you say. Consider other issues that may be dividing you before dumping it all on your mother-in-law's shoulders.

BE MONEY SMART
Discovering What Money Can and Can't Do for Your Marriage

———•———

Rare is the couple that doesn't fight about money. In fact, surveys have singled out money matters as the number-one trigger for everything from the occasional marital skirmish to all-out war. However, while couples are ostensibly fighting over how much to spend on new deck furniture, whether a bonus should go into high-risk stocks or safer mutual funds, or even whether to save or spend at all, they are really fighting about much more than simple dollars and cents. Understanding the hidden meanings inherent in money battles is essential for avoiding irreparable damage to a marriage.

Money is, and always has been, a symbol—for power and control, for love, for security, as well as for self-esteem and accomplishment. A husband may insist on managing the family finances, without

217

consulting his wife, because that's the only way he feels confident and strong. Or he may believe that he's entitled to sign off on all financial decisions because, well, that's the way money was always managed in his family. Then, too, in a culture that judges people by their paychecks, husbands as well as wives who don't make as much money as they'd like may discover that shaky self-esteem causes ripples of discontent and resentment at various times in their relationship.

Money battles may also mask buried but volatile issues—personal values, priorities, as well as each partner's emotional needs for independence or security. Personality and family background play a part: A fiscally cautious woman may prefer to pay bills as soon as they arrive. What happens when she marries a financial juggler who waits until the last minute before writing a check? Similarly, the man from a financially secure family who marries a woman whose parents struggled to make ends meet will most likely have strikingly different attitudes about, and ways of handling, money. Each partner buys or spends according to his or her own values and emotional needs, and when those needs differ from a spouse's, the ensuing arguments can be heated and long lasting.

In fact, too often, money is a weapon in marital battles, a means of instilling guilt or expressing anger. A shopaholic wife may run up charges on a credit card because it's the only way she can retaliate against a domineering or neglectful husband. A husband may balk at supporting a wife's children from a former marriage because he's furious that her ex-husband is reneging on his obligations.

However, this chapter shows that, while it's critical to understand the hidden meanings inherent in money arguments, it's equally essential to recognize how these symbolic meanings play themselves out against a shifting backdrop of social and economic change. Today, more than two-thirds of all wives work full-time—in many cases earning as much as if not more than their spouses. In some of these marriages, the assumptions and expectations about who is entitled to make financial decisions remain as traditionally divided along gender lines as they were a generation ago. In others, they are quite different. And if both spouses don't agree on the division of financial responsibilities, clashes are inevitable.

What's more, assumptions and expectations about money may change dramatically over the lifetime of a marriage and couples must be flexible enough to accommodate them. A wife, for instance, may work full-time for a few years, stay home while the children are small, then return to work. Divorce, remarriage, and obligations to stepchildren and elderly parents also create new and potentially explosive financial battlegrounds. Each new situation or new role demands new rules for money management, but unfortunately our attitudes and behaviors regarding finances are so deeply ingrained that sorting them out and striking a balance acceptable to both partners can be fraught with tension.

The current economic downturn, after a decade of unprecedented growth, has dealt a swift and painful blow to families across the country, sometimes causing seismic shifts in relationships. Couples with two incomes find that while they're working harder than ever, their paychecks buy less and less. Not much is left over for the good times— movies and dinners out, family vacations, or even child-free weekends away. Young dot-commers who had achieved a measure of financial independence find they must move back home with parents. Dreams bear little resemblance to reality, and that puts a strain on even the best relationship. Those couples who navigate best through the churning financial waters have made a conscious effort to chip away the emotional veneer surrounding money issues and, instead, talk openly about finances—what they need, what they want, how they can best attain these goals and how to live with the anxious uncertainty that they just may not. They've learned to brainstorm alternatives until they agree on a decision and, if that's impossible, negotiate a compromise.

In fact, *Seven Secrets of a Happy Marriage* highlights several characteristics common to couples who are able to keep money matters in perspective:

- Instead of assuming that their spouses' financial goals, habits, or ideas about spending and investing are the same, these couples have taken the time to discuss the following: What role does money play in our lives? What are our attitudes and beliefs about it? Is one of us a risk-taker, while the other one is security-conscious? Do we feel that money should be spent and enjoyed or squirreled away for emergencies?

- They've hammered out the logistics of budgeting and money management and they revise these decisions on a regular basis: Does a joint or a separate savings and checking account make sense? Who will actually pay the bills? Will we consult on all purchases or set a ceiling on personal spending? Will we use credit cards or pay cash?

- They've tracked any patterns to their money battles, noticing, for instance, when they are most likely to be triggered—when the bills come in, for instance, or at tax time.

- They've predicted and accounted for any financial changes that may take place at certain transition points in life—after the birth of a baby; when they buy a new house or when the kids go off to college; following the loss of a job. What's more, at each life stage, both partners are aware of and informed about the financial realities.

- When an argument does erupt, they are able to step back from the immediate quarrel and ask themselves: What am I really upset about? The fact that my husband spent money on a new stereo system or new set of golf clubs or the fact that he's not pitching in with child care?

Indeed, although we are a society that insists money doesn't buy happiness, the reality is that not having enough of it, or arguing over how and where to spend it, seriously disrupts many marriages. Money fights may on the surface be frivolous, but they are well worth attending to.

"We Always Fight About Money"

M ary Beth was proud of the way she handled the family finances in Jerry's absence. But the changes she made infuriated her husband—and set the stage for their current battles.

"Try to imagine how it feels to know your husband is sorry he ever married you," said Mary Beth, thirty, an apple-cheeked brunette with wholesome good looks. "Oh, Jerry doesn't say that flat out, but actions speak louder than words. For one thing, he keeps his money all to himself, just the way he did when he was single, and for another, he won't even talk about us having a baby. Does that sound like a man who has made a commitment?

"I admit I was the one who pushed for us to get married. We had been living together for two years and I was worried that, for all intents and purposes, my kids considered him their father. My daughter, who is eight, and my son, now five, were really little when my ex-husband deserted us, so they never knew him. So to them, Jerry was Daddy. For their sake, I felt it was time either to make everything legal or end the relationship.

"Jerry finally gave in. He was pushing thirty, and before he met me he had played the field. When he first asked me and the kids to move into his house, he told me he was surprised how much he wanted to be with me. He had always thought of himself as a confirmed bachelor. Well, the months turned to years, and it was clear that Jerry was

221

a wonderful man. Oh, we had our share of differences—he's a neatnik and I'm something of a clutterbug, and he's got more of a sex drive than I do—but basically we got along great. I wonder if we were both making assumptions and putting up with certain things back then because we hadn't tied the knot.

"I'll give you a for 'instance.' We never pooled our money. We never had any real reason to talk about finances since we're each pretty well set. Jerry has a good job as an airline mechanic. I do all right with my salary as a dental hygienist, plus child support. My ex-husband's employer garnishes his salary, so the checks come right on time. Still, I figured Jerry and I would put our money in one pot when we were husband and wife. One thing we did talk about was having a baby of our own, although the discussions were always kind of vague.

"Jerry finally gave me an engagement ring for Christmas, and we planned a spring wedding. But in January, the Persian Gulf War started, and Jerry, who's in the Marine Corps Reserves, was called to active duty. We sat up all night talking and crying. Jerry said we had to marry before he shipped out. He was afraid to leave me and the kids unless he knew we'd be taken care of.

"We found a justice of the peace who married us. Jerry insisted we open a joint account and arranged for me to have power of attorney.

Between his company and the Marines, Jerry would continue to get a regular salary, and he arranged to have it deposited directly into our account so that I'd have access if I ever needed it.

"Then he sat me down at the kitchen table and explained all the finances. Until then, I had paid for the kids' clothes and the food and laundry supplies, but Jerry had been handling big-ticket items, like the mortgage and the insurance.

"Three days later he was gone. I don't think I slept a full night the whole time he was overseas. But if I do say so myself, I did a great job of keeping things together. I even improved his bill-paying system and never missed a payment. I was sure he'd be proud of me.

"Now figure this. He gets home, we have this emotional welcome, and the very next day he closes out the joint account and says he's taking over again. He didn't thank me or say one word about how I had managed.

"In fact, he was furious that I had 'splurged,' as he put it, on a pair of recliners for the den. We had always talked about how much we wanted those chairs but that they were too expensive. I had handled the money so carefully I was able to use some of our income-tax refund to buy them. Instead of being thrilled, he accused me of being an impulse shopper.

"He said he'd had a lot of time to think during the war, and he'd changed his mind about our having a child; he couldn't handle the financial responsibility.

"I know Jerry grew up poor. His dad was a logger who made a good living, but with eight kids, there wasn't much to go around. Jerry was the youngest and he's always talking about how he had a paper route from the time he was seven and hasn't stopped working since. Fine, but the past is the past. I know many people were laid off at his company, but I don't think Jerry's job is in jeopardy.

"My family was a little better off than Jerry's since my parents owned a stationery store, but we weren't rich. I helped out in the store from the time I was little. It didn't scar me for life. He's frantic about money, as if we were going to starve to death.

"Anyway, at first I was very depressed about Jerry, but then I talked myself into believing he was having trouble adjusting to being back. I'd try to comfort him, but he never responded. Sometimes we'd have sex, but it wasn't lovemaking. Not the way it used to be. He could have been with any woman.

"In the meantime, I had to stop taking the Pill. For a while, we relied on a diaphragm, but that drove us crazy. Jerry didn't want to use a condom. Finally, my doctor suggested I try the new implant. Though it's been in use for about fifteen years in Europe, it's only been available here for a few years. Supposedly it's safe, with minimal side effects. Well, maybe it's just me, but I think gaining ten pounds, feeling bloated, and growing a mustache qualify as more than minimal. But I put up with all that because the doctor assured me the side effects would subside. Secretly, though, I hoped Jerry would agree to have a baby.

"I started to get more and more resentful of the way he was treating me. He's on my back about everything—cleaning the house, doing the laundry—and nothing I do is right anymore. The other day I was late going to a meeting at school and I ran out and forgot to lock the door. I never heard the end of that one.

"I really thought this time I had made the right choice. But our life is a charade. There's no love, no affection, just constant bickering. I'd rather be alone with my kids."

JERRY'S TURN

"Mary Beth has got it into her head that I wish I hadn't married her, but that's not true," said Jerry, thirty-one, a handsome man with a full beard. "The war didn't force me into anything; it just made me do it sooner. I loved her too much to leave her a single mother, and I can't understand why she doesn't see that.

"But I suppose the war did get us off to a weird start. As she said, I gave her power of attorney so she could handle everything while I was gone. But I never meant for things to stay that way. Look, she did a fine job, but it was foolish to spend an entire tax refund on two chairs. I don't believe in splurging unless you have the resources to do it. To be blunt, I don't think Mary Beth is responsible enough to make important life decisions. I love her, but she's flighty. She seems to have more than enough on her hands just keeping the house clean and the meals on the table without burdening her with other responsibilities. Besides, I make most of the money and I think I should handle it. It's a man's responsibility to be the provider and I intend to fulfill my obligations.

"That's one reason I stayed single as long as I did. I didn't want to end up like my father, always struggling to feed a huge family. I hated being poor and, Catholic or not, I don't think you should have kids if you can't give them a decent life.

"So I sowed my wild oats in my twenties. But when I hit thirty, I wanted to settle down with someone special. I met Mary Beth at a friend's party, and she was so bubbly and pretty, I let myself fall in love. The fact that she had two little kids scared me a bit, but once we started living together, I fell in love with them, too. They mean as much to me now as if they were my own flesh and blood.

"When Mary Beth saw how good I was with the children, she started lobbying for one of our own. I never said yes, and I never said no. I was pretty sure, though, that in this economy, two is all we could handle. What about college? I have no idea if her ex-husband will pay for that. What about a wedding for Stacy? Add one of our own . . . forget it. Sure, my job seems secure. But you see these pink slips all around you and read the horror stories in the paper; if you're smart, you don't live beyond your means. Besides, if Mary Beth had a new baby to care for, she'd have to cut back on her hours, and that means even less money.

"This baby thing is ruining our sex life. Mary Beth has this idea that if you're not going to have a child, then you shouldn't make love. I heard all that when I was growing up, too, but I don't agree with it. Besides, I was celibate in that desert for five months and I admit I came home wanting to make love two or three times a day. Of course, I don't want her to be feeling sick because of the birth control, but that means we'll just have to find a method that works for us.

"I know I haven't been myself since I got back. I'm jumpy and I have nightmares. I don't know what to do about it. But I do know she's making a mountain out of a molehill about this money stuff. Before I went away, we did just fine.

"To be perfectly honest, I think I've put up with a lot of things other husbands wouldn't. The lack of sex is one thing; there's also the fact that Mary Beth is a total, well, slob. It's not just that she leaves junk everywhere. She does stuff that is totally irresponsible and sometimes even dangerous. She'll leave her curling iron plugged in all day or the front door unlocked. I've talked to her over and over again about this, but nothing changes. Which is why I'm not thrilled about letting her handle the money. I still think she was rising to the occasion, so to speak, and on a regular basis, I'm not convinced I could trust her.

"You know, now that I'm here saying all this, I really don't know what she's all worked up about. I don't want a divorce, although Mary Beth seems intent on heading us toward one."

THE COUNSELOR'S TURN

"I would have phrased it differently than Jerry did, but this marriage did get off to a bad start," said the counselor. "However, this couple would have had problems even if the war hadn't pushed up their wedding date.

"Although they had lived together in what they honestly believed was a trial marriage, like many couples in a similar position, they had not actually given their relationship a fair test. Assuming that love conquered all, they had failed to discuss the nitty-gritty aspects of their marriage—primarily issues relating to money and children—that are key to a strong relationship.

"For instance, they had never talked about money or how it would

be handled, how much they should save or what kind of budget they needed. If they had, Mary Beth would have realized early on that Jerry's need for financial security, as well as his entrenched belief that a man must be the provider, had to be confronted. They might have realized that Jerry's reluctance to let Mary Beth handle the money had a lot to do with what he saw as her irresponsible behavior—leaving the door unlocked, for instance. They also had never discussed their hopes and dreams for the future, which included how large a family they wanted to have.

"My first job was to get both of them to identify the sources of their conflict and then help them learn to reach a mutually satisfying compromise. To do this, I asked each of them to write down their responses to a set of questions. Among the questions: Who should manage the money in your relationship? How much money should each partner contribute to the family account every month? Do you want to put your savings aside first? The questionnaire also touches on life-choice issues: How often do you want to have sex? How many children would you like to have? What personal habits of your partner do you find annoying? Which habits of yours bother your partner? The point of the questionnaire is not that you and your spouse should agree on everything, but that you should be aware of your differences.

Mary Beth and Jerry took this assignment very seriously. They not only came to the next session with answers to every question, but they had taken the time to highlight and talk about their disagreements. At this point, I was able to show them that Jerry's need for security was prudent, albeit slightly exaggerated. I suggested that they spend several weeks writing down how much they spent each day so they could see where their money went and then plan a workable budget. Once they did, Jerry was relieved to see that they were actually in better shape than he had imagined. He relaxed his grip on the purse strings and let Mary Beth share in the financial decisions. The one stipulation: She had to make every effort to prove her maturity by being less careless about those things that irked Jerry. Mary Beth agreed, since she now understood that her behavior, which she had always thought to be rather harmless, had seemed immature to Jerry.

"I then began some of the more difficult work: looking into the source of their conflicts. For several weeks we talked about their families, and it became clear that Mary Beth really hadn't felt the pinch of poverty the way Jerry had. Nonetheless, she was convinced their backgrounds were similar. 'Just because you were both raised in large Catholic families doesn't mean your experiences were the same,' I told her. Gradually, she felt more compassion for Jerry and was able to understand why the mere thought of having his money mismanaged could cause him anxiety. She was then able to reassure him that she respected his point of view and would be prudent and honest in her dealings with the finances. This simple assertion brought a visible look of relief to Jerry's face.

"At this point we were able to tackle the subject of having a child. Mary Beth told him that the biggest reason she wanted a baby was that she loved him so much and wished on some level beyond reason that she could bear his child. Jerry, the tough Marine, was moved to tears.

"Jerry was having real adjustment problems related to his service in the Gulf War. It isn't necessary to be engaged in combat to suffer stress from a war. At my suggestion, he joined a group for veterans led by another psychologist, and Jerry has found it comforting to talk to others in similar situations. His nightmares have ceased and he and Mary Beth have once again begun to enjoy a loving sex life.

"This couple ended counseling after a year. The last time I spoke with Mary Beth she told me she'd had the birth control implant removed—with Jerry's blessing—and she was hoping to become pregnant soon."

A CEASE-FIRE IN THE MONEY WARS

Many couples find that finances are a prime source of friction. And, like Mary Beth and Jerry, many couples never really discuss the financial facts of their lives: How do they each feel about money? What's a financial necessity and what's a luxury? How should money be handled and who should handle what? What are their long-range financial goals? If Jerry and Mary Beth had done this, they would have discovered that although they had very different ideas about saving and spending, perhaps they could have resolved these differences before they became too divisive.

If this couple's plight sounds all too familiar, take the time to sit down together with bank statements, pencil, paper, and calculator and draw up a workable budget that you can stick to. You may have to spend a few weeks jotting down what you each spend during the day so you can see where every penny goes. Most of us are aware of the big expenses, but it's the smaller ones—dry cleaning or drugstore items—that slip by but add up. Write down your fixed costs: rent, mortgage payments, child-care expenses, insurance. Then include costs that are more flexible: entertainment, clothing, food, and so on. What can you cut out or cut back? If you've made a realistic budget, you should be able to put aside money for savings every month as well as have money for emergencies. Determine who's going to handle which payments and be sure to put some money into a personal spending account for each of you so you aren't obliged to consult each other on every minor expense. However, always discuss significant purchases or investments. Revise your budget and investment plans if your family or job situation changes.

When discussing money, try to be businesslike, not emotional. Avoid blaming and labeling—calling your spouse a tightwad or saying he spends money like a drunken sailor, for instance, is not conducive to cooperation.

Most important, no matter how tight money is, reserve a small amount for pleasure. Even if you go out once a week to a movie or for pizza—just the two of you—you'll feel better about your relationship in general if you indulge yourselves once in a while.

"My Husband Is So Cheap"

Though Andy's desire to save money is admirable, he was doing so at the expense of Gina—and their marriage. Can two people who seem to have little in common work through their differences?

GINA'S TURN

"I used to carry a sandwich lunch to my office every day just to satisfy Andy," said twenty-four-year-old Gina, a deeply tanned blonde recently separated from her husband. "During our three years together, Andy told me how to dress, where to buy gasoline and groceries—and instructed me in every aspect of my existence. His objective was to save money.

"Andy's insistence on that sandwich lunch had a lot to do with our split-up. I supervise a stenographic pool in my section of a large insurance company. Carrying a package lunch made me feel like a lowly file clerk. My colleagues thought I was a tightwad and laughed at me behind my back.

"But Andy reminded me that he carried a package lunch to college, where he is a part-time engineering student, and got along very nicely with two shirts by washing one every night. This was quite true, but our budget was too restricted for comfort. It eliminated pleasure and the simplest recreation, and his indifference to my humiliation was outrageous.

"Andy's earnings—he held a job in a filling station, a second job in a supermarket—paid for our food, his tuition, books, and college incidentals. He was sinking my salary into payments and improvements on our huge old house. If I dared question him, he flew into a rage.

"From the beginning of our marriage, Andy took charge of all the money and I was too timid to argue. He bought my shoes and stockings and all my clothes, mostly at sleazy discount stores. Frequently I wasn't present. He bought my cosmetics through a wholesaler—brands I detested and often in unbecoming shades.

"Andy and I were also in the process of renovating our barnlike house without professional assistance—a colossal chore. We lived in perpetual chaos, stumbling over boards, wire, and bits of fallen plaster. I never felt I had a home. It seemed that there has been nothing in my life except hard work—no gaiety, no leisure, no freedom.

"I was the oldest of six children, the only girl, and my parents were extremely poor. My mother was terrifically ambitious for me and was determined I go to college. Her wages as a store cashier were badly needed at home, but she put aside ten percent a week for my education. Many times, Father got drunk and beat her to get at that college fund, but she never let him have it. At the age of ten I began washing dishes and vacuuming for neighbors, and every penny of my earnings also went into the education fund. During high school I studied so hard and had so many jobs that I had little time for boys. On Fridays, Mother and I visited the bank and made our deposits. It was the big event of the week.

"I was a college sophomore— a working student who lived off campus and missed the campus fun—when I met Andy. He proposed after one month. I told him no, but he wasn't one bit discouraged. At least once a week for two years he'd telephone. The message was always the same: I was the only wife he would ever want.

"Since he had professed to love me so much for so long, I expected a glamorous honeymoon trip when I finally said yes. It didn't happen. Andy convinced me it was impossible to take a short vacation or draw on his savings account, and he set up an immediate clamor for me to get a job. When I dillydallied—I wanted that one summer of freedom—he called the employment agencies and set up appointments for me. One week after my wedding, I landed a job and began turning over my weekly checks. Andy was so impressed that he decided he, too, should go back to school. He rearranged his schedule—Andy has always worked all the time—and started classes.

"Our only pleasure was sex, and there were times when Andy almost spoiled that for me. Terrified that I might get pregnant, he always checked my supply of birth control pills to make sure there had been no slip-up. To me, his lack of trust seemed like a lack of love.

"Another thing I soon discovered about my husband was that he did not believe in celebrating special occasions—Christmas, birthdays, anniversaries. I turned twenty-one three months after our marriage, but Andy forgot my birthday. Gregory, a man I work with, is the exact opposite of Andy. The day after we had our first office lunch I found on my desk an orchid and a sweet little note. Soon Gregory and I were lunching nearly every business day. He was easy to talk to and a wonderful listener.

"When I told Gregory about Andy's stinginess, he said the situation was ridiculous, that every wife, working or not, was entitled to a personal allowance. He said I ought to make some other living arrangements and he would help any way he could. One Saturday, I ran into him on the street and he took me swimming at his apartment house, which was designed for swinging singles. By coincidence, there was a vacancy in the building, a furnished sublet. Gregory introduced me to the manager and I halfway agreed to rent it. When I got home, Andy was on his knees laying tiles. I spoke to him very quietly before he had a chance to yell at me.

"I told him I was leaving him and I told him about Gregory. To my amazement, Andy didn't bellow or shout. In fact, his voice sounded terribly hurt. I could hardly believe it. We talked all night and in the end we compromised. Next morning Andy helped me move, but he picked the apartment. It was fairly near our house and miles away from Gregory.

"For the last six weeks, ever since the move, I've been totally confused. The first time I collected my own check I bought four new dresses in a single morning, but then I remembered a big payment was due on the house and realized how worried Andy would be. I returned two of the dresses that afternoon and sent the money to him. He came around and thanked me. However, when I suggested we go out to dinner he turned into the same penny-pinching Andy. He said a sandwich was all he wanted.

"I'm still seeing Gregory, though not as much. At the moment, I'm more than satisfied with the joys and freedom of single life."

ANDY'S TURN

"I have loved Gina since the very first time I saw her," said Andy, a curly-haired, broad-shouldered young man of twenty-five with fierce blue eyes and a pugnacious jaw.

"Gina has no sense of values—about money or people. She can be conned by anyone. She needs somebody, she needs me, to protect and look after her. When she took off six weeks ago, I'm almost sure I could have changed her mind if I'd known the right things to say.

"Gina can easily be talked into acting against her own principles and her own best interests. To see her influenced by a guy like Gregory, to hear her quote his 'wise' remarks, drives me nuts. I know how his type operates. Regardless of his fast line of chatter, he has no real concern for Gina's welfare.

"Until six weeks ago I thought Gina and I had everything going for us. Gina encouraged me to go to college and I encouraged her to find a job. I took a lot of personal pride and interest in Gina's career. I regarded her income as important in building, for us both, a financial program for the future. On a few occasions I guess she did beef a little, but I was too stupid or too busy to pay much attention. Together we were creating something of value.

"Everything I planned was planned for Gina. I thought she understood that my sole desire was to provide for her security. All that was required of her was a little patience.

"My folks would have made out okay financially—they had only three kids, with me the oldest—if not for the extravagance of my mother. My father sold and installed air conditioners, earned good wages, and occasionally even spoke of sending me, the only boy, to college. Mother's wastefulness and silly buying habits drove him into bankruptcy. In disgust, he left her one night and, of course, left me. I was nine.

"Until I met Gina, nobody ever gave a damn for me. At one time she did love me, but now I guess she has changed. I don't know why. I will always love Gina, but I don't know how to tell her so. She means more to me than anybody or anything in this world."

THE COUNSELOR'S TURN

"The appearance of a man like Gregory on the scene of this marriage was almost inevitable," the counselor said. "Gina quickly realized that although she didn't care for Gregory, he represented a handy exit from an existence that had become intolerable.

"When I first met Gina she had only recently retired from the thankless role of 'the girl who can't say no.' In her formative years, an ambitious and doubtless well-intentioned mother systematically robbed her of initiative and virtually all power of decision. In such circumstances, independence of action later could hardly be expected.

"Andy and Gina were bright young people, but both were very emotionally immature. The lack of communication between them was complete. When Gina married Andy, she expected to enter a world of romance, fun, and freedom. Instead, she had merely exchanged the prison of her girlhood for the prison of marriage.

"Andy had no understanding of Gina's feelings or her increasing bitterness and boredom. After all, with her assistance, he was achieving his dream. Gina was unaware that

Andy's concern for her inspired and fired all his actions. She had only the vaguest conception of his financial plans and future projects and she regarded his prudence in money matters as meanness.

"Although Andy deplored the wobbly quality of Gina's disposition, he had been quick to take advantage of it and on occasion bullied his unprotesting young wife unmercifully. Subconsciously, he was reacting to Gina as if she were his free-wheeling, wasteful mother. Once Andy acknowledged that Gina bore no resemblance to his mother, he was on the way to maturity.

"At times, Gina had made half-hearted attempts to speak to him about her unhappiness and very legitimate grievances. Unfortunately, on the occasions she rallied the courage to talk honestly, Andy was either too preoccupied or too overworked to listen. Andy had set himself a work schedule that would have been difficult for six men to follow. Most of the time he was exhausted. In fact, to a certain extent, Gina's complaints that he was a laggard lover were justified. Andy poured such an enormous store of intellectual force, muscular strength, and vitality into his work that his energy and interest in lovemaking were seriously reduced.

"Eventually this marriage was salvaged, but the task took more time than I anticipated. Gina was exhilarated with her newfound freedom and loath to part with it, but Andy was a fighter. From the beginning, he shouldered ninety percent of the blame for the separation; he was dissatisfied with himself and eager to improve.

"He deliberately maintained a curtailed workload, which was tough on a young man of his temperament, and dipped deeply into his savings, which was even tougher, to spend lavishly on the entertainment and recreation Gina fancied. For several months, she was treated to the courtship she had previously missed. Andy did his best to relax and enjoy himself along with her. When he was rested, he and Gina began to rediscover the passion of their lovemaking. Andy has also just about mastered his anxieties of a pregnancy that neither he nor Gina desires at the moment.

"Gina and Andy have now learned to talk freely to each other, to listen, and, most important, to try to understand each other's feelings. Gina was urged to talk about what's bothering her instead of retreating into teary silence.

"The big break came, however, when Andy was given a chance to sell their house, which was still unfinished, at a modest profit. When he consulted Gina, she advised him to reject the offer. With considerable indignation, she reminded him of all the time and toil they had invested in the place—and the next day she moved back home.

"Gina and Andy have now completed the remodeling job, and they expect to find a buyer soon for their

home. They will invest half their profits in another real-estate venture and spend the other half on a trip to Europe. Both are delighted with their plans and prospects for the future.

"In fact, once Gina and Andy had more opportunities to know and understand each other more intimately, they discovered that they were quite a bit alike."

HOW TO DEAL
WITH A CONTROLLING PARTNER

This is a classic example of how money equals power in a marriage. When either partner feels controlled, the result is a back-flow of resentment that can destroy love. What's more, the way your parents handled issues of power and control directly affect the way you behave as an adult.

But although these early patterns can be difficult to break, they can be changed. Do you often feel that your partner's wishes and needs come before yours? Do you feel put down and bossed around? It helps to take a look at how decisions were made in your family when you were growing up. By recognizing certain patterns, you can learn to do things differently now.

Below is a list of common family decisions. When you were little, were these decisions made by your father, your mother, or both? Who had the final word?

- Decisions about how to spend money.
- Decisions about whom to socialize with, which relative to visit, etc.
- Decisions about childrearing.
- Decisions about where to live.
- Decisions about how to spend vacations.

Is your list lopsided? Now, go over the questions again and ask yourself: Who makes the decisions on these issues in our home? If that list is also lopsided, your marriage may be at risk for financial power struggles. Does your partner feel weak if you earn more? Does he believe the man should always make financial choices? Is he open to change, or are his beliefs rigid and etched in stone? Do you feel entitled to talk about changing the way money is handled, or are you afraid to mention it? In a marriage that works, the deal is always being renegotiated.

"My Husband Is Having a Midlife Crisis"

Jo was frantic when Aaron kept postponing his job hunt. But while financial problems precipitated their current crisis, other long-buried issues were also driving a wedge between them.

Jo's Turn

"When you hear what I have to say, you're not going to like me at all," said Jo, forty-four, a beautiful woman with an uncanny resemblance to actress Sigourney Weaver.

"I've been married for almost twenty-five years to the absolutely most wonderful man in the world. I love him very much, but three years ago Aaron's parents died, and he quit his job soon after that; now he refuses to look for another. I'm afraid our marriage is not going to survive.

"I met Aaron the summer after I graduated from high school. I was working at the five-and-ten-cent store. My best friend was dating Aaron's first cousin, so they got us together. Aaron is one of the genuinely good, kind people in this world. He makes me feel very loved, very needed; I never felt that way with my parents.

"I was the younger of two girls. My sister, Anna, was very bright and I always felt I had to be as good in school as she was. But school was a struggle for me; I'm dyslexic, though we didn't know it at the time. So while my parents never

came right out and said 'You're not as smart as Anna,' I knew they felt that way.

"But Anna was also very depressed—when she was in her teens, she was diagnosed as being schizophrenic. My parents were always so wrapped up in her and her problems that I was ignored.

"My parents were happily married until my father's hardware business went bankrupt, when I was about twelve years old. Then the fighting started between them, the harsh words, always over money.

"When I met Aaron, I believed there was no doubt that our marriage was different from my parents. We dated for about a year, got engaged when I was nineteen, married when I was twenty. We went to Florida on our honeymoon. It was a wonderful trip, although we were both inexperienced sexually. In fact, our sex life has always been so-so. But it's not an issue for us. I think we're asexual. We make love maybe once a month.

"So anyway, we moved into a small apartment, and really, our life was perfect. We had two beautiful daughters, Susan and Tricia, three years apart. When our apartment became too small, we moved to a nice split-level on a corner lot in a new subdivision. We lived the typical suburban life. Then the girls grew up, went away to college, got married. They both live nearby. I was starting to get a little bored, so when my friend suggested I work in her

store selling tennis and exercise clothes, I said terrific, what a great idea. I've been there for over three years now, and I really love it.

"Like I said, things were going along just fine until Aaron's parents died. First his father, and then, a few months later, his mother suffered a stroke. She was ill for about a year before she passed away.

"Then one day, out of the blue, Aaron tells me he's decided to quit his job. For years he'd worked in the office-supply business owned by his uncle, his father's brother, for whom Aaron's father had also worked. He said he was going to manage his father's so-called investments and look for something—and I quote—'that allows me to be my own man.' And he insisted we move into his parents' house, which is falling down.

"Well, it's been almost two years now and he mostly sits around the house, staring at the TV. He complains that I talk on the phone too much, but what does he do all day? Why, he plays the stock market! I think we should keep our money very safe. This is not the time to take chances. Even though our expenses are much lower these days, my salary is not enough to live on. What about retirement? And although I'd never bring it up, I think it upsets Aaron that I'm supporting us now.

"A few months ago, I told him I wanted to sell the house and move to an apartment. The repairs here are astronomical and we really don't need all this space.

"Well, Aaron refuses to sell. He won't even discuss it with me. It's always been hard to find out what's on Aaron's mind or what he's really thinking about, but now he's more distant than ever.

"What makes me nuts is that Aaron acts as if we don't have a care in the world. Here I am, worried sick about money, and we'll go to dinner with friends—and he'll pick up the check! Or he'll go grocery shopping and buy fresh pasta that costs three times as much as the packaged kind.

"We've been fighting a lot, but mostly going around in circles. So ten days ago I walked out. How else was I going to get through to him? I went to live with my daughter Susan.

"Aaron went crazy when I did that, so I came back but insisted we get counseling. Is this what they call a midlife crisis?"

AARON'S TURN

"I just can't sell the house," said Aaron, a tall, distinguished-looking man of fifty. "I don't mind doing the repairs. In this house, I feel like a king.

"Of course, that's of no importance to my wife. All she worries about is money. I know her insecurities stem from her father's losing his money and all. But look, financially speaking, this house is a good investment. Okay, so the real estate market is down right now, but I'm sure it's going to bounce back. You just have to be patient and hang in there.

"I can't seem to convince Jo that there's no reason to panic. We'll never be rich, but we have enough money. We can afford to buy fresh pasta. It really burns me up the way she gets on me for things like that. If I go out for dinner with friends, it makes me feel good to pick up the check once in awhile.

"Jo was always hyper—I fell in love with her energy—but now all that's left is the anxiety. Some days I can't stand to be around her.

"You know, these are the years we looked forward to when the girls were little. Time to enjoy being together, to travel.

"Look, I'm not going to lie to you, I'm not crazy about Jo's working. I was brought up to believe that the man is the provider. So now I'm down on my luck a bit. That'll change. But she's a maniac lately, racing around, always on the phone. She doesn't even acknowledge me when I walk in.

"Jo mentioned our sex life. Well, the simple truth is, I'd like to have sex more often than we do, but Jo's never in the mood. Once she gets going, I know she enjoys it, but I get tired of trying.

"We never used to fight like we do now. Oh, sure, we'd argue about the usual routine domestic things, but we never had any major problems. Over the years we saw many of our friends get divorced, but I think we always felt like we, and our marriage, were forever.

"Maybe it's me. I've been feeling unhappy for quite awhile now. Things got bad when my father died, worse when Mother passed away. My father had taken a lot of, pardon the expression, crap from my uncle, whom he worked for, and I hated the way my uncle patronized my father all those years. He continued to treat me the same way—like dirt. But what was I supposed to do? Quit? With a wife and two kids?

"Still, I inherited a bit of money from my folks, plus this house. It wasn't a fortune by any means, but it was enough that I could stop working, take six months, and figure out what I really wanted to do. What's so bad about that? The girls were done with school and were working on their own.

"Okay, so it's been longer than six months. A lot longer. I've been fooling around a little with the stock market. I've always enjoyed it, and I'm damn good at it if I say so myself. The way Jo talks, of course, you'd think I was into some heavy-duty trading on margin.

"I'm not thrilled with my life, but I don't know what to do with myself. I can't stand the thought of going back to that office grind. I've always wanted to be more of my own man, but . . . I don't know.

"Anyway, I don't need Jo harping on me every second: 'You're lazy . . .

you're not motivated.' 'Did you call about this job? Did you look in the paper?'

"Then, last week, Jo walked out and went to stay with Susan. That hurt. I love my daughters and the one thing I can be truly proud of is the relationship I have with them. Now Jo goes there, talking about me, tarnishing it all.

"Maybe we got married too young. People change, grow apart, right? Maybe that's what's happened."

THE COUNSELOR'S TURN

"Yes, Aaron is having what has come to be known as a midlife crisis," said the counselor. "But although Jo and Aaron feared their marriage was ending, I felt strongly this was not the case. When I looked at this couple, I saw a long-term caring relationship, and a tremendous amount of love behind the anger.

"I also told them I did not think they would need to be in counseling for a long time. With many couples who have an acute problem—when a husband loses his job, for instance, or when a new baby arrives—I use a form of counseling called crisis intervention. Couples come for a brief period, perhaps eight to ten sessions. We shorten the time spent exploring their individual backgrounds and focus attention on the immediate problem.

"With this form of short-term therapy, I begin by drawing a time line—an actual chart that indicates changes that have taken place over the years. This enabled Jo and Aaron to understand more clearly how events in their lives—and the way they reacted to those events—had slowly brought them to a crisis point.

"As far as they were concerned, the immediate problem facing them was whether or not to sell their house. While Jo had no emotional connection to it, for Aaron, the house represented not only ties to his parents but success and achievement, a sense of himself as a man.

"When I first met him, Aaron was clearly depressed and phobic about going back to work. An only child, Aaron had been a mama's boy, although he also identified with his father, a kind but passive man who had always been beholden to his brother. While Aaron had bristled at his uncle's treatment of his father, he nevertheless did what he thought was expected of him and took a job in his uncle's business when it was offered.

"Things went on this way for years. Then, within a short period of time, there were many changes in Aaron's life: his parents died . . . he quit his job . . . the children moved out. And finally, his wife, who had always been content to lead the traditional life of the suburban mom, was suddenly working. He felt paralyzed.

"On the other hand, Jo was filled with nervous energy. Her anxiety about money probably started when her father lost his hardware business,

but fueling that insecurity was a deep-seated lack of self-confidence.

"As a child, Jo was constantly forced to put her own needs aside; when a person does that, those needs accumulate, often resulting in tension and agitation. Then, too, since she was dyslexic, school was a struggle for her. Though she worked hard, she never felt truly capable.

"Like most women of her generation, Jo looked forward to getting married and having children, and until the girls left home, all this was enough. But for every couple, the empty nest creates an enormous hole in the family, as well as an imbalance in the relationship between husband and wife. Jo and Aaron were now forced to relate to each other as individuals. Problems that in the past may have been overlooked rose to the surface.

"What's more, with her daughters on their own, Jo had fewer channels for her energy. Her concern about money grew as she watched her husband whiling away his time day after day, propped up in front of the TV.

"It was to Jo's credit that she, in a sense, instigated the couple's current crisis. She was in effect saying, 'This isn't good enough. We must make some changes.' First, I asked Jo to promise not to involve her daughters in her marital problems. That was unfair to them as well as to Aaron. Then I told her that she had to be more sensitive to small things, such as the tone with which she spoke to her husband.

"My next goal was to help Aaron find the confidence to embark on a job hunt. (Jo had agreed to postpone any decision about selling the house if Aaron would promise to look for a job.) Like many men today who took early retirement or were forced out of a job due to industry cutbacks, Aaron was too young and energetic to sit around doing nothing.

"The fact that I was there to listen to Aaron and not judge him helped shore up his confidence and refocus his goals. With Jo's help, he drafted his résumé, set about calling former colleagues and employment agencies, and checked the ads in the newspaper. To his delight, he received several positive responses, and within one week he had scheduled three interviews.

"Aaron's self-confidence carried over into his relationship with Jo. Soft-spoken by nature, he rarely told her when something bothered him. Now, if Jo flew off the handle because he bought an expensive brand of pasta, he pointed out that they could afford it, and besides, it gave him pleasure.

"Jo was thrilled that her husband was finally doing something. But she had a long way to go in learning how to relax. I suggested she buy a small notebook and, throughout the day, jot down all the things she could be happy about—something funny that happened at work, a beautiful garden that she saw, anything that gave her pleasure. Although it may sound simple, this exercise helped Jo track the positive things in her life and stop projecting disaster.

"Jo was also suffering from what we refer to as inhibition of sexual desire. She was so tense that she was unable to feel desire. However, once her anxiety lessened, she was more responsive.

"Jo and Aaron ended joint counseling after three months, although Aaron continued to visit for more career counseling. At his last session, he told me he had been offered a position as a stockbroker trainee at a small, well-regarded firm; he was planning to take the licensing test soon. 'It's a beginner's spot,' he said, 'but I'm my own man. And people trust me. I'll do fine.' There was no doubt in my mind that he would."

WHEN MONEY MATTERS MAGNIFY MARITAL WOES

Aaron and Jo needed to understand exactly how outside events can affect a marriage. Recognizing the importance of life stressors, such as losing a job or the death of a parent, is critical in solving marital problems. In this case, the children's growing up and moving out created the first imbalance in the relationship. The death of Aaron's parents created another. Problems that may have been overlooked in the past rose to the surface and swamped them both. Instead of facing them together, they blamed each other.

Played out against this backdrop was the immediate problem of Aaron's unemployment and Jo's fear that his failure to look for another job would send them careening toward bankruptcy. Marital problems are often magnified when one or both partners are worried about money. And, since money means different things to each of us, we often respond to financial crises in conflicting ways. For Jo, money meant security; without it, she was frantic and lost. For Aaron, money meant self-esteem and a sense of himself as a man. Instead of understanding each other's perspective and working together toward a solution, they decided the marriage was over. If similar issues loom large in your marriage:

1. Remember that your spouse is probably just as upset as you are, but he may be dealing with the issues differently (i.e., not talking about it).

2. Acknowledge the strengths your relationship has. Couples whose problems are, in fact, a minor part of their lives sometimes let them overshadow the positive aspects of the marriage. Give yourselves credit for what's good between you.

3. The only person you can change is yourself, so focus on what you can do differently. Jo had to relax and concentrate on those things that gave her pleasure throughout the day instead of dwelling on what her husband was or wasn't doing. Aaron needed to have a more positive attitude about his abilities, to shore up his confidence and redirect his goals so he could get back to a job he finds challenging. Looking for a job in the stock market, which had long fascinated him, was his answer. Once he did find a job, Jo felt less anxiety about money and they started enjoying being together.

"My Compulsive Shopping Is Ruining Our Marriage"

Kelly assured Rich that her spending was under control. What happens when one partner discovers that the other isn't telling the truth?

KELLY'S TURN

"Last night Rich told me he wants a divorce," said Kelly, thirty-two, a media buyer with an advertising agency who has been married for ten years. "I had just told him I'd gotten us in debt for more than twenty thousand dollars. Over the last couple of years, I've been buying things for our home and for myself—and lying to Rich about it all. I'm mortified and scared.

"We each handle all our personal bills, so Rich never knew what was going on. When I maxed out on one card, I used another—I had about twenty cards going.

"It's hard to explain the rush, the feeling of euphoria that I'd get when I was buying something. Later, I'd sometimes feel anxious and ashamed, but not enough to keep me from buying something else the next time I wandered into a store on my lunch hour. I never wanted to hurt Rich; I just wanted the world to know that we'd done well.

"I'm the youngest of seven kids—a mistake, my mother always told me. My father was a Navy pilot whose whole life was the military until he retired. Then drinking became his life. My mother has a history of mental illness; the doctors diagnosed her as schizophrenic, but she always

241

refused to take medication. She did bizarre things: One day she gave away my beloved dog with no explanation. She just took him to the pound, and by the time I found out, he'd been put to sleep. I was eleven.

"Money was always an issue; we just never had enough. I couldn't go to the movies or bowling, because I couldn't pay. We never got birthday presents, and only rarely got new clothes. If my father ever found out that Mother had taken one of us shopping, he'd fly into a rage.

"I met Rich in tenth grade, and by our senior year, we'd started dating. We have so much in common. In some ways, his family life was very similar to mine, so we could help each other deal with the past.

"We were married a month after we graduated from college. Rich found a job as a civil engineer with a construction company. I worked at an ad agency downtown, and we bought a charming fixer-upper.

"When we married, I told Rich I didn't want a joint checking account because I didn't want to answer to him for things I wanted to buy, the way my mother always had to. We split all the joint bills. Rich has always made more, but we never argued about money, except when Rich refused to use a penny of our savings to buy a nice bedroom set. Our savings were for retirement, he'd insist.

"Look, there's a difference between being smart and being cheap. We've never gone on a vacation because Rich hates to spend money. When my nephew got married in California, Rich refused to go with me because he didn't want to buy two plane tickets.

"Four years ago, Rich was offered a position with a terrific company based in the Rockies. I was very reluctant. I didn't want to sell our house or leave our friends. I also knew if we made a move, he'd find out how much I owed. Finally, I just asked him to sign the mortgage application forms for the new house, and I filled in the rest later.

"My husband loved his job, loved being away from the grind of the city. I hated it. After a couple of years, my old company offered me a better position, and after much discussion, we moved back to Denver a year ago.

"Even though I was happier being back in Denver, my spending just went out of control. Sometimes I justified my purchases as a way of getting back at Rich. He's clearly upset with me for making him move, though he never comes right out with it. He refuses to go anywhere or do anything. All he wants to do is sit home with a video or putter around the house. I can't make him understand how lonely and unhappy I am.

"We've also been trying to have a baby, but after an ectopic pregnancy when I was twenty-six, the doctors don't think I'll be able to get pregnant. We've talked about adopting, but we just can't make a decision.

"I ended up having to tell Rich about the debt when I couldn't make even the minimum payment on a single card. I know I need help desperately. Rich means more to me than anyone else. Will he ever trust me again?"

RICH'S TURN

"Even though I told Kelly I wanted a divorce, by morning, I realized we should at least give counseling a try," said Rich, thirty-three, a civil engineer. "I do love her, but I feel completely betrayed. Everything that happened to my dad seems to be happening to me.

"My mother, like Kelly's, struggled with psychiatric problems. She's manic-depressive, and for long periods of time when I was growing up, my two brothers and I had to live with my grandparents. Mother was never physically abusive, but she'd scream, throw things, curse us out. Dad owned a dry-cleaning business, and he tried to be both mother and father to us. My parents fought constantly, and when I was fifteen, they finally divorced. Mother moved to Oregon, and my brothers and I stayed here in Colorado with Dad.

"Money was one of the main reasons my parents split. My dad worked very hard to build up his business, and Mother worked equally hard to spend every penny he earned. Once, when I was about seven, she took off on a three-week vacation without telling Dad—she sent us a postcard from the Caribbean. So you can see why Kelly's spending made me crazy.

"In the beginning, our relationship was so special. Kelly and I could talk about anything, and we had so much fun! She was interested in things, too, things that didn't involve money. But over the years, she's changed. She's become almost single-minded in her determination to buy what she wants when she wants it.

"I hate the city, I hate traffic jams and waiting for an hour to eat in a restaurant. But, I loved everything about our life in the mountains, and I thought Kelly agreed with me—especially since we were trying to have a baby. But right now we seem to have so many problems, I don't think that's such a good idea.

"I also loved the job I had out there. But before we'd even been there a month, it was clear Kelly was unhappy. When she started talking about going back to Denver, the quarreling began. I eventually gave in. I didn't have trouble finding another position, though I'm not thrilled with my work.

"It's ironic: When we were first married, Kelly told me she didn't want a joint checking account, and I was actually relieved. I thought that meant she'd be spending her own money, not frittering away mine. We've never been able to discuss budgets or savings—she always gets very testy when I bring it up.

"Sometimes when she'd come home with a new dress or pillows for the couch, I'd be suspicious. But she always assured me she had the money. Besides, to be honest, I don't know how much these things cost, and I assumed I could trust her.

"I'm not very keen on being here. But I want to save my marriage. I guess some of the problems we're having are my fault, too. Besides, what do I have to lose?"

THE COUNSELOR'S TURN

"Although Kelly tried to deny to herself as well as to Rich that she was a compulsive shopper, reality finally caught up with her," noted the counselor. "For Kelly, it was a way of filling the well of emptiness she'd struggled with since childhood, as well as a weapon against Rich's restrictive attitudes about money. However, while money was the main issue for them, it wasn't the only one. These two had to start communicating not only about finances but about their feelings as well.

"Kelly was depressed and deeply ashamed about her overspending, but she was also defensive: She felt that because her husband wasn't there for her in many ways, she was justified in her actions. Of course,

she never imagined they would lead to such disastrous consequences. My first goal was to help this couple redefine the problems they were facing, to find the real causes for Kelly's overspending—and how Rich contributed to the problem.

"Kelly grew up in a dysfunctional home, dominated by a mother who was mentally ill and an alcoholic father, who, when he was around, was often verbally abusive. So she found comfort in material things.

"Rich's background was strikingly similar to Kelly's, and it's not hard to see why financial security loomed so large for him. Rich hadn't been shown much love as a child either. Remembering his mother's destructive overspending, he feared he and Kelly ultimately might be facing the same dismal future. What's more, having endured his mother's abrupt mood swings, Rich learned to shut down when he felt emotionally threatened. Instead of addressing the issue of Kelly's spending or his own anger and unhappiness about returning to the city, Rich ignored problems. By doing so, he unwittingly shut Kelly out of his life, refusing to talk or engage in any of the activities that had brought them so much happiness early on.

"Understanding this connection was a key to getting this marriage back on track. I recommended that they consult a financial planner to consolidate and pay off their debts, and set rules for spending and saving. Although keeping separate checking accounts was important to both of them, Kelly cut back to only one credit card, to be used only in emergencies and paid in full every month. If she wants something, she saves until she has cash. Once a month, the two of them sit down together to review the bills. The planner assured Rich that since their 401(k) plans were intact, they were on solid ground for the future.

"Part of the financial strategy involved setting aside money for personal spending and for fun. 'When Kelly feels deprived,' I pointed out, her internal regulator goes awry. If she feels she has some control over purchases, and she feels a connection with you, Rich, she has less need to overspend.'

"One homework assignment helped significantly. Every Thursday was date night for the two of them, and each took turns choosing the evening activity. This wasn't easy for Rich, since he was acutely bothered by crowds and traffic. But Kelly was thrilled that they'd be doing something together and that Rich would be involved in setting it up.

"Once Rich and Kelly began following their new plan, Rich's anger subsided, and he was able to examine the part he played in Kelly's spending cycle. In time, they were able to build back their old trust. Over the course of several months, they wrestled with the issue of adoption and decided finally not to have children. 'Given our childhood problems, we want to pour all our energies into the marriage,' explained Kelly. 'I'm not sure we'd have enough left over to raise a family, too.' Rich still worries that the mail may bring some unexpected bill. 'It's going to take time,' he said. 'But at least we are working together on this now.' I told them that the important thing was the open, honest discussion and the fact that they were finally really listening to each other. That's what will help them overcome the legacy of family problems—and build a happier future."

SEX, LIES & MONEY

Hidden debt, like a clandestine affair, can rock an intimate relationship. Is honesty always the best policy? That depends, experts say, on several factors such as: the general nature of your relationship (have you always sworn never to deceive each other on anything?), the intent or motive behind the silence, and, not incidentally, the amount of money involved and the effect of its discovery on your financial future.

Kelly's continued deception could easily have catapulted this marriage into the divorce statistics. For Rich, and for many couples, deception is as much of a betrayal as infidelity—and it's a red flag that there may be other serious issues in the marriage that must be addressed. If your gut tells you a spouse will be very angry if he knew what you did (i.e., never mentioned that large, outstanding student loan; smashed the car to the tune of $4,500; took a risky business gamble that tanked), or if you are obsessing about your secrecy and it's making you miserable, speak to a therapist or trusted member of the clergy to help you untangle your conflicted emotions. In this way, you can find the right time to share your secret sensitively and carefully work through the issues the revelation may trigger.

Needless to say, some partners feel they don't have a choice. If you're seriously afraid that a spouse's profligate ways will leave no resources in case of a medical emergency or job loss, or if your marriage is very rocky, you may need a separate account to ensure your independence and sanity.

However, on a less serious note: Does your spouse really have to know how much that new handbag cost? A distinction must be made between secrets and privacy. We are always making decisions large and small about what to tell a partner, a friend, or a colleague. We consider whether some things might be best left unsaid because the result might cause more problems than it's worth. The bottom line: If finances are particularly tight and you've agreed to cut back across the board, then yes, 'fess up. But if it won't make a huge dent in your finances or lifestyle, you don't need to be accountable, literally, for every thought or action.

"My Job Makes Me Happier Than He Does"

Shelly was successful and respected at work but Larry accused her of abandoning him and their kids. Can a working mother ever have it all?

"My husband told me he was moving out—I haven't stopped crying for a week," said Shelly, forty-one, president of the American division of a large Japanese manufacturing company, and mother of Amanda, fifteen, and Max, eleven. "I know I've been preoccupied with work but I didn't realize things were this bad.

"Up until now, Larry, who's a pediatrician, had no problem with the way we lived. He never told me what he wanted to do on weekends, so I assumed it was my job to make the decisions. And he never objected to my work hours. I thought we had a tacit agreement: I'd be the major breadwinner, and he'd take on the home chores. If Larry wasn't happy, if he didn't like our arrangement, well, how was I to know if he didn't say so?

"Last year, my company merged with a huge conglomerate, and I had to hunker down even more than usual. But it's much more rewarding to be in the office, where I'm in control, than at home, with a husband who's moody and uncommunicative. It's no fun being around someone who can't even tell me what he wants for dinner. At least the men I work with are powerful, successful, and happy.

247

"I work hard because I have to. Things between us started to sour after the pediatric practice Larry had been with for fifteen years folded—another casualty of managed care. I was upset and worried. I knew I'd have to make a lot of money and be very successful since I was the sole breadwinner. It took nearly a year for Larry to figure out what he wanted to do, so it was my responsibility to pay the bills. Even now, I make more money than he does. I don't feel safe without extra money in the bank; I guess that's the way I was raised. My dad, a businessman, made a good salary, but we lived modestly; we rarely took vacations or went to movies. I attended a state university, though my younger sister and brothers later went on to private ones.

"No one does anything halfway in my family. My siblings are all lawyers or scientists, and our mother is our role model. She was president of the hospital volunteer group and chairperson of every school committee, and she earned her college degree when she was in her fifties. Dad tended to see the negative in things. If I got a B, he asked me, 'Why not an A?' I had great expectations for myself, and I wanted him to be proud of me.

"Until recently, I loved my job. My colleagues were fabulous—we were almost like a family—and I zoomed up through the ranks. It was great to earn a good living and be in a position of power. At the same time, I stayed connected to my kids by going on field trips whenever I could, driving carpools and not missing recitals or school plays. I adore Amanda and Max, and it's awful to hear Larry accuse me of not making them a priority.

"But while I don't want to quit working, I do admit that it's getting harder and harder trying to do it all. I need more time with the children, especially now that my relationship with Amanda has fallen apart. Hardly a day goes by without the two of us getting into a screaming match.

"Larry and I used to be best friends. I knew from the moment we met that I wanted to be his wife. But lately, I've been saying irrational things to him that I really don't mean, like the business about the postnuptial agreement. Once, I even told Larry I didn't love him the way I used to. It must be all the stress I'm under. I'm still not sure why I even brought up the topic, but he hasn't stopped using it as proof that I don't love him or trust him to care for our kids.

"I can't accept that it's too late for us. I just need to learn how to show Larry how much I care."

LARRY'S TURN

"When I told Shelly I was moving out, the news hit her like a ton of bricks," said Larry, forty-two.

"I don't know why she's so surprised—we've barely had a marriage for the last five years. I've tried to tell her how much the kids and I love and need her, that it gets lonely looking at her empty chair at the dining room table every night. But all Shelly cares about is her work.

"When she's not traveling, she's out every night wining and dining corporate hotshots. She's smart and accomplished, and I'm proud of her success, but I hate the way it's changed our marriage for the worse.

"Folding my practice was a tremendous blow to my self-esteem. It didn't help that Shelly, instead of being supportive, was furious. She actually criticized me for going into pediatrics in the first place, saying it didn't pay enough. That really hurt.

"Eventually, I helped establish the children's health clinic where I work now. But just as I started to feel good about myself again, Shelly distanced herself, working up to eighty hours a week. She hardly ever has time to kiss or hug me, much less have sex. Late at night, when I'm half asleep, she spreads papers all over the bed and make calls to London. She never turns off her cell phone, even at school events. It's not that she ignores our kids, but we all know her job comes first.

"To compensate, I became the perfect husband. I picked up the kids from school, helped with homework, went to every school conference, band concert, and softball game.

I absolutely love being a dad, but I want a wife, too. I miss the sweet, affectionate woman I know Shelly still is at heart.

"When I was growing up, my mother used to tell me, 'Bad love is better than no love.' Maybe that's why I've put up with this for so long. I was only seven when my father died. Within a year, my mother married a man who treated me and my two younger brothers like dirt. I tried hard to please my stepfather, and by everyone's standards but his, I was pretty successful. I had a lot of friends and did well in school.

"Shelly and I started dating during my senior year of college. I loved her beauty, intelligence, and independence. We married while I was in medical school, and during my residency, she entered business school. Shelly's amazing: She took a few weeks off after she had Amanda, and still managed to finish fourth in her class.

"Those first years went as smoothly as you could wish. Even now, we don't really fight—but we don't really talk either. Shelly barks orders at me as if I were her assistant; for instance, she'll tell me what we're doing over the weekend without even asking if I agree. A few months ago, I told her I wanted to attend a medical seminar, and she didn't object to it. Then two days before the conference, she told me that she'd organized a surprise birthday party for her father on the same day.

She was furious when I didn't cancel my plans for the meeting.

"Though Max misses having his mother around after school and at night, he's an easygoing kid and seems fine so far. Amanda is a different story. In the last year her grades have slipped, she's argumentative, and she's been hanging out with a rowdy group of kids.

"Recently, when Shelly and I were discussing our wills, she announced that she wanted a post-nuptial agreement saying that if she died first, her money would go the kids and not to my future wife. Did she really think I was going to neglect our children? That's when it dawned on me: This is not the woman I married. She doesn't care about me or my interests. I play sax in a band, but she's never come to see me perform.

"I told her I was moving out. Now Shelly's pleading with me to patch things up. I hate to throw away twenty years of marriage and ruin our kids' lives, but I don't think I can live with her anymore."

THE COUNSELOR'S TURN

"Although Larry was dumping most of the blame onto Shelly's shoulders, it takes two people to tear a marriage apart and two to make it better," said the counselor. "I wanted to help them tap into the love they used to feel for each other.

"Shelly held herself to high standards, and it was through success and money that she defined herself as a person. Now she had achieved her professional goals, but like many executives in demanding jobs, she had developed tunnel vision in order to survive, and her family moved to the periphery. Larry's moving out was a harsh wake-up call.

"I told Shelly, 'The old marriage may be over, but you and Larry can work on a new one. The ball is in your court.' My words touched a chord, and her eyes welled with tears. I urged, 'What would you do differently to build a new marriage?' She said, 'I'd make more time for my family.'

"I learned that Shelly's father had once experienced a job setback. This, coupled with his tendency to withhold money from his family, instilled in her a deep anxiety about financial security. When Larry's medical practice folded, Shelly's fears resurfaced. Understanding the source of her anxiety helped ease the problem. 'I still get panicky sometimes,' she said, 'but I've found that if I stop and consider the reality of the situation—we have plenty of money in the bank—I can come back to earth.'

"After thinking it over for a few months, Shelly quit her job and, with a colleague, formed her own consulting firm. It's a less stressful position, and her flexible hours allow her to spend much more time with her family, doing things she likes.

The cold war between Shelly and Amanda has begun to thaw.

"I also helped Shelly see her husband in a new way: 'Maybe he's not the man you fell in love with, but that's because your relationship has shifted so dramatically,' I explained. 'When a marriage slips into a dominant/submissive power structure, the submissive person—Larry—becomes depressed and the dominant one—you—turns angry and impatient.'

"Knowing the root of his moodiness helped Shelly act less critical and bossy. She started going to Larry's band gigs and dropping by his health clinic. Seeing what a compassionate, respected doctor Larry was made her proud, and she stopped comparing him to the people she used to work with.

"Feeling unloved and unworthy from a young age, Larry behaved toward Shelly the way he had with his disapproving stepfather. Rather then stating his own desires, he let Shelly have her way on most issues.

"I suggested that he practice small acts of self-assertion: telling Shelly what he wanted for dinner, what he wanted to do on the weekend, and so on. The couple also learned to use a three-part decision-sharing exercise for issues large and small: First, check your personal agenda. What do each of you want? What's in your best interest? Next, explain the concerns underlying your desires. Finally, find a mutually acceptable solution.

"For example, Shelly likes to know well in advance when she and Larry will do something fun together, while Larry prefers not to be held to a rigid schedule. Their solution: On Mondays, they check their calendars and make plans, some definite, some tentative.

"Shelly was right when she said that Larry's moodiness made it unpleasant to come home at night. He needed to lighten up a bit. Happily, that was easy once he saw that Shelly was making the effort to spend more time at home and share his interests. And once they began communicating openly again, it wasn't long before the affection naturally returned to their relationship.

"Larry moved back home after six months, and they ended counseling after a year. 'We went to a business dinner the other night,' Larry reported. 'A woman said to us, "I'll bet you two just got married—you act like newlyweds." Well, that's exactly how we feel.'"

WHEN SHE EARNS MORE THAN HE

Anything that runs against the societal grain holds the potential for triggering anxiety. And when that something has to do with money, entwined as it is with a man's self-confidence and ego, budget battles may brew. These days, the opportunities for such clashes are more numerous than ever: According to figures from the Bureau of Labor Statistics, in almost one-quarter of dual-income marriages today, she earns more than he. While many couples take the disparity in stride ("It's not my money or his money, but *our* money"), the reality is not always so rosy. The way you handle these issues depends largely on how you were raised, and the expectations you've brought to the relationship. To keep budget issues in balance:

1. Pay attention to your feelings. Are you starting to resent being the primary breadwinner? A wife whose husband can't hold a job, or whose career ambitions are several notches below hers, may bristle or silently seethe. Similarly, the husband who willingly stays at home may, in time, feel abandoned as a wife's business dinners or travel needs erode family and couple time. First consider whether the current situation is due to factors out of his control—plummeting stock market, a company bankruptcy—or due to his temperament. The first? Give it time. The second? He is who he is and chances are you will not change his basic character on this point either.

2. If disagreements surface, identify the real bottom-line issue. Even when you work longer hours, does he still expect you to shoulder the childcare duties? Or, on the other hand, are you unable to delegate any household decisions? It's time to renegotiate the division of labor. Keep a diary for one month, detailing everything each of you do. If things are unequal, rework assignments based on interests and abilities.

3. Focus on what you each bring to the marriage. Identify areas of the relationship in which he is making a significant contribution. Maybe he's a stay-at-home dad who shoulders most of the parenting and nurturing responsibilities. Maybe he's decided to go back to school or start a new business. Or maybe he's an artist, musician, or social worker whose chosen field will never yield as much income as his attorney wife. As long as you both can appreciate the balance, you'll avoid money battles.

4. Don't flaunt your success or fling it in your spouse's face when arguments erupt. And be sure to let family, friends, and colleagues know if this is a sensitive subject for you and your mate.

"HE SPENDS TOO MUCH"

*C*harlie loved treating *family and friends to expensive gifts and dinners, but Terry was afraid they'd never have enough to pay their bills. What happens when one spouse always feels shortchanged?*

"*C*harlie has always had champagne taste and a beer budget, but this tops everything," said Terry, an at-home mother, clenching her hands nervously. "He knows how I worry about money, yet he just threw a very expensive party in a fancy hotel suite for my thirtieth birthday.

"When I flipped on the lights, there were twelve of our friends yelling, 'Surprise!' Charlie had arranged a buffet, with cake, and champagne. I was very touched—until I started calculating the bill. 'This must have cost a fortune,' I whispered to Charlie. 'You're worth it,' he said, hugging me.

"I know I must sound hideously ungrateful. Charlie's a romantic man who's always doing thoughtful things for me and our two little girls, Erica and Brittney. And I love him for it. But I don't need a four-star hotel or a gourmet dinner to make me feel good. We simply can't afford it.

"I'm tired of fighting with Charlie. Every month when I sit down to pay the bills, I get panicky. We pay only the minimum on our credit cards, so we owe a ton in interest. I feel calmer and in control when I can keep track of finances down to the penny. Charlie, on the other had, has no idea how much we have in our joint checking account.

253

"I know Charlie always dreamed of owning his own business. But the electronics store he part-owns and manages barely breaks even, and since it's so small, we don't have health insurance or a pension plan. I used to be an executive administrator for a catalog company, but I left five years ago, after Erica was born. I did the math and even if I went back to work part-time, all my salary would go toward child care.

"You can't spend money you don't have. For Valentine's Day two years ago, Charlie bought us matching leather jackets. They looked great, but they were totally frivolous. Last year, he bought a brand-new sport-utility vehicle without consulting me. Of course, we had to sell it because we couldn't make the payments.

"I've always had to be careful about money. When I was four, my alcoholic father walked out on us, leaving my mother and grandmother to raise me. Mom, a dental hygienist, had a string of boyfriends, all unreliable. I learned my lesson early: You can't count on a man, so you'd better learn how to survive on your own, or else.

"I was waitressing at a diner to pay for college—I have a degree in business administration—when I met Charlie. He used to come for lunch every day and draw me into conversation. He can be so funny, charming, and thoughtful, it was easy to fall in love with him. I didn't think much about his spending habits then; it just seemed nice that he picked up the check when we went out with friends.

"We agreed that I would quit my job after we started a family. Much as I enjoyed working, I loved being there to watch Erica and Brittney, who's now three, grow up.

"Back then, Charlie was working for a general contractor and making pretty good money. But he got tired of reporting to other people, so he quit. I wanted him to be happy, but not having a regular paycheck made me anxious. Now Charlie has the store, though he's not really cut out for management—he's too nice. He pals around with his employees; then if they slack off or miss work, he doesn't feel right about reprimanding or firing them.

"Charlie has the same careless attitude about everything. Our landlord gives us a break on the rent when Charlie does repairs on our house. He'll begin to replace the siding, or paint a room, and then quit halfway through.

"What happened two weeks ago was the last straw. Charlie got home late, exhausted and depressed, then began going on about some new business scheme. I was tired, too, and I said, 'Charlie, I can't listen to this. You've got to get a real job.' He stormed out of the room, packed a bag and flew to Florida for a week!

"He just doesn't get it—and I'm worn out from trying to make him come to his senses."

CHARLIE'S TURN

"Terry doesn't talk, she lectures," said thirty-one-year-old Charlie, shifting uncomfortably in his seat. "I love her, but I don't know if I'm in love with her anymore. She makes me feel like a loser. That's why I went to Florida; I had to get far away to empty my mind and calm down. Okay, it was a rash move, but I had hit bottom. I'm so stressed lately that just hearing my kids play too loudly can make me lose it.

"When I first met Terry, she was so sweet and encouraging—a far cry from the woman she's become. Her reaction to the surprise party was so typical. She can't lighten up and enjoy herself, even on her own birthday. I wanted to do something special, but she used it as yet another weapon to humiliate me. I can never win.

"Terry is forever harping on me about the home repairs. I recommended aluminum siding to our landlord because it's practical and lasts a lifetime, but Terry thought it looked cheap. Maybe that's why I don't seem to be able to finish those projects. Why should I even try if I can't make her happy?

"Unlike my wife, I had a pretty contented childhood. My mom stayed home with my older brother and me, and my father worked for the same clothing manufacturer for thirty years. We didn't have very much when I was growing up, but I never felt deprived.

"In high school, I dreamed of becoming a Major League Baseball player. The coach told my folks I had enough talent to try out for the state team. But things didn't work out—something to do with the expense and Dad having to take time out from work to drive me to the away games. After a while, I grew more interested in girls than in sports.

"There was only one time when I know I disappointed my mother and father. I dropped out of college to get a job—I was never a great student—and then moved in with a woman whose religion was different from ours. My parents were so upset, they didn't talk to me for almost a year. After my girlfriend and I broke up, though, everything was fine, and Mom and Dad never said a word about the way they'd acted.

"In fact, I don't recall ever hearing my parents argue. Maybe that's why I'm so shocked by the way Terry and I get caught up in these stupid fights about money. Neither of us knows how to put the brakes on. We've never been as desperate as Terry makes us sound—she exaggerates everything. It's not like we're headed for bankruptcy. I know I've changed jobs a lot, but I've always found something else, and Terry's so happy being home with the girls that I'd rather not see her go back to work. It would be nice if she had some faith in me. Instead, she shoots down all my ideas.

255

WHEN MONEY STYLES CLASH:
Three Critical Steps

Seemingly unstoppable money fights can swamp the good feelings you have for each other, especially at life's transition points, such as the loss of a job, the birth of a child, or a move to a new home. And topping the list of cash conflicts is a clash of money-handling styles. Different spending habits means different priorities and values—and that's something you must discuss and resolve. Unfortunately, money is often the one subject that even happily married couples have difficulty addressing.

These steps can prevent cash clashes from sabotaging your marriage:

Step 1: Recognize your distinct money personalities.
Everyone has his or her own attitude about money. Some are born savers, others committed spendthrifts. As increasing numbers of couples wed later in life, more people than ever before are bringing a complicated money history to the marriage. Having different financial objectives can be a plus—your ability to save will be crucial as family expenses grow, while his cajoling you to take that Caribbean holiday may enlighten you to certain experiences that are more valuable than extra money in the bank. Still, it's important to know who you are: *Money worriers* are convinced that the next market crash is imminent. They obsess about money all the time, even if the piggy bank is full. Why are they working so hard? They can't enjoy the fruits of their labor. *Money hoarders* can't bear to part with a penny. Every purchase is suspect, probably frivolous. For *money avoiders,* simply talking about finances can trigger an anxiety attack. Though ignorance is bliss, they may inadvertently overspend since they never balance their checkbooks. *Money spenders* can't save. Shopping brings a rush of pleasure, and they never prioritize, let alone budget. *Money bingers* are part hoarder, part spender. They save and save, then blow it all on something they can't resist. Which category do you fit into?

Step 2: Talk about your money concerns.
Set aside time on a monthly basis to talk about the bottom line—from your current finances to your early money memories growing up. The best time: When money isn't the issue. When are you most relaxed—Sunday afternoon? During dinner out? After the kids are in bed? The worst time: When you're paying bills or signing your son's college tuition contract.

Listen to each other's dreams without dismissing them as stupid fantasies. At the same time, be clear about how a partner's overspending or inability to part with a penny affects you. Share what you admire about your spouse's attitudes ("You know, I wish I could enjoy myself more in-the-moment, like you do. I'm always fretting that I'll be a bag lady when I'm seventy"). But don't be afraid to bring his or her attention to specific examples that leave you uncomfortable ("I know we're both working hard, but eating out every night, or having takeout feels extravagant to me." "I know we got that tax refund, but why did you go ahead and buy a new car stereo when you know I've been wanting to refinish the basement?").

Step 3: Talk about your future goals.

Where do you see yourselves in ten years and how can you get there? Address current needs as well as those that will change at each stage of your life (music lessons for the kids? orthodontist bills? retirement savings?) and try to devise solutions before you hit problems.

Finally: If you are such opposites that compromise feels as elusive as peace in the Middle East, enlist the aid of a financial adviser or marriage counselor to help you uncover the deeper concerns that the money worries are masking.

"Yes, I appreciate having certain things. I work hard, and I don't see the point in pinching pennies. If we go out to dinner with friends, I shouldn't have to catch hell for picking up the check once in a while. If my daughter wants a pack of Pokémon trading cards, I'll spend the four bucks. That doesn't mean I'm not concerned about bigger issues. I know we need health insurance, but I also believe that things will come together one day soon.

"I've always wanted to own a business, but this past year at the store has been the worst. I'm burned out. I want to spend more time with my daughters, but I'm putting in over eighty hours a week with no vacation days. Maybe Terry's right; I'll never be a success. Is the only answer going to work for a big company, where I'll be a nobody? Do I have to give up my dream for the sake of a benefits package?"

THE COUNSELOR'S TURN

"Although money is a major trigger for marital discord, it can also mask other important issues," said the counselor.

"For Terry, money represented the emotional support and trust she never had as a child. Deep down, she didn't believe she deserved nice things. Abandoned by her father, Terry projected her distrust of men onto Charlie.

"Though Charlie did have an impulse-spending problem, he was right when he said Terry tended to magnify problems way out of proportion. I gently pointed out to her that she could have set up a savings plan herself, rather than waiting for her husband to do it. Terry admitted that they weren't really in dire financial straits, and that she was being too critical of her husband.

"Charlie approached money with an I'll-worry-about-it-tomorrow mind-set. However, spending did little to boost his sense of self-worth. Charlie got the unspoken message from his parents that his needs didn't matter and that there was no use discussing anything that was important to him. As a result, he didn't know how to express his feelings.

"Before working on this, however, I suggested Terry and Charlie join the gym at the YMCA, or go bowling once a week—fun, relatively cheap, stress-busting activities that would help them focus on the pleasurable aspects of their relationship. Sure enough, they began to fight less and laugh more.

"At this point we were able to start honing their communication skills. 'No matter how good your ideas are,' I explained to Terry, 'Charlie will tune you out if you nag or belittle him.' She worked hard to take the scolding tone out of her voice, and to stop assuming that none of her husband's ideas could possibly work.

"To address the money issue, I suggested they attend a free seminar on money management offered by one of the local banks. The seminar leader helped them get their budget in order. They also learned that paying even just a little more than the minimum balance on their credit cards each month would help them get out of debt much sooner and avoid high interest payments.

"Budget in hand, Charlie and Terry discovered that it wasn't as hard as they'd feared to start putting aside money while still keeping up with the bills. Charlie also promised not to charge any more big-ticket items without talking to Terry first.

"Charlie is still at the store, but he's looking to sell his share and find a contracting job with a construction firm. He hasn't ruled out opening another business later on. Next year, when Brittney is in nursery school, Terry plans to work part-time in catalog sales, which will further ease their money worries.

"Terry came to our last session with two airplane tickets, 'We found these low fares on the Internet, so Charlie and I are going to Puerto Rico for a long weekend!' she announced. 'We've saved up enough, so I think we deserve a little treat.' Now that these two are back on track, neither one feels shortchanged about money."

"My Husband Is a Compulsive Gambler"

—

Nick had lied to Kim for twenty years. Although he swore he'd changed, can she ever learn to trust him again?

Kim's Turn

"Six months ago, I kicked my husband out of the house," said Kim, thirty-seven, her voice shaky. "Nick is a compulsive gambler and, although I've adored him for twenty years, I can no longer continue to be married.

"Except to discuss our kids, Nick and I have barely spoken—he's living in an apartment across town. Then last week, he called to tell me he'd gone to Gamblers Anonymous. He promises he's going to stick with it this time and he begged me to let him move back in. I don't know what to do. How can I ever trust him? I thought asking Nick to leave was the hardest thing I'd ever have to do, but healing our marriage seems impossible.

"I met Nick when I was sixteen. My family—I was the youngest of four girls, all far prettier and smarter than I was—had just moved to New England from Milwaukee, and I was finding it hard to make friends. Nick was a senior. Handsome and charming, he was clearly the smartest, most popular boy in high school. It was love at first sight for me and I was astounded that a guy like him was actually interested in a girl like me.

"After one date, we were inseparable. Although my parents wanted me to go to college, I couldn't wait to marry Nick, settle down, and raise a family. We were married two months after I finished high school. By then, Nick had a job working for a shipping and packaging company and I was a secretary for a businessman in town. I thought my dreams had come true.

"For a while, they had. Nick's family welcomed me with open arms. We moved into a small house down the street from his folks and his mother treated me like the daughter she never had. She was always there to help out and when the kids came along—Kelly will be eighteen next spring and Sean is thirteen—she volunteered to baby-sit so I could go back to my old secretarial job. She was generous with her money, too, popping over regularly with shopping bags filled with new clothes for the kids.

"Nick put in long hours on the job. His shifts changed every few months. He took lots of overtime and, since the company is a round-the-clock operation, he could conceivably be working all hours of the day or night. When he told me he had to work late, there was no reason not to believe him.

"But I started to get increasingly anxious about money. We never seemed to have any, even though Nick was working all the time. If I dared ask about it, he'd fly into a rage. 'That's my job,' he would shout, 'the home is yours. That's the way my father did it, and that's the way I do it. The bills are getting paid, aren't they? You have food on the table, right? So leave me alone.' I was never allowed to see his paychecks. Whenever we were low on cash, Nick had a ready explanation. I learned not to ask too many questions or I'd unleash the Irish temper.

"For years, I convinced myself that things were really all right. After all, my husband wasn't a goof-off, or an alcoholic like my father was. My sisters and I adored him, in spite of his outbursts. Mother always made excuses for him, anyway. She always forgave him: 'Oh, I know Daddy didn't mean that,' she'd tell us. She insisted we all love each other, never fight or argue.

"So, like my mother, I white-washed my life, literally. I became a cleanliness fanatic. The kids were immaculate, the house was immaculate. I could calm myself that way for a while, and then I'd feel anxious again and start yelling at my kids. Of course, Nick was the good guy. He'd come home and say, 'Guess where we're going? Disney World!' My stomach would churn. Where, I wondered, did the money for this trip come from?

"Then, one night, my worst fears came true. Nick came home and told me he had gambled too much at the racetrack. He explained that it was near the office and he had stopped off with the guys now and then to try his luck. I asked how much he lost, but I never got a straight answer. It was enough, he said, that we had to take out a second mortgage on our house.

I was hysterical, but Nick was so remorseful and promised it would never happen again. So we took out a second mortgage and I tried to forget it ever happened.

"This became a pattern. Things would be fine for a while, then I'd notice that money I was sure I'd deposited in our joint account was gone. When I asked Nick about it, he again always had a ready answer. And, as I said, if I even hinted that I thought he was gambling, he'd deny it vehemently. My daughter told me—just recently, in fact—that Nick used to borrow money she'd earned from baby-sitting. She was covering for him, too.

"I never thought of Nick's gambling as an illness. I just thought there must be something wrong with me, something I wasn't doing or giving him. I fooled myself into believing that each time was really the last time. If I ever mentioned anything about gambling, he'd accuse me of blaming him for one mistake for the rest of our lives.

"But I found a bank statement stuffed in the drawer that proved he'd squandered the money we had gotten from a personal loan—money earmarked for Kelly's college education. I told him he had to go to Gamblers Anonymous to get some help. He refused, but the children and I started going once a week to Gam-Anon, a support group for the families of compulsive gamblers.

"Those meetings opened my eyes. I can't describe how relieved I felt to hear the stories of all those other people whose problems were so much like mine. I realized that compulsive gamblers always have a ready answer or excuse for what they do. I realized I was actually encouraging his addiction by ignoring it. These people gave me the strength to do what I should have done a long time ago. I gave Nick an ultimatum: Get some help or leave.

"It hasn't been easy, but I've managed okay. At this point, I don't know how I feel. How can I be sure this won't happen again? I told him the only way I'd ever consider getting back together was if we first went for marriage counseling so we could at least learn to speak to each other. I love him, but I don't know if I can live with him."

NICK'S TURN

"I've been living a lie for years," said Nick, thirty-nine. "But I've learned my lesson. I've changed, and I want Kim and me to be together again.

"To me, gambling was always second nature. I grew up in a small town and as far back as I can remember, I rarely told the truth. It was a knee-jerk reaction, a way to protect myself, I guess. I remember my father whacking my younger brother and I if we did or said anything that displeased him—even something as

261

minor as being late to dinner. He was an iron worker, a real physical guy, and he'd hit us with his hand or a wooden paddle. I felt so protective toward my brother that I'd race home from school or bring him with me when I hung out with my friends just to get him out of the house in case Dad came home in one of his bad moods.

"Dad was an alcoholic, and a violent one, too. My mother didn't do much to help him either. Theirs was a pretty traditional relationship. Dad gave my mother a certain amount of money to run the house, and that was it. I wasn't close to either of them. I can't remember talking to my father about anything of any substance. He wasn't around a lot and was private with his own time. I know he had a regular card game and, although he made a good salary, from time to time, money would be tight. At one point, when my father lost his job, we had to move in with relatives for a few months. I assumed he gambled, but no one ever talked about it. Neither one of my parents ever shared his or her feelings and I certainly didn't think they cared much about mine. Although I was captain of the football team, neither one ever attended a game. But I had a close group of friends—guys I'd grown up with. They were a second family.

"When I was a freshman in high school, I took a job as a stock boy in a department store. I worked after school and on weekends so I could have the things my friends had—clothes, a new baseball glove, money for the movies. After high school I wanted to be a teacher, but my father wanted me to be an engineer and he refused to help with tuition unless I went to the college he wanted me to go to. I felt I had no choice, but my heart wasn't in my studies and I dropped out my junior year. I found a job with an international packaging company; the salary was good and the benefits excellent. Since Kim and I planned to get married, I thought it was a good move.

"The first few years, I did well. I moved up fast and, by the time I was twenty-five, I was in charge of a department of one hundred and fifty people. I'm not sure what happened to me then. Maybe I can't handle success. I started to feel overwhelmed. I had a hard time delegating and yet there was too much work for me to do. I hated to reprimand people, and having to fire someone—forget it. I couldn't do it. I developed an ulcer.

"I started to get anxious about money when Sean was born. I felt tremendous pressure to give my children a better life than I had had. I also lost touch with my old friends. When I worked the two to ten P.M. shift, I fell into the habit of stopping off at the track on the way home.

"At first it was a lark, something to do. I felt less lonely at the track. I would catch the last two or three races. The first couple of times I won decent money—two nights in a row, I came home with over five thousand dollars in my pocket. The next night, I gambled it all away.

"That became a pattern. Winning, losing, winning, losing. All the time I was betting, I was trying to pay off the bills, too. When I was short, I'd get cash advances on my credit cards to use at the track. Or I'd borrow from my mother, even my daughter once or twice. I didn't want Kim to know. I was secretive and defensive, and when she confronted me or asked about money, I'd clam up or lash out at her. And I adamantly denied I was gambling.

"As time went on, I got deeper and deeper in debt. I lied through my teeth and told her I'd never do it again, but all I was waiting for was another chance at the track.

"I did attend one meeting of Gamblers Anonymous, but I didn't even stay till the end. I thought the program was ridiculous. 'I'm not as sick as these people,' I told myself. When Kim laid down the law and kicked me out, I was indignant at first. But I knew she was right. I started going to GA after work in the evening and vowed to stick with it—and I have. But I can't make Kim believe that I've changed for good. She keeps throwing my past mistakes back in my face. She blames me for everything. When she does, I can't help getting mad. I'm afraid it might be too late to save our marriage, but I want to try.

THE COUNSELOR'S TURN

"As in any relationship where trust has been broken, Nick and Kim had to rebuild their marriage from the foundation up," said the counselor. "At Gam-Anon meetings, Kim realized how badly she had been hurt by Nick's addiction. She had been burned too often to freely trust her husband again.

"Although Nick insisted he'd changed—if he hadn't already been going to GA meetings, I would have insisted he begin—it was going to take a long time, and require a lot of effort on both their parts, for Kim to feel that he had.

"As I do with all couples, even those who are living apart, I asked Nick and Kim to make a commitment of at least three months of weekly counseling. By that time, couples have usually hit upon at least one issue that makes them both want to call it quits. If they can get past this point, however, they usually have enough confidence as well as the essential tools to cope with problems as they arise.

"Once they made a commitment, I wanted to make sure they understood about addictions in general and how they destroy a relationship. Anyone growing up in a family with addictions, especially if the addiction is not addressed, is also at high risk for developing an addiction. It's not uncommon for the children of addicted parents to avoid feelings and instead tap into a quick feel-good mechanism, anything to help them make sense of an unpredictable world. The child of an alcoholic may become an alcoholic, too. Or he may become addicted to gambling, sex, or even to work. Rather than learn the skills needed to deal with stress, Nick used gambling to camouflage his inadequacies and give him a false sense of power and control. Understanding this helped Kim be more compassionate about the obstacles Nick had to overcome.

"It was also important for Nick and Kim to understand themselves and their own feelings better. Kim, especially, had little sense of herself. She grew up to be a replica of her mother, an uncomplaining woman who never felt entitled to express her feelings, opinions, or needs. Kim was a pleaser. Despite the obstacles thrown in her path, she was determined to make everything work, and for many years she did.

"It's not surprising that Nick and Kim were attracted to each other. Kim saw her charming, handsome father in Nick. And in Kim, Nick found all the love, acceptance, and appreciation for his accomplishments that had been missing from his childhood. Because of their childhood experiences, however, any show of anger, be it their own or their partner's, was frightening and to be avoided at all costs. One of our early goals was to help them both recognize when they were angry, and then learn to deal with that anger in a constructive way.

"I told them both, 'Tune into your own body; when you're upset, what happens?' Kim realized that anger made her anxious: Her stomach would churn, her heart race, and she'd squirm in her seat. Assuming she was to blame for their troubles, she'd either keep quiet or give in. Nick tended to pull away emotionally and physically when angry. He'd cross his arms, get a distant, glassy look in his eyes, and when pushed to his limit, he'd explode in rage.

"Once they could recognize the early signs of their anger, they set about learning to deal with anger that arose in the middle of their often incendiary discussions. 'Conflict in marriage is not the problem,' I told them. 'It's how you deal with conflict that makes the difference.' I also told them not to get hung up on who's right and who's wrong. 'You don't have to debate each other or try to have the last word in every conversation. But you do have to listen and try to empathize with what your partner is feeling,' I advised.

"To do this, I taught them a structured speaking and listening technique called The Dialogue, developed by Harville Hendrix, Ph.D., a psychotherapist and founder of the Institute for Imago Relationship Therapy in Winter

Park, Florida. The technique can be especially helpful for couples dealing with addiction problems. In such cases, partners' needs may be very different, yet they must talk calmly to each other. For example, Nick was told at GA, quite correctly, that, once he recognized his problem and made amends to those he had hurt, he must forget about the past and live in the present. Kim couldn't do that. She had been so damaged by his deceit that she needed to talk, over and over again, about her pain. Nick had to be able to listen, empathize, but not react defensively or angrily. Although it sounds simple, it's not. Few people really know how to listen to another person and feel what they are feeling without jumping in with their own ideas, opinions, or hidden agendas. Couples like Kim and Nick, who have been fighting for years, are so locked into their adversarial roles that fighting becomes the only way they can relate to each other. They don't know how to handle differing opinions about even the most elementary things—which restaurant to go to, which TV show to watch.

"I told this couple, 'This process will prevent every interaction from becoming a "you" versus "him" battle. It will allow you to experience angry feelings and understand them, instead of running away or ignoring them.'

"This technique was especially useful when Nick and Kim had to talk about volatile money matters—buying a car, renting a new apartment (their home was foreclosed due to Nick's gambling debts, and Kim had to move out), making a budget. Kim found this very painful, but with my coaching she was able to say, 'I feel threatened. I was so naive, and you took advantage of me over and over again.' Nick listened, repeated verbatim what she had said, and empathized with her anxiety and frustration without reacting defensively. 'I can imagine you felt really scared and alone,' he said. Kim melted. For the first time, she felt he understood. Nick, too, learned to express his feelings to Kim whenever he felt he was being unjustly accused or if he was under a lot of stress and overwhelmed by responsibilities. 'Instead of running to the track, I talk with Kim,' he told me at one of our last sessions.

"Learning to share feelings and experiences helped Kim and Nick develop an intimacy long lacking in their marriage. After four months, Kim invited Nick to move back home.

"I still see Nick and Kim periodically, and they are both continuing to attend meetings of their recovery groups. 'Just like an alcoholic can never have one drink, I know I can never place one bet,' said Nick. 'It's too easy to slip back. But you know, I have more confidence now. I don't have the urge to gamble anymore. I don't need it.'"

EASING MONEY ANXIETY WHEN TIMES ARE TIGHT

Layoffs, bankruptcies, plummeting stock prices, and rising unemployment . . . the current economic downturn affects traditional white- and blue-collar workers as well as dot-commers. Who isn't worried? Uncertain times make it all the more imperative for couples to find ways to temper money anxiety and make sure it doesn't spill over into other areas of the relationship. These strategies can get you started:

• Don't panic. Is your self-esteem and self-confidence wrapped up in your professional title or the amount of your paycheck? Remind yourself that you are much more than your job. If you lose it, you, like everyone else, can adjust to change and pressure. Positive thinking works wonders.

• Feelings often follow behavior. If you act like you're in control, you'll feel more in control.

• Sharpen your job skills. Take new courses; research which positions are in demand; polish that résumé. Should the inevitable happen, you'll be prepared and won't be gridlocked by indecision and fear.

• Set financial goals with the realization that you may not be able to achieve all of them. Sometimes even worthy goals can conflict and you may have to make tough decisions about which will bring the most benefit. Separate "needs" from "wants" and narrow your focus to goals that are essential and imminent (paying off credit-card debt or creating an emergency reserve fund) and those that can be put on the back burner (buying a matching living-room set).

• Take advantage of your employer's tax-deferred retirement plans but don't put all your savings in a company-controlled plan or stock. Thousands of laid-off Enron employees lost their retirement savings when the company imploded; to make sure that doesn't happen to you, diversify. If your employer's contribution to your fund is in the form of restricted stock, be sure that the money you put in is divided among a broad range of funds that don't rise and fall with your company's fortunes. Once or twice a year, check how these funds are doing, and if you're not happy with the results, switch.

• Research automatic savings plans. Most mutual fund firms (the easiest way for financial beginners to diversify) will electronically transfer a specific amount from your checking account to purchase shares on a regular basis.

• Get money smart. Contact the National Center for Financial Education, a nonprofit organization that publishes books and money management guides. Contact them at P.O. Box 34070, San Diego, CA 92163.

MAKE LOVE

Keeping the Marriage Hot

———◆———

A couple's sex life is in one sense a barometer of their marriage. Over the years it will fluctuate, depending on a host of factors. The stress of juggling work and family obligations can be so physically and emotionally exhausting that husbands and wives forget the importance of expressing love and tenderness not only outside the bedroom, but inside, too.

External events and problems—having a baby, losing a job, a death in the family, as well as chronic worries about money, health, or work—also take their toll. In fact, about half of all couples, even those who are happily married, struggle with a sexual problem at some point during their marriage.

We see consistently, however, that when husbands and wives complain that the sexual aspect of their marriage is less than satisfying, the impact is usually felt in other areas of the relationship.

Unexpressed anger and resentment, for instance, can haunt the bedroom like ghosts, inhibiting or extinguishing sexual interest altogether. The mother of young children who feels her husband is not

267

doing his fair share around the house, and who believes she's not entitled to speak up or, when she does, is ignored, may feel less than loving later that evening when her husband, oblivious to her feelings, initiates sex. Or a husband, tired of being the target of his wife's sarcastic, critical remarks may assert, "Lovemaking? Forget it. I can't be in the same room with her, let alone make love." In countless cases, sex is the weapon with which one spouse punishes another.

Sometimes a partner's general unhappiness and dissatisfaction with his or her own life triggers a crisis of intimacy. Although this can happen at any time in the course of a marriage, in *Seven Secrets of a Happy Marriage* we see it frequently in the stories of couples in their late forties and fifties faced with an empty nest. When the focus of a marriage shifts from raising children and being a family back to being a couple, both men and women may feel a painful void. Personal doubts as well as lack of confidence or self-esteem can quickly translate into low sexual desire.

Whatever the trigger for trouble, the results are the same: Routine, mediocre sex replaces the fireworks of the earlier years. As doubt deepens, it's a short leap to questioning the validity of the relationship altogether. Interestingly, when relationship problems spill over into the bedroom, couples are evenly divided between those who say that they are so furious with their partner they can't imagine making love and those whose sex life thrives despite difficulties and animosity in other areas. For the latter couples, sex is the only way they can feel close. Unconsciously they may be hoping that, by reconnecting in bed, they can restore the harmony in the rest of their marriage.

Seven Secrets tackles the spectrum of sexual complaints. We meet physically exhausted and emotionally depleted wives who yearn for tenderness and physical affection—"Why does every kiss have to lead to intercourse?" they want to know. When they are in the mood, many wives wonder if their husbands ever learned the definition of foreplay; "What's the rush?" they gripe.

We also meet men who not only want sex more often, they also want their wives to make the overture—"Why can't she be more spontaneous, more adventurous?" is a common lament. Clearly, women who enjoy sex, who initiate and respond to lovemaking, turn their husbands on.

Chief among sexual complaints throughout the decades has been the inability of couples to reconcile different levels of sexual desire and arousal—although the reasons for the differences have changed somewhat. Thirty years ago, therapists focused on psychological factors-problems in the marriage or a strict upbringing—as culprits. Although there is no doubt that these issues heavily influence desire, recent studies in human sexuality have highlighted the key role hormones play in sexual arousal throughout our lives. While many women enjoy sex and are orgasmic, men in general have higher levels of testosterone, the hormone responsible for sexual arousal in both sexes. Understanding the effect of hormonal changes on each partner's desire for sex is important in decreasing the arguments about when and how often to engage in lovemaking—and in increasing intimacy in general.

Seven Secrets also reveals that men and women still have a very different take on their sexual relationships. Like the couple in Woody Allen's *Annie Hall* discussing with their therapist the frequency of their sexual encounters, he typically says they have sex "Hardly at all," while she insists, "All the time!" Women almost always put sex in the context of a relationship: When a woman feels good about her marriage, she's interested in sex. For women, feeling connected emotionally is an essential prelude to lovemaking. But for men, sex affirms their virility. It may also be the only way they know to be intimate.

Whatever the cause, ignoring the lack of a satisfying sexual life, hoping sexual problems will disappear, or making excuses for the lack of passion in a marriage because a couple is reluctant to deal with their other problems is a prescription for disaster. Couples who have successfully kept their sex lives vital understand that the passionate, romantic love they felt in the beginning of their relationship gives way to a more enduring, but equally satisfying love.

These couples make their sex life, and their marriage, a priority. That means creating the opportunities to be intimate: romancing, and flirting with each other, whether it's calling during the day, making lunch dates, or better yet, escaping for a weekend alone—and yes, even scheduling time for sex. It means paying attention to each partner's individual needs, because intimacy cannot flourish when either partner is tense, angry, or resentful.

Making sex a priority also means that, if either partner is dissatisfied, instead of turning complaints into a power struggle, they talk about them candidly. Ironically, talking about sexual problems can actually be a turn-on. When couples resolve the underlying issues that are dividing them and air their differences directly instead of acting them out in the bedroom, they break the sexual stalemate—and, ultimately, discover the right balance between intimacy and autonomy.

"HE'S NEVER IN THE MOOD"

Newlyweds Cindy and Dan were baffled when bedroom battles put a chill on intimacy. What happens when one partner wants sex and the other doesn't?

CINDY'S TURN

"I know this sounds ridiculous, but after three years of marriage, my husband and I no longer make love," said Cindy, twenty-four, a pixie-faced woman with curly brown hair. "I don't mean our sex life has diminished; I mean it no longer exists, period. Although we care deeply about each other, Dan has completely lost the ability to make love to me.

"What's so ironic is that sex was wonderful before we were married.

Dan and I started dating in high school, and we shared an apartment all through college, which adds up to five full years of healthy, happy, wonderful lovemaking. We were married right after graduation, and six months later, Dan started having problems maintaining an erection.

"I really can't believe this is happening to us—we were the perfect couple—and now I'm afraid my marriage will disintegrate and end just like my parents' did. They fought constantly and kept right on fighting after they finally divorced, when I was five years old. During my teens, everybody in my family seemed to be getting divorced and remarried.

"My father stepped out of my life completely when I was seven, and I was raised by my mother. Mom worked in a local department store and we lived with my grandparents. I had a happy enough childhood; I breezed through school, had many

271

friends, and went out for all the extracurricular activities. I dated a lot in high school, too, but I made it a policy to play the field and not let myself get attached to anyone. I sort of flitted here and there—that is, until I turned sixteen and met Dan.

"We met through friends, and if you asked me what it was that hooked me so quickly, I wouldn't know quite what to say. In many ways, we're opposites. I'm gregarious and outgoing; Dan's quiet and introspective—very solid, thoughtful, and responsible. The moment I saw him, I felt I had known him all my life. I chased him until he caught me. From then on, neither one of us ever looked at anybody else.

"I never thought much about what I wanted to do after high school, but when Dan applied to college, I applied to the same one. We shared an apartment and scheduled our classes so that we could have lots of free time together. That was a happy period for us. I majored in psychology, Dan majored in economics, and we had grants and scholarships to help us along financially.

"During college, our lovemaking was wonderful. We were so much in love, sex just seemed so natural. And since we were virgins when we met, we learned together.

"After our wedding, we settled down to live happily ever after. I found a job doing personnel work and Dan went into the management-training program at the same department store where my mother worked. We both also started taking graduate courses at night—I very much wanted to finish my master's degree in psychology and Dan was working toward his M.B.A.

"It seems to me that from that point on, we hardly ever saw each other. My job was a piece of cake, but Dan's was a nightmare. He had a full hour's commute each way, which was time-consuming enough, but on top of that he was always being asked to work overtime and to come in on weekends. When he did have a free night, it was invariably one of the nights I was in class. Dan was also constantly being sent off on buying trips. Sometimes his boss would give him a day's notice, sometimes just a few hours.

"Dan hated his job—he was disgusted by some of the store's unethical business practices—and I knew that the stress was affecting him emotionally. So I never complained. I didn't want our marriage to become a battleground the way my parents' had been, but I couldn't stand the lonely evenings. Since I'm not the type to sit and watch TV for hours, I decided to start a part-time business designing and custom-making clothes—a hobby I had always hoped would lead to something.

"It was during that period that our sex life took its initial nosedive. In college, we made love at least once a day, but on our new schedule, we were lucky to fit sex in twice a week.

Then, one night, to our horror, we tried to make love and it just didn't work. We couldn't believe it! This had never happened before. We kept trying and finally got so frustrated we just gave up.

"Three months later, the very same thing happened. Dan was fine during foreplay, but then, when he was getting ready to enter me, his erection collapsed. From then on, things worsened. I was sure his problem was caused by stress, and when Dan lost his job at the department store I was actually relieved.

"Dan found another job that very same day, working for a competing department-store chain, and although it wasn't quite what he would have chosen, at least the hours were decent. Now we did have a lot of time to spend together, but Dan was never able to maintain an erection again.

"We've tried everything, and I do mean everything, to work through this problem. Dan has had physicals by two different doctors and been told by both that he's in perfect health. He takes huge quantities of vitamins every day. I went on a crash diet to make myself more attractive and started wearing lacy black negligees to bed at night. We read a lot of sex books and did all the things they suggested; we took bubble baths together, burned incense in the bedroom, and tried making love by soft candlelight. Dan even bought and mounted mirrored tiles on the ceiling over the bed, but we had to take those down because they kept coming loose and falling on us. We both dropped out of grad school, thinking we were pressuring ourselves too much. That didn't help either.

"By unspoken agreement, we almost never try to make love anymore. We're too scared. We keep ourselves busy, so on the surface we're still happily married, but the knowledge of what we once had and have now lost has created a barrier between us. I feel I'm losing my husband emotionally as well as physically. I love him so much, I don't think I can bear this much longer."

DAN'S TURN

"I don't know what is the matter with me," said Dan, twenty-five, a serious young man with short, neatly cut hair and tortoiseshell glasses. "I'm crazy about my wife, and I'd do anything to be able to prove it to her physically, but I just can't seem to do it. It's frustrating and embarrassing and scary.

"But to be honest with you, I'm not very comfortable sitting here talking about sex with a stranger. My family is pretty straitlaced; Dad, who worked as a clerk for an oil company, and Mother, who was a secretary, are serious, quiet types. I certainly never talked with them about sex. I have two sisters. The older one suffers from Down's syndrome, and I think because of that I absorbed a strong sense of responsibility. We were a family that shared a common problem. As a kid I was quiet, inquisitive, interested in different things: the stock market, scientific inventions, nature, and animals. I wasn't particularly social. I had only one girlfriend before Cindy, and I never even kissed her; we were good buddies. Cindy's the only girl I've ever loved.

"Since we're both bright academically, college was a playground. It wasn't until after we graduated and got married that the real world finally caught up with us. My first full-time job was a disillusioning experience. The department store where I was taking retail-management training was part of a major national chain that I had always thought was on the up-and-up. Instead, I discovered they were a total rip-off. At one point, I had a large commission coming and they tried to cheat me out of it. I wouldn't permit that and was never forgiven for having stood up for my rights. From then on the manager did everything possible to make life miserable for me. One day, on the manager's whim, I was fired. I was never given a reason for my dismissal and the manager's nephew was given my job. I would have initiated a lawsuit except I was afraid they'd take revenge by discharging my mother-in-law, who also worked there. I didn't want that to happen.

"It was while I was working at the store that I started having problems performing sexually. The first time, I really wasn't worried. I'd been away on a long buying trip, and although Cindy had never actually said anything, I could tell she was ticked off about my being away. Neither of us was much in the mood for lovemaking that night. But the second time it happened I didn't take it so lightly.

"When I lost my post at the department store, though, it was the end of everything. Of course I went straight out and found another job, but I still felt I'd been kicked in the teeth.

"Counseling was Cindy's idea, but I'm going along with it because it represents our one final chance to save our marriage. Truthfully, I don't have much hope. We've already tried everything. And I have to admit, the whole idea of sex therapy gives me the creeps. But Cindy knows more about this sort of thing than I do. She said you're fully accredited, but even so, if she and I are supposed to get into bed in front of you and, well, do a sort of show-and-tell thing, there's no way I'll go through with it."

THE COUNSELOR'S TURN

"Dan's apprehension about entering therapy for a sexual problem is very common," said the counselor. "Most of my clients are highly relieved to find out that the only bed they will be using during the course of therapy is their own, and that all sexual activity between them will take place in the privacy of their bedroom.

"Dan and Cindy were as solid a couple as I have ever had as clients. They loved each other very much and were committed to preserving their marriage at all costs, even if that involved the embarrassment of discussing the most intimate part of their relationship with a stranger. As almost always happens in these cases, however, once our initial session was over, the embarrassment vanished.

"During our first counseling session, we reviewed Dan's medical history to make sure there wasn't a physical reason for his impotence. Since he had already been examined by two physicians, this did not seem probable, but I wanted to make sure there was nothing wrong with his diet, that he was getting enough rest, and that he didn't have any serious illnesses, such as diabetes, that could affect his ability to sustain an erection. Certain medications, including the antidepressants commonly prescribed for mild anxiety, can also lower the libido, but Dan was not taking anything.

"As we talked, one point soon became obvious: Dan and Cindy had made their lives so busy that there was little time for sex. Young and energetic, they believed they could juggle everything. Ironically, when problems developed they piled on still more projects to ward off emotional pain.

"My first goal with this couple was to relieve the pressure they were under by helping them realize how common their problem was. Although most people do not talk about it, periods of sexual dysfunction occur in almost all marriages at one time or another, especially when one or both partners are under unusual stress. These problems generally right themselves automatically once the immediate problem is resolved, but sometimes a couple begin to panic about the situation, which in turn creates a separate but equally disturbing problem. The anticipation of not being able to perform sexually can actually create that situation, causing a man to have erection or ejaculation problems or a woman to be unable to reach orgasm. This frustrating experience increases their fear of failure the next time and soon, like Dan and Cindy, a couple may find themselves locked into a pattern they can't break.

"During our initial sessions we viewed some educational films about impotence that showed how a couple mastered techniques, such as non-genital touching, to help them overcome their problem.

"Once Dan and Cindy became more relaxed about their situation, I described to them various intimacy-enriching experiences they could

SECRETS FROM SEXY MARRIAGES

In every relationship, levels of sexual desire for both partners fluctuate. Some stages are predictable: when you first marry, after you have a child, when the kids leave home, when job pressures persist. These are all times when sexual moods and patterns of lovemaking may shift. Knowing this, and being confident enough to talk about it, strengthens intimacy. Those with the sexiest marriages:

1. Remember that sex problems are sometimes red herrings. Understanding that impotence is a common problem at every stage of marriage is the first, and highest, hurdle most couples have to clear. Talking about the problem can be reassuring and often lessens the anxiety for both partners. In fact, the more both partners worry about the problem, the more intractable it becomes. However, wise couples recognize that impotence can also be a wake-up call, a signal of stress somewhere in the relationship. Instead of banishing feelings of frustration, unhappiness, or emotional overload—at work, at home, with your kids or other family members— ask yourselves if something is bothering one or both of you. Sit down and talk about issues in a nonconfrontational, nonjudgmental, and unhurried way. Once Cindy and Dan found the courage to talk, the episodes of sexual stage fright disappeared.

2. Don't save affection for the bedroom only. Couples whose sex lives bring them the most happiness eroticize their lives—that is, they give affection physically and verbally through the day in different ways. They touch. Whether it's reassuring or frantically passionate, touch makes the difference between making love and having sex. Touch is a reflection of what you feel inside: You can convey desire, appreciation, delight, a sense of safety as well as boredom, resentment, or anger.

3. Make time for love. Sexy wives know that lovemaking is a habit: The more you do it, the more you like it, and the more you like it, the more you do it. They make lovemaking a top priority, and if that means scheduling sex, so be it. It won't be any less exciting just because it's planned. Sexual excitement feeds on itself. Just do it.

4. Talk every day. Even if it's just ten minutes in the morning and ten at night, voice your love. Call each other pet names, remember to say good-bye and good night. Be sure that you don't fall into the mind-reader trap of assuming your partner knows or should know what you're thinking and feeling simply "because he loves me." Those in a healthy, sexy marriage make a point of expressing their feelings and their attraction to each other on a regular basis.

5. Kiss often. We're not talking a perfunctory peck on the cheek but a deep, sensual, teasing kiss. Many longtime couples rarely kiss at all, going straight to intercourse when they have sex. Don't you remember the backseat? The cool, dark movie theater, and the thrill of making out? Steal a kiss!

6. Have adventures. Instead of sex behind a locked bedroom door, these couples make love at the beach, in the car, in the shower, on the living room floor. They keep their eyes open during sex—and sometimes leave the lights on—because they know that watching their partner's eroticism makes sex easier.

7. Break the rules. Ask yourself: What ruts have we fallen into and how can we get out of them? Explore changes, even small ones, with which you both feel comfortable. Don't nix ideas automatically; instead, be willing to experiment with videos, sex toys, and magazines.

8. Learn what pleases. Know what you like and don't like in bed—and make sure your partner knows, too.

---

have at home that would get them more in tune with their sexuality. In the beginning, these activities simply involved touching and closeness so Dan would not be threatened by the challenge of having to perform. Gradually, the exercises were increased to include the caressing of genitals and then actual intercourse. In one exercise, Cindy was instructed that when Dan had an erection she was to wait and allow the penis to become soft again before continuing sex play. Many men are fearful that if an erection is lost once, it won't come back. By having some experiences in which his erection was purposely let go but was then regained, Dan became less threatened.

"Along with actual sex therapy, we also worked on increasing other areas of this couple's intimacy, particularly their verbal communication. Cindy's unhappy memories of her parents' battles made her reluctant to demonstrate any outward signs of anger in her own marriage. As a result, she rarely expressed her negative feelings, allowing them to build up inside her. Dan was sensitive enough to pick up on Cindy's anger, but was frustrated in his efforts to respond appropriately. His family life had been so quiet and so introspective that he had never been encouraged to specifically voice his concerns. By practicing getting their feelings out into the open, they took a second major step in reducing stress.

"Another subject we spoke about at length was the fact that good sex doesn't necessarily have to be spontaneous. Dan had complained during therapy that Cindy was not willing to plan time for sex because she felt that to do so was unnatural and unromantic. When we discussed this, Cindy realized she was being unrealistic; when people's lives are as busy as hers and Dan's, it is not only okay but absolutely necessary to set aside time for sex.

"The more Dan and Cindy shared of themselves, the more relaxed they became, and the less difficulty Dan had maintaining his erections. Because this couple were so highly motivated and committed to working at their relationship, their progress was fast and steady. Inevitably they hit plateaus, but lost distance was quickly regained, and counseling was terminated after ten weekly sessions. A follow-up session six months later found them still satisfied with all areas of their life together.

"One year later, I contacted Dan and Cindy to ask their permission to propose their case as a possible subject for the *Ladies' Home Journal's* "Can This Marriage Be Saved" column. During the course of our conversation, Cindy told me that they were 'abstaining from sex these days,' but for a very happy reason: Cindy's doctor had told them to wait six weeks after the birth of their baby daughter before resuming intercourse."

"He Had a One-Night Stand"

Jake insisted his affair meant nothing to him, but Allison refused to believe it. Does it take a crisis to teach us how to forgive and move on?

ALLISON'S TURN

"As horrific as the terrorist attacks were, I take some solace in the fact that they helped my husband realize how close he had come to losing everything he loves," said thirty-one-year-old Allison.

"One day last summer. I found a piece of paper in Jake's pants pocket as I was doing the wash. It was a note from a woman, raving about what a special night they'd just had. I nearly fainted right there. I called Jake at work—he's a manager at a steel-manufacturing plant just across the river from Manhattan—and told him to come right home. From the tone of my voice he knew I'd found out he'd been with someone else, yet even as he apologized, he had the nerve to tell me it was no big deal. 'Just a onetime fling,' he kept saying. His words of remorse seemed so hollow, I just didn't believe them.

"In eight years of marriage, we've certainly had our problems, but I never imagined infidelity would be one of them. I need to figure out what went wrong, and why. I'm just devastated. Jake thinks it's possible to erase what he did and move on. 'Can't you get over it already?' he asks. Well, no, I can't. He makes me feel that I'm wrong for being so angry. Until recently, he hadn't even been interested in going to counseling. Then came September eleventh, and everything changed.

"As I watched the news on TV, Jake called to say that he was going to help with the rescue efforts. I didn't hear from him for almost eighteen hours, and though I was sick with worry, I kept calm for the sake of our seven-year-old twins, Megan and Amber. At last, Jake walked in the door at around four A.M., covered in ash. Holding me close, he said he loved me and was sorry for hurting me. But how do I know he means it? How can I trust him again?

"The stress in our marriage, coupled with the grief over what's happened to our country, is overwhelming. Some days, I go into a frenzy of mothering just to keep busy—baking cookies, sewing costumes for the class play. Other times, I barely have the energy to get out of bed.

"Though I'm furious at Jake, I hate making scenes, so I walk on eggshells. Jake and I have never been that great at communicating. In arguments, he becomes loud and insistent, and I can never win.

"Sappy as it sounds, I once believed Jake and I were meant for each other. We met through his sister Stacy, who used to be a co-worker of mine. I thought he was adorable, funny, and a real gentleman, and I just knew he was the one. I wanted my marriage to be just as happy as my parents'; I think they've had all of two fights in their thirty-three years together.

"Jake and I had a huge wedding: I'm an only child, but he has a big extended family. We moved to a place not far from my parents. We didn't expect to have children right away, but we were delighted when I became pregnant with twins. Fortunately, Jake's job supports us very nicely, so I can stay home to raise the girls. I thought we were a terrific team. Now I feel like a fool. I don't see how I can make love to a man when I don't believe he really loves me.

"Jake told me he slept with the other woman because he was looking for some excitement in his life. Does he expect fireworks every day? He likes to think of himself as spontaneous: I'd call it impractical. He'll announce on Friday morning, 'The airfares are low: let's go to California for the weekend!' Of course, I'd love to—we used to take little last-minute trips when we were dating—but when I have to run the school book fair and take the girls to soccer matches, I can't just drop everything. He makes me feel like a wet blanket just for fulfilling my responsibilities as a mom. When I say no, Jake sulks.

"I keep asking myself what I did wrong. I haven't asked Jake for the specifics of this fling, yet there's a part of me that wants to know every detail—what she looks like, who made the first move. I still check every pocket and phone bill for evidence I don't want to find. While I'm glad Jake seems to be serious about repairing our marriage, the damage has been done, and I don't think we can ever go back."

JAKE'S TURN

"I'm a different person now from the one I was on September tenth, and I wish I could make Allison understand that," said Jake, thirty-one. "I've told her how sorry I am that I cheated on her, but she keeps obsessing about it. Why can't we move on?

"It was a stupid, stupid mistake, one I'll never repeat. I was feeling trapped, both at work and at home. One night after going bowling with my friends, we stopped for a drink, and this sexy lady at the bar flirted with me. I admit I didn't resist much, and I wound up sleeping with her. She sent me a note at work the next day, and like an idiot I put it in my pocket and forgot to throw it away.

"But everything's different now. Going to Ground Zero was a reality check. My blood froze when I saw the first tower being hit. Some of the older guys in my plant helped build the World Trade Center, and we all know it well. Realizing that the rescue workers would need people with our skills with steel beams, several of us raced to the scene.

"There are no words to describe seeing the towers reduced to ash. We helped pass buckets of debris, listening for signs of survivors, but it soon became clear that we wouldn't find any. We were there only two days; after that, the rescuers were more in need of heavy machinery operators.

"I'm grateful that Allison and I didn't know any of the victims personally, but I'm still shaken. Driving home that first night, it hit me: I have something so wonderful, and I've taken it for granted. I wanted, needed, to be with my wife and family.

"I know it sounds lame, but I didn't mean to hurt Allison. It's just that I've been feeling so separated from her. We hardly ever have sex, and I don't get the sense that she loves me the way she once did. Allie is so wrapped up in the girls and all her committees that there's no time for us to do anything spontaneous anymore.

"I have wonderful memories of throwing a few clothes in the car and driving to New England just because we felt like it. When we were dating, we were always on the go. I know we can't be as carefree now, but do we have to act like old fogies? Is it such a big deal to go to Atlantic City for a couple of days? Allison looks at me like I'm a moron for even mentioning it.

"I thought I'd always have time for fun. I had a happy, if chaotic, childhood. I'm the youngest of five, raised by a divorced mother who worked a variety of jobs to support us. We didn't have much, but I never felt deprived. We moved around the country each time Mom needed a new job, so I had to deal with a lot of change growing up. Now, of course, I see what I missed. I want my kids to have stability and roots.

WHO CALLS THE SHOTS?

The bedroom is often the setting for power struggles in a relationship. Though conflicts rarely erupt when love is new, daily life has a way of fogging up those rose-colored glasses. Little inequities pile up: You feel that your spouse always controls the purse-strings. You sense that in the bedroom, you're always submitting to his sexual style and preferences. He thinks you're the dictator when it comes to your social life. If you consistently shy away from acknowledging these stresses, in time you may find them intractable and difficult to change. While no marriage breaks up because one partner feels he never gets to pick which movie to see on Saturday night, the fact that one of you feels voiceless and vote-less weakens the foundation of the union and diminishes that partner's self-esteem. For a power check, agree or disagree with the following statements:

1. When I am really upset about something that my mate has done or said, I'm not afraid to say so.

2. I'm comfortable talking about my vulnerabilities and weaknesses with my spouse.

3. On weekends, we check with each other about plans before carving them in stone, taking each other's desires and schedules into account.

4. My mate respects the fact that I have a career that's important to me.

5. We discuss finances openly and decide together what to spend our money on.

6. We take turns initiating lovemaking.

7. In bed, I feel relaxed telling my partner what I like and what I don't like.

Did you both agree with most of them? If so, then you probably don't have a power imbalance. But if one of you primarily agrees and the other primarily disagrees, it's time to examine the imbalance. Remember, in a good marriage, power is always shifting:

- Renegotiate the deal. Just because you always did things one way, doesn't mean you must continue that way.

- Remember that your partner may be surprised, even upset, if you bring up your desire for change. If you've never told your spouse that you feel he doesn't support your career as much as you think he should, he may react negatively at first to your wish for change. Pick a quiet, peaceful time to explain your feelings and make some suggestions that would work for you. Do you want him to check with you before making weekend plans in case you have a project you need to finish? Do you assume that he will always accompany you to out-of-town business meetings, without checking with him first?

- Do something different to make your point. If you feel that you've said everything you can, but your message isn't being heard, perhaps it's time for action. Is he chronically late? Stop haranguing him; tell him you will simply leave for your scheduled appointment, be it a dinner date with friends, or a movie, by yourself. Then do it.

"After high school, I joined the Army for two years. When I got out, I took a job at the same factory where one of my brothers worked. I would occasionally drop by my sister Stacy's office, and that's how I met Allison. I knew from day one that we'd get married. There was something so loving about her, and until recently, she was a terrific listener. She made me feel like a better person.

"Allison thinks I yell too much, but that's just the way my family talks, and it doesn't mean I don't love her.

"Riding toward lower Manhattan the day after that terrible morning, I saw all these people cheering the firefighters and police. The outpouring of love from New Yorkers was overwhelming. It gave me a sense of hope about a lot of things in this world. I'd like to think there's hope for Allison and me, too."

THE COUNSELOR'S TURN

"Every tragedy reminds us of life's fragility, but the terrorist attacks were a catalyst for Jake and Allison," said the counselor. "They realized they needed therapy in order to renew the strength of their marriage.

"Though their relationship was solid at heart, the affair caught both of them off guard. I felt sure that once this issue was addressed, the rest would fall into place, and that short-term therapy would set them on the right road within a few months.

"Like many victims of infidelity. Allison found that her fears spun out of control as she tried to make sense of what had happened. Much as she wanted to save her marriage, she despaired of ever being able to love a man who had hurt her so deeply.

"However, I suspected that Allison's inability to assert herself might have contributed to the distance between them. As an only child with loving parents who never fought, she'd had little practice with disagreements. As an adult, she avoided conflict entirely. So instead of challenging Jake when he was angry or made unreasonable demands, she bent over backward to please him. Over time, he lost respect for her.

" 'Let Jake see your outrage.' I told Allison. 'Make it clear that he caused you pain and that you won't tolerate anything like that again.' Jake, in turn, had to be patient and willing to answer Allison's questions. He also had to truly feel, and show, remorse for the pain he'd caused.

"As Allison began to speak out, Jake began to listen to her. 'Now I'm starting to feel I can trust him when he says he'll never cheat again,' she said.

"Jake needed to examine his discontent and why he automatically assumed that Allison, and his marriage, were the source of it.

"The upheaval of the moves cross-country he'd experienced as a child made Jake expect life to be full of change, but this is hard to sustain in a romantic relationship. It was certainly not wrong of him to want excitement in his marriage. Still, he had to realize that compromises had to be made.

"What's more, both Allison and Jake had unwittingly begun to take their marriage for granted. 'If the spark has gone out of your marriage, it may be because you're not lighting it,' I told them. 'You both must work to make it happen.' This could mean anything from holding hands to snowboarding.

"Allison and Jake began to make small changes that had a big impact. Instead of announcing unrealistic travel plans, Jake now makes a reasonable suggestion, and together they see if it's feasible. Recently, they went away for a long weekend.

"I also suggested that Allison make a list of small things that Jake could do to make her feel loved, appreciated, and secure—gestures like calling if he was going to be late. This injected new energy into their marriage. Allison found it easier to be intimate with him, as well as to begin to forgive his infidelity.

"As Jake said during one of our last sessions: 'We realize now, more than ever, how lucky we are to have this marriage, and how right we were to fight for it.'"

"We Haven't Had Sex in Years"

Marcy and Rick adored each other, but her inability to have sex frustrated both of them. What happens to a marriage when love hurts?

MARCY'S TURN

"I don't know what's wrong with me," Marcy, a thirty-five-year-old elementary-school teacher, said softly through her tears. "You see, my husband and I hardly ever make love.

"It's not that I don't find Rick sexy, and I do enjoy foreplay. But every time he tries to enter me, I tense up and can't go through with it. It's awful having to say, 'Stop—it hurts' night after night and watch Rick sigh and roll over. We've found other ways to please each other over the last eleven years, but intercourse is all but impossible.

"Rick is the most devoted, generous, patient husband anyone could ask for, and I want to show him how much I love him. But he's at the end of his rope, and so am I. We're fighting about everything now: not just sex, but also work, our three-year-old twin sons, and especially my parents.

"I'm the oldest of three in a strict Catholic family from the Cincinnati suburbs. Mother is a homemaker who's involved in community and church activities; Dad is a lawyer. They're cold and rigid, concerned far more about appearances than about my feelings. As long as I was the good, responsible little girl, nothing else mattered. And when Dad gave orders, we followed them, or else.

"No one in my house talked about sex except to forbid us to watch certain off-color movies or TV shows. I learned about menstruation from my best friend's mom. I wasn't allowed to date either. When I was thirteen, my father reprimanded me just for sitting on the front lawn with a boy.

"Even now, my parents still try to control me. They call every day and come to visit whenever they please, regardless of whether it's convenient for us. Rick keeps saying, 'How can you let them run your life?' and he's right. I just don't know how to change.

"Rick and I grew up in the same neighborhood, but it wasn't until I was a college senior that we really got to know each other. He was home for a few months before going back to grad school in Boston, where he was studying for his teaching degree. I fell in love, and we dated for several months.

"Then, after Rick went back to school, he told me we should see other people. I missed him terribly, but we stayed in touch. On the rebound, I dated Steve, a guy I knew from college, and he became my first lover—for some reason sex didn't hurt me back then. But we were careless, and sure enough, I learned I was pregnant shortly after Steve and I broke up.

"I panicked; I wasn't ready to have a child. Despite my religious beliefs, I wanted an abortion. There was no way I could tell my folks, so I called Rick, who was incredibly supportive as I talked through my decision. I had the procedure, and immediately tried to put it out of my mind.

"When Rick came home for Christmas vacation, we started seeing each other again. On New Year's Eve, he proposed; we married the following June, and I moved into Rick's house in Boston.

"Sex with Rick was excruciating from the start, which surprised and dismayed me, since I hadn't had any problems sleeping with Steve. As you can imagine, trying to have a baby wasn't easy, though we managed to have intercourse with a lot of patience and teeth-gritting on my part. After three years of trying to conceive on our own, I was artificially inseminated with Rick's sperm. It worked on the first try.

"We knew there was a small chance of a multiple birth because of the fertility drugs I had taken, but we were stunned when my first sonogram showed I was carrying quadruplets. We didn't have the financial or emotional resources to raise four children at once. The doctors urged us to consider selective reduction for the sake of my health and the babies', and after much agonizing, Rick and I agreed it would be best. I went on to have two sons, Colin and Tyler, who are the joy of our lives.

"I thought that giving birth would help me make love like a normal woman, but it hasn't. It hurts even to use a tampon. I'm so humiliated. Gynecologists and marriage counselors haven't given me any good answers.

"I know Rick is fed up, and I can't say I blame him. We've drifted apart. When he's not playing with the boys, he's glued to the TV or surfing the Web. He doesn't want to have anything to do with me.

"I feel like a failure, and I'm terrified that my husband won't want to stay in a sexless marriage much longer."

RICK'S TURN

"If something doesn't change, I don't think I can keep this marriage going," Rick, a forty-year-old college professor, said wearily. "I love Marcy and my sons deeply, but I can't live this way anymore. Every day, my wife pulls further away from me.

"I'd never had much of a sex life before—Marcy was my first serious girlfriend—so for a long time our difficulties in bed weren't a big deal. I figured it was just another problem we had to get through. There were many other things, like our children, that held us together and brought us joy.

"But now I can't say a word without upsetting Marcy. She takes every little comment as a personal affront, and gets hysterical at the thought that she isn't 'normal' sexually. She claims I badger her but what choice do I have? Marcy is so closed off that I don't know any other way to get her to talk.

"When we tried to start our family, the bickering and tension got worse. I knew Marcy hated making love, and I admit I was frustrated at times, too. It was a relief when we found out the insemination was successful. Deciding to reduce the pregnancy was extremely difficult, but to me, the safety and health of Marcy and the remaining babies was the most important thing.

"I know that having a child, let alone twins, can put a damper on even the most passionate sex life. But it's been three years since the boys were born, and having Marcy reject me time and time again makes me feel inadequate. And considering my family, that's an emotion I know well.

"My dad, an executive at a manufacturing company, was constantly busy with activities and friends, ignoring me and my two older brothers most of the time. Mom was considerate to a fault, always more concerned about other people's feelings than her own. She and Dad fought a lot, and since my brothers were already in college when I was a kid, I was the one who literally came between them.

"Shy and awkward, I never felt I could live up to Dad's expectations. He always told me what I was doing wrong, but never how to do it right. He was a great mystery to me until the day he turned to me in a rage and said: 'You're nothing more than a mistake after a wild night.' I was stunned at first, but then I felt strangely calm—I knew why he treated me like dirt.

"Though I'd been living near Marcy in Ohio for years, I didn't actually get to talk to her until I was home on break during grad school. That was a pleasant surprise: The cute little girl next door had grown up! I broke up with her after a few months because I thought I was too young for a commitment. I was wrong: As soon as I left, I realized I was madly in love with her. Marcy was wary of dating me again after her abortion—she was afraid I would consider her 'damaged goods'—but I persisted and finally asked her to marry me.

"Yet as much as I loved Marcy, I wasn't prepared for the way her parents injected themselves into our lives. Whenever any issue comes up—whether to move, what to name our kids—they weigh in with an opinion. I think her mother and father are mean and manipulative, but Marcy won't stand up to them; she feels she has to keep everyone happy.

"I'm worn out from trying to ignore our problems. I play with the boys, turn on the TV, or go online to block out the rest of the world. I don't know if this sex clinic will work, but I don't want to be bitter in twenty years because we're still fighting and unable to make love."

THE COUNSELOR'S TURN

"Marcy cried during that first session," reported the counselor, "None of her doctors or therapists had told her that her problem had a name: vaginismus, and involuntary spasm of the outer muscular wall of the vagina (the pubococcygeus, or PC, muscle). Experts estimate that as many as two out of every thousand women and at least 20 to 40 percent of those who seek sex therapy, suffer from it.

"Marcy's dysfunction stemmed from several factors. When Rick nagged her to talk about her feelings, she felt resentful and overpowered, just as she had as a child. Subconsciously, Marcy was shutting down sexually in order to gain some control over her life. Of course, Marcy's strict, repressive upbringing compounded her problem, as did her deep grief over the pregnancies she had chosen to terminate.

"Rick, sensitive and kind, had grown up in the role of peacemaker and problem-solver. Like his mother, he pushed aside his needs and the pain of being rejected by his father, becoming a martyr and a victim in his attempt to feel loved and important.

"Marcy first needed to take charge of her life, which meant that Rick had to stop jumping in and pushing her to talk. 'By doing that, you allow her to stay a little girl, not a marriage partner,' I said. Rick now states his feelings calmly to Marcy, and then directs his energies elsewhere; going for a walk or doing yard work.

"It wasn't long before Marcy felt much more self-confident, especially where her parents were concerned. Recently, they told her, 'We're coming to stay with you over the July 4 weekend.' She replied, 'I'm afraid we already have plans. Let's find another time for you to visit.'

"Treating the vaginismus involved teaching Marcy a series of Kegel exercises to control her vaginal muscles, as well as relaxation techniques, like deep breathing and muscle isolation, for her and Rick to perform together. I also gave them a helpful book: *A Woman's Guide to Overcoming Sexual Fear and Pain* by Aurelie Jones Goodwin, Ed.D.E., and Mark E. Agronin, M.D. (New Harbinger Publications, Inc., 1997).

"To help Marcy feel more comfortable with penetration, I recommended special creams that would allow her to insert a tampon easily. Next, she graduated to a series of increasingly wider vaginal dilators.

"I told the couple to focus on gestures of affection—massage and touching—instead of sex for a few weeks. Afterward, they were to give each other three compliments and one constructive criticism; this helped them talk honestly about what they did and didn't like. However, when the two were ready to try making love again, Marcy still found it painful.

"That's when I helped Marcy deal with her heartache over the pregnancies she had terminated. Even after all this time, she still hadn't found a way to achieve closure for those losses. I suggested that she pick up three pretty stones from the beach, one for each baby. 'Carry them around with you for as long as you need to,' I said. 'When you feel ready to say good-bye to them, put them on a shelf.' In just a matter of weeks, Marcy had taken the stones out of her purse. It was time to move on.

"Once Marcy came to terms with her past, she and Rick were finally able to enjoy a full and rewarding sexual relationship. Vaginismus can almost always be cured if couples are committed to working it out."

SEXUAL SELF-DECEPTION:
Why You Can't Figure Out What's Wrong

Sex in a good marriage is complicated. There are highs and lows, good times and lousy times. But too often, too many people settle for predictable sex when they could have passion. They settle for the status quo when they could have a sexual life that is constantly being renewed and recharged. And they do this because they're too afraid to admit to themselves or their partners that something is just not quite right.

What causes sexual deception? Several factors: fear of hurting a partner's feelings, fear of rejection, fear of intimacy, fear that it wouldn't make any difference if you did acknowledge a problem. While Marcy and Rick's problems were extreme, there are lesser secrets we all keep that need to be aired and addressed. After all, sex can only get better if you communicate both in and out of bed. But after years of ignoring, minimizing, or rationalizing a sexual self-deception, how do you even begin to open up? Think about the following questions. If you have concerns or doubts about any of them, consult your physician, or a professional counselor, for help.

1. Do you worry that you're not having sex as often as other people?

2. Have you had, or are you thinking about having, an affair?

3. Do you have pain when you make love?

4. Do you have difficulty becoming, or staying, aroused?

5. Has it been a long time since you made love?

6. Do you fake arousal or orgasm more often then you truly feel it?

7. Do you worry about whether you're pleasing your partner?

8. Does it take much longer for you to become aroused than it used to?

9. Do you frequently feel tired or depressed?

10. Are you embarrassed about the way you look?

11. When it comes to sex, do you feel that you could take it or leave it—and more often leave it?

12. Do you feel sexually out of sync with your partner? (Do you want to make love when he doesn't and vice versa?)

Being willing to take an inventory of your secrets, willing to seek the medical or psychological help you may need, and willing to talk about it all with your partner is the real secret to great sex.

"We Can't Have a Baby"

Cathy and Wayne dreamed of a large family, but their five-year struggle with infertility not only dashed their hopes for a child, it threatened the very existence of their marriage.

CATHY'S TURN

"Ever since I was three years old, I've wanted to be a mother," said Cathy, twenty-nine, a tall, thin woman with shoulder-length blond hair. "It's not that I didn't think anything else was important—I went to college, got my degree in accounting, and found a wonderful job in the city. I've been there seven years now and I still enjoy the work. But to me, being a mother is the most important thing in the world.

"It's kind of ironic, I suppose, because I had a terrible relationship with my own mother. She devoted herself to my father and us kids—I have three younger sisters—and used to tell me proudly how she and my father never took a vacation alone because she didn't want to leave us with a baby-sitter. She was always reminding me of the sacrifices she'd made for me, but I found her very distant, very critical. My father was just the opposite; he was an administrator with the local school district until his death two years ago, and I had a great relationship with him.

"Of course, he had certain ideas of how I should lead my life. He'd often tell me that women should stay home and raise their kids. I feel every woman has to make that choice for herself, but I know my father's message sank in.

"My parents' marriage seemed happy, though, and I had a typical suburban upbringing. I was the good

291

kid who studied hard and never dreamed of rebelling. I was twelve when my youngest sister was born and I practically raised her.

"I met Wayne at work. My desk was right behind his, and we became pretty close. Wayne is five years older than I am; he'd been in the Army for several years, stationed in Europe, and was trying to earn enough to get his own place.

"Well, the friendship blossomed into romance. Our first date was New Year's Eve. A bunch of us went for a drink after work; neither Wayne nor I had plans that night and, well, the rest is history.

"Wayne was everything I had always hoped for in a man: He was smart and ambitious, yet kind. He also wanted to have a lot of children and a wife who would put aside her career and raise them. In March, on my birthday, he proposed, and we were married in June. We went to the Caribbean for two weeks and a few months later we moved into a beautiful seventy-year-old three-bedroom Colonial on a small lake about an hour north of the city. We didn't know anyone there, but it was a picture-perfect town, a wonderful place to raise kids.

"We started trying to have a baby the day we got married. Having children was the focus of our married life, at least it was for me. But I just couldn't get pregnant.

"I'd read in a magazine that if you've been trying for six months and you still aren't pregnant, you should speak to your doctor. I was anxious; my gynecologist told me not to worry, but I made her promise to give me a fertility drug if in a few months I still hadn't conceived.

"Although I had no adverse reactions to the drug, I didn't get pregnant either. My gynecologist referred me to a fertility specialist. The doctors did the basic workup—they tested Wayne, too—but nothing yielded a clue. I started taking my temperature every morning and keeping a detailed chart.

"Now I feel like a laboratory specimen. My whole life revolves around my menstrual cycle. The first two weeks of the month I'm nervous but still hopeful. Then I'll get my period and sink into despair. Every time I see a baby on the street or in a commercial, my heart aches.

"I thought Wayne would be bothered by the sperm tests, but he's taken the whole thing in stride. Maybe that's why I get so upset; I want him to be more involved on an emotional level, but he's an automaton. Sex isn't fun anymore, it's business, and even that doesn't faze him.

"Meanwhile, about a year after we were married, Wayne found a better job at a small company closer to our home, and he's moving up fast. But the more involved he gets, the more oblivious he seems to what I'm going through. Wayne's sister-in-law, Kelly, said something to me at her baby shower last year that I will never forget. 'Cathy, you come stand by me,' she said. 'Maybe some of my fertility will rub off on you.' It took everything in me not to burst into tears.

"Wayne doesn't understand why I was upset. He insists I'm too sensitive and implies that I'm crazy to feel the way I do. That's why I'm so happy, I joined Resolve—it's a nationwide organization of couples who can't get pregnant. We talk and share information on fertility treatments. Wayne comes with me occasionally, but he never says anything.

"I'm afraid our marriage is falling apart. Wayne is working night and day, often seven days a week. If he's working late, he rarely calls. Or he calls, says he'll be home in an hour, and then he shows up three hours later.

"When Wayne spends so little time at home, it makes me feel worthless. It would be nice if once he did something that made me feel special. He never brings me flowers or gives me a little hug. Not that he ever did, but I'm feeling particularly needy now.

"I'm also tired of spending all my evenings, and most weekends, alone. When we moved here, it didn't bother me that it was far from my friends—I knew it was the ideal place to raise kids. But now I have no babies, no friends, and no husband. I sit in front of the TV and eat.

"I know I should go out and make new friends, but how? Most of our neighbors are older and the women

my age are busy with their families. All my friends at work live close to the city and it would take me an hour just to get to their homes.

"The worst is that Wayne and I hardly talk anymore. We went for a rare dinner out last week and I tried to tell him about a new fertility technique I'd read about, but he tuned me out. That happens all the time. Lately, he thinks nothing of criticizing me—my cooking is terrible, the house isn't neat enough.

"It's been five years now. I feel as if there's no purpose to my life. I've started thinking about adoption, but Wayne won't even discuss it.

"I dread waking because the first thing I have to look forward to is that thermometer."

WAYNE'S TURN

"I'll do anything to make my wife happy," said Wayne, thirty-four, a muscular man with a neatly trimmed beard. "But this baby business has taken over our lives. I'm sick of it.

"So maybe we won't have a child—that's not the end of the world. Cathy says I don't care, that I'm not involved. That's not true. But I see myself as just a player in this game; she's the boss, the one who sets the rules. If she says tonight's the night, well then, we make love. I go to the doctors' appointments with her; I listen. If they tell me I have to ejaculate into a little plastic jar, I do it. Maybe it's my strict upbringing, or learning to follow orders in the Army. I just don't understand what I'm doing that's so terrible.

"I will tell you one thing: I don't feel like spending every waking moment talking about having a baby. Cathy's incapable of having a conversation about anything else. That's why I tuned out in the restaurant. I know Cathy also loves going to these Resolve meetings, but I'm not thrilled to talk about my sex life with total strangers.

"And we never do anything as a couple anymore. We used to go out to dinner or to catch a hockey game. But now Cathy refuses to do anything in the evening because it might conflict with some test she has to have, or maybe we have to make love that night because it's her fertile time. She won't even go away on a vacation—she can't bear to miss a doctor's appointment.

"Let's talk about this not-calling business. I used to call, but every time I did we'd get into a twenty-minute argument about why I had to stay late. Everyone in the office would hear me fighting with my wife. And when I do walk in the door, no matter what time it is, she starts screaming.

"What can I tell you? I love my work. I love the pressure, the challenge. It's very demanding, but it stretches me as a person every single day. How many guys these days can honestly say that they love their job?

"I guess I got this strong work ethic from my parents. My father was a commercial fisherman and my mother was a housewife, and they instilled in me and my four brothers the importance of hard work. We had a strict Catholic upbringing: blue collar, old values. Dinner was at five on the dot every night and we ate huge Sunday dinners with all our aunts and uncles. We were close, even though no one talked very much—especially about feelings.

"If I had a problem when I was a kid, I'd never go to my father. It would embarrass him to talk about personal things. But I tell you this: I never saw my parents fight. That's why it's so hard for me now. Cathy and I fight constantly, but we never get anywhere.

"I didn't have a lot of friends when I was young. The neighbors used to call me Lone Ranger because I'd hang out by myself. I got decent grades in school and I went on to a local college, but then joined the Army. During my tour of duty, I worked in the accounting department at military headquarters and caught the accounting bug.

"After the Army, I moved back home while I looked for a job. By the time I met Cathy, I was ready to settle down. I wanted a big family, too, but if it's not meant to be, it's not meant to be. Now Cathy's on my back about adopting, but I'm not sure it's right for me.

"Look, I know how hard this is for my wife, but living with someone who is hysterical and anxious most of the time is not easy either. She's way too sensitive, takes offense too easily, and overreacts. She needs to see you more than I do. That business with my brother's wife is a perfect example. I don't know why Kelly said what she did, but I don't believe she said it to be hurtful.

"Also, if I make the slightest comment—like maybe the chicken was a little dry—my wife slams the plate down in front of me, marches upstairs, slams the door, and broods for hours. Cathy is not Susie Homemaker. My mother used to get up at five A.M. to cook my father a hot breakfast, and then she'd spend the rest of her day thinking about dinner, and never complain. Do I resent the fact that Cathy's not more like that? Yeah, sometimes, and if we're having one of our fights, I will say something to that effect.

"I know I'm not the perfect husband, but I love my wife very much. It's getting harder and harder to live with her, though. Maybe you can calm her down."

THE COUNSELOR'S TURN

"Like many couples, Cathy and Wayne placed a tremendous strain on their marriage," said the counselor. "Every problem they had was magnified by the infertility issue.

"Cathy and Wayne's inability to conceive was a blow to their egos, to their sense of themselves as a complete woman and a complete man, but they handled their disappointment in different ways. Wayne put his pain in a little compartment and insisted the whole business never really bothered him. To admit that he was having difficulty dealing with his problems would mean talking about them—something Wayne had never been able to do. His frustration and anger were manifested in other ways: He threw himself into his work, criticized his wife, and was insensitive to her feelings.

"The favorite son, Wayne had been babied by his mother most of his life. Although he maintained it didn't bother him that much that Cathy was not an ideal homemaker, his disappointment was evident, and when they fought, he hurled little insults at her. This further weakened Cathy's self-esteem. Although Wayne insisted his family was close, in reality they adhered to the trappings of closeness but not the substance.

"Cathy's struggle with infertility was more obvious than her husband's: To be a mother was her main goal in life, and her inability to reach it was devastating. Her frustration was compounded by the physical stress of having to monitor her temperature and blood counts, the surgeries and procedures she had to endure, as well as feeling that her

RECOGNIZING THE INFLUENCE OF OUTSIDE PRESSURES

As many as one in six women experience infertility, and about half that number eventually complete a successful pregnancy. Most often, infertility can be traced to a medical cause, but in about 3 percent of cases no cause can be found. The impact on both partners can be profound. Self-esteem evaporates, sex becomes mechanical, and a couple may experience a flood of feelings not unlike the stages of grief associated with a death. Shock or denial, guilt, anger, and helplessness are all too common. What's more, spouses rarely feel the some emotions at the same time, and as a result struggle to find their own coping mechanisms. Understanding what's normal for yourself and your partner is critical as you wind your way through the various medical treatments available to you.

Also, as more women wait longer to marry and establish their careers, what doctors call secondary infertility is on the rise. These couples may have one or more children—conceived with little or no trouble. It's only when they try to have another that they bump up against the frustration of not being able to conceive. The disappointment can be profound (Why is my body failing me?), but such couples often receive far less sympathy from family and friends. "You already have such a lovely child," they hear time and again, "some people have none." And while they know that's true, it can't replace the emptiness of what they don't have. To get the help you need:

Get a second opinion. RESOLVE, a nonprofit national support group for infertile couples can recommend physicians or clinics in your area. Call the National Helpline at 617-623-0744. Check that a clinic or doctor is recognized by the American Society for Reproductive Medicine, 1209 Montgomery Highway, Birmingham, AL 35216 (205-978-5000). When you begin treatment, consider a stress reduction program or couples counseling.

This couple's inability to conceive was a piercing blow to their egos and was placing an enormous strain on their marriage. Cathy dealt with the stress by obsessing about it. Wayne withdrew and numbed himself with work. Together they used this technique to short-circuit their emotional response to issues and to ease the tension between them:

At a quiet moment, think about an argument you had with your spouse recently. Ask yourself: What was I really feeling when we were fighting? Was I really uncared for? Guilty? Unworthy? Can I remember having that feeling before? When? Try to isolate the events or comments that triggered your emotion and think about how it might be similar to the way you're reacting to a comment or action on your spouse's part now. Share these discoveries with your partner. The important part of this exercise is to learn how to put the brakes on your emotions before events sweep you along. Once Cathy and Wayne were able to do this, they could more calmly discuss their inability to have a child and refocus their energies on adoption.

husband was unsympathetic to her unhappiness.

"Although she had never felt fully wanted or accepted by her critical mother, Cathy felt loved by her father, and she expected her husband to cherish her the way Daddy had. To some extent, her sense of self was also defined by her father's views about women's place in the home. Instead, Wayne was a closed-down guy, more like her mother than her father. Furious and disappointed at his lack of sensitivity, she bottled up her emotions.

"The biggest problem for both of them was learning to recognize and deal with their anger. We spent many sessions simply talking about this, and in time, they both learned to recognize that some of the things

they did and said could be handled in less destructive ways.

"For instance, I told Wayne he had to learn to stop scapegoating Cathy, to pay attention to her feelings and respect them even if they didn't seem logical to him. 'Just because you don't feel the way she does,' I said, 'doesn't mean she's crazy.' In time, Wayne learned to listen when Cathy talked rather than immediately dismiss her as hysterical. Once she felt her husband was really listening to her, Cathy didn't feel the need to constantly repeat herself.

"Next I told Cathy she had to stop defining herself as wife or mother and start forging her own identity. Although we agreed that it's very hard to refocus the way you think about yourself, and particularly hard to meet people and find new interests when you feel so down, I insisted she push herself. She signed up for a ten-week aerobics class at the local YMCA and has started to lose the pounds she gained by overeating. She's also met other neighborhood women there, and next month she will start pottery classes on Saturdays. Over the past few months, she has become less lonely and happier with herself. As a result, she has interesting things to talk about, so their conversations are no longer one-note monologues.

"Wayne also began to realize that part of the reason he and Cathy never did things together was because he was always unavailable. I told him he had to stop putting work ahead of his marriage. Now he's making an effort to give priority to Cathy. If he does have to work late, he is more diligent about calling. I also pointed out to Cathy that Wayne can't possibly say to the minute when he is coming home, and she has tried to be reason-

able. They've also agreed to reserve every Wednesday for dinner out.

"Once the hostility and tension between them eased, Cathy and Wayne were able to confront more calmly their inability to have a child. We spent several sessions discussing their feelings and fears about adoption. Finally, I said to them: 'What is more important: to be pregnant or to be a parent?' Once the issue was phrased like that, they both agreed that as much as they longed for a child of their own, it was more important to be a mother and a father. They began to face the problem more realistically and decided to pursue adoption.

"Cathy and Wayne stopped coming to see me after ten months, although Cathy visits every once in a while to touch base. Last week she told us with joy that she and Wayne hope to fly to Texas at the end of the month to adopt a baby. I'm confident that in spite of other pressures, they have finally learned to put their marriage first."

"My Husband Is Impotent"

For twenty-six years, Janet and Ken had a wonderful life. But now something was very wrong and their search for an answer was driving them farther and farther apart.

JANET'S TURN

"It's very hard for me to talk about my sex life with a stranger," said Janet, forty-four, a striking woman who sat forward in her chair as she spoke. "It's such a private thing. But I love my husband very much . . . and I want our marriage to be the way it was. I hope you can help.

"Counseling was my idea. Ken would never have called you if I had not insisted. That's the way he is . . . Ken brushes problems under the rug. Even now, he'll probably tell you things aren't so bad.

"But there's no question this is tearing us apart. We are fighting more than we have in our entire marriage because Ken can't sustain an erection. And I have to say it isn't a once-in-a-while thing. This has been going on for nearly two years. I'm at my wit's end.

"You see, we've been married for twenty-six years and sex has always been a very important part of our lives. I met Ken when I was only fifteen; he was seventeen. We were both doing volunteer work at the community center. We started dating, and as soon as Ken graduated from college we were married and he began teaching English at the local high school. Two years later I finished my college degree and became pregnant with our first child.

"Over the years, we've raised three terrific kids; of course, there have been rough times along the way. Our youngest, Greg, who's eighteen, was born with a clubfoot. He's fine now, but you can imagine how hard it was dealing with one specialist after another. The point I'm trying to make is that through all the years of bringing up kids, when you read about people not having time for sex and their love life fizzling, ours was fine. That's why it's so difficult to figure out what's wrong now.

"Of course, with a man like Ken, it's always difficult to know what he's feeling, and hard as I try, I can never get him to tell me outright what's bothering him. This problem he's had recently with the school board is typical.

"Ken is a wonderful teacher and he's been acting as assistant principal for several years. About two years ago, the principal retired. Now, Ken was the ideal candidate for the job. In fact, they pretty much promised he'd get the position. But the school system is so political and people on the board threw a monkey wrench into the process. It was really awful and Ken had to fight for himself. After months of wrangling, they ended up giving the job to someone else.

"Ken didn't even tell me right away. I found out from one of the other teachers. And when I asked him about it, he just shrugged and said, 'Janet, it doesn't really matter. We'll manage.'

"I know he was torn up by it. He's worked hard his whole life—

Ken's family was very poor. He put himself through school, getting honors all the way. As usual, though, he pretended everything was fine. And when he does that, I always feel so closed off. Doesn't he want to share things with me?

"We're such opposites in that respect. I worry a lot and it helps me to talk things out. But whether it's a problem one of our kids is having in school or an argument I've had with my mother I often feel Ken just doesn't want to hear about it. I start to talk and he tunes me out. The best I ever get is, 'Janet, I'm sure you'll work it out.' I get so angry that before I know it, I'm yelling my head off.

"I've always had a sense that Ken's there for everyone except me. He's a very generous man, very involved in the community. You name a committee or board and he's on it, probably as chairman. Everyone knows they can count on Ken to help out if they have a problem.

"So why has it taken him so long to get around to doing something about his own problem? Ken just makes up excuses instead of seeking help. He'll bring up our vacation in Vermont last summer and the trip we took to Mexico last Christmas to prove that there isn't really anything the matter. Yes, sex was great on both those trips, but as soon as we got back home . . .

"In fact, lately, sex has become a major ordeal for me. I've started to dread it. It's frustrating, not being able to let myself go and enjoy it, but how can I? I never know if Ken will be able to make love or not. And when he can't, I feel so unsatisfied, so alone, I want to cry.

"I guess after all these years Ken isn't attracted to me anymore. I don't think he's having an affair or anything like that, and I know I'm not as young or as thin or as pretty as I used to be. Last Valentine's Day, Ken bought me these flimsy nightgowns and teddies; I knew he thought it might give our love life a boost, but to tell the truth, I feel very silly wearing them. And none of that stuff ever mattered before, so what difference can it make now?

"You know, we've been through a great deal together. I guess we'll manage to get through this, too. But we're at this impasse. Everything is so confusing, I don't know what to expect."

KEN'S TURN

"I'm tired of having sex be the sword of Damocles hanging over my head," said Ken, forty-six, a handsome man who spoke in a soft, deliberate way.

"I'm perfectly aware that I have a problem. And I'm also sure I'm a lot more uncomfortable being here discussing all this than she is.

"Look, I may not talk about it, but I think about sex plenty. I'm not used to having a problem and not being able to solve it. But Janet is

exaggerating. When we're on vacation, when we get away, sex is super. Last year in Mexico we had night after night of terrific sex. I don't get it. Same plumbing.

"But what's this business about my not being there for her or talking to her about problems? Janet is a very bright, capable woman. She knows exactly how to handle any situation, always has. It's not that I don't care; she simply doesn't need my help.

"Look, I've never said this before, but sometimes Janet carries on so much, discussing every minute angle and detail of whatever it is that's bothering her, that I just can't take it. If I didn't tune her out, frankly, I think I'd go out of my mind. I wish she wouldn't yell so much, too, but that's just the way she is.

"And how can she say I'm more involved with other people than I am with my own family? For years I've worked hard, sometimes at two jobs, so we could have a nice home, raise three kids, send them to camp. When Greg had to go to the doctor because of his foot, I always took off from school to go. What does Janet want?

"This constant arguing is wearing me down, too. My parents fought a lot, and though it was mostly about money, I swore that in my own house we would never have such conflict.

"Besides, lately I've had to deal with more than my share of fighting.

As Janet mentioned, I've been having some difficulties at school. I was up for a principalship, which I thought I deserved, but I didn't get it. Unfortunately, the whole process dragged on for a long time and there was nothing I could do about it. It wasn't that I didn't want it or wasn't upset that I didn't get it, but what good would it do to lose my temper after the fact?

"Right now, I'm not sure what I'm going to do. Should I keep on working at my same old job? Should I look for another one? I guess I could do some consulting; several people have approached me about working for them, but I don't know if I'll be able to make enough money doing that. I hate this feeling of being in limbo. But look, we'll work it out, we always have.

"I'd like to think we can work out this sex thing, too. I feel terrible that Janet is so unhappy with me. She's a wonderful wife and she deserves better. But sometimes when I start to kiss her, she pulls away. Wouldn't that get any guy upset? Other times I can tell she's just not into it. If the phone rings, she'll even get up and answer it, and by the time she's finished talking, well, forget it. My desire is gone and it's impossible to continue. So I figure it's best to just get up and focus my mind on something else.

"But it's gotten to the point that every time I touch her, I'm terrified I won't get an erection. I find myself thinking about it all day long. I tell myself, 'Tonight, it'll be different. Tonight, we'll try something new and different.' I even bought Janet some sexy nightgowns, but that didn't do any good.

"Still, all I want is for Janet to be happy. I don't want to let her down, and I hate it when she's this mad at me. So I'm hoping you can help."

THE COUNSELOR'S TURN

"Ken and Janet knew intellectually that fighting about sex could only make things worse, but they were still unable to stop," said the counselor. "I wasn't surprised. No matter how well-read a couple is on sexual matters, impotence is such a volatile issue—reaching, as it does, to the core of a person's self-image and self-esteem—that many couples find it extremely difficult to deal with it on their own.

"Impotence is usually psychological in origin, but it's important to rule out any physical causes. Structural or hormonal abnormalities may be responsible. So I suggested that Ken see his doctor for a complete physical.

"Once Ken received a clean bill of health, we discussed some facts about impotence in general. First, I explained that certain changes in sexual responsiveness as one ages are perfectly normal. A man in his forties may need more stimulation to achieve and maintain an erection than he did in his twenties. Medication, such as the kind many men take to lower their blood pressure, can also adversely affect sexual responsiveness.

"But by far the single most common cause of temporary impotence is stress, such as Ken had on his job. Sometimes, simply recognizing that fact can go a long way toward reducing anxiety. But unfortunately, one episode of impotence often shakes a man's confidence so much that it becomes a self-perpetuating condition.

"That's precisely what was happening to Ken: Unable to find a solution on his own, he felt ashamed and he dwelled constantly on his failure. 'I didn't link my problems in bed to my problems at school,' Ken admitted during one of our sessions, 'but that's probably why things were better when we were away on vacation.'

"Interestingly, the fact that Ken and Janet were finally talking about their problem in a nonjudgmental atmosphere was an enormous relief to both of them. As often happens, this initial recognition was followed by a honeymoon period of several weeks in which their sex life was mutually exciting. Some couples stop therapy at this point. However, I reminded Ken and Janet that there had been other times during their marriage when sex had been fine for a period of time, only to have the impotence resurface, and I suggested they remain in counseling to determine what factors might be contributing to their difficulties. They agreed.

"Since Ken and Janet had been married such a long time, their life together had a much greater impact on their current problem than their early background did. So we concentrated on how they had developed a pattern of relating to each other that discouraged honest communication.

"For instance, Ken tended to avoid conflict of any kind; if Janet had problems at home or if he had them at work, he kept his own counsel. This greatly upset Janet, who dealt with her own anxieties by analyzing everything.

"What's more, Ken so keenly felt the need to be a good husband and provider that over the years he had completely lost his ability to assert himself. Since he truly believed he didn't deserve much happiness, Ken had to learn what I call healthy selfishness, that it was okay to express his own needs and desires, in bed or on the job. At the same time, however, he had to heed Janet's concern that he wasn't there for her emotionally. By expecting her to read his mind about problems in their relationship, he was actually pushing her away.

"Quick to anger, Janet had to realize that you can't force someone to communicate. As she learned to control her temper and to talk calmly about something that bothered her, Ken started to speak up more. He

WHEN SEX IS SIDELINED

Although impotence has emerged from the shadows in recent years (doctors estimate that more than half of all men suffer from it at one time or another), the topic is still so fraught with embarrassment that many are unable to speak to their doctor, let alone their wives, about it. Sex (or the lack of it) becomes the forbidden topic, a plague that troubles the most loving marriages.

While impotence is usually psychological in origin, it's vital to see a physician for a complete physical checkup to rule out any medical conditions—cardiovascular disease, diabetes, or prostatis— that may be triggering the problem. The most common cause of temporary impotence is stress. It can block the body's response to stimulation and cause a decrease of blood flow to the penis. The more chronic type of male sexual dysfunction, however, is caused by a drop in testosterone levels. Studies indicate that these levels slump gradually with age, sometimes as much as 30 to 40 percent between the ages of forty-eight and seventy. This drop can lead to fatigue, depression, muscle atrophy, as well as impotence. But that doesn't mean that a diminished sex life is an inevitable result of aging. It *does* mean that men need to be aware of what's normal and what's not at different ages.

While impotence is usually correctable (a variety of treatments are available, from drugs such as the much publicized Viagra, to injections and pumps), it's essential to examine any relationship issues that may be contributing to, or resulting from, sidelined sex. When a man loses his ability to make love, his wife loses something too. It's critical that a woman understand that her husband's problem is not her fault. At the same time it's important that she find ways to encourage communication and show him how much she still loves him by diffusing his anxiety with patience and understanding, and giving positive feedback during lovemaking. You might say: "Whatever the problem, we can overcome it because we love each other." Until you do, focus on pleasure, not performance. If you stop equating sex with intercourse, you will both learn to enjoy being aroused while cuddling, kissing, showering together, and just being close. Instead of having sex at the end of the day, try getting up an hour earlier in the morning (after a good night's sleep, blood vessels in the penis are relaxed). Or try taking a vacation with the goal of simply having fun. Needless to say, Viagra and other so-called miracle drugs are not the be-all and end-all of sexual problems. As doctors point out, these new medications improve the capacity to make love, but do nothing to reawaken desire. He may want, or need, to have sex right now—but she may balk at being pressured into something she believes should be spontaneous and infused with romance. What's more, a pill can't fix long-unresolved issues of anger and resentment. And while Viagra may help him maintain his erection, it won't help him in the affection department if he's not committed to his wife's sexual fulfillment, too. Doctors report that it's not uncommon for wives to protest that the quantity of sex may be greater, but the quality worse, after some impotency treatments. Regardless of the method used for restoring sexual potency, the greatest marital benefit occurs when a couple starts truly communicating so that they can address the emotional climate of their marriage. Don't be shy about seeking couples or sex therapy.

In the meantime, the following exercise helped Janet and Ken renew the playful side of their relationship so that performance anxiety didn't permeate their marriage:

On separate sheets of paper, make a list of the physical things you would like to do together—everything from holding hands and taking showers to making love. Studies have shown that touch is very important in triggering emotional closeness, and when a couple is physically close it's often easier to recapture the exuberance and spontaneity they used to share. Compare lists and come up with a third master list composed of ideas from each. Select at least one activity from the list to do each week. At first, this exercise may sound silly. You may think: We have serious problems and you're telling us to take a shower together! Although it certainly won't make problems go away, it does make them seem less monumental—and you will be more willing to press for resolutions.

finally admitted how unhappy he was at work, and after some discussion he decided to take an early retirement from his teaching post to accept a more lucrative consulting job at an educational research foundation.

"This decision was a turning point for Ken and Janet. Now that Ken was no longer burdened by concerns about his future, the tension at home eased considerably. This allowed them to start talking honestly about their sexual feelings for the first time.

"As Janet described how abandoned she felt when he couldn't make love, Ken finally understood how frustrating sex had become for his wife. Because he was so upset by his impotence, Ken had gotten into the habit of abruptly ending their lovemaking sessions, leaving Janet hurt and unfulfilled. With only harsh words and very little discussion between them, it was not surprising that Janet started to withdraw sexually as well as to doubt her own physical attractiveness. My next step was to give them homework assignments designed to make sex a truly communicative experience for them both.

"First, I instructed them to set aside time at least twice a week to shower together, to massage each other with lotion or oil, to fantasize together if they wished. They had to abstain from intercourse for the first week. I urged them instead to talk to each other about what pleased them as well as to focus on their own sensations and the joy of being together without worrying about performance.

"During the second week, I told them they could have intercourse only if they both wanted to, but they were to incorporate their massage and shower techniques into their lovemaking.

"These exercises proved very successful; Ken and Janet realized that if Ken lost his erection one night, it was not the end of the world, nor did it signal a major problem. This gave them the confidence to vary their lovemaking; Janet learned how pleasurable it could be to try new sexual techniques or to wear a sexy nightgown if her husband asked her to. Ken learned that instead of leaping out of bed if he was unable to have an erection, he could satisfy Janet in other ways.

"After thirteen months, Ken and Janet ended counseling, thrilled with their success and confident that they can solve any future problems."

"He No Longer Thinks I'm Sexy"

Amy tried everything from skimpy lingerie to romantic vacations but still couldn't reignite the passion. What happens when he always has the headache?

AMY'S TURN

"With my husband, there's never any right time to have sex," says a furious and depressed Amy, thirty-seven, a lawyer who works for a city environmental agency. "If I had my way, we'd make love three or four times a week, like we did when we were first married. Seth was a wonderful lover, even though I was usually the one to initiate sex.

"The problem started right after our first child was born. We have two boys—Michael is six; Kevin, three. When the doctor gave me the green light to have sex after my six-week checkup, Seth had no interest. Six years later, it's the same dance every night. I reach over to touch him in bed, and he pushes my hand away and mumbles some excuse: he's too tired, he had a hard day, the kids will wake up. Sometimes he'll give in, but I know he's just going through the motions.

"I've tried everything: renting X-rated videos, buying sexy nightgowns. Nothing works. Seth usually just clams up—once in a blue moon he'll explode, and we'll get into a screaming fight. And then maybe we'll end up making love. But I don't want to have to beg my husband to make love to me, or pick a fight in order to get sex.

"When Seth started to reject me, I blamed myself. I thought he didn't find me attractive anymore—I had gained about thirty pounds. So I went

307

on a diet and styled my hair the way I used to wear it. I did everything I could to look exactly as I did before I had the baby. It made no difference.

"Maybe Seth just stopped thinking of me as a sexual being. I'm not one to let anything go without a discussion, but whenever I sit Seth down and pour my heart out, he simply nods off. Can you imagine? It would be comical if it weren't so tragic.

"I grew up in a very traditional Italian home. My brother always had so much freedom, while every move I made was scrutinized. My father, who worked for the post office, was unbelievably critical and demanding. He was also very smart and musical, and he could actually be quite funny. But he was horrible to my mother: I'll never forget, when I was about eleven, he came into my room and handed me the key to the safe-deposit box. He said my mother was too stupid to hang on to it.

"Though I made straight A's in school, my father didn't hesitate to undercut just about everything I said or did. There were constant, subtle messages that I could never do anything right. I love my dad, but more than anything I did not want to marry a man like him.

"My mother was your basic housewife: cooking, cleaning, talking on the phone—that was her life. Mother and I have always had a very prickly relationship, and she still says things like, 'Look what a wonderful husband you have, Amy; he does everything for you'—always with the implication that I don't deserve him.

"After law school I went back to Boston, got my own apartment, and started working for the city's environmental protection agency. I met Seth at a bar where I had gone with friends after work. He was looking at me the whole night, but he didn't have the nerve to start a conversation. So on my way back from the ladies' room, I marched up and said, 'Well, when are you going to talk to me?' We dated for six months, and on my birthday he proposed.

"We were able to resolve problems so easily then. Now, I find myself constantly nagging. Seth likes the fact that I work, but he is not willing to do his share. He's a wonderful father, and he does do a little laundry. But the big stuff? Forget it. Do you know how often I have asked him to fix the porch steps? How about the time he asked me to make a casserole for the Boy Scout dinner, and when we got to the empty gym, he remembered the date had been changed?

"But what hurts me the most is that I feel duped. If I had known then what I know now, I don't think I would have married him."

SETH'S TURN

"Amy is just too much," says Seth, thirty-nine, a handsome man who works as a manager at an electric company.

"She's too pushy, too demanding. In the beginning, I was captivated by all that energy. Now, she's worn me down.

"Even as a teenager, I never had the sex drive Amy has. She wants it all the time—several nights a week—whether or not I'm in the mood. When we were first married, I was turned on by her wanting sex so much, but even then it was hard to keep up.

"I can't make love on demand—or when I'm worried about work or the bills, or when she's screaming at me because I haven't done one of a thousand things on her list.

"Amy is a tough taskmaster. We've been restoring our old Victorian house ever since we got married, and she expects it to be done yesterday. If it takes longer than I thought to fix the porch because it's full of termites, she hits the roof. She makes a federal case out of everything. So maybe I got the date wrong for that dinner. It's not the end of the world.

"Most of all, she expects me to do her bidding in bed. You have no idea how many times I've made love when I really didn't want to. It's not that I don't think Amy is sexy, but I have so much on my mind that sex is just not a priority.

"The boys delight and enchant me, but being a parent is tougher than I thought. And for a few years, I was floundering professionally. Some nights I still feel as if I have the weight of the world on my shoulders.

"My folks are first-generation Irish Catholic. There were seven kids—I was the second youngest. I don't remember my dad being around all that much, but my mother was very overprotective. One of my older brothers died of a brain tumor at five. Less than six months later, I contracted rheumatic fever and was in the hospital for two months. I had a relapse when I was nine and another when I was fourteen; I still take medications.

"I became a bit of a loner. School was a struggle, but I managed to graduate from college with a teaching degree. I have a gift for working with kids. But when I met Amy, I was at a low point because I had recently lost a teaching job I loved due to cutbacks.

"I made the worst possible career choice: I went to work for my father even though we never got along. Both he and my mother were alcoholics—functioning drunks. Dad owned two auto-body shops, but he was a terrible businessman. He needed someone to get the place in order. I figured I'd try, but working with a man I could never please was hell.

"At the time, I was still living at home to save money, even though I was almost thirty. One night my mother told me it was time for me to stop moping around and start socializing. I noticed Amy the minute I sat down at the bar. I couldn't tell whether she was with anyone—not that I would have had the nerve to talk to her. When she finally came over, we hit it off immediately. It sounds melodramatic, but she made me feel alive again.

"It was at Amy's urging that I mustered the courage to quit working for my dad. My brother-in-law had connections with the electric company, and he helped me get my foot in the door. I've been there ten years now, and I love it.

"But I can't come home every night to a wife who doesn't hesitate to tell me I'm letting her down in every area of our life. When she treats me like dirt, I withdraw. Amy's whole family is so emotional: When they're mad, they explode; five minutes later, they're hugging you and urging you to sit down to a huge feast. When I'm upset, I brood until the issue gets resolved.

"You know, it wasn't easy coming here. I think we're both committed to the marriage, and we're nuts about our kids. But I feel like I'm walking on eggs to please her."

THE COUNSELOR'S TURN

"This was a classic role reversal," said the counselor. "Amy's sexual appetite was much stronger than her husband's, though the passion of the early years masked this. Unfortunately, neither understood that even in the best marriages, it's impossible for a couple's needs, sexual or otherwise, to coincide all the time.

"I explained to this couple that the most common cause of lack of sexual desire is anger. Indeed, it was my suspicion that Seth—the child of two alcoholics, who grew up lacking confidence and never really trusting those around him—was finding it difficult to stand up to his articulate, demanding wife. Unable to express his hurt and fury, he withheld sex as a subconscious payback for the way Amy treated him. It became one of his weapons—in much the same way that he never got around to fixing the porch or paying the bills.

"A sensitive and kind main, Seth prided himself on being the involved father his own dad never was, but he'd begun to feel overwhelmed. Even in bed, he found it difficult to put aside his worries. His wife's badgering made matters worse.

"But Amy was furious and anguished, and she focused her disappointment about her marriage on their unsatisfying sex life. In her eyes, Seth could do nothing right—and she didn't hesitate to tell him so. Then, when he rebuffed her, she felt unattractive.

"Having grown up with a father who made her feel inadequate, Amy vowed she would never marry a man like Dad. But she never dealt with her anger toward her father. Instead, she took on the characteristics she least liked about him: This allowed her to distance herself from her mother, but her need to control was destroying their marriage.

"Seth wondered if his medication was blocking his sex drive; a visit to a physician confirmed this possibility, so he switched to another drug. However, in therapy, he admitted that he masturbated regularly. 'That lets out a lack of sexual desire,' I told them, 'but there are obvious marital issues here. It takes far more work emotionally to make love to someone else than it does to masturbate.'

"Seth described how hard it as for him to stay organized, to remember to do things and follow through with plans he started. We spent weeks discussing how he could handle things more efficiently. As he began to finish tasks long left undone, one major area of friction between them eased. Meanwhile, they agreed that if Amy asked him to do something, they'd set a deadline and she wouldn't bring it up again. If the task was left undone, she'd call a repairman.

"Seth also discovered that some concrete steps, such as writing in his personal appointment book that he was going to make love that night, helped him get in the mood,

'Thinking about sex during the day got me primed for the evening,' he said.

"As the tension eased, the door toward greater empathy was nudged opened. While Amy kept pulling the conversation back to the bedroom, I told her that if she wanted her sex life to improve, she had to, paradoxically, stop zeroing in on it. 'The way the two of you treat each other outside the bedroom determines what goes on inside,' I explained. 'And just as you feel entitled to a rich and rewarding sex life, he's entitled to say no.'

"Gradually Amy accepted the fact that her husband wasn't programmed for sex the way she was, and that this was not a personal attack on her. I taught them massage and touching techniques that did not include intercourse, which further helped him. Amy enjoyed the creative ways he touched her, and once she stopped pressuring Seth, she found that time spent cuddling often led to sex. Instead of focusing on what she was not getting from her husband, Amy began to think about how much things have changed. 'Now I'm thinking quality,' she says, 'not quantity.'"

THE DOS AND DON'TS OF GREAT SEX

Good sex shaves the sharpness off life's edges. With a little planning and imagination, passion can grow throughout your marriage. You can't have great sex unless you are true to yourself and honest with your partner. Still, despite great strides, one adage largely holds true: Women need love to get in the mood for sex. Men need sex to be receptive to love. Work with this:

DON'T:

. . . consistently have sex if you're not physically ready. Over time, giving in—because you feel you must, or because time is short—can breed resentment that will seriously erode any good feelings you have for each other. Instead, transform the moment: Tell him you're thrilled that he wants you, and suggest a better time.

. . . criticize him for trying something new that doesn't work.

. . . have sex when your mind is mulling over how to handle the problem with the contractor, your son's failing math grade, or whose turn it is to take lacrosse carpool on Saturday.

. . . use your fear or resentment as a weapon and avoid sex. Find a way to talk about what's really bothering you outside the bedroom, so it doesn't ruin what happens inside.

DO:

. . . pay attention to the pace at which your body responds. If you're not aroused enough for sexual activity, let him know.

. . . tell your partner what you need and like.

. . . keep in mind that it can be difficult moving into new sexual arenas. If a spouse's suggestions are uncomfortable for you, don't automatically refuse. Tell him what scares you but try to modify it in some way that will please both of you.

. . . give him a chance to fix what bothers you about your sex life. Give him feedback but avoid critical remarks, especially in the moment. Try to sandwich a negative between two positives.

. . . be the seducer. Trading roles will help you both empathize with each other, not to mention boost passion. Surprise him by showing you're thinking about him when he least expects it.

"MY HUSBAND KEEPS CALLING THOSE SEX HOTLINES"

Beth was devastated to discover that strait-laced Michael was regularly phoning prostitutes. Would she ever be able to trust him again?

"How could he do it?" asked Beth, thirty-one, her voice rising in anger. "How could Michael call a sex service and talk to some prostitute on the phone, for God's sake? What's wrong with him?

"Never in a million years would I have imagined that my dependable, straight-arrow husband would do something like this. One reason I fell in love with him was that he represented a life so different from the one I had known.

"My childhood was pretty intense. My father was a writer and professor, very dynamic but also moody. There was no question that he was the boss in the family and that he wanted to mold us (me and my older sister) in his image. I always had a sense that I was disappointing him.

"I was shy and insecure as a kid and I stayed by myself a lot. Dad was totally wrapped up in himself and his work, and Mother was always trying to control my rebellious older sister. I was good little Beth, pretty much forgotten.

"I was nineteen and a sophomore in college when my mother got sick. She came down with viral pneumonia first, but soon we learned she had lung cancer. Until the last few weeks, when she entered the hospital, I fed her, bathed her, held her hand, read to her. When she died, I flipped out.

"Just before Mother died, my father started an affair with one of his grad students. I never forgave him. Four years later, when he had a heart attack and died, I flipped out again. I was alone.

"After college, I didn't know what I wanted to do, so I took this secretarial job with a large corporation. It's drone-type work and I hate it; I come home from work with my stomach all tied up in knots. Anyway, Michael is in charge of ordering supplies for another division of the same company. He works downtown and he called me one day to check on a shipment.

"It turned out I had to be in his office the following week for a meeting. I walked in the door and I fell madly in love. He asked me to lunch and from that day on we dated steadily.

"Michael is a diabetic and at first I didn't understand the seriousness of that. Sometimes he'd say, out of the blue, 'I'm really hungry, I gotta eat now.' I'd think, 'Fine, I'm hungry, too.' But the truth is, Michael has to eat regularly throughout the day. He has to test his blood-sugar level two or three times a day. And if he's not careful, he can die.

"Once, in the very beginning he casually mentioned, 'Oh, I'm diabetic.' I remember asking, 'What does that mean?' and he said, 'Nothing, really. I take insulin.' End of discussion. Michael appeared perfectly healthy, so I never thought anything more about it. Not once did he say, 'I am seriously ill and if I start to have an attack get me some orange juice or something else with sugar.'

"Anyway, we'd been dating about six months when we flew to Chicago for a friend's wedding. We had some time to kill, so we went to the Museum of Contemporary Art. All of a sudden, Michael got very quiet. It was about one o'clock and we hadn't eaten since breakfast, but back then I didn't know to pay attention to that.

"We walked outside and Michael started weaving and bobbing and looking as if he were going to pass out. I thought, God, he's a lunatic. Then it hit me: He's got to eat! I raced to a phone and called the emergency medical squad. I told them where I was and they told me to get him some orange juice. So I ran to this snack bar, but Michael was so far gone he couldn't even get the juice down. Finally the EMS guys arrived and gave him an injection. After an eternity he started to come out of it—fine, but embarrassed.

"That was the beginning of our problems. You see, Michael refuses to take his disease seriously. In fact, he refuses even to talk about it. Each time he has an attack, he promises it will never happen again—as if it were a question of willpower.

314

"Meanwhile, we'd become engaged and I'd moved into his apartment. We had a beautiful wedding at a small hotel in the city—we paid for it ourselves—and then went to Spain for a three-week honeymoon.

"But the honeymoon was over before a week was up. One night, after a long day of sight-seeing, we fell asleep early. Around two in the morning I woke up and realized Michael was having a severe reaction. It was horrifying, trying to communicate with the emergency medical people in my high school Spanish, thinking my husband was going to die right there.

"He came out of it, but I was devastated. I felt as if my whole future was crashing down around me. How could Michael do this? How would he be able to take care of me and the children we dreamed of having if he wouldn't take care of himself?

"We came back from our honeymoon early. That was four years ago and things between us have just gotten worse. Our marriage is a sham.

"When we come home from work, I rush around and get dinner ready and we usually eat in silence. Then Michael goes into the living room to watch TV and I go into the bedroom to unwind. I'm so angry at him now that there are nights I can't even stand to be in the same room with him. I certainly don't want to have sex.

"I'm tired of pleading with him to take care of himself. Lately we've been fighting about everything. I'll buy a new sweater and he'll hit the ceiling. Look, I'm not frivolous. I don't buy four-hundred-dollar shoes. We both make very decent money, but Michael is an incredible pennypincher, yelling at me to hurry up and close the refrigerator door so I don't use up electricity. He is so overly meticulous that he even gets upset if I don't put something back in the refrigerator in the exact same place it was before. His stinginess even extends to the baby we've talked about having—he's so hung up on how we'll be able to afford it that even that discussion goes nowhere.

"When Michael gets angry, he does things like refuse to take me to the grocery store. I hate to drive. The first year we were married I had an accident—nothing serious, but it left me terrified to get behind the wheel. And now when he's mad he uses this driving thing to get back at me.

"But as I said, our problems don't stop there. Last Sunday I was sleeping late. I woke up because I heard Michael talking to somebody on the phone in the hall. I peeked out the door and heard him say, 'So when was the last time you had sex?' and other things. I could see he had an erection. Something clicked in my brain; I remembered that the husband of one of my dear friends had been calling these sex services and seeing prostitutes—my friend found the charges on their credit-card bills.

"Later that day, while he was watching the football game, I went on a search-and-destroy mission. I pulled out all the credit-card receipts, and sure enough, there were hundreds of dollars' worth of calls going back for over a year and a half to things like Entre-Nous and Dial Desiree. I stormed into the living room. Michael didn't know what to say.

"I insisted we get help. I won't give up without a good fight, but I don't know what to do anymore."

MICHAEL'S TURN

"I'm glad Beth finally found out, I really am," said Michael, thirty-four, in a voice barely above a whisper. "It's a relief to have it out in the open. I know I have a problem. I'm very embarrassed. But at least I didn't go out and have an affair.

"Beth is wonderful; I don't want to lose her, but she's pushing me away. She won't let me be close. I can tell she's angry with me, but she won't tell me why. At least now we're here talking.

"Our problem is very simple: Beth doesn't want to make love. She says no so often I've stopped trying. You should see her when we get home from work. She's a maniac, whirling around the kitchen, throwing things into pots—you'd think she was trying to set a world record in dinner preparation. At the end of the day I like to relax. I know she thinks I don't help her enough, but if she took half an hour to unwind first, I'd help.

"Then, after dinner, instead of sitting and talking like normal people, maybe watching a little TV, Beth disappears into the bedroom. Or she'll rant and rave at the top of her lungs.

"She thinks I try to get back at her by not driving her all over the place. That's ridiculous. I'm not that kind of guy. I know she was very shook up after her car accident, and I was sympathetic. But that was three years ago. It's time she got over this hang-up.

"The only time we talk is when we argue over how much money she spends. I cannot understand why she has to buy a sweater a week. Both of us have good jobs, but we also have a lot of expenses. And if she wants to have kids in the future, we have to start saving today. I'm not saying she shouldn't buy any clothes; I'm saying she should be realistic. Buy what you need.

"Maybe my money worries are left over from my childhood. Dad was in the dry-cleaning business; he made a decent living, but we never really had much.

"I guess you could say it was a fairly traditional home: Mom stayed home and took care of my younger brother and me, while Dad was the boss, very strict, with lots of rules.

My parents were so overprotective it made me crazy. I know they were very concerned about my health, but they never let me make any decisions on my own. I fought with them a lot. They didn't think I was studying hard enough, they didn't like the colleges I was applying to, they thought my decision to major in psychology was dumb.

"I was first diagnosed with diabetes when I was seventeen. I'd started to lose weight; I'd get very tired, hungry, and thirsty, and I'd urinate a lot. I had to go to the hospital for tests. When I got out, my parents said I shouldn't tell anyone about my diabetes. What did I know? I was a kid; I did what they told me to do.

"But I guess I was angry. I didn't want to be sick, and for a long time I relied on my mother to give me the injections. Beth's right. I don't know why I don't take better care of myself.

"Look, I don't know what else to say. I don't know why I started calling phone-sex services. I got the number from the back of a porno magazine. And yes, at first I denied it. I was scared. I'd never seen Beth so angry. But something drastic had to happen."

THE COUNSELOR'S TURN

"Although this couple first came to see me about a sexual problem, that issue quickly became framed in the broader context of Beth's anger and resentment over Michael's refusal to own up to his illness, as well as their inability to resolve issues of control in their marriage," said the counselor.

"Michael had never made peace with the fact that he has diabetes. Like many people with a chronic illness, he hated to think of himself as anything less than a whole, well person. Sadly, his parents had made him feel ashamed of his illness. Michael grew up in a home suffused with what we call a Depression-era mentality, the belief that the world is a dangerous, terrible place, and as a result, safety and security must be your paramount concerns. Michael was convinced that Beth would reject him if she knew how sick he was. Because he had functioned in this pattern of denial for so many years, Michael was truly unable to see that his frequent attacks were directly linked to his unwillingness to deal responsibly with his disease.

"At the same time that his parents encouraged his denial, however, they also pampered him—his mother took on the responsibility of managing his illness and, later on, Michael expected his wife to do the same. His parents tried to control his life in other ways, too, issuing edicts on everything from where to go to school to what profession he should choose. Although Michael thought he was rebelling against such strictures, with few exceptions he did what they told him to do.

WORKING THROUGH
THE TOUGHEST SEX PROBLEMS

It's understandable that Beth would be shocked at such a disclosure—and not surprising that she would immediately begin to doubt herself, her sexuality, and her marriage. Any wife in a similar circumstance would wonder: What does he get from these calls that he doesn't get from me? Is he sick?

While such behavior need not signal the end of a marriage, it does indicate a serious problem that must be resolved. Sexual problems left unspoken can ruin a relationship. Women like Beth need answers: What's behind such secret calls? The proliferation of sex hotlines clearly indicates that many couples are not able to talk honestly about sexual concerns and desires. Indeed, most men who resort to phone sex are afraid to express their deepest sexual fantasies to their wives, out of fear of being ridiculed or rejected. Simply bringing these concerns into the open, however, can enrich your sex life in general. Perhaps there are things you can do differently in bed that will please your husband as well as yourself. On the other hand, if he confides sexual fears or desires with which you are uncomfortable, you might consult a sex therapist for guidance. In either case, seek professional counseling to shore up your own self-esteem and feelings of confidence so you don't wallow in what's-wrong-with-me feelings.

"Not surprisingly, as an adult, Michael had a compulsive need to control all areas of his life, no matter how minute. Even his arguments about having a child broke down into dollars-and-cents issues.

"In the beginning, Beth willingly played the role of rescuer—just as she had nursed her dying mother—because it made her feel needed. But those good feelings soon gave way to a simmering rage, and just as she couldn't express that anger to her autocratic father, so, too, did she have trouble telling her husband.

"When Michael refused to take care of himself and Beth was forced to witness his attacks again and again, she grew terrified of losing him just as she had lost her parents. Her anger was further fueled by his

. . . AND A WORD ABOUT CYBERSEX

Though numbers are impossible to tally, experts believe that thousands of people from all socioeconomic levels are addicted to online sex. The Center for Online Addiction in Bradford, Pennsylvania, estimates that one in five Internet addicts are most likely online for sex. Easily available, inexpensive, and anonymous, online sex eliminates slinking around in sleazy bars, spending a lot of money on costly 900 hotlines, as well as the dangers of unprotected sex. Yet the repercussions, especially in a marriage, can be devastating. According to Kimberly Young, Ph.D., director of the Center of Online Addiction, cybersex is "the crack cocaine" of sexual addiction. While most Internet sex users tend to be "recreational" users—checking out a site to satisfy a passing curiosity—increasing number of victims, men as well as women, become so dependent on Internet sex that their marriages and their lives fall to ruin. Are you or a partner facing potential trouble? Young has developed a series of questions to assess your situation: How much time do you routinely spend in online chat rooms or surfing the Internet for the purpose of finding sexual contacts? How often do you prefer cybersex to sexual intimacy with a partner? How often do you neglect other responsibilities to spend more time having cybersex? Do you fear that life without cybersex would be boring? Young also offers suggestions and counseling for those who fear that their partners are engaging in cybersex. For more information: www.netaddiction.com.

nit-picking control over her life: 'How can he bug me about closing the refrigerator door,' she demanded, 'when he refuses to take care of his health?'

"Beth was similarly conflicted at work. A bright, creative woman, she was stifled by a routine job but was afraid to ask for more responsibility. By the end of the day, she was wound so tight she couldn't relax.

"The first step in counseling was to insist that Michael take responsibility for his illness. When he finally realized that their success hinged on this issue, he began to change. He started to watch his diet, monitor his blood sugar, and take his insulin. Beth pulled back and stopped reminding him to eat properly. At one point, his doctor advised him to check into the hospital for a three-day evaluation.

319

This was difficult for Michael to do, because it meant that his disease might be getting more serious and could involve a whole new set of instructions. But he went ahead with the tests, and as a show of support, Beth, who had signed up for a refresher course in driving, drove him there.

"Once the issue of Michael's illness was out in the open, this couple made progress very quickly. By talking about the connection between her childhood and her fear of losing Michael, Beth was able to label her anger for what it was and no longer had to act it out sexually. As she became more loving and responsive to him, Michael stopped calling the sex hotlines.

"We encouraged Beth to speak up in other ways. When Michael questioned her about a pair of shoes, she learned to say, 'I'm a responsible adult. I know whether I can afford these shoes. I resent the way you interrogate me.' She spoke up at the office, too, and when she did, her supervisors were impressed with her ideas and broadened her duties. Happier at work, she arrives home calmer and more available to her husband.

These two ended therapy after a year. 'I get anxious about Michael's illness,' Beth told me at her last session, 'but I trust him to stay on top of it now. We've found that old closeness. I really couldn't ask for anything more.'"

TEAM UP

Balancing Parenthood with Partnership

————•————

Whether they have one child or five, whether they've known each other since grade school or met online a year ago, most couples are still unprepared for the enormous changes that come with the transition to parenthood. In fact, one of the most common dilemmas that plagued the subjects of "Can This Marriage Be Saved" when it first appeared in 1953 continues to be a paramount concern a half-century later: How can men and women be both partners and parents?

The very arrival of children and their can't-be-ignored demands often propels couples into a therapist's office in the first place, as differences that may have appeared insignificant become magnified— and sometimes unmanageable—through the prism of parenthood. Some people enter counseling because they simply can't decide when, or even whether, to have children. If infertility is an issue, they may struggle with the question of adoption. Everyone discovers that the joys of parenthood can be quickly erased by battles over who handles which chores, whose work is more important, how financial resources should be allocated—not to mention why sex is a distant memory. Everyday, routine decisions are no longer routine, and can become the kindling for nasty, white-hot arguments. For many, the difficulties of raising young children often pale in comparison to the clashes and conflicts during a child's teenage years. We may know that intimacy needs to be cultivated, but when parenting feels like an extreme sport, connecting demands time and energy, and who has either?

Current research confirms how tough it is: Marital dissatisfaction, especially for women, often drops precipitously with the birth of each child. Unless each person works hard to be sensitive to his own (as well as his partner's) need for respect, attention, and love, self-esteem crumbles and resentment builds. A marriage that is cracking may start to collapse.

Seven Secrets of a Happy Marriage also makes clear that a couple's relationship is their child's blueprint for intimacy. By watching how you and your spouse get along, kids learn about themselves and relationships. But according to a report from the National Marriage Project at Rutgers University in New Jersey, much of what they see is discouraging: Today's teenage girls show a pronounced pessimism about marriage; only 64 percent of high school girls expect to stay married for life.

Equally telling is the growing body of research that underscores the fact that children raised in high-conflict homes—where there is overt arguing as well as a climate of underlying anxiety—often become unsure, emotionally needy adults who may have trouble fielding life's curve balls and settling into their own committed relationships. "Marital conflict is a more important predictor of child adjustment than divorce itself," reports the National Marriage Project, "and the most important predictors of child adjustment are the intensity and frequency of parent conflict, the style of conflict, its manner of resolution, and the presence of buffers to ameliorate the effects of a higher conflict."

One direct result of parental battles, researchers add, is that kids never learn the skills they need to be and stay close. Time and again in *Seven Secrets* one or both partners learn through counseling that a key reason their own marriage is failing is that they never witnessed a healthy marriage in action. They don't know that fighting is normal even in a good marriage; that parents can argue and make up; that divisive issues can be negotiated. Had they seen a model for good partnering then, perhaps they wouldn't be in counseling now.

Every column in this book echoes that theme. Whether it's the legacy of infidelity, addiction, and abuse or the unspoken assumption that Dad is the boss and Mom's feelings don't really count, kids' antennae are always tuned to what's happening on and under the surface of their parents' marriage. And the messages they pick up have a resounding impact on their lives.

So what can you do? The evidence is just as clear that the positive things children see at home affect them as strongly as the negative. Husbands and wives who show affection, express empathy and support, listen and debate solutions to problems, and possess a sense of humor about themselves and their marriage are also sending messages to their kids—positive ones. Likewise, you can choose to build a better relationship and make your marriage a priority.

Look at your marriage, or any relationship, from your child's point of view. What messages are you sending? Some are obvious: The way you and your partner speak, touch, fight with each other . . . whether arguments are resolved in calm, conciliatory voices or with tempers flaring and fists flying. Others are less so: Who makes the important decisions? Are family members allowed to disagree, and what happens if they do? Who works outside the home, and who does what chores inside?

Next, picture the relationship you truly want. When couples get stuck in hurtful, destructive patterns, it helps to pull back and think about what your lives would be like if you weren't wrestling with the same old problems or fighting the same fight for the 652nd time. Keep an image in your mind of your ideal relationship; this will allow you to concentrate on the work that needs to be done in order to make it happen.

Once you've made a commitment to achieve that goal, act as allies not adversaries. Find ways to resolve conflicts before they escalate. If you can't, consult a professional—right now. Besides making time to visit a counselor, make time for the two of you, away from the kids, at least once a week. It's important for each of you to be alone, too—away from work, away from the family—to recharge your emotional batteries. Even a ten-minute walk around the block when you get home from the office but before you walk in the front door can ease stress. Or better yet: Pencil into your week some time for exercise, time with friends, and time to do whatever you please.

Don't forget one more important ingredient in preserving a relationship: enter laughing. Have a sense of humor. When you're frazzled from the whining and exhausted from all the fetching and schlepping that having kids involves, it's hard to find anything funny. Still, if you can manage to share even a giggle over something your child has said, you'll not only strengthen the bond between you and your spouse, you'll find more joy in parenthood.

"He's a Super Dad but an Awful Husband"

J eannie yearned for Joe's attention, but her daughters were getting it all. What happens when the kids always come first?

JEANNIE'S TURN

"I have friends who complain that their husbands don't spend enough time with their kids," said Jeannie, thirty-nine, a small, fine-featured woman with long, honey-colored hair. "But with us, it's just the opposite. Karisa, fifteen, and Meghan, fourteen, monopolize Joe's attention. It's as if I don't even exist. Lately, we're either fighting all the time about the girls or we're simply not speaking to each other.

"Joe was always the most loving, giving person. We met on a ski slope seventeen years ago—I had careened off course, landed in a snowbank, and badly twisted my ankle. Joe, who had been skiing right behind me, raced over to help. We started dating soon after that, and before long, I had fallen madly and deeply in love.

Joe is nine years older than I, a professional singer whose voice you hear on many radio and TV commercials. I had never met anyone so fascinating; he introduced me to music, books, poetry, foreign films—being with him was always so stimulating, I was miserable when we were apart.

Even though I was very busy with classes, I had almost completed my M.B.A. in accounting, Joe and I still managed to see each other often.

325

One night, after he picked me up at the library where I was studying, we stopped for a snack at a McDonald's close to campus. When I opened my Big Mac container, I found a beautiful diamond ring inside!

We were married the following summer. From my side only my parents and grandmother attended the wedding, but Joe had dozens of sisters and brothers, cousins and nieces, all joking around with him and having a great time. Joe's parents had been poor and his father was often away searching for work. But obviously, those kids had formed their own close-knit family.

My own father was a lawyer—a true workaholic who used to stay at his office well past seven o'clock every night. And my mother, always in the kitchen or busy with something around the house, never seemed to welcome my help or even my company. Usually she'd tell me brusquely, 'Go study.'

So I did; I worked hard throughout school, and Joe was one of the first men I had dated who seemed to understand my commitment to my work.

"After we were married, we moved into a small apartment near campus, and for the first few months our life was just as I had hoped and envisioned. The only sore point was that I never really felt a part of Joe's family, and I suppose I resented the fact that they all felt free to call on him at any time for just about everything. Being second place in Joe's life hurt a lot, but whenever I felt bad, I simply buried myself in my work.

We had been married just a little more than two years when I discovered I was pregnant. Joe was absolutely thrilled, and although I was a bit nervous, I felt very grown-up and important as a mother-to-be.

I wanted so much to be a good mother, a perfect mother, but I have to admit that when the baby arrived, it was Joe, not I, who turned into Super Parent. In fact, I felt inadequate. I adored Karisa, but by that time I had completed my master's degree and started my career as an associate at one of the Big Eight accounting firms in the city—a dream job. When I got home from the office each day—usually around seven o'clock—I was often so tired I could barely see straight.

"When Meghan was born about a year later, though, the pressure at work really escalated. I was all the more grateful that Joe was such a terrific father. In fact, over the years, Joe was always there to fill in the blanks, introducing the girls to all sorts of exciting activities and interests just as he had done for me the years before.

"The problem is, it's gone too far. Now that I've reached a level of achievement at work that allows me to take a breather, I see Joe is too indulgent—to the point of not disciplining the girls at all. And quite frankly, when I look at my two girls trying to dress like Britney Spears with the hair, the barely there midriff tops, and tight skirts, I'm terrified they're turning into wild tramps.

"Even their fascination with music, which initially pleased me very much, has gotten way out of hand. They are positively addicted to MTV—they do their homework in front of the television and venture downstairs only to eat. When I tell Joe I'm afraid the girls' grades will start slipping, he either dismisses my comments quickly or tells me that they're just going through a harmless stage so I should quit worrying.

"Last year, Karisa and Meghan kept hounding us for their own television. Without consulting me, Joe went and bought them their own set for Christmas, and even hooked up the cable in their room! I was livid and demanded that the girls at least assume more chores around the house to earn their new privilege. Joe finally agreed to that, but of course, my efforts turned out to be a farce.

"The 'N Sync concert last year was the final straw for me. The girls had begged to attend, but I had heard plenty of reports that it was going to be a very wild scene.

"Instead of taking my no as their final answer, they called Joe at the recording studio and asked him. You'd think he'd have backed me up on something as important as this, but no, Joe actually stopped off at the box office on his way home from work, found out the concert was sold out, and paid scalpers $100 each for three tickets, volunteering to take the girls to the concert himself.

"I don't want to have to compete with the girls for Joe's attention. Last week, when I suggested we go for a drive after dinner, just the two of us, he said 'Great idea.' But when we told the girls we were going out and Meghan asked if she could go, too, Joe said yes. Doesn't he enjoy being alone with me at all anymore?

"Right now, I don't know what to do. I don't want my children to think I'm an ogre, but I also don't want them to grow up to be self-centered and spoiled.

"I've actually thought of packing up and moving out with the girls-my work load is much more manageable now, and perhaps that's the only way to get my daughters back on track."

JOE'S TURN

"With Jeannie, I always feel as if I'm between a rock and a hard place," said Joe, forty-eight, a tall, rugged-looking man with warm blue eyes. "I've loved Jeannie since the day I yanked her out of that snowbank, but I can't seem to get that through her head. And just because I want to give my kids the best of everything, she thinks my feelings for her have changed.

"Jeannie is right about one thing, though: Lately I really don't enjoy being with her. Her constant complaining about Karisa and Meghan and her insisting that I'm a bad parent because I don't discipline the kids enough are driving me nuts. I know we must come to some agreement about the girls, but as far as I'm concerned, she is much too harsh on them.

"One day Jeannie will go on a rampage because the girls haven't cleaned up their room as they had promised they would; the next day she'll complain about the way the girls dress. For Pete's sake, has she opened her eyes lately? All the kids dress like that, and besides, before you know it, they'll be into something else, some other fad. Has it been so long since Jeannie was young herself?

"Jeannie has been getting so uptight. I often feel I have to protect the kids from her martial law. I just don't think our kids are that irresponsible. But Jeannie can't let up on this discipline bit.

"She still complains—constantly, I might add—about the television I bought Karisa and Meghan last year for Christmas. What more can I say about that darned TV set? Karisa and Meghan are two smart kids, and they continue to bring home good report cards.

"Jeannie thinks they spend all their time glued to the TV; I know they don't. She's not home as much as I am. What's more, she insisted that the girls practically scrub floors like Cinderella to earn their television. Jeannie told me that her mother and father were never very warm or giving when she was growing up. If that's true, you'd think she'd bend over backward to be just the opposite with her own daughters.

"My dad disappointed me so many times, I swore I would never be that way to my own kids. I want to be there for my children in every way possible. Isn't that how a mature, loving parent should be? Parents have got to give of themselves. So what if Meghan comes for a ride with us; after all, Jeannie and I can talk anytime.

"I think Jeannie's the one who's been acting self-centered lately. In fact, she has always had a tendency to want things her own way.

"When we first met, she was very perky and charming, but only for as long as she had my full, undivided attention. If a niece or cousin called, for example, and asked me to do something, Jeannie would immediately become clingy and wistful.

"I think that's what's happening now, too. Of course, we have wonderful times together, and if we lived on some desert island, we could spend every second being alone. But we don't and I can't understand her resentment. I love my wife and I want to be a good husband. But does that mean I can't be a good parent, too?"

"Joe and Jeannie were caught in a vicious circle," the counselor said. "The more Jeannie said no to Karisa and Meghan, the more Joe said yes—and the girls were taking full advantage of the situation.

"This was happening in part because Jeannie was jealous of her own children—a common feeling for a woman with very low self-esteem—but there were other factors aggravating the situation, among them Joe's failure to recognize that he was not giving his wife the emotional support she needed and unquestionably deserved.

"Our first task in counseling was to help Jeannie and Joe come to some agreement about raising the children. During an early session, I pointed out to Joe that, although it was normal for mother-daughter conflicts to arise when a daughter reaches puberty, he was intensifying the battles each time he stepped in the middle. By doing so, he reduced Jeannie's status from being parent to being one of the girls. I stressed the need for Jeannie and Joe to discuss all potential conflicts in private and to agree to back each other up in front of the children.

"Joe insisted that any tendency he had to overindulge the girls was in response to Jeannie's rigidity, but I asked him to take a look at the factors in his background that might also account for his attitudes and behavior.

"For example, Joe had come from a large and affectionate family, but while there were lots of children to play with, he had always felt a keen and secret sense of deprivation because his father had never been there for him.

"Joe vowed to treat his children differently, a plan that made it difficult for him to see Jeannie, or himself, for that matter, as having any legitimate emotional or psychological needs. It took him awhile to truly understand that adults, like children, have emotional needs, too . . . that both he and Jeannie had a right to set some priorities that had nothing to do with their daughters.

"When Joe finally realized this, he was ready to work with Jeannie to create some rules that would make both of them feel comfortable as parents. First, when a problem arose with one of the girls, I suggested to Jeannie that she say, 'Why don't you ask your father?' instead of automatically saying no to them. That way, Joe would see firsthand just how often, and to what extent, the girls were making demands, and he would then have to use his judgment about setting rules. What's more, Jeannie wouldn't always be the bad guy.

"Much to Jeannie's surprise and relief, Joe agreed to set some limits on the amount of television the girls could watch. Together, they decided to allow one and a half hours of television, either MTV or some other program, each weekday night, but only after the girls had completed their homework assignments.

"They both informed Karisa and Meghan of the new rules for watching television and, predictably, there was a fuss. However, once the girls realized that both Joe and Jeannie were standing firm on the matter, their rebellion became more muted and, sooner than Joe and Jeannie would have imagined, it ceased entirely.

"Our next step was to take a closer look at Jeannie's problems. For an adult, Jeannie was a very emotionally needy person. Her parents had been so cold and rejecting that she had grown up with an almost insatiable longing to be loved. She married Joe, an older man who seemed like a wonderful caretaker— and he was, but not to her. As a result, Jeannie panicked when her daughters, in adolescence, began to fight her on many fronts.

"I told Jeannie that it was absolutely essential for her to start sharing time with Karisa and Meghan, to juggle her work schedule so she could spend time and plan special activities with them. Even if the planned activity didn't seem to be going well, Jeannie was not to retreat into work.

"I also thought it would be helpful to see Karisa and Meghan, and the four sessions we had were indeed productive. I invited them to look at their mother not as a parent but as a person, one who had not been treated very lovingly herself as a child but who loved her daughters greatly and wanted them to love her, too.

"The results of these simple steps were very positive. Within several weeks, Jeannie told me she and the girls actually looked forward to being together. Jeannie was also pleased that Karisa and Meghan seemed more willing to listen to her and not so quick to run to Joe for everything. Though she is still not delighted with their current style of dress, Jeannie finds it easier to relax about it because she is happier with herself and more confident in her relationship with Joe as well as the girls.

"Joe and Jeannie stopped coming to counseling sessions about four months ago, but we still speak occasionally by phone. Jeannie recently called to tell me that she and Joe had planned a week's vacation out West to go skiing: 'And this time, I know I'm on course,' she said with a laugh."

PARENTING AS PARTNERS

Although she expressed it the wrong way, Jeannie had a point: Parents have every right to have their emotional needs met, and if that means setting priorities that have nothing to do with the children, so be it. To make up for his own emotionally barren childhood, Joe was giving to his daughters at the expense of his wife. Jeannie deserved more. But as this case illustrates, disciplining adolescents can bring out the worst in even the best parent. Consider the following:

1. Expect a teen to be moody, sulky, and short-tempered. There will be days when a simple "Hi, how are you?" seems like too personal a question for you to dare ask. Remind yourself that your teen's behavior often has nothing to do with you—although you may be the target, you're not the cause. Give them time to work things out themselves. Despite their growing independence, even teens want to know that there are guidelines and that you're there for them when they need you.

2. Your emotional bond with your child is your most effective parenting tool, so make yourself available. Insist that she eat meals with you as often as possible (ask her friends to join). Volunteer to drive the carpool, even if it's late at night. Make your home a safe haven where your teen feels comfortable being herself.

3. Listen, but don't lecture or judge if your teens come to you with a problem. That doesn't mean you condone rude or disrespectful behavior. Explain what you will tolerate and accept, listen while they express their feelings, then compromise until you reach a solution you can still live with.

4. Don't micromanage your teen's life. By focusing too much on what you want a teen to accomplish and how she can accomplish it, she may grow up thinking that she isn't good enough just the way she is.

5. If punishment is in order, make sure both parents agree to it and that it fits the crime. Consequences for missing a curfew or failing to do a homework assignment should be logical. Grounding for a week makes sense; doing so for six months doesn't.

6. Pay attention to signs of stress: withdrawal or lethargy, a drop in grades, abrupt changes in eating or sleeping habits. Gently describe to your teen what you've noticed. Make it clear you want to help, not condemn. If your child reacts angrily, table the conversation for another time. It's easy to get sucked into an irrational argument with a highly emotional teen. Keep your feelings in check and talk about strategies for bringing the pressure down a few notches: planning a weekend away or an afternoon at the movies; cutting back on activities; carving out time to do nothing at all.

"MY STEPDAUGHTERS ARE DESTROYING OUR MARRIAGE"

Rona expected her stepdaughters to resent her initially, but she thought that in time they'd all get along. How can a marriage succeed when others seem hell-bent on destroying it.

RONA'S TURN

"I try so hard to be a good stepmother, but I always feel like a failure," said Rona, thirty-eight, as she slowly twisted the strap of her shoulder bag. "The girls are at best distant; we fight all the time, and I'm afraid I'm losing Patrick, too.

"I grew up in a rural community in Pennsylvania. My father was a fireman, my mother was a home-maker, but ever since I can remember she was very sick. She had a stroke when I was twelve and was totally disabled after that. I took on all the household chores.

"My father was very strict. Although he never hit us, my sister and I were absolutely terrified of his temper. I was a lonely kid, and most of the time I felt so angry that all I wanted to do was get out of there. I had to pay for college myself, so I worked during summers and vacations to save money. I also won a few scholarships, which helped a lot.

"One of my jobs had been with a large marketing company, and when I graduated from college, they offered me a position in the person-nel department. I liked the company, so I stayed, and now I head the department. The company agreed to pay for me to get my master's in management training. Patrick was in the same program.

"Ours was a two-year program; you went one weekend a month, plus two full weeks spliced in there somewhere. It was pretty intense and we all got very close. I'd had a series of relationships that never worked out—mostly with married men, and I'm not very proud of that. When I met Patrick, I wasn't thinking marriage; I was happy being single.

"But slowly the relationship changed; we fell deeply in love and got married two years ago.

"Patrick had always told me about his first marriage and his two daughters—Jen, who's now sixteen, and Hilary, twelve. He and his ex-wife, Cheryl, have joint custody. Although Patrick and Cheryl had been divorced for five years, the girls were wary of me from the start. That didn't surprise me, but I wasn't prepared for the continued hostility.

"It's hard to know where to begin. The girls don't treat me with any respect. From what I can determine, they had few rules when they were growing up. Even now, when they're at their mother's house—the girls spend one week at our house, one week at hers—they never make their beds or do any chores. I've always worked and feel it's important for everyone to be a full participant in family life. But they don't even set the table or put their own dishes in the dishwasher.

"The girls don't respect my things either. They think nothing of borrowing my shampoo or of shuffling through my drawers for a sweater or a piece of jewelry without asking. They just assume it's okay, and although I ask them not to do it, they still do.

"What makes me angry is that Patrick never comes to my defense. He promises he'll speak to the girls, but he never follows through.

"I can tell they think I'm a real bitch. I lose my temper, but sometimes they do very hurtful things. Last month I organized a sweet-sixteen party for Jen. I cooked an enormous amount of food for all her friends—and I didn't even get a simple thank-you. Last Mother's Day was probably the saddest day of my life. Neither one even gave me a card or wished me Happy Mother's Day.

"Patrick lets his kids do whatever they want. Oh, he'll tell Jen she has an eleven o'clock curfew, but if she waltzes in at midnight, he leaves it to me to punish her.

"This past year has been particularly bad with Jen. She recently announced that she wanted to live with her mother full-time—she hates switching houses. Patrick doesn't know whether to let her go, and we're all fighting about it constantly.

"But most of the time, Patrick is in a state of blissful oblivion about all this. We talk about what the rules should be concerning homework or having boys over and agree on something, and then Patrick just doesn't follow through.

"And as I said, I'm afraid that soon I won't even have a marriage. Oh, our sex life is fine, but I just feel Patrick isn't there for me anymore. I try to discuss problems at work, but he doesn't listen. He cuts the conversation short by saying, 'Rona, you can do this and you can do this.'

"I love these girls, but sometimes I feel that maybe I don't love them enough. I resent the fact that I do all those things a mother does yet they don't feel close to me. I don't want children of my own, and I know that Patrick doesn't want to start over either, so that's not the issue. Having a close relationship with my stepdaughters means the world to me. Why can't I do anything right?"

PATRICK'S TURN

"Why is everyone on my case?" asked Patrick, forty-nine, a lanky, bearded man with bright red hair. "I know it's not easy for Rona, but to tell you the truth, I don't see what the fuss is all about. Jen and Hilary are good kids. Okay, maybe if we're going by Emily Post's book of etiquette, my daughters should ask permission to borrow a sweater. But, hey, that's what teenage girls do.

They rummage through their parents' closets. I don't mind; what's mine is my kids', too.

"Look, I raised my kids a certain way. Maybe my ex-wife and I were too laid-back, I don't know. I think Rona is too strict and expects too much. Right now, the girls are very upset. From their point of view, the rules are changing in the middle of the game. Rona also makes a big deal about presents and cards. I know she is upset about last Mother's Day and birthdays and such, but I just can't get worked up about things like that.

"Rona talks a lot about what the girls should do to change. Well, I think she should make some changes, too. I want Rona to be more tolerant. I want her to share the responsibility and discipline with me. If the girls take stuff she doesn't want them to take, then she should tell them right away, and not expect me to handle it for her later.

"Rona's right, though: I do say I'll talk to them and then I don't. I guess I just don't want any trouble. I want us all to be happy.

"You know, I was so unhappy growing up, I wanted life for my kids to be different. I grew up the oldest of four in a middle-class suburb of Boston. My dad was a manager in a steamship company. He was very cold and unaffectionate. I knew he wanted me to excel academically and become a model child, and I did. He went to work, came

334

home, had dinner, and read a newspaper. I desperately wanted to know him, but I never knew him at all.

"My mother was an alcoholic. I'd come home from school and find her still in bed. I tried to take care of her, but she got worse, and when I was in high school, she died of a heart attack. "I started dating my first wife in high school, went to college nearby, got a degree in marketing, got married, and had two kids. Pretty standard stuff. But after fifteen years, we had grown apart.

"After the divorce, Cheryl and I did everything to make our daughters' lives as stable as possible. I had hoped the week-to-week arrangement would work; I'm very upset that Jen wants to move out.

"Rona and I used to have an extraordinary relationship. How can she say I'm not there for her? Has she told you that when she gets upset she won't talk to me for days? She plays the silent martyr. I ask what's wrong and she says, 'I don't know.' That's why I walk away. I tell myself, 'If and when she figures it out, she'll tell me.'

"I love Rona very much. She's tremendously capable and her new boss does expect a lot of her. So when she becomes agitated, I help her figure out exactly how she can manage her time—after all, I make my living as a strategic planner! Why, when I'm trying to help her, does she see me as uncaring?"

THE COUNSELOR'S TURN

"The problems Rona and Patrick were having are typical of stepfamilies. Although they also needed help dealing with such marital issues as communication and lack of intimacy, Rona's problems with her stepdaughters proved so divisive that it was vital to tackle those first.

"Rona's childhood in a home devoid of love, warmth, and emotional closeness did not prepare her well for her new role. She grew up feeling alone, unloved, and insecure, but with a steely determination to make her own way in life.

"Underneath that strong exterior, however, there was a frightened little girl who yearned to be loved. Her history of affairs with married men reflected her lack of self-worth; she didn't feel she deserved to have a full, rich relationship of her own.

"When I first met him, Patrick was sad and confused. He had no idea how to handle the conflicts between his wife and his children, and after some feeble attempts and many broken promises, he chose not to deal with the problems at all.

"Like his wife, Patrick grew up in an emotionally empty household. With no one to talk to, this quiet, sensitive little boy would simply retreat to his own room. Patrick learned to turn inward and deny his emotions; he was totally divorced from his feelings.

335

"Interestingly, Patrick unconsciously became the same kind of absentee parent to his daughters that his own parents had been to him. He and his first wife had a very laissez-faire attitude toward disciplining children, and that proved to be a serious obstacle in his marriage to Rona.

"The problems began when Patrick started to date Rona and escalated when they married. I explained that when children reach their teens, many stepfamily problems, especially those involving joint custody, intensify. Teens are very concerned with their social lives; they want their friends to know where they are. And their emotional state is so chaotic that they often need the structure and stability of one home. There is also a desire at this age to live with the same-sex parent.

"As a family therapist, I felt it was important to meet Jen and Hilary. I saw the girls in separate as well as joint sessions with Patrick and Rona, and this gave me the perspective I needed.

"The girls were clearly angry at seeing Rona take over their father. They told me Rona was snarling, stiff, and formal, which was all true. In fact, Jen felt that the only way she could find herself was to leave. She didn't have enough of a history with Rona to be able to yell and fight, then come back loving, as you could do with a natural parent.

"I told Rona she was expecting too much of herself and of the girls. In most cases, a stepmother will never love her stepchildren the way she would love biological children, and they will never love her in the same way they love their biological mother. She should stop berating herself and feeling guilty for something that is a fact of life. I also told her that she should not expect to change her stepdaughters' behavior. That was the job of the biological parent.

"Then I turned to Patrick and told him that it was his job to discipline his daughters, not Rona's. Any stepparent who disciplines a stepchild without a long history with them is doomed to failure. If Hilary doesn't do her homework, then Patrick, not Rona, must say something to her. If Jen misses curfew, then Patrick must speak up. However, if Hilary refuses to help clean up the dishes after dinner, it's Rona's responsibility to make her feelings known. She should say, 'I don't like it when I ask you to do something and you don't do it.' The first situation involves discipline in general; the second relates directly to Rona and Hilary's relationship.

"Many stepfamily problems simply take time to work out, but at the very least, Patrick had to ensure that the girls would treat Rona with respect. He also had to tell the girls that if they wanted to borrow something, all they had to do was ask, but that asking was very important. And they were required to pitch in with the housework.

"I told Rona that some of her problems with her stepdaughters would ease if she could learn to be more flexible. She had lived alone for many years and she was not used to compromising. When Hilary used her shampoo, borrowed a sweater, or left a mess in the kitchen, she had to try not to feel threatened. Once Patrick made it clear to the girls how important it was to Rona that they ask before borrowing something, and once they started to clean up their rooms and help with the dishes, Rona's anger subsided—as did the family fights and tears.

"Then, in meetings with Patrick and Rona, we discussed the pros and cons of honoring Jen's wishes. Finally, Rona and Patrick decided it would be best for everyone not to fight her desire to move out of the house. At the end of the school year, Jen will move in with her mother; Hilary will stay with Rona and Patrick.

"It was time, then, to focus on the marriage. Rona and Patrick wanted a more intimate relationship but were at a loss as to how to build one. This was a couple that didn't know how to have fun together. So, although it may sound silly, we tried scheduling some fun. Patrick and Rona took turns planning evenings out, finding a restaurant or getting tickets for a show. They've started to make friends as a couple and travel.

"When Rona was upset, she'd refuse to talk. I suggested that Patrick follow her and insist she tell him what was bothering her. In time, Rona stopped walking away. Or, if she felt she needed some space, she learned to say, 'I need time to pull myself together. I'll be back in half an hour.' By working together, a disappointment or hurt was settled in a matter of hours instead of dragging on for a week.

"I also tried to help Patrick learn to listen when Rona was upset instead of leaping in with a solution. Like many men, Patrick was oriented toward solving problems and saw her many comments about work as mere complaining.

" 'Rona doesn't need help in solving her problems, at least not right now,' I told Patrick. 'Right now she needs nurturing and reassurance.' And in one session, when Rona was extremely anxious about work, Patrick leaned over, put his arm around her shoulder and said, 'Rona, everything is going to be all right. And you know why? Because I love you.' No one had ever said anything like that to Rona before. I could see her whole body instantly begin to relax.

"This couple was in counseling for two years. They worked very hard, and they've learned that it takes a long time to forge new bonds as a family. And they have far exceeded my, as well as their own, expectations."

WHEN PARENTS REMARRY:
Smoothing the Way for the Kids

It's not unusual for children, even those who are adults themselves, to be suspicious, if not resentful, of a parent's remarriage. They may wonder: What will my relationship with this new person be like? How will my relationship with my parents change? How will holidays and other special occasions be celebrated? Which rituals will be continued, and which forgotten? The first task in dealing with such issues is for both partners to acknowledge that they are real and will happen. Keep these pointers in mind:

1. Give peace a chance. Experts in stepfamily problems remind us that a stepfamily, by definition, is born of a loss. It can take years (the Stepfamily Association cites seven as average) to resolve conflicts, so don't be too hard on yourselves. Remember, too, that all families, even intact ones, fight. The Stepfamily Foundation, Inc., is located at 333 West End Avenue, New York, NY 10023, 212-877-3244. Their 24-hour information line is 212-799-STEP.

2. Remind yourselves that you have the power to change the way you act and react to others. Acknowledge your stepchildren's feelings. While you can certainly hope that they will feel close to you in time, you can't legislate love. You can insist, however, that they treat you and your belongings with care.

3. Expect children, especially teens, to be rebellious and at times undermining. Don't be surprised, either, if a stepfamily situation that seemed to work when the youngsters were grade-school age suddenly goes awry when they enter the teenage years. It may be time to rethink family rules and procedures, even custody arrangements.

4. Make it clear to stepchildren that you have no intention of supplanting their biological parent. Meanwhile, give them time and space to develop their own relationship with you. Be a friend or mentor first. Spend time with each child, one-on-one if possible, so you can learn to enjoy each other and share interests. Keep promises and confidences. Once they know they can trust you, the rest will follow.

5. Make sure children know the rules, and and when they have gone too far, leave discipline to the biological parent. While stepparents should never swallow their anger when a child misbehaves, trying to be the major rule enforcer, especially with a defiant teenager, will likely backfire.

6. Don't expect to love your stepchildren the way you love your own. Maybe you do, and that's great, but don't feel guilty if you can't.

"He's Spoiling Our Son"

Neil and Marcia were thrilled to be parents, but arguments over how to handle their son punctuated their lives. Is it possible to resolve discipline dilemmas when both parents think they're right?

"What happened at my friend Maxine's Christmas party last week was a perfect example of how Neil and I can't agree on anything related to our four-year-old son, Sam," announced Marcia, thirty-nine, a former counselor who's been married for seven years. "Sam refused to eat the food he was offered, and when I handed him a peanut butter sandwich, he shouted, 'This is disgusting!'

"All the while, Neil was trailing me, stage-whispering what I should be doing. Then, just as I thought I'd calmed Sam down, Neil marched him out to the car, leaving me to mumble an embarrassed good-bye.

"I was mortified. Having to discipline Sam in public was hard enough; having all our friends see us out of control drives me crazy.

"I'm the oldest of three girls. My father is an attorney, but Mom, who worked part-time as a secretary, was the real family boss. I know they loved me, but they were always rushing to do everything for me, making me think I was totally incompetent. And while my sisters excelled in school, I managed only B's. I can almost hear my mother saying, 'Honey, I don't think you're truly giving it your all.'

"Going away to college was my first taste of making my own

decisions. I got a master's in psychology and had been working as a counselor for several years when I met Neil. He reminded me of all the good parts of my father-the kind, accepting parts. He was so easy to talk to. We married within a year.

"Those first few years were terrific. Then, when I was thirty-five, I had Sam, and from the moment we left the hospital, the tension between us has been rising.

"We agreed I should quit my job, and I plunged into motherhood with enthusiasm. Very few of my friends had kids, though, and the mothers in the kiddie gym classes and nursery school were all much younger.

"Neil didn't feel comfortable feeding Sam, putting him to bed, or giving him a bath. So I stepped in and did everything. When Sam was little, I was nervous about leaving him with anyone else, so I never had a moment to myself or time to meet a friend for lunch.

"The tension between Neil and me escalated when Sam started preschool last year. Sam's teacher told us he acts up in class, has trouble following directions, and shoves the other kids. Every other word out of his mouth is no. He's very physical, too—he doesn't walk when he can run, and he throws things when he's mad.

"Neil kept insisting that Sam is just being a boy. But I can't handle our son, and what if his behavior is a sign of something more serious? Frankly, I can't believe that Neil and I, who used to agree on just about everything, could be so far apart. I want the toys put away before we sit down to dinner. Neil steps over all the stuff and says, 'What's the big deal? Let's eat!' I make a rule that we eat or drink only in the kitchen or dining room. The next thing I know, Neil and Sam are lying on our bed, watching a game, eating pretzels. But then he'll come down incredibly hard, like taking TV away for a month, if he thinks Sam is being fresh.

"It doesn't help that Neil's hours are insane. Last year he left his position at a software firm to start his own company. I know that he has to put in long hours, but Neil gets home, sometimes at nine or later, and just as I'm getting ready to turn out the light, he waltzes in for a pillow fight. And puts me down for being a rigid fuddy-duddy.

"The bottom line is I'm worried about my son and scared my marriage is over."

NEIL'S TURN

"Most people would agree that I did the right thing by removing Sam from that party, but not Marcia," said forty-two-year-old Neil, looking harried. "As far as she's concerned, I get an F in parenting.

"I don't like to disagree with my wife in public, but she had already made a scene. It was obvious that nothing short of removing him was going to calm him down.

"My wife is bossy and controlling. I'll never forget the day we were taking Sam home from the hospital. While Marcia was in the bathroom, I got the baby ready. Well, she practically had a coronary because I put on the wrong outfit.

"But when I do ask for help, Marcia snaps at me. A few weeks ago, I went into Sam's room to help him get dressed, and he had a huge tantrum. When I asked Marcia what to do, she told me to figure it out myself. And she wonders why I don't want to get involved.

"Marcia is right; I wasn't particularly comfortable with Sam when he was an infant. But I resent the fact that she makes almost every decision related to our son without consulting me—and criticizes my attempts to assert an opinion.

"More and more, I'm convinced she's handling him all wrong. He is defiant, but I don't think he has learning problems. I think Marcia is simply too rigid. Does it really matter if he's not in bed at the precise hour she deems acceptable? The world won't come to an end, either, if his toys aren't put away in their color-coded bins. Of course, whenever I try to tell her to be more flexible, she accuses me of not caring about our son or about her.

"I didn't really have a childhood; my mother abandoned me when I was an infant, and my father left me with my grandmother. I was too much for her to handle, so when I was eight, she placed me in a foster home, where I was very unhappy. I had no real family until tenth grade, when a farm couple with no children adopted me. My new parents were kind, but they weren't very demonstrative. I don't see them anymore. After college—I won a scholarship to the state university—I found a job with a large firm. I worked for them until last year, when I finally decided to try setting up my own business.

"Before Marcia, I kept my relationships casual; there was something about her, though, that attracted me powerfully. We were deliriously happy in those first years of marriage, I know she loves Sam, but I think she's much too emotional and dramatic.

"Look, I wish I could be more involved with Sam, but I have to put in long hours and do some traveling. Marcia insists she understands, but I get these dirty looks and silences when I walk in. At the same time, she asks me every other day whether I really think I can make my company work. Why does she have so little confidence in me?

"The bottom line is, I love Marcia. But she sees me as the enemy, and I'm frustrated that I can't break through that defense."

THE FINE ART OF DISCIPLINE

Daily battles over discipline try our patience, test our wills, and eventually destroy our ability to really enjoy the good times with our kids or spouses. It doesn't have to be that way.

Approach discipline as a preventive medicine. Just as you need to take certain steps to keep your family healthy, you must also take steps to avoid power struggles. Check out these common scenarios:

Scenario #1: SIBLING TUG-OF-WAR

Your five-year-old refuses to share anything with her brother, aged two, and proceeds to bop him on the head when he tries to play with her stuff.

What's really going on: Your daughter feels ignored and replaced. She's jealous of the attention she perceives baby brother has stolen from her. An older sibling may also think that Mom and Dad allow younger kids to get away with far too much.

Emergency advice: Though they do know how to share, most five-year-olds can't finesse such a difficult situation for more than an hour. Acknowledge the legitimacy of her feelings: "I know it's a pain when your brother messes up your things. You don't have to share if you don't want to, but it's not okay to hit." Give her strategies: "Next time, tell him, 'Please, don't touch that, it's mine.' If that doesn't work, come to me or Daddy for help." If she deems certain things off-limits, put them high on a shelf or hide them. And if the squabbling continues, separate them until they can play cooperatively.

Long-range planning: Shore up your older child's tolerance quotient by offering plenty of opportunities for your undivided attention. Help her develop empathy and patience when she is two or three. You might ask: Did that make you feel angry? Sad? As she gets older, you can add: How would you feel if someone grabbed a toy out of your hand? How do you think your brother feels when you hit him? Help her understand that her brother is not acting maliciously but is simply too young to play nicely like she can.

Scenario #2: FAMILY DINNER DISASTER

You're both anxious about whether your eighteen-month-old can make it through a holiday dinner. How can you prevent a meltdown with the whole family, in-laws included, present?

What's really going on: Don't expect too much. At this age, a child could last in this type of situation for about thirty minutes. By the time he's three or four, he could probably last forty-five minutes to an hour, tops, but with a lot of your attention.

Emergency advice: Bring along a bag of supplies—favorite toys, some toys he's never seen before, and small packs of favorite foods. Sit next to him at the end of the table so you can make a gracious exit if necessary. Don't ignore behavior that seems to be escalating. Remember, family members often think they have more license than others to lecture you about parenting. Without trying to defend yourself, cheerfully announce, "Well, I think we've gotten about as much as we can expect from this eighteen-month-old!"

Long-range planning: Give your toddler advance warning, even though he may not fully understand it; it lays the groundwork for the future. When he behaves well, compliment him. And consider enlisting a teenage baby-sitter or an older cousin as a mom's helper.

Scenario #3: THE WHINING WARS

Your kids deserve Olympic medals for whining. Or maybe a spot in *The Guinness Book of World Records.*

What's really going on: Younger children whine because it may be the only way they can express that something is bothering them; older children whine because they know it works. Most likely, it's caused you to waffle over rules in the past. Whiners stop whining when they know you're serious.

Emergency advice: Use the broken record approach. In a firm voice, repeat your rule until your child complies. Or, try the one-two-three method: "TV must be off by the time I count to three. If it's not, you'll be punished." Then count slowly until he does. If he storms out in a huff, ignore it until he stops whining. If this behavior continues, issue a punishment that makes sense: no TV at all tomorrow.

Long-range planning: Clear rules that you consistently uphold are your first line of defense and you need to start setting limits early. "I know it's hard to turn off a favorite show; I don't like to either, but we agreed on a family rule and sticking to it helps everyone." When you decide on rules, be sure they really make sense for you. Will another half hour at the end of the day let you relax and prepare dinner in peace? Give yourself permission to modify a rule if situations change.

"This is a classic story of how a marriage can be pulled apart when baby makes three," said the counselor. "By the time these two sought counseling, their days were filled with battles over discipline and they were clueless about negotiating compromises.

"One of the first things I did was ask them to discuss their expectations for marriage and family life. When Marcia and Neil took the time to describe their dreams and plans, they saw that they had similar values and goals but different means of achieving them. Realizing this made both of them feel optimistic about solving their problems.

"Next, I suggested that they bring Sam to see me. A series of standardized psychological tests revealed no learning disabilities and no evidence of attention deficit hyperactivity disorder. I suspected that Sam's problems grew in part from the tense atmosphere at home. The way we parent is often linked to the kind of parenting we received, and recognizing this was a key step for Marcia and Neil to begin to change the way they dealt with Sam.

"We spent several sessions drawing a genogram—a psychological family tree that describes family members across several generations, outlining the characteristics, strengths, and weaknesses of each person. By highlighting connections, the genogram can point out patterns and suggest why we behave the way we do.

"Until he was fifteen, Neil had no real concept of a loving family. Because he yearned to give his son the kind of childhood he never had, he tried to be a fun-loving dad and he often bristled at Marcia's rules.

"Nevertheless, Neil had no patience with his son's back talk—something he had rarely witnessed as a child. Resentment of his son's defiance, combined with the desire to be close to him, turned Neil into an ambivalent parent. Ignorant of appropriate discipline, he sometimes came down too harshly.

"There were no horror stories in Marcia's childhood, but neither could she remember many happy times. Her parents were obsessive worriers. As a result, Marcia's own self-confidence was shaky, and she became intent on controlling every element of her family's life.

"Having a headstrong child could would test any parent. When Neil disrupted Marcia's routines, she became even more upset. As much as she wanted her husband to take charge, she felt undermined when he handled the situation differently. My job was to help her see that his way was simply different—not a criticism of her.

"Once these two calmed down, both of them admitted to inconsistency with Sam. An exhausted Marcia admitted that although she expected Neil to follow endless rules and schedules, she allowed Sam to manipulate her. Instead of turning off the TV when she said she would, she'd let him wheedle five more minutes, then another five. It was the same with his so-called time-outs; Sam never wound up spending any time in his room, because Neil and Marcia both caved in. They were astonished at the difference in Sam when they stuck to their guns. He had balked at first, but once they began to follow through, it was only a matter of weeks before he began to toe the line.

"Clear communication between parents is crucial. Marcia had no trouble voicing criticism, but she wasn't able to tell Neil what she needed from him. She simply stewed about it and snapped at him. She had to learn to say, for example, 'I need you to help me follow through on Sam's bedtime routine, because if we do this, his needs will be taken care of, and so will ours.'

"As Sam's behavior improved, tensions eased. Neil's business continued to do well, and he was able to come home earlier and spend more time with Sam. Marcia has joined a book club at the library, and meets friends for lunch or tennis. 'When I'm happier,' says Marcia, "I'm nicer to my son and to my husband.'

"I cautioned them not to forget that when parenting demands pile up, you have to work even harder on your relationship. Neil and Marcia now get a sitter every Sunday afternoon so they can play tennis for a few hours. Finally, Marcia reports, they feel like a real family."

"Our Daughter Is on Drugs"

Their child wasn't just hurting herself, she was tearing her parents' marriage apart. What happens when a couple can no longer fix a child's problem?

Julia's Turn

"I should have known," said forty-one-year-old Julia, reaching for another tissue to wipe her red, tearing eyes. "We'd suspected for some time that our daughter, Ariel, was smoking pot, but we had no proof. Then one day last year I found a joint in her jacket pocket when I took it to the cleaners. As if that wasn't bad enough, a teenage neighbor told us, 'I thought you should know: I saw Ariel snorting coke at a party.'

"I'll never forget that awful night when we confronted her. I said, 'Ariel, are you using drugs?'

"She shot back, 'Are you crazy?'

"My husband, William, could barely control himself. He yelled, 'Don't pull that garbage on us. Mom found a joint in your coat!'

"'That was my friend Sherry's,' she lied. 'You never trust me! You never believe anything I say!'

"At last, Ariel admitted sullenly, 'Okay, I get high sometimes, but it's no big deal.' Since then, we've tried everything to help her. We've taken her to psychologists and experts on teen drug use; she's been in and out of treatment programs. But she's eighteen now and still using. My older sister, Helen, had a drug problem in college, so I should have recognized the signs earlier.

"I don't know if our marriage can survive this strain. I love William dearly, and up till now he's always been there for me, yet suddenly he's become remote and cold. How can he act like this when our daughter's life is at stake?

"Still, I never thought we'd have any serious problems with Ariel. She was popular, always excelled at school, and was very close to her brother, Matt, who's eleven now.

"The trouble began when those devastating floods hit Iowa a few years ago. We barely had time to throw a change of clothes into the car and evacuate to a motel in a nearby town. The entire first floor of our house, including Ariel's bedroom, was destroyed. On the surface, Ariel seemed to be coping. But soon she grew moody and started hanging out with kids we knew had dubious reputations.

"Then Ariel began cutting classes. She seemed lethargic. Occasionally I'd find a bottle of eyedrops or decongestants in her room, not realizing that she was trying to hide her telltale red eyes and runny nose. Yet any time we confronted her, she'd shout, 'Get off my case!' It was always 'the other kids.'

"Once we discovered the truth, our whole family was turned upside down. Matt was devastated. Then William started to shut me out. Actually, he flip-flops. Some days we'll talk about nothing except Ariel. Then at other times he'll clam up and look as if he'll explode if I say another word.

"I can't stand it when William and I fight. Why, in my family, we barely raised our voices. I really did

have a picture-perfect Midwestern childhood. Dad taught high school math, and Mom stayed home to raise the three of us. We didn't have much money, but I never felt deprived. I remember picnics on the lake, sightseeing trips to nearby cities, church every Sunday. Everything was wonderful until my senior year of high school, when we found out my sister was on cocaine, heroin—you name it, she tried it. Thank God, she's been clean for fifteen years.

"College was a welcome escape for me after the grief my family went through that year with my sister. I met William toward the end of my sophomore year, and it was love at first sight. After our first date, neither of us dated anybody else.

"I'm a program coordinator at the local community center, and I love it. But William has never been happy with his work in the sales division of a manufacturing company here in town. I wish I had a nickel for every time I've suggested we work on his résumé so he could look for a more exciting job. He just never makes the effort.

"Things get even worse between us when we visit my parents. I know my dad is pretty conservative and Mom speaks her mind. But William now refuses to visit them at all. Why can't he just ignore their remarks the way I do?

"Another area we've always struggled with is our sex life, which is terrible. Frankly, I don't think

347

about sex all that much even in the best of times, and right now, it's the farthest thing from my mind. But William is always ready, and if I refuse, he gets upset and thinks I don't love him.

"Somehow Ariel managed to finish high school, and she's living at home. She's been good about doing her chores and respecting her curfew. Plus, she seems to be sticking with this latest outpatient treatment program, and she's been working as a clerk in a video store. She hasn't expressed any interest in going to college, but we're hoping she'll be ready if and when she cleans up her act for good.

"We may not be able to save our daughter, but please tell me there's something we can do to save our marriage."

WILLIAM'S TURN

"I am just as upset and guilt-ridden as my wife is, but I cannot for one more hour, one more minute, listen to her go on and on about Ariel's problems," sighed William, forty-one, a handsome man with thick, wavy hair and piercing blue eyes. "She literally follows me from room to room—even into the bathroom—repeating the same things. I know Julia can't turn it off completely. But couldn't she at least turn it down a few notches? She spends half the day sobbing.

"Not a night goes by that I don't wonder whether I could have done something to prevent this. We tried to be such good parents. But we can't wring our hands forever. Funny, I say that, but I don't know how to stop either, do I? I know I need to control my anger. I don't mean to scream, but I'm feeling brittle these days.

"Spending time with my in-laws leaves me even more crazed. My wife may say her childhood was perfect, but to me it sounds like it was dictatorial. Her parents constantly tell us, 'You shouldn't have been so lenient with Ariel' and 'You should have noticed her problem sooner.' Isn't it hypocritical for my mother-in-law to blame me, when the same thing happened to her own daughter? Julia's mom once cursed me out because I expressed an opinion she didn't agree with—and Julia expected me to swallow it. Well, I can't do it anymore.

"My folks couldn't have been more different. Dad sold farm machinery; Mother helped him, but mostly she raised us—I was the youngest of five. My parents were active in the community and our church, politically moderate, and very tolerant of other people's ideas. I was close to both of them and wanted to be the same kind of father to my children. Obviously, I've failed.

"I know Julia wants to help when my job stresses me out, but it's a touchy subject for me. I never knew what I wanted to do with my life.

I was recruited right out of school, and I've stayed with the company for years. But my salary is too good now to turn my back on it, and besides, at my age, what would I do?

"I love my wife, but we've lost that closeness we always had. We certainly aren't intimate in bed. It's such a struggle to figure out when she's in the mood, I've just about given up.

"I always considered myself the kind of guy who could figure out what to do on my own, but our marriage is getting worse. We can't even get away for a night. A few months ago, when we went out of town to my sister's birthday party, Ariel had some friends over, and we think they got high in the house. She's not allowed to have guests anymore, but Julia is still afraid to leave her or Matt alone at home.

"We're both so frightened—for Ariel and for ourselves. It's time to get some help."

THE COUNSELOR'S TURN

"For the past two years, Julia and William have been struggling with every parent's nightmare," notes the counselor. "Their conflicting ways of reacting to stress made things worse. Julia needed to talk about her fears all the time; William tended to withdraw.

"It was clear these two loved each other very much, but the only way they could preserve their marriage and their individuality was to be a little selfish and refocus their time and energy on each other.

"First, I referred Julia to a psychiatrist, because she had the classic signs of clinical depression: anxiety, weeping, sleeplessness, and an inability to concentrate. The doctor prescribed an antidepressant, which helped her face her problems.

"While the goal was to get these two communicating, we also discussed how unproductive it is to live in constant regret and self-doubt. 'Sometimes we just don't know why a child takes drugs,' I told them. 'It happens in the best of families, and you've done everything you can for Ariel right now. As long as you stick to the rules you've established for her, you must stop heaping blame on yourselves. It's time to move on.'

"It was also time for them to start paying attention to Matt, who had been lost in the shuffle. They encouraged him to invite his friends over so they could get to know the boys better. William and Julia keep in touch with the boys' parents, and several of the families meet regularly for potluck dinners. 'We plan to do this all through high school,' explained Julia, 'so we'll feel comfortable enough to call one another for help or to ask an opinion.'

Their next challenge was to manage their intrusive in-law problem. I helped the couple understand the concept of boundaries—defining what they wanted and needed and letting

WHAT EVERY PARENT NEEDS TO KNOW ABOUT KIDS AND DRUGS

Make no mistake: The widespread use of alcohol and drugs—including a cornucopia of designer drugs, such as Ecstasy (MDPD), and prescription painkillers like Vicodin and OxyContin, which weren't even invented when today's parents were navigating their own rebellious paths—has triggered a seismic shift in the quality of teenage life today. According to an annual study of high school students conducted by the University of Michigan School of Social Research, 37 percent of high school seniors have smoked marijuana, the most widely used illicit drug. Six percent smoke daily. (Note: This is not their mother's weed. More potent than it was twenty-five years ago, it's usually laced with other chemicals that render its effects unpredictable.) The use of Ecstasy, a cousin of speed, rose sharply at all grade levels, even among eighth graders. Heroin usage, which fell significantly among younger kids, zoomed among their older brothers and sisters. And the use of anabolic steroids, which athletes use to bulk up their muscles at the expense of their physical and mental health, has skyrocketed among eighth- and tenth-grade boys.

But don't just ask the pros: In a survey conducted by the National Center on Addiction and Substance Abuse at Columbia University (CASA), kids themselves cited drugs as their biggest problem for the sixth year in a row. Most concede that drugs are a cell phone call away. Some buy off the Internet. When asked which was easiest to get—cigarettes, beer, or marijuana—33 percent said marijuana. (The hardest? Cigarettes.)

Still, alcohol remains the drug of choice. Some teens drink to feel grown-up, some drink to fit in, and some drink because they're bored. Nearly one-quarter of eighth graders reported drinking in the month before the Michigan survey was taken. Half of all seniors made the same admission. Fifty percent of adolescents had their first drink between thirteen and fifteen years of age. The average binge drinker (defined as a girl who downs four, or a boy who downs five, drinks in a row) is sixteen years old. While these figures have remained steady for the last few years, the social context of drinking has shifted from one of rebellion ("Let's sneak a six-pack into the party") to acceptance ("Everyone does it; what's the big deal?").

Make sure your child doesn't become a statistic: Say no. That's probably the hardest word for parents, especially those of the baby-boomer generation, to say. Parents don't want to be hypocritical: They rationalize that since they smoked marijuana when they were in college, it's something of a rite of passage. So instead of being clear and firm, they fudge their answers: "When you get older . . . maybe then you can make your own decision [about drugs]." Or they offer the equally ambivalent "Don't use drugs, but if you do, be careful." The trouble is, kids translate that to mean "She said it was okay." Parents need to adopt a zero-tolerance policy when it comes to alcohol and drugs—and then enforce it. You can say: "Marijuana is a dangerous and illegal substance. It's not carefully monitored so you really don't know what you're smoking. It's far more potent than it used to be— and far more psychologically addictive."

On a more practical front: Get the community involved. Call parents in your child's grade, or at least his immediate social group, and ask them to sign pledge agreements banning unsupervised parties in their home. If they refuse, tell your child he's not allowed to socialize at that house. Make sure your teen knows that the legal blood-alcohol limit in every state is lower for them than it is for adults. (Research shows that these laws have a significant impact on keeping tipsy kids off the roads.) Insist that he phone you rather than get in a car with someone who has been drinking. And also make sure he knows to call you or dial 911 for immediate medical help if a friend is so intoxicated that he passes out. Though you may not approve of his behavior, let your child know that you are there for him and will come and get him wherever he is, no matter how late he calls.

Meanwhile, educate yourself about the signs of substance abuse. Kids who have two hands-on parents are the teens who make it through unscathed.

others know when their behavior crossed the line. It wasn't easy, but Julia started standing up to her parents, which has strengthened her self-esteem as well as her marriage. 'I couldn't believe it,' William exulted at one session. 'Julia actually told them we weren't coming to Sunday dinner because she couldn't tolerate the way they spoke to me. Victory!'

"Julia's deeply religious childhood had also sent her the message that sex was not something good girls enjoyed, so she found it hard to be intimate with the man she loved. Defining her boundaries would help in bed, too: 'If you tell him exactly what you want,' I said, 'you'll feel more in control, and more sexually free.' Seeing that William respects her on nights when she says she just wants to cuddle, she has become more responsive—and adventurous—on other nights.

"Another area we addressed was Julia's need to talk about Ariel all the time. Understandably, William was feeling swamped. The couple now takes twenty minutes every day to discuss whatever is on their minds; knowing she can count on that time, Julia can think about other things instead of wallowing in her worries all day.

"Discussing his work situation with Julia helped William realize that he didn't want a new job, after all. 'I'm not ready to make a change,' he decided. 'But I've asked for a few new projects, which has helped me to stop moping about which path I should have taken.'

"Though the couple suspects Ariel still gets high occasionally, she's doing well at her job and is sticking with her outpatient therapy. 'I'm sad that our dreams for her—going to college, raising a family—may never be realized,' Julia said. 'But the fact that William and I are so much closer keeps me grounded.'

"Julia and William ended counseling after six months, having realized that you have to let your grown children take responsibility for their lives, while you work on the one thing you do have control over—yourselves."

"I Wish I Had an Empty Nest"

After years of tension, Jeanette and David were looking forward to time alone together. What happens to a marriage when grown kids move back home?

Jeanette's Turn

"I wouldn't be here if my divorce lawyer hadn't made me come," fumed Jeanette, still lithe and attractive at fifty. "This lawyer seems to think there's a chance that David and I could make a go of it, but the truth is, I don't even want to save my marriage at this point. I've been living on my own for six months, and I'm happy and peaceful for the first time in years. Why in the world should I go back to a man who treats me like a second-class citizen, plus two freeloading adult children who are either watching TV or out partying?

"The amazing thing to me is that David doesn't see anything wrong with this picture. Look, Matt is twenty-six, and Becky is twenty-four. They both lived at home while they were students at the University of Colorado, here in Denver, which saved us room and board, and both of them got a year in Vail as a graduation present. But after that year off they just plunked themselves down here again with no intention of getting lives of their own.

"Every time I try to bring the subject up, though, David just says that it's tough finding jobs in this economy, and why should we push the kids into anything when we can afford to give them time to make choices? It's true, we can. But so what? You feed your baby birds, and then they fly away on their own, right? I'm tired of being a mother.

"But David has this calm, steady way of contradicting me that drives me up the wall. My reaction is—always has been, actually—to start screaming. It's his tone of voice: totally patronizing, as though he thinks I'm a crazy woman.

"It's funny. You'd think mere words could never hurt me, considering what I went through as a child. To be blunt, my father beat me regularly. Both of my parents were lawyers, and we lived in the best neighborhood in Chicago. My two younger sisters and I went to a private school, and we had all the 'right' lessons—ballet, piano, horseback riding. And my father never touched my sisters, not once. As far as everyone outside the family knew, I was just 'accident-prone.' That's how all the bruises and burns and broken fingers got explained away.

"By the time I was eleven, I had dropped all my other activities to go to ballet every day after school. My father objected, but this was the one issue my mother supported me on, and he gave in. So the ballet school became my refuge in every way. The minute I opened the door, I'd smell the sweat and the resin and the tulle and the satin shoes, and I'd hear the music and my teacher's voice saying 'Girls! Girls! Pay attention. Ready? Arms, one and two . . .' I'd get tears of relief in my eyes every single day.

"I still do: One thing I've done for myself since I moved out on my own was to start taking class again. I hadn't done more than two exercises at the barre before the teacher came over to me and said, "You're a dancer, aren't you? Your arms are really lovely. Welcome home.'

"A switch flipped in my head. I knew I couldn't go back to David and the kids. Finally, it was going to be my turn. See, I had run away from home after college, with some vague plan about going to Hollywood to be a dancer. I ran out of money when I got to Denver, and I met David while I was waitressing at a ski resort. I gave up my dream and decided to marry this nice, safe man. He came from a solid, Jewish family with a doting stay-at-home mother and a doctor father.

"So I got my teaching certificate, had two babies, went back to teaching full-time when they were in school, and the rest is history. A couple of times I tried to fit in some ballet classes, but then I couldn't stand how my body looked. So I'd starve myself and take diet pills, and David would really get on my case. He said I had an eating disorder! I'm more healthy than he is. He eats meat and potatoes, and he's way overweight.

"After awhile, though, I was so frustrated and bored, I gave up on my diet. I put on twenty pounds, chopped off my long hair, and resigned myself to being a menopausal matron. What I hadn't counted on, though, was having my kids be permanent fixtures! And did I mention the dogs? Matt and Becky each brought two huge dogs home from Vail, none of them housebroken!

"But back to the present. As I said, I've got an apartment of my own, and I've lost fifteen pounds. I'm dancing every day and dating every weekend. I've been running away all my life, and I've finally gotten to someplace that I like. Why should I give this up to go back to a life I hated?"

DAVID'S TURN

"I'm probably one in a thousand men who could still be married to Jeanette after more than twenty-five years," sighed David, fifty-seven, a large, handsome man with the look of an aging linebacker. "She's flighty, quirky, quick to anger, a spendthrift—but I love her so much. I knew it the minute I met her. She's a real looker, with red hair and those dancer's legs. She was so different from the nice, plain, hometown girls I had been dating. We got married after only about six months of seeing each other, and the first couple of years were fun. We went out a lot, she introduced me to her kooky, artsy friends, and I didn't care that she wasn't all that domestic. Actually, I enjoyed the contrast to my own mother, who had been the perfect housewife.

"But then the kids were born and everything started to go wrong. Jeanette wasn't prepared for what it's really like to be a mother. She felt tied down, so I encouraged her to go back to teaching as soon as the kids were a little older.

"But she was still miserable, because she has such a distorted body image. She always thinks she's fat. Eventually, Jeanette really wigged out and started doing some really unhealthy things. She took diet pills—amphetamines, speed, actually—and laxatives, and she went through periods when she wouldn't eat anything but vegetables. The dinner table got to be a battleground, and I finally just started staying late at the office, eating on my own. We never sat down as a family anymore. I felt so sad about that. I think family life falls apart if you can't share the dinner hour.

"There was never a time when one of the kids wasn't still living with us—the year Becky left was the year Matt came back home. He's trying to decide whether to go to grad school. All he has now is a liberal arts B.A. with a major in sociology. What kind of job will that get him?

"Anyway, Becky came home after Vail also, and it's the same thing. She majored in French and earned a teaching certificate, but she's having second thoughts. She wishes she had gone into law or medicine. I can't see pushing her into a teaching job when we have the means to let her make a more satisfying life choice.

"But Jeanette is a wild woman over this. She wants those kids out of our house and on their own in no uncertain terms. When I try to talk with her rationally, she flies off the handle and says I have always loved the kids more than I love her, that I spoil them and pamper them and that they'll never be able to stand on their own two feet.

"You know, it's not that I love the kids more than I love Jeanette. It's that I've always felt I had to be their champion. Jeanette has no patience. She feels she's put in her time, and she wants to get rid of them.

"As for the dogs, Jeanette globalizes everything. One of Matt's dogs is old and incontinent, and yes, that's a problem. But the other three dogs are no trouble, and the kids really love them. One night I tried to talk to her about the possibility of having the old dog put to sleep, and she started ranting and raving about how she was going to pick up the phone and call the vet and make an appointment to have all the dogs put to sleep.

"Well, I guess the whole thing is academic, since Jeanette seems to have no intention of coming home— unless you can talk some sense into her. I admit, I'm kind of enjoying the peace and quiet—but I love Jeanette. Is there anything I can do to convince her to give this one more try?"

THE COUNSELOR'S TURN

"These people had gotten to the point where they couldn't have a civilized conversation about the weather, let alone about areas of conflict in their relationship," says Susan Hietler, Ph.D., a clinical psychologist at the Rose Medical Center, in Denver.

"Since both of them ski, I used the sport as an analogy, telling them they had to start on the beginner slope and discuss a totally unemotional topic—say, the furniture in my office. I wasn't surprised that they managed to end up arguing. David said, 'The couch is beige.' Jeanette said, 'Yes, but the throw pillows are really colorful.' David responded, 'I never said there wasn't any color in the decorating scheme.' Jeanette said, 'No, but it's just like always. You hate bright colors. You're forever making fun of my wardrobe, just because I like bright colors.' David said, 'I don't care what you wear!' Jeanette said, 'Right. You don't care about anything except the kids.' David said, 'Well, somebody has to! Because you certainly don't.'

"Even in that short exchange, their typical pattern had emerged. So I gave them a simple conversational tool. I told them to start over with David's opening remark about the couch. From there on, neither of them was allowed to use the word 'but,' which creates the impression of rejection and criticism. If that word came to mind, they were to substitute the word 'and.' With that as a guideline, the conversation went like this."

"David: 'The couch is beige.'

"Jeanette: 'Yes, and the throw pillows are really colorful.'

"David: 'You've always loved bright colors.'

"Jeanette: 'That's true. My whole wardrobe is bright colors.'

"David: 'Yes, and they look great with your red hair.'

"Jeanette: 'Do you really think so? You never said that before!'

"David: 'No, but that's because I can never get a word in . . . I mean, no, and I . . .'

"At that point he was stymied, because the technique was so new to them, and they both burst out laughing. Obviously, this first attempt at a positive conversation was a little artificial. Even so, it was a great start, and I gave them a homework assignment in which they were to set aside two five-minute time segments per week. They'd take turns bringing up a topic. The other spouse would respond in an 'additive' manner—that is, using 'and' instead of 'but.'

"At first, I cautioned David and Jeanette to stick to neutral topics such as the weather. After that, they graduated to the 'intermediate slope' and could discuss which restaurant to choose for dinner—potentially volatile since Jeanette does in fact have an eating disorder. After months at this level, we graduated to the 'advanced slope' and dealt with the issue of the adult children in the household. David ultimately conceded that both kids—for their own sake as much as for his and Jeanette's—needed to get on with their adult lives as quickly as possible.

"Within a few weeks, Becky came to the conclusion that she did indeed want to be a French teacher. By fall, she had gotten a job in a prestigious private school with a respectable salary, and she had gotten an apartment of her own.

"Matt was harder to bulge, which made David see even more clearly that allowing the young man to waffle on his life decisions was not helpful after all. Eventually, I suggested that Matt be given an ultimatum. David thought this cruel, but he agreed to give it a try. The result was gratifying. Matt actually seemed relieved to have someone take a stand, and he said he wanted to apply to graduate schools in social work. By September, Matt was enrolled in a master's program, and Jeanette and David had an empty nest at last. Not until then did Jeanette move back into the family home.

"Both David and Jeanette easily gave up their outside relationships, which they admitted were not at all satisfying. The last time I saw Jeanette, she said to me: 'I was wrong about David in a lot of ways. I thought he was putting me down, but he wasn't really. He's a good man, a kind man, and he likes the fact that I'm a little different. I'm definitely glad we're together forever.'"

ZEROING IN ON MARITAL STRESS POINTS

Just as your kids pass through different stages as they grow, so, too, does your marriage. And just as some of those childhood passages can leave you frazzled, guilty, or angry, the stages of a marriage can be so pressure-filled that partners who aren't aware of them, much less know how to handle them, may be left wondering if all those negative feelings means the relationship isn't meant to be.

What's more, even happy, positive milestones—a promotion to a new job, winning the lottery, getting pregnant—can upset the balance of a marriage, causing marital fissures to crack wide open. What to do? First, recognize the time bombs that can detonate a relationship. While every couple charts its own course, *Seven Secrets of a Happy Marriage* illustrates that there are some fairly predictable stress points:

1. The first year.
No longer can you just do what you want; now you must make decisions based on what's best for both of you. Decisions may seem trivial (Should we buy Coke or Pepsi?) or global (Do we have Thanksgiving dinner at my parents' house or yours?). Handling these early negotiations creatively and carefully ensures that you become a committed couple without losing your individual selves in the process.

2. The birth of your first child.
Now you really start to feel like a grown-up. It's time to reexamine your dreams and goals and make sure they're in sync with your current needs. Your key decisions about money, where to live, how to pay the mortgage, and who watches the baby, are fraught with long-range consequences. You're also more tired, more worried about money and possibly less tolerant of each other's needs, emotionally and physically. Sex? You'd rather get a good night's sleep.

3. The seventh year.
The seven-year itch is more than just the title of an old Marilyn Monroe movie. The latest research reveals that more marriages break up during this period than any other. Perhaps you are the parents of two or more kids by now. And perhaps, without even realizing it, you're running on two sets of parallel tracks instead of side by side on the same ones. When was the last time you had a complete conversation?

4. Your children's teenage years.
You thought having a two-year-old was hard until you had a fourteen-year-old. Tensions rise as you try to set reasonable limits for your kids and struggle to make the rules up fast enough. If you and your spouse aren't

on the same page when it comes to parenting an adolescent, simmering resentment may boil over and you may discover, to your shock and horror, that you've turned into your mother. Pay attention to whether you're rehearsing old scripts, and, instead, write new ones that work for your family.

5. The empty nest.
The stress of caring for elderly parents or grown children who need your financial or emotional assistance can place increased demands on couples at a time when they thought they'd have fewer, not more, problems. As Jeanette and David learned, the prospect of spending the rest of your life with someone you feel you don't really

know anymore can bring an end to longtime marriages.

6. Milestone birthdays.
While you're blowing out the candles, you may also be wondering if you've accomplished what you set out to achieve. Perhaps you're thirty, married for several years, but still not sure you're mommy material. Maybe you're forty and, having spent the last fifteen years raising your children, you wonder what to do with the rest of your life? As couples take stock of where they are and where they want to go, marital problems surface. It can be easier to blame a spouse for personal disappointments than to take responsibility for problems and work together of resolving them.

You can survive these eruptions if you create daily rituals of connection, even if it means simply splitting a bagel and talking for five minutes. Marriages that last are those where companionship and commitment go hand in hand, where couples trust each other to say what's on their minds and in their hearts. To superglue your relationship, concentrate on your successes rather than your failures; and figure out what makes the other feel especially cherished.

"WE HAD TO GIVE UP OUR BABY"

———◆———

After losing the battle for little Haley, Jamie wanted to adopt again, but Ben couldn't risk another heartache. How can a couple understand that no one grieves exactly the same?

JAMIE'S TURN

"I never thought we'd lose Haley," wept Jamie, thirty, a former librarian. "Everything had been wonderful in the two weeks since we had brought her home. Then one afternoon two months ago the counselor who had arranged the adoption called. 'Jamie, I have some terrible news,' she said. 'Haley's birth mother changed her mind. I'm so sorry.'

"'Come get her right now,' I wailed, 'or I'll never be able to let her go.' Ben and our kids, Tommy and Samantha, bolted upstairs, and we all hugged and cried. The counselor arrived early that evening. I can still remember how sweet my baby's hair smelled as I kissed her good-bye. I thought I would die of grief.

"Ben and I are both so weary. I don't know how we can go on. And we're terribly worried about our children. Tommy, our other adopted child, is five, and he keeps asking, 'Is my birth mommy going to take me away, too?' Samantha, three, is our biological child, and she's simply confused.

"It doesn't help that Ben and I have been arguing constantly, which has never been our style. He actually told me he'd never wanted another child in the first place! How can he say that? Being a mother is my life, what I dreamed about since I was little.

360

"I grew up in Washington, D.C. My parents divorced before I was a year old, and my dad moved to Chicago. I saw him only sporadically after he moved away; when I was twelve, he died of a heart attack.

"Mom went on to marry a divorce lawyer with two sons, and when I was sixteen, we moved to Denver. My stepfather verbally and sometimes physically abused me, but Mom was too preoccupied with taking care of him and the boys to intervene.

"I met Ben my freshman year of college. He was just so much fun to be with, so passionate about everything. Once we began dating, we quickly fell in love.

"After graduation, I moved to New York to get my master's degree in library science, while Ben launched his career as a stockbroker. After I completed my studies, I moved back to Denver, and we were married.

"After a year of trying to have a baby, we started infertility treatments. From that day on, our lives became totally focused on having a child. With each procedure, surgery, and miscarriage (I had two), we freaked out more and more. Yet each disappointment made us even more determined to have the large family we'd always dreamed of. We tried artificial insemination several times without success, but we drew the line at in vitro fertilization because of the cost. That's when we decided to consider adoption.

"We expected the process to take years, but scarcely two months after registering with the adoption agency, we were told about a pregnant college student who wanted to meet us. That's how Tommy came into our lives. From the very beginning, we were open with our son about his birth, and we're in touch with his birth mother and her parents. I left my job so I could care for him full-time.

"But while we were ecstatic about Tommy, we never gave up hope that I might have a baby naturally. After two years I finally became pregnant with Sam. Of course I was thrilled, but I still wanted more children. I went on to have yet another miscarriage. I told Ben, 'I refuse to give up on having a third child.'

"Three weeks after that conversation, the agency told us about Vicky, a pregnant twenty-nine-year-old student who already had a son from a failed marriage. We visited Vicky every weekend throughout her pregnancy. Ben and I were present for the birth, and Vicky introduced me to all the nurses as Haley's mom.

"In Colorado, there's a forty-five-day period during which a mother can legally reclaim her baby before the adoption is deemed final. I never thought it would happen to us. When Vicky took Haley back, it was like a death in the family.

"Nothing is the same anymore. Ben's always been very conscientious about providing for us, but now he's become a workaholic. And every time I try to bring up the subject of adopting again, he says he doesn't want to do it. It's as if he's put Haley right out of his mind.

"Look, I know Ben. He's going to adore a third baby as much as he loves Tommy and Samantha. Why is he being so stubborn?"

BEN'S TURN

"I had a gut feeling from the start that something about this adoption was all wrong," said Ben, thirty, a soft-spoken man with warm brown eyes. "Vicky kept changing her mind about when and how she would give us the baby. But the few times I mentioned my doubts, Jamie went nuts. 'Oh, no. You're imagining things. Nothing's wrong!' she'd insist. I didn't press the issue. She was in love with that baby from the moment we first found out about her.

"Jamie is so desperate to have another child that it breaks my heart to even suggest otherwise. But I told her after we adopted Tommy that I didn't know if I could go through such an emotionally charged procedure again. Maybe I was afraid that because everything had gone so perfectly, we were bound to be disappointed if we took the risk one more time.

"Then there are the huge demands of raising a large family. I'm one of six myself, and we're all very close. But my parents were saints who managed a bustling, happy household with few problems, and I don't know if I can handle that. I feel incredibly selfish just thinking that way, let alone admitting it to Jamie.

"In fact, I've never been good at saying no to my wife. She's always had a strong need to control things, and I've tried to be patient and understanding. Many times, especially after her miscarriages, I'd wonder: Is this worth it? We tried not to let our lives revolve around making a baby, but it happened anyway. In the last few years, the spontaneity of our lovemaking has disappeared. Before we adopted Haley, I was always worrying whether I'd be able to perform on the required night.

"I can't take it anymore. Jamie's blaming me for things that aren't my fault, and she's furious because I don't feel the same way she does. I tell her that I love her and will always be there for her, but she's clearly not listening. She calls me cold and heartless, or threatens to leave me if we don't have another child. How can she say things like that? Why should I want to be with someone who is constantly ripping me apart? So maybe I am pulling away, and maybe I do spend more time at work. At least my colleagues don't put me down.

"I think I've been pretty darn understanding. But I will never comprehend why Jamie stubbornly insists on putting all of us through this pain again. We have two beautiful, healthy children. I think our family is complete. Why doesn't she? And how dare she accuse me of not being upset about Haley? I lost a baby, too, and it tears me apart, even though I'm not crying every day over it. It's time to stop this so we can all move forward."

THE COUNSELOR'S TURN

"Jamie and Ben were emotionally stuck, both inconsolable in their own ways," the counselor said. "Grief and their inability to resolve the issue of having another child made them impatient and argumentative.

"I suspected that Jamie's preoccupation with having more children was aimed at filling a deep void within herself. Jamie had lost her biological father to divorce, neglect, and finally death, and then her mother abandoned her emotionally. Not surprisely, Jamie tried to ease her anxiety by keeping control over her life, and she yearned to love and be loved by a houseful of children.

"But things don't always turn out the way we expect. When life went awry for Jamie, she became belligerent, which quickly pushed Ben away. She needed to recognize when she did this and to acknowledge that Ben had legitimate feelings, too.

"Ironically, Ben didn't think he had a right to his own feelings either. As often happens in large families, he had learned early on that his chances of getting his own way were slim. His need to be a people-pleaser came from his desire for attention in a chaotic household.

"I challenged Ben: 'Can you force yourself to refuse to do things you can't or don't want to do?' He came to trust and voice his inner feelings, and to find his priorities.

"We spent many sessions discussing the loss of Haley. I pointed out to Jamie that people grieve in many ways. 'Just because Ben doesn't share your emotions exactly or respond the way you do doesn't mean his feelings are any less important or that he's heartless,' I said.

"I asked Ben a tough question: 'Did you feel relieved in any way when Vicky took Haley back?' After several minutes, he softly said, 'Yes.' It was a painful secret to confess, but it showed the couple how torn Ben had been about an adoption he had always feared would go wrong. They learned how to empathize and help each other through the grieving process, until they were at a point where they could discuss having another child.

"After much soul-searching, Ben realized that his reluctance was more about adoption than it was about adding to their family. However, he was willing to try having a baby naturally, which was still possible and safe for Jamie.

"We discussed waiting six months before trying to conceive.

'You need time to heal,' I said, 'and if you start right away, that child will always be connected to the loss of Haley.' They also agreed to stop trying after a year.

"Tommy's and Samantha's fears about losing their parents needed to be addressed honestly but simply. 'Tell them: "Families are created in many ways,"' I suggested. '"You're our children, and no one can ever take you away from us."'

"Counseling ended after six months. I didn't expect to hear from the couple after that, but recently Ben called to share two unexpected bits of news. First, the daughter of a

dear friend of theirs had passed away suddenly, which made them realize anew how precious life can be.

"Shortly after that, they got a call from their adoption agency: A baby boy was available. Ben's reaction surprised both Jamie and himself. 'I wanted this child more than anything,' he said. He assured me that he hadn't been pressured into the decision, and that he and Jamie were prepared to face whatever might happen. Happily, the addition of little Zach recently became final.

"It's not easy to open your heart after a difficult ordeal, but those two have the skills to try—together."

SILENCE ISN'T ALWAYS GOLDEN:
Getting Him to Open Up

Until the counselor pointed it out, Jamie and Ben didn't realize that the clash between her articulate, assertive style and his inability to give voice to his feelings was at the heart of many of their problems. She's certainly not the only wife to find herself in a conversational tango when trying to get her husband to communicate. To help him express his feelings:

• Understand the silences. It can be hurtful and infuriating to try to talk to a man and feel as if you're talking to the wall. But while women often find silence uncomfortable, men find solace in it. What's more, we often read into a partner's silence our own desires, fears, and past experiences. If your parents endured long icy periods when they were angry and didn't

speak, you may infer that your husband's lack of response means he's upset with you. His silence may simply mean he really has nothing particular on his mind. Similarly, a man whose father left the office behind when he walked in the door may believe it's inappropriate to talk about business issues or problems at home. Many men have reported that they don't tell their wives things because they don't want to worry them. That protectiveness, however, may be misinterpreted as disinterest. Also, when he talks to others but not to you, it may be because he views having to make conversation and relay factual information as work. At home, he wants to relax. And that may mean sinking into his own thoughts or reverie.

• Ask directly for what you need. Men and women have different definitions of the word "commun- ication." Men problem-solve, often silently. They proceed directly from Step 1 ("Here's the issue") to Step 3 ("Do this"). Of course, you believe in Step 2: bouncing suggestions and possibilities around before coming to a solution. If your man is not the bouncing type, try presenting a specific agenda: "I'd like to talk about Jake's terrible behavior lately" or "We need to figure out how we're going to handle Amanda's ballet practices during the school week."

• Challenge yourself to phrase your questions so they can't be answered with one-word responses. "How was your day?" won't jump- start a conversation. He may just say "fine" or "terrible." "Tell me about your presentation to that new client," might engage him more fully.

• Learn to argue constructively. Many men are afraid to say anything because past experience has taught them that they'll be criticized or blamed for past crimes and misde- meanors. He may have learned to

disengage as soon as you start talking, which makes you talk even more. Someone has to break the cycle; try counting to yourself if he's silent, or give him a friendly look to encourage him to respond.

• Appreciate the silences. More likely than not, your spouse will never be as loquacious as your best friend. And you probably don't want him to be, either. So learn to listen to the silence. When he takes you in his arms for a long hug, shares in a joyful whoop with you when your son scores his first hockey goal, or reaches for your hand as you ride in the car, he may be saying a great deal.

• Pick the right moment. You prefer talking when you get into bed because it's the first time all day you can relax; your husband falls asleep the minute his head hits the pillow. You like chatting over morning coffee, his brain doesn't get in gear until an hour later. Men often feel ambushed and tend to clam up unless they have a say in the timing of talks. They may also feel cornered when the whole agenda of your conversation is "the problem." If you try raising issues while doing an activity (playing backgammon, cooking a special dinner, or gardening), the talk will flow more easily. Another tactic: Ask him to come to you when he's ready to talk. You might try saying: "We don't have to discuss this right now, but I really want to understand what you're thinking about our moving to a bigger house. Talk to me when you're ready."

"I LOVE MY KIDS MORE THAN I LOVE MY HUSBAND"

After twenty-eight years and twelve children, Joan refuses to be Nat's doormat. Can a marriage survive when both partners feel like they're last on the list?

JOAN'S TURN

"Nat and I have been together so long, I never thought it would come to this," said Joan, forty-eight, a tiny, soft-spoken woman. "We knew each other in grade school, and we married when I was twenty and he was twenty-two. Twenty-eight years and twelve children later, we're talking about getting divorced.

"I come from a large family, so it's not unusual that I wanted one of my own, is it? But mine wasn't a particularly happy family. My father, who owned a house-painting business, was an alcoholic. Back then, no one acknowledged that sort of thing. He was abusive to my mother, not to us kids, but there we were, always anxious about how he would be when he came home. He could be very loud and very mean; I was terrified of his explosive rages. He ultimately lost his business and never recovered from the shock.

"Nat and I lived near my folks when we first married, but after our third child, we moved to a house about an hour away, in a nice community with a lot of other young couples. I devoted myself to my family. We have eight biological kids and four adopted. I know, I know everyone wonders how I manage. What can I say? I started having kids when I was very young. I've always had tremendous energy; I don't need a lot of sleep.

"After the eighth child, I decided not to have any more. But I was only thirty-nine, and I didn't know what to do with the rest of my life. I sat down to think about it, and when I wrote down all of my strengths and weaknesses I realized that, more than anything, I love, and am very good at, being a mother.

"So when I read in the newspaper about the need for homes for children that nobody wanted, I spoke with Nat, then with our children. They were all in favor of adopting another child. We spoke to the social services people, and soon we were parents of six-month-old Christine. In the next few years, we added three more kids to our family: Linda, fifteen; Nat Jr., eleven; and John, who's seven, still live with us. We adopted John when he was just a few months old; the authorities think he may have been abused by his birth mother.

"We both adore John, but he has demanded more of my attention than all the other kids combined. One problem we're struggling with now is that he insists on staying in our bedroom at night. He sleeps on the floor, wedged between a dresser and my side of the bed. We've tried endlessly to get him to move to his own bed, and he's been seeing a counselor, but sleeping alone is a frightening experience for him. He and Nat are actually very close, but Nat thinks I'm too indulgent with him and says I should demand that he leave the room. How can I do that? The child is scared.

"I was always active in the community and at school—I was a Cub Scout leader for about twelve years, and coached the basketball and soccer teams as well as the cheerleading squad; I can't even remember what else. Now I also volunteer at a soup kitchen.

"It hasn't always been a Hallmark-card kind of life, though. We've had our share of difficult times. A few years ago, one of our daughters had cancer, a rare form of lymphoma, and it's a miracle she's alive. In spite of the chemotherapy treatments, she was able to have a baby last year. One of our sons was in a bad hiking accident. Part of his leg was severed and he walks with a limp, but he can do pretty much everything he did before.

"What got us through? Faith, I suppose. For me, I could always cry and talk things through with others. It has always been much harder on Nat. He thinks it's a sign of weakness to show emotion—with the exception of anger, that is.

"I really can't say when the problems started. Over the years, I just got more and more engrossed in the children, and we slipped farther apart. Nat is a workaholic; he isn't home all that much.

"I should explain about his apartment in the city. We live about a two-hour drive from Nat's office. He is a vice president of a large metallurgy company. When our oldest son decided to live in the city, he asked Nat if he wanted to split the rent with him. The idea was that Nat could stay there one or two nights a week to break up the long commute, or if he had to entertain clients late at night and didn't want to face the long ride home. So we discussed it and all agreed that getting the apartment sounded like a good idea. But now Nat spends the whole week in the city and comes home only on weekends.

"By the weekend, so much has happened it's hard for him to catch up. I know it's not fair of me, but I'm tired. Sometimes I just don't want to take the time to explain things, to go through it all. He complains he feels closed out, that he's the last on my list of people to pay attention to. What does he expect? He's a grown man. He can't always be number one.

"Sometimes I really resent his comments. When he comes home and says 'How could you let Nat Jr. do that?' or 'Why did you give that to Marie?' my back goes up. I tell him, 'Look, you're not here. When you're away, I make the decisions.' I've been handling everything and everybody for so long, who is he to criticize me? What else could I do? I had to make a life for myself.

"He wants to fight, but I'm not going to argue. He screams and yells

so, sometimes I think he's going to burst. What can I possibly say to this man?

"What makes him the most upset? Money. He's always yelling at me for keeping terrible records. He says he can't understand how we can still be in debt, when he works so hard. I don't think Nat has any idea what it costs to run a home. And if our children need money, even though they're on their own now, I want to give them a hand. I don't think that's terrible, do you?

"So either he's screaming at me or there's silence. We never talk anymore. I go about my business; he goes about his. We've grown apart.

"I guess I'm angry. I still care about him, but I'm not in love with him anymore—not like I used to be.

"And I know the kids are worried. They hear Nat yelling, and they ask questions like 'Are you and Daddy going to get divorced?' We can't go on like this. We have to resolve things one way or another."

NAT'S TURN

"Number one? Are you kidding?" yelled Nat, fifty, a large man with a booming voice. "Number seventeen is more like it.

"She's right. I am angry. She's a good, loving woman, but she has no room for anyone but the kids. I'm a stranger in my own home. Just because I work long hours doesn't mean I don't care about my family and don't want to know what they're up to. I ask about what's happening, and she tells me, 'Oh, nothing.' I ask why she did something, and she either gives me a blank look or gets mad at me. I'm not interrogating her. I'm the father, remember?

"You know, when we got married it was a different era. We both come from large Catholic families—I was the oldest, like Joan—and having lots of kids was no big deal.

"But Joan and I are opposites. I'm very outspoken and outgoing. I say what I think and don't like to hold things in. Joan is quiet and keeps her feelings under wraps. She's always positive, never says anything bad about anybody. I think I'm realistic; she thinks I'm negative.

"The problem is, I can't talk to her. If I get the slightest bit agitated, she clams up. I believe that if you have a problem, you discuss it. She won't.

"I feel like a money machine, not a father or a husband. I make a good living, but there is never, ever enough. Joan is spending it faster than I can make it. I don't know where it all goes, and when I try to get her to keep track, she either forgets or deliberately deceives me. Sure, she told me she was giving our married daughter some money. I figured fifty, sixty dollars, right? It was six hundred dollars! Did she think I wasn't going to find out? She's gotten our credit rating all messed up because she's put off paying bills.

"Look, I know she doesn't spend money on herself; she spends it all on the kids, but it's gotten so out of hand it makes me crazy. I think I have a right to be upset about that and also about how permissive she is with the kids. This has been going on for years. She never says no. They're basically good kids, but she never asks any of them to do anything around the house. She shouldn't be their servant.

"This apartment business has gotten blown way out of proportion. I thought having a place to stay in the city would ease the stress because I wouldn't have to go back and forth. It's gotten to the point now that the apartment is another source of tension. She's exaggerating: I do not spend the whole week there. I have never stayed there more than two nights a week at the most.

"But even at home we never have time together. We have absolutely no privacy. Joan leaves the bedroom door wide open. All the time. The kids just march right in. I'm probably closer to John than I am to any of them, but I'll be damned if I want him sleeping on my bedroom floor.

"What can I say? I have a wife and twelve kids, and I'm lonely. I feel like I don't have a friend in the world. Joan is a wonderful mother, but once in a while it would be nice to have her say I love you. If she can do it for the kids, why not for me?"

369

"These two people were so alienated from each other that our initial counseling sessions served as a sounding board as well as a vehicle to help them break the communication barrier," said the counselor. "The marriage had been rocky for the last five years but had deteriorated rapidly in the last two. Though they shared a home, Joan and Nat were able to talk to each other only in my office, where I could act as referee.

"As the oldest of five children of an alcoholic father and a passive mother, Joan had stepped into the role of family caretaker early on. A surrogate mother to her siblings, she continued to nurture everyone after she had married.

"However, having endured her father's abusive rages, Joan was terrified of confrontation. In her marriage, she avoided arguing at all costs and would gladly suppress her own feelings if it meant avoiding a fight. Joan is one of those rare women who sincerely loves being a mother; she sees this as her purpose in life and is not ambivalent about her choice.

"Nat is a hail-fellow-well-met kind of guy: gregarious and hearty, in sharp contrast to his demure wife. If he has something on his mind, he's not afraid to say it. He is also an openly affectionate man—again, in stark contrast to his shy, restrained wife. However, he had an explosive temper that terrified Joan; it reminded her of her father.

"When they came to see me, Nat and Joan each insisted they were right and refused to see the other's point of view. While it was a positive sign that they continued to come week after week and talk about their situation, we were at an impasse until the fifth session.

"Here's what happened: Even though they lived in the next town, Nat kept getting lost every time he drove to my office. One evening, after riding around in circles for the better part of an hour because of yet another of his 'shortcuts,' they ended up by the town duck pond. They both burst out laughing. It struck me then that if you know someone for such a long time, plenty changes. You get old, get fat, you get bald—but if you can keep your sense of humor, you'll be okay. In fact, as a prelude to their sessions, they started to drive to that same duck pond purposely, just to sit and chat before they came to see me.

"Over the next few months, Joan and Nat were able to understand and know each other in a way that had eluded them for almost thirty years.

"Joan had lost sight of the importance of putting her marriage first. I told her forcefully: 'Your marriage must always be your number-one priority. It is the best gift you can give your children, too.' Joan was genuinely puzzled to hear Nat say he didn't feel loved. Even though she was not overtly affectionate, she was sure that he knew: 'I've always taken such wonderful care of him; I keep the house clean and launder his clothes. I plan the meals around foods he loves. That's an expression of love, isn't it?'

"I told Joan that, yes, it is, but that it wasn't what her husband wanted. 'You need to say I love you outright, to give him a hug, to become more fully involved in love-making.' Joan listened and said she understood, but for some reason resisted making the changes.

"That's when another break-through occurred: During one of their talks at the duck pond, Joan reminded Nat that after their eighth natural child, she had been very upset that he had refused to have a vasectomy. "I think I have resented you—unconsciously, maybe—all this time because of that. I asked you to take some responsibility for birth control, and the fact that you wouldn't do that for me hurt.' For many years, Joan had avoided and repressed her hostile feelings. Recognizing this was the first step in beginning to change their relationship.

"During another session, Nat spoke in touching terms about how mechanical his life was. Rather than complain or attack, he revealed his sadness and his loneliness. This confession had a huge impact on Joan; she realized for the first time that he was hurting as much as she was. Many couples have this problem.

"At the beginning of our next session, Nat burst into the room, beaming. 'She did it all,' he exulted. 'She closed the door, she got out a sexy nightgown, and we had sex—twice.'

"That was a courageous step for Joan, the first of many. In the following weeks, she did, indeed, issue a rule that from now on, the bedroom door will close at nine P.M. After that time, unless it is a true emergency, the children have to respect their parents' privacy. They have understood and accepted this with much less difficulty than anticipated. For the first week, John slept on the floor outside their room. 'Now he's sharing a room with Nat Jr., and they are fine about that,' Joan reported.

"Nat appreciates how difficult establishing this rule, and making all the other changes, has been for Joan. He has committed himself to controlling his temper. Now that Joan has put their marriage high on her list of priorities, now that she lets him know he is loved, he doesn't get as angry as he used to. Joan also has worked hard to stick to her budget and refrain from using credit cards. When the family finances are under control, Nat feels much more relaxed. He is thinking, though, about switching jobs: "It's not going to be easy at my age, but I want a life that's less demanding, less stressful. I love being with my wife.'

"Joan will never change her permissive attitude toward her children, but, as Nat said in one of our last sessions, 'Some battles you have to stop fighting.' Indeed, they are both so much more attuned to each other in so many ways that this complaint has dramatically decreased in importance.

"'You could say that now I'm number four,' Nat said. 'That's progress!'"

WHEN YOU FIGHT IN FRONT OF THE KIDS

When you and a partner fight, you may not be the only ones who want to walk out the door. Children are sensitive to the emotional ups and downs of their parents' relationship, and research has shown that even the youngest can sense the subtleties of conflict—whether you're withdrawing emotionally, feeling contemptuous of each other, or defensive. While you know it's important to present a united front, you just don't know how:

1. Remember that no two people are carbon copies of each other. The way you raise your kids has a lot to do with the way you were raised. Disagreements are bound to arise. When they do, keep in mind that it's not whether you fight but how you handle the fight that's important.

2. Never resort to name calling, insults, or sarcasm. Avoid angry silences too. Your kids can't always read the silence, making it scarier to experience than outright yelling matches. Make certain to assure them that it's not their fault and that you are both committed to working it out.

3. When you're really livid, agree that you're not getting anywhere and call a time-out until tempers cool.

Always revisit the issue, though, so you settle it once and for all. Make sure the kids see that you have either resolved the problem or agreed to disagree.

4. Don't threaten to leave or get a divorce. Kids don't know that, in the heat of the moment, we often say things we don't mean. They are easily frightened by such threats.

5. Remember, there isn't one right way to handle discipline problems. It's not that you're right, and he's wrong; it's that you feel differently. Respect the fact that you are each entitled to your opinion. Does one of you feel more strongly than the other about a particular issue? Implement that person's suggestion first. If it fails to work, try another idea.

CHECKLISTS AND STRATEGIES

A Workbook for the Two of You

———•———

Y ou're fighting again . . . about spaghetti sauce: You like the imported gourmet brand; it's more expensive, but you think the taste is worth it. Your husband insists the generic sauce (the same one his mom always used, thank you very much) is just fine. You are yelling at each other now, loudly, and you're doing it in front of the kids. Neither of you really understands why you're so furious about a jar of spaghetti sauce, but you're both quite sure it's for a perfectly good reason.

You've hit a marital land mine—one of those hidden time bombs that detonates when one of you treads on a buried but deeply felt issue leaving both of you hurt, disappointed, or resentful. But these hidden issues aren't really about marinara. They represent our emotional needs and hopes—our desire to feel loved, respected, and accepted. And they must be recognized and addressed before problems can be fully resolved. Unmet needs can fuel a host of negative emotions, ranging from anxiety, frustration, and boredom to resentment, anger, or apathy.

How can you tell if you've struck a land mine? Whether you're fighting about tomato sauce, how to discipline the kids, money, or sex, if you find yourselves arguing until you're hoarse but getting nowhere, if you avoid important topics fearing that you'll rock the proverbial boat, or if one or both of you mentally keep score about who did what to whom, chances are you're in some trouble. And whether you are dating, engaged, newlywed, or long married, want to make a wobbly marriage stronger or a good marriage great, you need to know where the dangers lie as well as how to steer around them.

To help you, we've included a companion workbook to this collection of the best of "Can This Marriage Be Saved?" Culling advice from top marital experts across the country, we've created self-appraisals to help you and your partner determine which areas of your relationship may harbor hidden land mines. Once you've located a trouble spot, neutralize it. Choose an exercise from the ones we've provided and find out what works for you. (A few of these are similar to ones used earlier in the book; we've included them here for your convenience.)

Most of us never really think about improving the most important relationship of our lives, especially in such a seemingly academic way. We assume we know how to "do" marriage—at least until our own begins to show signs of implosion. So before you begin, a caveat: For some of you, these exercises may seem elementary or downright awkward at first. For others, thinking about your behavior, both past and present, as well as what did or didn't happen when you were young may provoke anxiety, stirring up emotions you haven't felt in years. It's not easy to take a hard look at your past, but you won't be able to fully understand yourself, or your partner, unless you investigate it. So hold on to those feelings and stay with the exercises until you've processed them fully.

There's a reason that this column has been so popular for half a century: The advice it provides works. Give it a try.

RECONNECTING—WITH YOURSELF AND YOUR PARTNER

O nce you've agreed to make your marriage a priority, put that commitment in writing and sign it; this is your marriage contract.

Next, take the husband and wife quizzes on the following pages. Why separate quizzes for each sex? Men and women look for and expect different things in marriage. You may find that you are strong in several areas, weak in others. As we've discussed throughout the book, there are seven such areas that are vital for a healthy marriage. To refresh your memory, these are the ability to:

- trust—to feel safe emotionally, sexually, intellectually, and spiritually with each other
- communicate—to talk heart to heart as well as head to head
- express angry feelings and resolve conflicts effectively
- balance issues of power and control
- make smart choices about money
- keep passion and affection alive
- be good companions and make the partnership a priority

After you've taken the quizzes and calculated your scores, check the exercises targeted to specific areas. Relating to each other in new ways takes practice, just like anything else, but in time, being more attuned to your partner's needs—not to mention feeling entitled to express your own—will become second nature.

A QUIZ FOR WIVES

Answer True or False for Each Statement

1. I trust my husband with my thoughts and feelings. ❑T ❑F

2. I feel sure my husband is faithful to me. ❑T ❑F

3. It's unusual for my husband to do or say something he knows will embarrass me. ❑T ❑F

4. My husband talks easily and often about his feelings. ❑T ❑F

5. When I talk about myself, I feel I have my husband's complete attention. ❑T ❑F

6. In my marriage, it's easy for me to express myself and feel understood. ❑T ❑F

7. We rarely stay angry for long periods of time. ❑T ❑F

8. My husband and I rarely bicker. ❑T ❑F

9. I feel safe expressing my angry feelings toward my husband. ❑T ❑F

10. I rarely hide my true feelings to avoid a fight. ❑T ❑F

11. I don't feel controlled by my husband. ❑T ❑F

12. We are able to compromise when we differ on issues. ❑T ❑F

13. When important decisions have to be made, my needs and opinion count. ❑T ❑F

14. There are very few things about me my husband would like to change. ❑T ❑F

15. My husband treats me like an equal in our relationship. ❑T ❑F

16. I get a lot of praise from my husband. ❑T ❑F

17. I rarely, if ever, feel married to a critical parent. ❑T ❑F

18. We have a comfortable sexual relationship. ❑T ❑F

19. I rarely, if ever, feel pressured to have sex when I'm not in the mood. ❑T ❑F

20. I get affection outside and inside the bedroom. ❑T ❑F

21. My husband cares about our emotional intimacy. ❑T ❑F

22. My husband is my best friend. ❑T ❑F

23. It's easy for us to play and have fun together. ❑T ❑F

24. I am willing to try activities that my husband enjoys. ❑T ❑F

SCORING

0–6 FALSE: *Your marriage is in good shape, but read on—even good relationships can be improved.*

7–12 FALSE: *Your marriage could probably benefit from a tune-up.*

13 OR MORE FALSE: *Your marriage appears to need substantial work; you should consult a professional for counseling.*

A QUIZ FOR HUSBANDS
Answer True or False for Each Statement

1. I don't worry about my wife being faithful. ❑T ❑F

2. I trust my wife has my best interests at heart. ❑T ❑F

3. I fully trust my wife's love for me. ❑T ❑F

4. It is easy to talk to my wife, even about difficult subjects—such as money, in-laws, my job. ❑T ❑F

5. I feel my wife knows and understands me. ❑T ❑F

6. When I have problems, I know my wife will be a good sounding board. ❑T ❑F

7. My wife and I don't stay angry for long periods. ❑T ❑F

8. I feel safe expressing angry feelings to my wife. ❑T ❑F

9. I rarely hold my anger in just to keep the peace. ❑T ❑F

10. My wife and I rarely say hurtful things to each other. ❑T ❑F

11. My wife doesn't have to have everything her way. ❑T ❑F

12. When major decisions have to be made, we work well together. ❑T ❑F

13. I believe marriage is a partnership between equals. ❑T ❑F

14. Our marriage works because we know how to cooperate with each other. ❑T ❑F

15. My wife rarely finds fault with the things I do. ❑T ❑F

16. I rarely feel unfairly blamed or attacked. ❑T ❑F

17. My wife frequently expresses her appreciation of me. ❑T ❑F

18. My wife doesn't use sex as a weapon when she's upset with me. ❑T ❑F

19. My wife lets me know she desires me. ❑T ❑F

20. My wife is eager to make love-making special. ❑T ❑F

21. Sex is something we don't fight about. ❑T ❑F

22. Having fun together is a strong part of our relationship. ❑T ❑F

23. I'm eager to try out things my wife likes to do. ❑T ❑F

24. My wife is my best friend. ❑T ❑F

SCORING

0–6 FALSE: *Your marriage is in good shape, but read on—even good relationships can be improved.*

7–12 FALSE: *Your marriage could probably benefit from a tune-up.*

13 OR MORE FALSE: *Your marriage appears to need substantial work; you should consult a professional for counseling.*

TRUST

————✦————

Trust—personal integrity and truthfulness—is the foundation of a healthy marriage. In the fifty years that the *Ladies' Home Journal* has reported on cases in "Can This Marriage Be Saved?" couples have repeatedly singled out trust as their most important value.

Unfortunately, too many couples think of trust solely in terms of sexual faithfulness. While that's certainly important, there are six dimensions of trust that must be present and unquestioned for a marriage to remain strong. Most couples trust each other in some of these areas and are less trustful in others. In a solid marriage, you should both be able to say an unqualified yes to the following:

1. I trust and expect that you will be sexually faithful.

2. I trust that you will not harm, reject, or control me.

3. I trust that you will love me without ulterior motives.

4. I trust that you will keep our marriage top priority.

5. I trust that you will not abandon me in the face of anger, conflict, or disagreements.

6. I trust in my own capacity to do the same for you.

However, if you cannot trust your partner, you may place coercive expectations on him. For example: *If I expect you to behave in a certain way (the way I prefer) or to do things in a particular fashion (the way I think is right), then I'm placing a coercive expectation on you.* Such expectations are felt as demands and cause friction.

SELF-APPRAISAL

Ask yourselves the following questions. Discuss your responses openly and honestly.

1. What was the emotional climate in the family you grew up in? Was it comforting or unpredictable?
2. Did you feel loved and accepted by your mother and father?
3. Did you see your parents act with honesty toward each other?
4. Did your parents encourage you to trust or mistrust others? Were they accepting or suspicious of people?
5. Were your parents abusive to each other? To you?
6. Was one or both of your parents addicted to alcohol or drugs? If yes, how did you cope with this?
7. In your relationship to the parent of the opposite sex, did you feel safe and comfortable? If not, why?
8. In your marriage, do any of these same feelings come up?
9. As a child, was there trust between you and your siblings? If not, why?
10. Did either parent ever have an affair?

NOTES

1. TRUST CHECKUP
Turning Inward

In a trusting relationship, you feel comfortable to let your spouse into your world. You let him know the whole you—with all your vulnerabilities and imperfections. How much do you trust your partner? Let's start with an exercise you may recognize. In the box next to each question, rate whether it is A) easy; B) somewhat difficult; or C) difficult for you to get help from your partner when:

	A	B	C
1. You feel indecisive	❑	❑	❑
2. You're depressed	❑	❑	❑
3. You're exhausted	❑	❑	❑
4. You feel guilty	❑	❑	❑
5. You feel humiliated	❑	❑	❑
6. You need encouragement	❑	❑	❑
7. You need advice	❑	❑	❑
8. You feel like a failure	❑	❑	❑
9. You're in physical pain	❑	❑	❑
10. You're in a money crisis	❑	❑	❑

Share your responses with each other. By taking the time to think about these basic situations, you can begin to make critical connections that affect how you think and feel about yourself now.

2. IF YOU REALLY LOVED ME
Making Unrealistic Expectations Realistic

It's impossible to live without expectations, but when those hopes and dreams bear little resemblance to reality, they can easily create or perpetuate unhappiness. Too often we blame our partner, or the marriage itself, when we feel this way. "How could he do this to me?" you might say; or, "I thought she'd always be there for me." In truth, perhaps you set the bar too high all along. Learning to take responsibility for creating your own happiness is a two-step process of change that can strengthen your own self-confidence and deepen the trust between you and your spouse.

STEP ONE: Make a list of all the expectations you have for your spouse—from the silly to the serious. Your list might include:

- I expect that you would never do anything to upset me.
- I expect that you will pick up the baby's toys by the time I get home from work.
- I expect that you will call me when you're going to be late.
- I expect that you will make love to me whenever I want you to.
- I expect that you will spend time with me on the weekends.

STEP TWO: Think of a recent time when your expectations weren't met and you felt disappointed or let down. How did you react? Describe the scenario that followed. Now ask yourself: Was your expectation realistic? Did it show that you loved your partner, or did it show that you were trying to control him or her? How can you rewrite your expectation so that your spouse doesn't feel criticized and you feel cared for? How would your thoughts be different? Discuss your individual lists and responses.

Once you do this, your marriage will benefit. Your confidence will help you weather misunderstandings and crises—and your sense of yourself as worthy of love will allow you to love each other more freely.

3. SOS
An Emotional Lifesaver

Here's another exercise you may remember. Tell each other about one family or social situation that makes you feel particularly vulnerable and where your partner has not been as helpful in the past as he or she could have been. Maybe Thanksgiving dinner at your in-laws' is tough for you; perhaps your husband has problems socializing at school functions. This is a good exercise for when you feel you need someone to give you a little extra support.

Once you identify an SOS situation, work out a way of signaling to your partner that you need help. It could be a touch of the elbow, a raised eyebrow, a whispered pledge of support.

WHAT ARE SOME OF YOUR SOS SITUATIONS?

_____

_____

_____

_____

_____

_____

_____

_____

_____

_____

_____

_____

_____

4. LEAN ON ME
When Being There Means a Lot

This is a playful test to see how comfortable you are with each other.

THE FIRST PART IS FOR WIVES:
Stand in front of your husband, facing away from him. Let yourself free-fall backward into his arms and trust that he will catch you.

NOW FOR THE HUSBANDS:
Put on a blindfold and let your wife take you on a house tour; trust that she will guide you safely.

What feelings come up? Did she break the free fall by moving her feet? Did he take baby steps? Is either of you feeling anxious, out of control? If so, you may have a problem with trust.

NOTES

_____

_____

_____

_____

_____

_____

_____

_____

_____

_____

5. MARRIED TO A FLIRT
How to Tame a Roving Eye

Just because plenty of guys and gals like to flirt doesn't make it right. A partner's "innocent" flirtations can make the other feel anxious and emotionally unsafe. We've written the pointers below with masculine pronouns, but don't imagine that men don't get hurt by flirtatious wives, too.

WHAT CAN YOU DO?

1. **Give your partner the benefit of the doubt.** Perhaps he truly doesn't understand how humiliating his actions are. In a quiet moment, explain that his behavior hurts you deeply. Once he hears you speak calmly and without hostility, he may well act with more sensitivity.

2. **If he still has trouble relating to your feelings, ask how he would feel if someone made wisecracks or flashed a lewd look at his sister, or even his daughter, in the same way.** Express your feelings clearly. Make a date, go to a quiet restaurant, and discuss the problem seriously.

3. **Consider the impact your own anger has on his behavior.** While you are understandably outraged, could your fury be provoking him to prove that he is not under your control? What shortcomings of your own might be contributing to the problem? Are you too demanding or smothering? Too critical? Could your expectations for his behavior be unreasonable?

COMMUNICATION

———•———

A healthy relationship rests on two levels of communication. The first is the external, custodial level at which two people discuss the details of daily life: paying the bills, planning vacations, carpooling the kids, and related logistics.

In the best marriages, couples also communicate on the second tier—they talk about the interior, emotional aspects of personal experience. They share feelings, hopes, joys, fears, doubts. It's the sharing at this level that keeps passion alive.

Many husbands and wives communicated well when they were dating. But all too often communication falls victim to busy careers and the stresses of raising a family. Many women mistakenly conclude that if their husbands aren't expressing feelings, they have none. These women become angry at their mate's taciturnity. Often, the angrier they get, the more closed off their husband becomes.

WHAT'S YOUR COMMUNICATION STYLE?

In every marriage, partners display different styles of communication. What's your style of communication? Recognize anyone?

The Know-it-all

Ask these people for the time and they'll tell you how to make a watch. They enjoy showing off and giving unsolicited advice.

The Controller

One type of controller is always ready to take charge. Another is a more passive naysayer who controls by complaining.

The Pleaser

Quiet and timid, the pleaser rarely says what she means and often doesn't mean what she says.

The Victim

This person's main communication skill is reciting the most recent personal injustice to have befallen him.

SELF-APPRAISAL

Ask yourself:

1. How was communication handled in the family I grew up in? Was it open or closed, encouraged or discouraged?

2. Who was the better communicator, my mother or my father?

3. When I was upset as a young child, which parent was easier to talk to? Was Dad the strong, silent type, Mom warm and open?

4. Does my style of communicating resemble that of either parent? Which one?

5. If there was an upsetting incident at work, would I talk about it with my partner or more likely keep it to myself?

6. Do I encourage my partner to share feelings?

7. When upset, can I easily figure out what's wrong?

8. Am I a good listener? Would my partner say I am?

9. Are there specific situations when my ability to communicate breaks down? For instance: Do I have trouble expressing myself in a confrontation or when I have to ask for help?

NOTES

_____

_____

_____

_____

_____

1. REFLECTIVE LISTENING
Basic Training

This basic exercise is one many therapists use to help couples learn to better structure their communication so they don't find, as so many couples do, that one person is talking over the other or hearing the words but misinterpreting them.

Reflective listening is hard work, and it doesn't come nearly as naturally as most people assume it will, even when they love each other very much.

To be an effective listener, make direct eye contact, pay full attention, and listen to the feelings as well as the facts. Even harder, you must also shelve your ego—everything that has to do with your own feelings and thoughts, criticisms or judgments—so you can be fully attentive.

HERE ARE THE RULES:

1. When you have ten minutes of uninterrupted time, name one person the sharer and one the listener. Next time, switch.

2. The sharer has ten minutes to speak freely (set a kitchen timer if you need to). Share an event that happened that day, a conversation you had with a friend or relative, or your feelings about something. In the beginning, discuss only nonvolatile areas. Speak for yourself, using "I" phrases: *I feel, I believe, I think.*

As the listener, you may not interrupt, analyze, judge or rush in with solutions.

3. At the end of ten minutes the listener must feed back to the sharer two things: the facts that were told as well as the feelings behind those facts.

If at any point the listener becomes defensive, stop the process and ask: What did you hear me say? At some level, the other person has heard a personal attack, and this must be cleared up immediately. After one week, if you both agree you are communicating well on this first level, move on to issues that have been dividing you.

2. THE COURAGE TO SPEAK UP
What's Holding You Back from Holding Your Own?

If you crumble at criticism—whether it comes from a spouse, a boss, a parent or a friend—understanding the reasons behind that fear can boost your confidence. Below are three common fears.

1. You're afraid of abandonment. You think that if you speak your mind, you'll provoke your husband (or your friend or your parent) enough to leave.

2. You're afraid to confront because you've been burned before. Perhaps you've been met with an angry response in the past. The person may not have been able to really hear the message you were trying to deliver. The result: He topped you by getting even angrier and more critical.

3. You've been taught to placate others. Rather than assert your needs and desires, you allow yourself to be squeezed into someone else's mold.

WHAT TO DO:
When you feel blasted by another's words, ask yourself: What does this feeling remind me of? Consider whether speaking up will enhance communication or if it's best, for the moment, to say nothing. Sometimes, simply running these questions through your head will give you the courage to hold fast to your point if a discussion gets heated.

Next, wait until your anger subsides before confronting the person who's been critical. Listen to what he is saying and take mental notes so you can respond in a composed, unemotional manner. Be assertive but not offensive. Compromise on the unimportant things, but stand firm on issues that really matter. Once you start making your feelings known, you'll no longer feel like a doormat, and others will curb their critical comments when they recognize that they are stepping over the line.

3. REALITY CHECK
When Assumptions Lead You Astray

Remember the classic O. Henry story "The Gift of the Magi"? A young husband and wife yearn so desperately to make the other happy that they sacrifice their most precious possessions in order to do so: She sells her beautiful long hair to buy her beloved a chain for his pocket watch, but, unbeknownst to her, he's sold his watch to buy an exquisite comb for her hair. Like the characters in this story, couples need to realize that they gain nothing by hiding their feelings from each other, stoically keeping silent about hurts or frustrations, and pretending about what they need most. Though you may love each other deeply, communication still takes work— you can't assume that you know what a partner is feeling or thinking. You have to ask and listen, as well as risk letting your partner know who you really are. By answering the following two questions, and taking time to do a relationship reality check every six months, you can continue to shatter false assumptions that impede honest communication.

1. What three assumptions do you suspect you may be making about what your partner wants, needs or feels?

2. What are three assumptions you believe your partner may be making about you?

SOME STRATEGIES:
Set aside time to talk about each one. Compare perspectives and discuss the following questions.

Are the assumptions correct? Totally wrong? Partly wrong? Do you each see the big issues—sex, money, and commitment—in a similar way? What about the smaller issues—such as how you spend your free time, who does what around the house, and so on?

If there is a kernel of truth in one of the assumptions, you may unwittingly be giving each other the wrong signals. What can you do to communicate more clearly next time?

4. TALK TACTICS
Confrontation Isn't a Dirty Word

When unacknowledged anger builds up, it can trigger a host of physical and psychological problems. It's not easy to recognize this pattern, harder still to stand up to someone who is taking advantage of you and set proper limits. Try these suggestions:

SITUATION: Someone denies he has said or done anything wrong: "Where did you get that idea?" or "That's not what happened at all."

SOLUTION: Don't keep arguing. Instead, consider whether you might be overreacting or misinterpreting what's happening. If you're sure of your feelings, insist that your partner hear you out and address what's troubling you: "I'm not here to debate you. The bottom line is, I'm upset by the way you speak to me. If you love me, why don't you take the time now to talk this out?"

SITUATION: Someone constantly puts you down: "You're being ridiculous" or "You're so naive."

SOLUTION: Don't assume she's right just because you have always felt insecure. Let her know: "Maybe you don't think you're being critical, but it feels that way to me. I don't like it, so stop."

SITUATION: Someone is in a rage: "I'm sick of being blamed for everything that goes wrong in your life."

SOLUTION: Take a deep breath and calmly repeat your point. You can add: "I'm not trying to blame you, but I feel that you do try to control me. You're in a rage, and I find that intimidating. I want you to stop now, or I'll leave the room."

5. DO YOU DISCONNECT?
How to Get Close—and Stay There

In one way or another, we all distance ourselves from our partners. Below is a list of the behaviors we sometimes use in doing so. Check the ones you use and ask your partner to do the same. Then, check those you think apply to your partner.

HE SHE

❑ ❑ I often work late and on weekends.

❑ ❑ I don't tell my partner everything about myself that I really should.

❑ ❑ I'm often late.

❑ ❑ I nag and criticize.

❑ ❑ I'm often irritable or tense.

❑ ❑ I withdraw and shut down instead of responding to others.

❑ ❑ I'm silent more often than communicative.

❑ ❑ I embarrass my mate in front of others.

❑ ❑ I'm a perfectionist and insist everyone else be one, too.

❑ ❑ I spend more money than I should instead of sticking to our financial agreements.

❑ ❑ I'm judgmental and not a good listener.

❑ ❑ I interrupt my partner.

❑ ❑ I bark orders or lecture instead of stating how I feel.

If you checked many of these behaviors, you need to find ways to reconnect. It's never too late to replace the negative, push-away behaviors with the more positive, come-closer ones. Work on short-circuiting any negative thinking about your partner and begin to act more like the mate you want to be. Take the first step toward having the marriage you want by taking responsibility for your own actions.

ANGER

———◆———

Anger is inevitable in every marriage. When two people live together, there will always be issues they disagree about. The problem is not the occurrence or recurrence of anger but rather how well couples have learned to deal with it.

The way you deal with anger as an adult depends in large measure on the way your parents handled it. If your father exploded whenever he was mad, you may do the same. Or you may do the opposite, what psychologists call a reaction formation; you may brood or believe you're not entitled to angry feelings. There are three unhealthy ways people generally handle anger:

• *Some hold it in.* Nursing their anger gives them a false sense of power or strength, a way of protecting themselves. They think: If I'm angry, I'm less vulnerable. They may brood for days or weeks—sometimes even forgetting what it was that made them so angry in the first place. But that stored-up anger is just beneath the surface, ready to be added to whatever frustration or disappointment comes along.

• *Some people vent it.* Explosive screaming and carrying on are harmful, not only because hurtful things are said but also because the intensity of the storm can push a loved one so far away that the distance is impossible to close.

• *Still others deny it.* They may be conscious of their anger initially, then banish it from their minds. Sadly, it often surfaces in contradictory behavior and feelings toward their spouse.

What's the right way to handle this complex emotion? By being direct, immediate, and specific about the cause of your anger. Ideally, you will be able to tell your spouse what distressed you when it happens or as soon afterward as possible—without personally attacking him or her. Your goal is to be able to make a clear and direct statement: "I am hurt (angry, upset) when you say you will be home for dinner at seven, but then walk in the door at eight without even calling" is better than "You are always late."

But learning to do this is often a detailed and lengthy task. You need to identify your style of anger and how it needs to be changed, learn how to regain emotional control in the heat of anger, be willing to work hard to resolve the conflict.

SELF-APPRAISAL

1. How did your parents express their disappointment, frustration or rage, and how did they handle disagreements?

2. Did they fly off the handle, yelling or criticizing at the least provocation? Slam doors or throw dishes? Sulk, fume, and give everyone the silent treatment?

3. Did they spar and jab with sarcastic comments and chronic bickering?

4. How did your parents react to your expressions of anger as a child? Were you allowed to express your rage when your sibling played with your prized possessions or were your frustrations routinely dismissed? Were you expected to be the good little girl who never, ever got upset?

5. Of the three styles of anger management mentioned earlier, which best describes you—do you nurse, vent, or deny your anger?

1. THE DANCE OF ANGER
Changing the Beat

I f arguments are interminable, recognizing your own fighting style can be a first step toward ending them. The second: establishing rules for off-limits behavior. Below is a list of things we all do that inevitably make matters worse. How many are in your argument arsenal?

❑ **Exaggeration.** Stick to the facts. If your spouse was late in meeting you one night, don't insist that he kept you waiting in subfreezing temperatures for an hour.

❑ **Generalizations.** One mistake does not a character flaw make. If a spouse doesn't fulfill household responsibilities one day, don't announce that she's a slob who always passes the buck.

❑ **Name Calling.** Start in with nasty names and you immediately put someone on the defensive and sabotage any hope for a civilized discussion.

❑ **Replaying History.** Concentrate on the current problem, not what did or didn't happen last year or ten years ago.

❑ **Kitchen-Sinking.** You start off criticizing one thing, then another, then another. Before you realize it, you've thrown in everything that's ever bothered you. It's better to stick to one issue or problem at a time.

NOTES

_____

_____

_____

_____

_____

_____

2. WHAT'S YOUR EMOTIONAL M.O.?
Stress and Problem-Solving

People handle stress differently—call it their emotional modus operandi, or M.O. Some are *turtles*: It's hard for them to say honestly how they feel and they may not be entirely sure they're entitled to in the first place. As a result, they stifle emotions and do anything to keep the peace. Some are *controllers:* Precise and opinionated, they deny feelings and react in robotlike fashion to any emotional display. Others are *blamers,* chronic fault-finders who believe their problems are all due to the faults and mistakes of other people; or *gaslighters,* those who spend their time minimizing or dismissing problems and insisting anyone who doesn't agree is crazy.

How can you determine your emotional M.O. and make it work in tandem with that of your partner so that you solve problems as a team instead of as adversaries?

Try this two-part exercise:

1. Think of an issue that recently triggered great hostility between the two of you. Each of you should write down on a piece of paper a verbal picture of how you saw yourself handling the problem: What did you say to your partner? What tone of voice or gestures did you use? Switch papers to see how your partner perceived the same interaction.

2. Now, role-play. Try to reenact the situation, but this time, respond in the way your partner responded. How did it feel to walk in his shoes? What did you learn about your own M.O.?

NOTES

_____

_____

_____

_____

3. DEAR DIARY
The Importance of Writing It Down

An essential part of learning to deal with anger is understanding that it's okay to have negative feelings and to express them, no matter what the situation. Many people who have trouble expressing anger to their partner also have trouble expressing it to their friends, co-workers, relatives—even to the person who cuts ahead of them on line at the supermarket.

Once you learn to pinpoint your negative feelings, you can practice healthy ways of expressing them. In time, that skill will transfer to your marriage. Below are situations that often make people angry. Write down what you would like to say in each situation, or say it into a tape recorder.

• You call a friend. She's dashing out but promises to call you back later. She never does—and this happens over and over again.

YOU SAY: _____

• You have a dinner date with your husband and some friends, and he arrives twenty minutes late. In fact, he often keeps you waiting.

YOU SAY: _____

• You have plans to go to a movie with friends, but they cancel without an explanation.

YOU SAY: _____

• Your neighbor borrows $20 from you and never pays it back, so you have to ask her for it.

YOU SAY: _____

• Your sister begs you—at the last minute, as always—to baby-sit her kids so she can go shopping, and you want the time for yourself.

YOU SAY: _____

4. THE ARMISTICE
Resolving Conflicts Peacefully

Once the hot emotion of anger is dealt with, efforts to resolve conflicts can begin. Usually there are three choices: You can capitulate; you can compromise; or you can peacefully and lovingly coexist even though the disagreement is not fully resolved. That means that while you may not be able to settle an issue, you can at least come up with a temporary solution.

THINK: Recall a time when the two of you disagreed about an issue but were able to work it through. Was there anything you did then that you can do now? Sometimes just stopping to think can give you the impetus to try again. Is nothing applicable? Then it's time to brainstorm ideas.

_____

_____

ACT: Each of you should write down as many solutions to the problem as you can think of. Then go down each list and ask yourselves: Is this an acceptable or unacceptable solution as far as I'm concerned? If it is acceptable, can I live with it—without resentment? If the answer is no, then cross it off. Whittle your lists down until you have a solution.

_____

_____

REGROUP: Feel like you've hit a brick wall? If you're simply unable to reach a mutually satisfying solution, put your list of solutions in a safe place and agree to take it out in a week and look at it again. This gives you time to cool down, get a clearer perspective, and make resolution possible.

_____

_____

5. IN FRONT OF THE KIDS
Dial Down the Anger

Here's a scenario you may recall: You and your partner are fighting (openly or silently) and you're not the only ones who feel the earth quaking. Your children's antennae are finely tuned to parental discord, so remember that it's not whether you fight but how you handle a fight that's important. In fact, it can teach your children a valuable lesson about expressing feelings and resolving differences. Just keep the following in mind:

1. Promise you will not resort to name-calling, insults, or sarcasm. Nor will you cut each other off in mid-sentence, or draw your kids into your disagreements.

2. Try not to lapse into angry silences. Emotional distance can be scarier for kids than outright fighting because they just don't understand why Mom and Dad aren't talking. They assume it must be something they've done. It's better to say directly: "Mommy and Daddy are having an argument right now. Sometimes parents fight, just like kids fight. But we're trying to work it out." Make sure they see that you do.

3. Never threaten to leave or get a divorce. In the heat of anger, we often say things we don't mean. Kids don't know that and are confused and frightened by unfulfilled threats.

4. When you're really furious, agree to disagree. Call a time-out if tempers get too hot.

5. When you're calm enough to discuss strategies, respect the fact that you are each entitled to your opinion. Does one of you feel more strongly than the other about an issue? Implement that person's suggestion first. If it fails to work, try another idea. This shows kids the importance of sharing ideas respectfully.

6. Work on your marriage. Get a baby-sitter so you can regularly spend time alone together. If you keep your relationship healthy and nurturing, it will be easier to resolve disagreements.

POWER AND CONTROL

When either person in a relationship feels controlled, the result is a backflow of resentment that can destroy love. Such competition for power, whether overt or subtle, triggers continual game-playing. And if you think you are being manipulated, you end up feeling threatened and demeaned, rather than loved and cherished.

Marriage must be a partnership of equals. But if you were raised in a home where certain patterns of power were established, it can be difficult to break them. Also, if you feel insecure or threatened, we may try to make our world safe by striving for more control.

SELF-APPRAISAL

Part A

- In your parents' marriage, how was power and control handled? Was one clearly in charge or was there a balance?

- Did you grow up in a permissive or authoritarian atmosphere?

- Is it important for you to be right and hold center stage? In a group, are you more comfortable in a leadership role or as a follower?
- How does power work in your marriage? Is it in balance? If it is unbalanced, is that okay?
- Think about power with regard to sex, money, children, and parents. What thoughts and feelings come up?

Part B

Below is a list of common family decisions. In your family of origin, were these issues decided by your father, your mother, or both? Who had the final word in arguments?

	FATHER	MOTHER	BOTH
• decisions about how money is spent	❑	❑	❑
• decisions about whom to socialize with, which relative to visit, and so on	❑ ❑	❑ ❑	❑ ❑
• decisions about child rearing	❑	❑	❑
• decisions about where to live	❑	❑	❑
• decisions about where to spend vacations	❑	❑	❑

If the list you made is lopsided, there's a good chance you're bringing an unbalanced view of power and control issues to your current relationship. Go over the questions again with a different color pen. Who is in charge in your own marriage? Again, if that list is lopsided, a warning bell should go off.

NOTES

_____

_____

_____

_____

_____

_____

_____

1. YOUR TURN/MY TURN
A Delicate Balance

After you've singled out the areas of imbalance, identify three areas where each of you can give up some control. Pick one to focus on. For instance, if you recognize that your need to control takes the form of always criticizing your mate when he goes shopping ("How could you buy that tomato sauce?" "Those bananas aren't ripe!"), be conscious of that and graciously accept what you find in the grocery bags. Next week, pick another area. Remember: If you give your spouse responsibility for doing something, you relinquish control—and that includes the right to decry the fact that he didn't do it your way. Be sure to offer each other positive feedback.

HIS LIST

HER LIST

2. TALENT SHOW
Go With Your Strengths

No two people are equally talented in all areas. One way to reduce the resentment over control issues is to acknowledge each other's strengths and weaknesses. If you are good at record-keeping and your husband can't add up your checkbook, agree that you will pay the bills. On the other hand, if your husband is a better cook, agree that he will be in charge of family meal-planning.

HIS STRENGTHS	HER STRENGTHS

3. FREE TO BE YOU AND ME
The Give and Take

The opposite of feeling controlled by your spouse is a healthy degree of personal freedom in the relationship. You should each make a list of five things you like to do on your own. Perhaps you want to meet your women friends for dinner one night a week. Your husband must then agree to rearrange his schedule so you can do that—by being home by six-thirty to watch the kids, for instance, without leaving you in the lurch or making you feel bad. Let's say your husband has written down that he'd like to go on a hiking trip with his college roommate. Offer to take charge of all weekend parental duties so he can go camping, and don't make him feel like he's shirking responsibilities when he does.

HIS TIME-OUT

1.
2.
3.
4.
5.
6.
7.
8.
9.
10.
11.
12.

HER TIME-OUT

1.
2.
3.
4.
5.
6.
7.
8.
9.
10.
11.
12.

4. BREAKING AWAY
The Many Disguises of Control

You know that screaming is one way to boss someone around. But did you realize that partners control each other in many different ways and with many different types of behaviors? Below is a list of stonewalling tactics frequently used to dominate a marriage. Study them and discuss how you might both be unconsciously fanning the flames of conflict.

1. Control by compliance: You go along with what your partner wants, saying you want to avoid conflict. In reality, constant acquiescence can feel like control to your partner.

2. Control by instilling guilt or fear: You make threats to leave or withdraw financial support. You give your partner the silent treatment or use tears, blame, or sarcasm to make your points. You complain or use illness to get your way.

3. Control by indifference: You shut your partner out by refusing to have sex or by burying yourself in your work, the TV, a book, or your favorite sports or hobbies.

4. Control by indecision: By refusing to state how you really feel or what you want forces your partner to make decisions for you.

WHAT CONTROL TECHNIQUES DO YOU USE?

_____

_____

_____

_____

_____

_____

5. ARE YOU A YES-OHOLIC?
Getting to No

Many women are rescuers, taught to be the good girl whose job it is to please everyone all the time. Usually that means a person winds up feeling resentful that her own needs are never met. Such women have trouble saying no. If that's you, these strategies will allow you to feel more in control of your life:

1. Understand where the impulse to say yes comes from. Most women are taught from childhood to be cooperative and compliant. The truth is, if you want to get off the yes-track, you have to take a chance that someone out there won't like it. You can, however, learn to live with the uncomfortable feeling that you've disappointed someone. Sometimes that adjustment is necessary to hold on to your self-identity.

2. Practice saying no in relatively benign situations. For instance, the next time a telemarketer calls asking you to contribute money to a cause you have never heard of or couldn't care less about, politely but firmly say, "I don't want to talk to you." Then hang up immediately.

Remind yourself that you have every right to say no, even to a loved one or friend. The next time someone asks you to run an errand that you really can't or don't want to do, again, politely but firmly say no. Don't offer any detailed reasons either. Simply say: "I'm sorry, but it's just impossible for me to help out right now." No excuses necessary. If you find yourself on the verge of agreeing to bake one hundred brownies for the class bake sale, catch yourself by saying: "Can I get back to you on that?" There is no rule that you have to say yes to a request simply because it is made. It's smart to wait until you are sure you know your answer. Then, you'll be freer (mentally and physically) to focus on what you want to do and really shine at it.

SEX

———❖———

When partners keep each other a priority outside the bedroom and share themselves at a deeper level, passion can be renewed. Sex is a celebration of love, and it can be as varied as two people make it. Performance is less important than process.

A couple's sexual pattern will vary from time to time, depending on external events as well as physical health and well-being. When sex becomes a problem, it almost always signals a problem in another area. Such couples would do well to examine how connected they are in non-sexual ways. However, a complete physical examination, to rule out a medical cause, is also important.

SELF-APPRAISAL

Ask yourself the following questions:

- What message did you get from your same-sex parent about sex? Did your mother imply that six is dirty or that you just use sex to get a man? Or perhaps a man grew up hearing that the more women you score with, the more of a man you are.

- When you were a child, did you think your mother enjoyed being a woman? Did your father appear to enjoy being a man?

- From the eyes of a little girl, how did you see your mother? Was she tender and affectionate? Cold and domineering? From the eyes of a little boy, how did you see your dad? Was he warm and loving or distant and dictatorial?

- In the family you grew up in, were boys favored over girls, or vice versa?

- Are you comfortable with how you feel as a woman or as a man? What's your fantasy image of a female? A male? Are you satisfied with where you stand in relation to that ideal?

- What was your relationship with your siblings of the same and opposite sex?

Now, on a scale of 1 to 10 (with 10 being the highest), rate your sexual relationship in the following areas:

_____ frequency

_____ ability to talk about sex

_____ variety in lovemaking

_____ how and when sex gets initiated

_____ amount and duration of foreplay

_____ overall satisfaction

On a scale of 1 to 10 (with 10 being the highest), rate the sexual romance level of your marriage in the following areas:

_____ You tell each other about the special qualities that turn you on.

_____ You enjoy dressing up for each other.

_____ You give each other physical affection outside the bedroom.

_____ You look into each other's eyes and say "I love you."

_____ You surprise each other with treats.

Compare your numbers with your partner's. Pay particular attention to those areas where your perceptions differ.

1. GENDER ROLES AND IMAGES
How You Really Think

On a sheet of paper, draw a line down the middle and write Masculine on one side, Feminine on the other. List the personal characteristics you associate with each gender—emotional, sensitive, goal-directed, rational, caring, and so on.

Compare lists. It's important for both partners not to fall into the trap of stereotyping. For instance, if a man believes that only women are sensitive, how does that influence how he shows affection and tenderness? Look at your responses in terms of power and control, too. For instance, a man who sees women as sweet and compliant may feel his wife is not capable of making important decisions. On the other hand, a woman who thinks that men are space cadets when it comes to remembering things on the homefront, she may resist or criticize his child care efforts.

MASCULINE	FEMININE

2. YOUR CHOICE
Taking Turns

Once a month, pick a day and agree to do whatever your partner wants. The person in charge gets to decide everything you do that day—assuming, of course, it is not painful or humiliating. You want to go out for breakfast at a fancy restaurant? Have a bubble bath and drink champagne? Mountain bike across the dunes? Great. Next time, switch.

HIS DAY | **HER DAY**

3. REDISCOVERING INTIMACY
Starting Again

If you believe your sex life has become too routine, try getting reacquainted. First, agree to abstain from intercourse for two weeks. Kiss and cuddle, but do nothing more. Your main form of physical contact will be a full-body massage, excluding the genital area. Alternate, giving each other at least two massages. The person getting the massage must be specific about directions: what feels good, where she or he likes to be touched, how much pressure feels right, etc. Remember to focus your feedback on positive suggestions—"Please rub between my shoulders"—rather than negative comments, such as "Not like that." Your goal is to help each other become expert in giving pleasure. The second week, include the genital area. Again, be clear about what you like. Once the two weeks are over, choose a special time to put together all you've learned.

NOTES

_____

_____

_____

_____

_____

_____

_____

_____

_____

_____

_____

4. YOUR SEXUAL HISTORY
The Hidden Messages

Despite a society permeated by sex and sexual imagery, many people are still tongue-tied about their own sexual needs. They're also surprisingly lacking in knowledge about their own sexuality as well as that of their partners. The result can be a predictable and passionless sexual life at best, or one that is nonexistent. One reason: Emotional baggage weighs them down.

Take a few moments to inventory the messages you or your spouse may have brought into the bedroom. Consider nonverbal messages—behaviors and attitudes—as well as things your parents may have told you about sex and sexuality. These questions can be the catalyst for further thought and self-reflection:

1. Did you grow up in an affectionate, demonstrative family? Were you hugged by your parents when you were little?

2. Do you recall your parents being affectionate with each other as well as with their children?

3. Did your father make jokes about how cold or indifferent your mother was? As far as you knew, did either parent ever have an extramarital affair?

4. Did you sense or hear complaints from your mother that sex was a burden, something a woman must endure in order to raise a family? Did your mother caution you that "boys only want one thing from a girl"?

5. Did your parents warn you against premarital sex? What was their attitude about unmarried couples living together?

6. How did your parents' attitudes toward you change as you grew older and entered puberty? Was it a comfortable, joyous time, one you could warmly share with your parents? Or did you feel awkward and embarrassed by the changes in your body? Did your father pull away from you, giving you the impression that it was unseemly to hug and kiss an adolescent?

5. WHAT'S HOLDING YOU BACK?
The Top Three Sexual Inhibitions

In the past, some women found themselves passive particpants in bed. Today the opposite is often true: Many are counting orgasms and worry if they're not hanging from the chandeliers. On the other hand there are women who've become accustomed to less rather than more sexual activity in their marriage only to discover that the advent of drugs to help men overcome impotency has created a whole new set of pressures. Under these conditions, sex becomes a battle and every other issue in a marriage—be it money, disciplining the kids, or whether one of you is spending too much time at work and not enough tending the relationship—becomes ammunition in the war.

Needless to say, the secret to making sex come alive is to risk being emotionally naked. For some, that means shedding old assumptions and routines—a scary, often overwhelming step. Recognizing, and then dispelling, these three inhibitions is critical.

INHIBITION #1: ANXIETY Some people have such a high level of anxiety in general that they fear the loss of control necessary to giving and receiving sexual pleasure. These people have learned to function well in society by staying in control and it's hard, if not impossible, for them to switch gears in the bedroom.

STRATEGY: To help you relax the pressure you put on yourself, remember that sex doesn't always have to mean sex—not in the traditional sense, anyway. Instead of counting the number of times you have intercourse, count the number of times you are together and close physically—from holding hands, lathering each other up in a shower for two, or making out like you did when you dated. In this way, sex becomes a special time together when you and your partner invent the rules.

INHIBITION #2: GREAT EXPECTATIONS Others suffer from unrealistic expectations regarding what they should be doing and feeling in bed. When you believe you're not measuring up physically, you shut down.

STRATEGY: Remind yourself you're not competing in the sexual Olympics and the only impossible standards are those you set for yourself. Take small steps before you attempt the bigger ones. And don't fail to take the time to do things that make you feel good physically—enroll in a gym; take up a sport you always wanted to try but never thought you had the time for; or pamper yourself by springing for a manicure or pedicure or having your hair highlighted.

INHIBITION #3: FEAR OF BEING VULNERABLE Saying what you want in bed is always difficult because you're exposing your deepest, most private secrets. This is especially true for women reared to believe that good girls don't make requests of any kind, certainly not erotic ones. There are some women who think they're conveying their sexual wishes through body language or gentle verbal directions, but their methods are so oblique or their hints so subtle that their husbands would have to be mind-readers to decode them.

STRATEGY: If this is true for you, try slowly initiating conversations about sex in a neutral environment—take a walk together after dinner, or share a glass of wine after the children have gone to bed. Mention something that sounds like fun to you, and gauge his reaction. Then, when you do make love, you'll be that much closer to sexual rapport without having to resort to a lot of heavy, action-stopping prompts. During lovemaking, try to use simple, unequivocal language—"Harder please," "I love it slower," or "That feels wonderful." Or request something he's done before that pleased you: "Honey, it really turns me on when you touch me here. . . ." Far from being turned off, your spouse will most likely see your newfound assertiveness as proof of his power to arouse you.

MONEY

———◆———

Ask any marital expert to name the issue that most divides couples today (and yesterday) and money matters usually top the list. Having too little money—or being unable to civilly discuss how to spend what you *do* have—triggers countless arguments that can linger and erupt throughout the course of a marriage. That's because money is, pardon the pun, such a loaded issue. Ostensibly, you may be arguing over whether to put your tax refund into your savings account or spend it on a weekend trip to Paris. But you're really battling about what that money symbolizes to each of you: Power? Love? Revenge? It all gets mixed up in fights over dollars . . . and often it makes little sense.

SELF-APPRAISAL

What are your money goals? What would you like to do with the money you have? If you have trouble answering that question, you're not alone. Most people can't. They think they know, but they're often clueless about their real financial targets, mainly because they've never really taken the time to seriously think about money, other than worrying about it, that is.

Take a moment now to ask yourself the following questions:

Financially, what would I like to accomplish this year? Be specific. Do you want to put aside money for your child's college fund? Take a family vacation? Buy a new car? List them all.

What are your financial goals for the next decade? Do you hope to be promoted within your division? Have enough money to start your own business—or to take time off and write your novel? Do you hope to find a house in a neighborhood that has a better school system?

What are your lifetime financial goals? Did your father vow to leave a certain amount of money to each of his children, and do you intend to do the same? Have you been dreaming about retiring to a little cottage on Nantucket?

What are you doing right now to achieve each of these goals? Are you prepared to cut back on expenses or take on another freelance project or consultancy job to meet your financial goals? Realistically assessing what your dreams are, and how you might attain them, will help you focus on the things you need to do every day so you don't look back with accusations and regrets.

NOTES

_____

_____

_____

_____

_____

_____

_____

_____

_____

_____

_____

_____

1. A ROSE BY ANY OTHER NAME
Escaping Childhood Labels

Attitudes about money can divide partners into opposing camps that seem impenetrable. Sometimes we become emotionally and physically stuck in our beliefs and attitudes because we're functioning under old rules and labels from childhood, which really don't pertain to our lives now. While some labels accurately reflect a person's basic nature, strengths, or weaknesses, more often then not they are products of past experiences as well as parental anxieties, wishes, or expectations. It's nearly impossible to escape labels completely, but you can minimize their impact on your relationship.

First, be sensitive to the labels you each grew up with. Ask yourselves: What roles did you play in your family of origin? Were you the *leader*? The *baby*? *Daddy's girl*? The *selfish one*? *The brain*? Were you comfortable with those labels or do you believe they failed to describe you accurately? Were there alliances between siblings, or between a parent and a child, that affected the rest of the family? How did these alliances impact you? Does your partner have a different perspective or insight on the role you might still be playing?

Remembering early roles can help you consciously rewrite the script of your marriage now. What changes would you both make? Be patient, these fundamental changes take time and hard work.

NOTES

_____

_____

_____

_____

_____

2. DO YOU HOLD MONEY GRUDGES?
Letting Bygones Be Just That

Money fights can be particularly bitter and long-lasting—and making up can be hard to do—if you or your partner are grudge-holders. Grudge-holding also creates anxiety in a partner who may not understand what he or she has done to incur so much hostility. In either case, closeness is seriously eroded. In a healthy marriage, partners need to find ways to accept each other's mistakes, problems, and flaws. In that way, a partner knows that he or she may be imperfect, but in no way inadequate.

Whether you're arguing about money, sex, or the kids, consider the following: Do you nurse resentment for long periods of time, waiting for an opportunity to prove yourself right and your partner wrong? Are you unable to resolve issues because one or both of you continues to collect and nurture grievances? As each new "offense" is duly noted, resentment builds until the distance between you looms too large to bridge. Most grudges in intimate relationships serve a disguised purpose for the grudge-holder; in a way, it protects that person from being hurt in quite the same way again. Here's how you can tell:

1. Does the grudge give you an edge over your partner, a degree of moral superiority or security? How would you feel if you weren't still so angry?

2. Anger and power often go together. Does being angry with your partner help you feel more powerful? Are you feeling weak in general in other areas of your life—perhaps at work, or in relation to your parents or children, or with a friend? Try to put your anger into perspective: Where does the real problem lie?

3. Could you be protecting yourself against something by holding on to this grudge? If you let go of this grudge, will you feel vulnerable to another hurt? Think about what you're afraid of, and tell your mate you'd like to discuss it. Pick a quiet time when you can talk undisturbed and lay this grudge to rest so you are free to concentrate on other issues.

3. TAMING MONEY WORRIES
Easing the Anxiety That Drives You Apart

When you're having financial problems, it's hard to keep the rest of your life and your marriage on an even keel. Anxiety disorders—either temporary or longer term—affect as many as 20 percent of Americans, almost two-thirds of them women, and they manifest in different ways and in different degrees. For some sufferers, anxiety is an overwhelming feeling of looming disaster. For others it's a racing heart, tension headaches or back pain. Unpleasant as it is, anxiety isn't always a bad thing. It can motivate us to finally resolve a problem, make a decision about whether to look for a new job with a higher salary, or to confront a spouse or friend when we are upset or hurt by their actions. But chronic worriers push away their partners, who often feel that nothing they do or say could ever help. Try these strategies designed to help worriers cope better in stressful situations:

1. Keep a worry diary. For one week, record every fear, large or small, that passes through your mind. Then, put your diary aside for one week; when you take it out again, consider how many of your fears or concerns proved realistic. Most of the things we worry about never come to pass. Or schedule a worry break: Allot a certain amount of time, say thirty minutes every Monday night, to worrying. Fret about everything and anything, try to figure out what you can do about each dilemma and, when your allotted time is up, cap those worries until the next worry time. During the rest of the week, when you feel overwhelmed, take a deep breath and calmly tell yourself that you're saving this worry for later.

2. Focus on the present. Interrupt negative thoughts when they begin by focusing on an activity you enjoy: exercise, listen to music, or watch a video. Or concentrate your attention on something else: What people standing next to you in line at the bank are wearing, the sounds of the birds outside, the way the sunlight is bouncing off the car windows. When you do this successfully, you will break the cycle—there isn't room in your head to concentrate hard on two disparate things.

3. Eliminate the words "should" and "must" from your vocabulary. Worriers usually have a long list of things they believe they must accomplish or handle on their own. When you are overwhelmed by your to-do list, tell yourself: "I don't *have* to do this, I'd *like* to do it." The semantic switch takes some of the pressure off.

4. Silence your inner critic. Many worriers secretly believe they're not good enough. Whenever you hear that little voice, divert your attention so you can't hear it.

5. Exercise. Worriers benefit greatly from good health habits. Aerobic exercise at least three times a week for twenty to thirty minutes—even just walking around the block—triggers a rush of endorphins, chemicals in the brain that help you relax and put worries into perspective.

WHAT THINGS CAN YOU GIVE UP WORRYING ABOUT?

_____

_____

_____

_____

_____

_____

_____

_____

_____

_____

_____

_____

4. THE GOOD-ENOUGH APOLOGY
Love Means Saying You're Sorry

Maybe he just splurged on another piece of stereo equipment without checking with her. Maybe she bought toys for the kids when he's already feeling as if he lives in a Toys "R" Us warehouse. Arguments over money can get heated, and things said in the heat of anger, while perhaps not truly meant, can cut a deep wound. An apology, genuinely offered and graciously accepted, has the power to validate hurt feelings and restore even the most seriously damaged relationships.

Unfortunately, far too many people never apologize—or think they do but fail to offer enough security to their mate so that their mumbled words make a difference. There are four key elements to a good-enough apology:

1. For an apology to be meaningful, a person cannot simply recite the words "I'm sorry." Rather, he must account for his actions, specifically acknowledge another's pain, and empathize with how you are feeling. Empathy is the key, the bridge that allows a person who has done wrong the chance to prove that he understands and regrets the pain he has caused: "I was wrong to do that. I know I hurt you deeply."

2. The apology must include an acknowledgment of wrongdoing and a vow to change. This means not making excuses or justifying his actions. A good-enough apology must also speak to the future and offer a promise of specific things the wrongdoer will or will not do again.

3. An apology must be followed by a visible demonstration of changed behavior. The wrongdoer must extend herself in some way toward improving the long-term situation.

4. Finally, an apology must be appropriately timed. Said in haste, before the wronged one has had a chance to feel his or her rage or despair, the apology will feel insincere. On the other hand, if it is too long in coming, it can feel like neglect.

5. WE CAN WORK IT OUT
How to Get the Most Out of a Therapy Session

Even the best relationships can benefit from an occasional tune-up, a chance to bounce problems off a third, impartial party, or air grievances in a setting where neither feels one-down. Across the country, marriage workshops and courses are flourishing—for those about to be wed, newlywed, or long married. If you're considering counseling, remember that it will be successful only if a couple agrees that resolving their differences is their number-one priority. But even if you're both committed to the process, don't expect it to be easy.

How can you find a qualified therapist near you? Calling or visiting the website of the American Association of Marriage and Family Therapists (www.aamft.org; 703-838-9808) or the Coalition for Marriage, Family and Couples Education (www.smartmarriages.com; 202-362-3332) is a good starting point. Each has a state-by-state directory of counselors. Also, ask your physician, clergy,man, or trusted friend for a recommendation. Once you begin, keep the following in mind:

• Don't expect to change a partner who has no interest in changing. You can change only the part you play in a struggling relationship. And you can learn to negotiate and compromise. In fact, mastering the intricacies of compromise is the very essence of adult life, the secret to improving relationships in every arena, and a mark of emotional maturity.

• Stop being defensive. For counseling to work, you have to put your ego on the shelf and have the courage to admit that you may have been wrong. People who have the most trouble in counseling point fingers and expect to win an argument. With that attitude, you both lose.

• Use counseling constructively. If you focus on what you gained in the counseling process, you'll feel more empowered to make the necessary changes in your life and your marriage.

TEAM UP

---·—·---

We can't say it enough: If you don't make your marriage a priority, you're not only hurting yourselves, you're hurting your kids. But how do you protect a marriage from the havoc triggered by myriad problems large and small? How do you find the time to pay attention to each other, emotionally and physically, when you barely have time to finish a sentence? Whether you've been married for two years or twenty, you must work hard to make each other feel respected, accepted, and cherished. At the bottom of many marital issues is the fear that these basic needs simply won't be fulfilled—that, ultimately, you will be rejected for being you.

Are you doing everything you can to make your marriage special? It's easy to slip into bad love habits. Good love habits deepen and strengthen a marriage, bad ones chip away at its core. The following self-appraisal highlights habits you need to break.

SELF-APPRAISAL

Empathy, encouragement, and the ability to separate the person from the performance are fundamental in showing acceptance and working as a team. Are you working as a team? You're not if you . . .

1. Push your partner out of your daily life. Couples can become so involved in the minutiae of daily life that they stop telling each other not only what happened during the day—a business coup or setback, the fact that the baby turned over in his crib—but how they felt about it. While it's essential to talk about problems, it's equally important to talk in a let's-get-to-know-each-other way. Only then do you strengthen commitment and enrich your love.

2. Assume Mother/Father knows best. A division of labor is not only normal, it's necessary. However, many women take their responsibility too seriously and discount their husband's opinions and ideas because, quite simply, they're different from theirs. Guarding your turf can be dangerous for a marriage.

3. Reroute your hurt feelings. Rerouting disappointment or anger away from your mate and dumping it instead on a confidante not only puts a strain on your friendship, it robs you of the opportunity to use your anger constructively to solve problems with your spouse. Not that you should halt all conversations with trusted friends, but if you find that you're talking only to friends, you're not giving your spouse, or your relationship, a chance.

4. Wait for the perfect moment to discuss what's bothering you. That perfect time doesn't exist. And, if you're afraid to rock the boat or you assume that your partner will react the same way he always does, you're doing nothing to improve your marriage. Sometimes you just have to say: "This is hard for me to talk about . . ." or "I know you may get upset, but we really need to discuss . . ."

5. Always have the last word. The next time you are about to hurl a possible zinger, ask yourself: What do I hope to achieve by making this particular statement? Taking sixty seconds to think about your goal may be all the time you need to figure out a nonaccusatory way to say it, or perhaps, decide to say nothing at all.

1. WHO AM I?
Finding Yourself Within Your Marriage

You can't have a genuinely happy marriage unless you have a reasonably solid sense of who you are. Yet many struggle with marital problems because they can't figure out what they really need, as opposed to what other people—their parents, their spouses—want for them. If that sounds like you, take a few minutes to consider the following questions. By answering each one honestly, you will highlight events, circumstances, and patterns of behavior of which you might not be fully aware. You'll be able to understand the impact past experiences had on your self-esteem and your ability to trust your own judgment. What's more, some of these questions will jump-start your thinking about topics and issues you may never have considered before.

- Were your parents happily married? _____

- If they were separated or divorced, how old were you when the marriage fell apartt? _____

- Were your relationships with your siblings loving and friendly? Did you fight a lot as children? _____

- What is your relationship with them now?_____

- In general, did your parents accept you for who you were or did you sense you were never good enough in their eyes? _____ _____

- When you made a mistake, or were unable to do something on your own, how did your parents react? _____ _____

- Did your parents allow you to make your own decisions when you were growing up? _____

- Did they support your choices or insist you march to their drummer? _____

- Did you feel that their love was contingent on your success or achievement? _____

- In general, could family members speak their mind in your home or did they subscribe to the belief that people should keep their personal thoughts and feelings to themselves?

  _____

- In general, would you describe your parents as trusting, optimistic, and open or suspicious, negative, and emotionally distant? _____

- Did they exude a sense of satisfaction with their lives, or did they give you the impression that the grass was greener elsewhere? Or did they warn you that it was a jungle out there? _____

- When you are in a new situation now, do you find it easy or hard to talk to others? _____

- Do you enjoy traveling to new places and meeting new people?

  _____

- When was the last time you really felt joy—that soaring feeling that takes you above the mundane nitty-gritty stuff of daily life? How could you find it again? _____

  _____

- If you could print your personal life credo on a T-shirt, what would it be? _____

- If you had a lunch date with your twelve-year-old self, what would he or she think of you? _____

- If you could take a six-month leave of absence from whatever you do now, what would you do and where would you go?

  _____

- Are you living your life for you or for your parents, your spouse, your children? _____

- Ten years from now, if you had all the money you would ever need, what would you most like to be doing? _____

  _____

2. DO YOU LOVE ME?
Count the Ways

Intimacy is built in small ways, with simple, everyday acts of kindness. And while we all like to think that our partners know how much we care, be honest: When was the last time you were as thoughtful and considerate as you'd like to be?

Take a sheet of paper and make a list of all the things you would like your partner to do for you. Your list might include: give the kids their baths at night, watch my favorite TV show with me, arrange for a Saturday night baby-sitter, as well as ask me about my day, tell me that you love me. Exchange lists and ask your partner to pick one thoughtful gesture to do faithfully for one week. Add one more each week.

WEEKLY WISH LIST	HIS	HERS
WEEK 1		
WEEK 2		
WEEK 3		
WEEK 4		
WEEK 5		
WEEK 6		
WEEK 7		
WEEK 8		
WEEK 9		
WEEK 10		

3. ICEBREAKERS
Getting to Know You

The idea here is to rekindle the fun and playfulness you had when you first started dating, when you talked freely about anything and everything.

BLIND DATE
After the children are in bed, sit down in the most comfortable room in your home, turn off the TV, and take the phone off the hook. Take turns asking each other some interesting questions. Share the facts about what happened as well as your feelings. A few sample questions: What would you do if you won the lottery? What's the luckiest thing that ever happened to you? The most embarrassing? When was the first time you were kissed?

LET'S GET PHYSICAL
Make separate lists of the physical things you would like to do together. Include everything from making love or playing tennis, to taking ballroom-dancing lessons to sharing a shower. Now compare your lists and make a master list. Promise that you will select at least one activity each week from this list.

LOVES ME, LOVES ME NOT
Write down three things you admire most about your spouse. Then write down what it was that attracted you to each other in the first place. For the next week, consciously remember these points and compliment your spouse at least once a day on something—either on the way he looks, the fact that she did something special for you, an achievement at work, and so on. Be specific.

(continued on next page)

TIME FOR A VALUE CHECK

There are periods in every marriage when dreams no longer seem in sync—and loving partners become polarized in conflicting positions. Nevertheless, we all need to dream—and we need to know that our partners support our hopes even though they may seem totally impractical. Dreams connect us to childhood—when the world felt limitless—and promise a future that's a bit freer than we may feel right now. If you have a sense that the two of you no longer share a vision of the future, give this exercise a try:

On separate sheets of paper, write down the goals that are important to you. Include everything from having another child to buying a cottage by the lake or starting your own business. Compare your lists and talk about why these dreams are important. How many visions do you share? Where are you at odds? Why do you think your partner doesn't share your vision? What is preventing you from meeting each other's expectations?

You may discover that you really do share more dreams than you thought, even though you have different ways of fulfilling them. That revelation can give you the security and confidence to work through differences and come to a renewed appreciation for each other.

HOW ABOUT THOSE GIANTS?

Think about your partner and pick three topics you know he or she is truly interested in. Write them down and, beginning tomorrow, mention one every day. You may need to do a little homework for this one. For instance, if your partner is a football nut, take ten minutes to read the sports pages. If she likes to follow the stock market, check the business pages and ask if she thinks interest rates will go back up and why. Or if you know he loves the ballet, and a company is coming to perform *The Nutcracker* for the holidays, read some of the reviews and ask him about it. Or perhaps one of her concerns is restoring the neighborhood playground. Ask how the fund-raising is going.

Of course, after you've asked a pointed question, pay attention to the answer! Don't let your mind wander. Ask follow-up questions, too.

4. IS THERE SEX AFTER PARENTHOOD?
Ending the Stalemate

Many couples expect that adding children to the family equation will trigger seismic shifts in their prebaby lives. They just don't realize for how long: One Kinsey Institute study published in 1990 found that more than 50 percent of couples had not resumed their normal sex lives even a year after their first child was born. The key to breaking a sexual stalemate is to make sure you don't allow criticism, guilt, and blame to cloud the issues.

Does your marriage seem more like a good used car, chugging along and dependable yet suffering from neglect? While children will always trigger upheaval in a marriage, the patterns developed during the early years can be hard to break. In order to stay together when it seems you're being pulled apart:

1. Consider any outside stress that may be affecting one or both of you. Job woes, illness, concern about an aging parent, or a child's troubles in school affect your love life, too.

2. Change your definition of good sex. Be frank with your partner about it. Sex may be different now that you're parents, but that doesn't mean it can't be pleasurable if you make each other feel cherished in other ways. If you're not in the mood to make love, suggest variations and alternatives: You can perform oral sex, let him stroke you while he masturbates, or simply lie there luxuriously and be part of his fantasy.

3. Lighten up. Most people take sex far too seriously and forget that much of what happens, or doesn't happen, in bed can be funny. Laughing together can make you both feel more loving in general.

(continued on next page)

4. Treasure memories of your past. Recounting stories of how you met, your first impressions of each other, the jolt of recognition that this person was the one for you, can bring a rush of feelings and provide a link between past hopes and present needs. This can help you weather the changes brought by time, as well as the upheavals or disappointments inevitable in every relationship.

5. Don't berate yourself if your love for your children when they are small seems stronger than your feelings for your spouse. Young children can sap your energy and creativity. Being blinded by parenthood is a common state that will pass.

6. Book a baby-sitter once a week and pay her in advance, so you're not tempted to say, "Gee, let's forget about it." If you're both working, meet for lunch. You're paying for child care anyway—take advantage of it.

7. Acknowledge each other's feelings and needs. Simply saying "I know you feel neglected . . . I wish we had more time alone, too," makes both of you feel appreciated and in touch even if the reality of your life doesn't quite match. To make sure that doesn't happen, talk often about how you feel about the balance of parenting and marital intimacy and how you see yourselves and each other since becoming parents.

8. Make sure you each get your own needs met. What do you really enjoy doing? What do you miss from your prekid life? Going to the movies? Time to exercise? Time to flop on the bed and read a magazine all by yourself? Find a way to make it happen, even on a much-limited scale.

NOTES:

_____

_____

_____

_____

_____

5. SECRETS AND LIES
A Painful Legacy

A relationship built on secrecy is unhealthy. The truth is, life is actually easier when you face it. If secrets haunt your family, remember:

1. Some secrets are harmless—even necessary and helpful. You don't, for example, need to go into excruciating detail about the drugs you took in college or your sexual escapades in order to teach your children the obstacles and dangers they may face. You and your spouse should agree on what to tell and what not to tell.

2. It's natural to want to withhold information—protect those you love. Whether it involves divorce, alcoholism, sexual orientation or suicide, such secrecy can backfire if your kids hear about it from someone other than you. It's often healthier to share such information with children, at an age-appropriate time, than jeopardize trust and communication by holding back.

3. Kids are acutely sensitive to the emotional climate at home. Parents may be able to hide facts, but they can't hide intense feelings. Though children may be unaware of the specifics of a situation, they know that something is wrong. Don't deny that reality, or they may grow up doubting their perceptions. They may also harbor a belief that something they did caused the problem.

Before you decide whether to share information with a child, consider her emotional maturity and remember that information not directly related to her life probably isn't necessary to share. (The fact that Uncle Jack, who lives across the country and whom your child never sees, was arrested for shoplifting doesn't need to be shared; however, she should probably be told about a favorite aunt who may be seriously ill.) Always be honest—just proceed slowly and answer the questions asked. Also consider the consequences of asking your child to keep a secret within the family. Sometimes that request places too great a burden on a child—for example, confiding in a child and telling her not to tell a sibling.